The Origins of Globalization

T0302116

For better or for worse, in recent times the rapid growth of international economic exchange has changed our lives. But when did this process of globalization begin, and what effects did it have on economies and societies? Pim de Zwart and Jan Luiten van Zanden argue that the networks of trade established after the voyages of Columbus and Da Gama of the late fifteenth century had transformative effects inaugurating the first era of globalization. The global flows of ships, people, money and commodities between 1500 and 1800 were substantial, and the realignment of production and distribution resulting from these connections had important consequences for demography, well-being, state formation and the long-term economic growth prospects of the societies involved in the newly created global economy. Whether early globalization had benign or malignant effects differed by region, but the world economy as we now know it originated in these changes in the early modern period.

PIM DE ZWART is Assistant Professor of Rural and Environmental History at Wageningen University in the Netherlands. His publications include the book, *Globalization and the Colonial Origins of the Great Divergence* (2016). He was awarded the Thirsk-Feinstein Prize by the Economic History Society in 2016.

JAN LUITEN VAN ZANDEN is Professor of Global Economic History at Utrecht University, honorary Angus Maddison Professor at Groningen University and Honorary Professor at Stellenbosch University. He was president of the International Economic History Association. His many publications include *An Economic History of Indonesia, 1800–2010*, with Daan Marks (2012).

New Approaches to Economic and Social History

Series editors
Marguerite Dupree (University of Glasgow)
Debin Ma (London School of Economics and Political Science)
Larry Neal (University of Illinois, Urbana-Champaign)

New Approaches to Economic and Social History is an important new textbook series published in association with the Economic History Society. It provides concise but authoritative surveys of major themes and issues in world economic and social history from the post-Roman recovery to the present day. Books in the series are by recognized authorities operating at the cutting edge of their field with an ability to write clearly and succinctly. The series consists principally of single-author works – academically rigorous and groundbreaking – which offer comprehensive, analytical guides at a length and level accessible to advanced school students and undergraduate historians and economists.

A full list of titles published in the series can be found at:
www.cambridge.org/newapproacheseconomicandsocialhistory

The Origins of Globalization

World Trade in the Making of the Global Economy, 1500–1800

PIM DE ZWART
Wageningen University, The Netherlands

JAN LUITEN VAN ZANDEN
Utrecht University, The Netherlands

CAMBRIDGE
UNIVERSITY PRESS

CAMBRIDGE
UNIVERSITY PRESS

University Printing House, Cambridge CB2 8BS, United Kingdom

One Liberty Plaza, 20th Floor, New York, NY 10006, USA

477 Williamstown Road, Port Melbourne, VIC 3207, Australia

314-321, 3rd Floor, Plot 3, Splendor Forum, Jasola District Centre, New Delhi - 110025, India

79 Anson Road, #06-04/06, Singapore 079906

Cambridge University Press is part of the University of Cambridge.

It furthers the University's mission by disseminating knowledge in the pursuit of education, learning and research at the highest international levels of excellence.

www.cambridge.org
Information on this title: www.cambridge.org/9781108426992
DOI: 10.1017/9781108551410

© Jan Luiten van Zanden and Pim de Zwart 2018

First published 2018

A catalogue record for this publication is available from the British Library

ISBN 978-1-108-42699-2 Hardback
ISBN 978-1-108-44713-3 Paperback

For my parents, Maria and Wim – PdZ
For my grandson, Maarten Matthijs – JLvZ

Contents

Figures

Tables

Maps

Acknowledgements

This book is a work in global economic history and by implication a work of synthesis. Research into the economic development of all regions of the world has boomed in recent years, and, perhaps even more importantly, thanks to the development of a unified, quantitative framework for this research, has resulted in a high degree of comparability. This has been the result of collaborative research, often carried out by teams of scholars who used the same concepts to study economic change in the countries and regions of the world. One such team is the Maddison project, which continues the pioneering work by Angus Maddison to measure historical GDP per capita (and population). Our work draws heavily on the results from studies that have estimated long-run GDP for all parts of the globe. Scholars combined in the Maddison Project are Leticia Arroyo Abad, Bart van Ark, Jean-Pascal Bassino, Luis Bertola, Stephen Broadberry, Nicholas Crafts, John Devereux, Robert Inklaar, Giovanni Federico, Johan Fourie, Herman de Jong, Kyoji Fukao, Andre Hofman, Bas van Leeuwen, Peter Lindert, Debin Ma, Mikolaj Malinowski, Branko Milanovic, Sevket Pamuk, Leandro Prados de la Escosura, Pierre van der Eng, and Harry Wu, but especially the central role played by Jutta Bolt should be mentioned here. A related network, which has produced a similar dataset of estimates of real wages, has mainly built upon the innovative work by Robert Allen, and consists of, amongst others, Leticia Arroyo Abad, Jean-Pascal Bassino, Elwyn Davies, Bas van Leeuwen, Peter Lindert, Debin Ma, Tommy Murphy, Christine Moll-Murata, Sevket Pamuk, Jaime Reis, Klas Ronnback, Eric Schneider, Jacob Weisdorf and Jeffrey Williamson. Joerg Baten carried out a comparable international comparative with his co-authors, measuring the evolution of the biological standard of living for a large number of countries and regions, and a small team of Utrecht researchers, most notably Eltjo Buringh and Maarten Bosker, did much to quantify the long-term evolution of urbanization (data published in www.cgeh.nl/urbanisation-hub-clio-infra-database-urban-settlement-sizes-1500-2000). These and related datasets are now made available on the CLIO-INFRA website (www.clio-infra.eu/), and have been published in the OECD report, *How Was Life?* (2014).

The aim of this book is to integrate and synthesize this new research into a new interpretation of the development of the world economy in the 1500–1800 period. We are indebted to all those scholars whose studies on the economic histories of the various world regions we have employed extensively in order to be able to present a global overview. By referring to these works in this book, we aim to acknowledge their valuable contributions. We also have to mention a few colleagues who have been particularly helpful. For the chapter on Global Connections, we benefitted from collaborative work with Peter M. Solar on the speed of Dutch ships, while Leo Lucassen provided us with an early version of his paper on long-term global migrations. Geert Schreurs' research on Japanese mining was very helpful – it was the final building block that allowed us to make global estimates of silver and gold production and money supply; Jonathan Fink-Jensen collected the available data on silver production and flows, and Nuno Palma's papers on the impact of American silver helped us to better understand its role in European economic development. Discussions with Dennis Flynn further informed us about the silver flows to India and China. The section on commodity market integration of Chapter 2 was based on earlier research that would not have been possible without the data published by the Bookkeeper-General Batavia project headed by Gerrit Knaap. These data were also used in this book in the chapters on South and Southeast Asia. The chapter on Latin America partially results from recent collaborative work on Latin American GDP and real wages with Leticia Arroyo Abad and Elwyn Davies. The chapter on India was helped by insights from joint work with Jan Lucassen, while the chapter on Europe has benefitted from previous collaborative work with Alexandra de Pleijt on the 'Little Divergence' and with Maarten Bosker and Eltjo Buringh on urbanization and parliamentary activity. Angus Dalrymple-Smith, Kate Frederick and Pieter Woltjer provided helpful comments on the chapter on Africa, while David Richardson pointed us to data on African slave prices. Thomas Weiss and Joshua L. Rosenbloom provided us with papers on colonial American trade and growth. Data on wages and prices in North America were kindly made available to us by Robert Allen and Eric Schneider.

We are grateful to the Rijksmuseum Amsterdam, the Thomas Fisher Rare Book Library of the University of Toronto, and the Mary Courts Burnett Library of the Texas Christian University for granting permission to print the various illustrations shown in this book. We also acknowledge the kind permission given by Cambridge University Press to reprint the maps in this book, which had already appeared in earlier publications of the Press. David Cox did a great job in adjusting those maps according to our wishes.

We thank Michael Watson from Cambridge University Press who supported the project from the beginning, as well as the three anonymous referees for the 'New Approaches in Economic and Social History Series', whose comments on earlier versions of this manuscript have greatly improved it. Lisa Carter and Ian McIver of Cambridge University Press were very helpful in answering our endless stream of questions when we were finalizing the manuscript. Last, but not least, Liesbeth van Kuijk and Rex Panneman provided valuable research assistance. Despite all this help, we remain responsible for any errors that this work may still contain.

1 | Introduction

Globalization in the Early Modern Era

When archaeologists dig into Dutch soils, and in particular in the cess-pits that are usually their richest sources, they notice a clear break around the year 1600: after that year, Chinese porcelain, or the shards and pieces that have remained of it, is frequently found, especially in places close to Amsterdam (Ostkamp 2014). The influence of the Dutch East India Company (*Verenigde Oost-Indische Compagnie*, VOC), which began to import this luxury product in those years, can be noticed immediately. And then, in the 1640s, there is another discontinuity: Chinese porcelain suddenly disappears, and Japanese and Dutch copies arrive at the scene. The political troubles of those years – the large-scale warfare that brought about the transition from the Ming to the Qing dynasty – made it impossible for the VOC to continue importing from China. They turned to Japanese manufacturers who were eager to satisfy the growing demand from Europe; at the same time entrepreneurs in Holland – especially in the town of Delft – experimented with similar technologies to make a product that would be similar to Chinese porcelain; Delft blue was born, but it took a long time before Europeans managed to achieve the same high-quality product made by the Chinese. After peace returned, Chinese products took over the market again, but Japanese and Dutch products continued to occupy a small niche in this rapidly growing market. This is only one of many examples that show how integrated the world economy had already become in the seventeenth century. War and political unrest in China had serious repercussions for producers in Japan and Holland, and international merchants – the VOC in this case – linked these markets and producers into one global network.

Over the past decades, academic debate in history has focused on the question of whether the modern concept of 'globalization' could be meaningfully applied to describe this earlier period of global interaction. The answer to the question depends largely, of course, on one's preferred definition. The term 'globalization' was first included in an English dictionary in the 1960s, but its usage exploded in the 1990s.[1] In the public domain it is often understood as the process of a 'shrinking world', or the world becoming 'a global village', spurred by multinationals like McDonalds and technologies like the internet. Social scientists have studied the phenomenon extensively, but have yet to reach consensus on a definition. One influential scholar defined it as 'the intensification of worldwide social relations which link distant localities in such a way that local happenings are shaped by events occurring many miles away and vice versa' (Giddens 1990, p. 64). Scholars have looked at different dimensions of globalization – cultural, political, environmental, as well as economic – and have found traces of the process since antiquity (Held et al. 1999).

In this book, we focus on economic globalization and its effects on economic development in the early modern era. Among economic historians two definitions of globalization have been influential. On the one hand there are those who have adopted a rather broad definition of the process, like Dennis Flynn and Arturo Giraldez (2008, p. 369), who propose that globalization is the 'sustained interaction between all the world's heavily populated landmasses [i.e. Eurasia, Africa and the Americas] both directly with each other and indirectly through other land masses – in a manner that deeply and permanently linked them'. They suggest that a focus on purely economic globalization is 'doomed' and argue that globalization should contain ecological, demographic, cultural as well as economic elements. Flynn and Giraldez (2004) thus emphasize the Columbian exchange of plants, diseases and animals across the oceans in general, and the adoption of New World crops, by the Chinese in particular. Specifically, they point out the foundation of Manila in 1571 as the starting date of globalization, as that inaugurated the direct link between all continents and in a way, by connecting the Americas to Asia, closed the circle of global interactions. In his review of the globalization debate, Jan de Vries (2010, p. 713) christened their definition 'soft globalization'.

In opposition to such a broad definition, there is the more narrow definition of 'hard globalization'[2] as the integration of factor and commodity markets, as adopted by Kevin O'Rourke and Jeffrey Williamson (2002a). In this definition, globalization is driven by declining transaction costs: transport costs, information asymmetries, monopolies and other barriers to trade. These costs drive a gap between prices in purchasing and selling markets and the best evidence of a decline in these costs taking place, and thus of the integration of commodity markets, is the decline in the price gap across the globe. Price convergence is therefore the crucial test of a globalizing world. On the basis of this definition, and the data available to them, O'Rourke and Williamson (2002a) suggest that there was no globalization before the 1820s, as global commodity prices did not convergence before that decade.

This book is centred around the question of how global interaction created the global economy and led to crucial transformations of its various components in the period between 1500 and 1800. While we will also discuss some of the trends in regional migration and trade (e.g. that between China and Southeast Asia), our focus is on long-distance overseas trade – connections between the world's continents. Compared with the overland trade across the Silk Road that dominated during *Pax Mongolica*, overseas trade was in general faster, cheaper and, perhaps most importantly, less vulnerable to political instability across Eurasia. It is clear that from roughly around 1500 onwards, for the first time in human history, all major parts of the globe were in consistent contact with each other. This was a period of sustained global interaction and, as a result, many components of this newly created world economy were profoundly transformed. We suggest that this 'soft globalization' was almost everywhere, and as a broad process, its consequences could be far-reaching. In some cases, this also led to global economic integration, or 'hard globalization', as measured by price convergence, but not always. However, our main point is to show the many different ways in which societies were transformed; these differences were influenced by a combination of geographical and institutional factors. In some cases, global interaction played only a limited role in such transformations. This was the case for, e.g., India – although integrated in the global economy (as measured by price convergence – see Chapter 2), change was largely domestically driven; while Latin American societies, on the other hand, were completely transformed as a result of external factors. For Europe, the creation of networks of global connections had entirely different consequences than for China or for Indonesia – or for sub-Sahara Africa for that matter. These many faces of globalization are the subject of this book; we try to explain why different parts of the world had such remarkably different development trajectories between 1500 and 1800, and what role the growing global interactions played in these trajectories. We will ask the fundamental question of who benefitted, and who lost from global interaction; not only on a continental level, but also within the different regions: often, elites in Africa and Asia benefitted from a globalization that hurt most of the people, as well as the long-run economic prospects, of their region. We look at the direct effects that globalization may have had, as well as the indirect effects and, in doing so, we will move beyond the dichotomy of hard and soft globalization.

For our story, we will systematically make use of three kinds of data to chart the societies we study: GDP per capita, real wages and urbanization ratios. GDP (Gross Domestic Product) is the measure of the economic output of a country, and of the level of real income of its inhabitants, as production of goods and services normally equals the amount of goods that can be consumed or invested. Economists and economic historians have since the 1930s used this concept to measure the productive capacity of a country or a region (see Maddison 2007 and Bolt and Van Zanden 2014). The concept has, however, been criticized because it covers only one dimension of well-being, and does not take into account the inequality of the income distribution (economic growth can mean that only the rich become richer) (Van Zanden et al. 2014). Discussion about the standard of living often focuses instead on real wages, the income earned by the working class. We have included in the various chapters the estimates of the real wage of unskilled construction labourers, as they have become standardized in economic historical research (see Allen 2001, Allen et al. 2011). The way in which these real wages are measured is as follows: for the society and period concerned data of nominal wages were collected, as well as data on the prices of the most essential consumer goods. The value of a standard low-cost budget of a family of four (two adults and two children) was estimated, and it was calculated how many of such 'barebones' budgets could be purchased with the wages of the unskilled labourer (assuming 250 working days per year). These estimates have been made for many societies and time periods, offering an alternative measure of real income (of the less well-to-do) of these countries. A third measure of economic performance that we use is the urbanization ratio, the share of the population living in cities (with at least 10,000 inhabitants).[3] It is well known that there is a clear link between urbanization and levels of economic specialization – and

GDP per capita – although the correlation is far from perfect. But for many pre-1800 societies, we do know the urbanization ratio, whereas other data are often unavailable (see Bosker et al. 2013). Finally, in some cases we also make use of the available data on the stature of the population involved. Human stature tells us about food availability in the first years after birth, but also about health and disease environment (Baten and Blum 2014).

Historical estimates of income and well-being are admittedly not without problems; they are based on assumptions that may not always hold or rely on limited data that could raise questions about reliability or representativeness (see e.g. Deng and O'Brien (2016) for a critique on real wage studies of China). We agree that historical data should continue to be scrutinized and if necessary revised by further studies. However, we also believe that the methods that are used to produce the figures are sound, and that the scholars who produce these estimates are regional experts with a deep knowledge of the wider histories of the regions they have assembled the data from. The results that have come out of these studies are plausible and are generally accepted by most economic historians. Furthermore, we often use a variety of estimates for several economic indicators, which allows us to check for consistency.

By combining these indicators with trends in trade, we demonstrate how different parts of the world developed during the period of early globalization, and we can try to compare patterns of change between the different parts of the world economy. This, we believe, has led to a nuanced and empirically sound restatement of the role of early modern global interaction in the creation of the modern world economy and its diverse effects on the global income distribution.

Early Globalization: The Capitalist World System

The focus on how international trade pushed different economic development trajectories across the globe is not new. In the 1970s and 1980s an influential literature on the historical roots of the global economy (and the winners and losers in that economy) arose from the ranks of world systems scholars and dependency theorists. While this literature did not discuss the concept of 'globalization' *per se*, it is clear that the idea of the world as one capitalist system hints at something similar.

According to Immanuel Wallerstein, founding father of the world systems approach, the 'modern world-system' originated in Europe in the long sixteenth century (*c.*1450–1640). This world system was based on three key elements: (1) a worldwide division of labour; (2) an international political order based on states of different strengths; and (3) a dynamic element that creates opportunities to create new profit-making enterprises (Wallerstein 2011 [1989], p. xiv). The key element that defines the modern world system as a capitalist system is that it is built 'on the drive for the endless accumulation of capital' (*ibid.*). This, Wallerstein argues, is an important requirement; there are 'mechanisms in the system to reward those who operate according to its logic, and to punish those who operate according to other reasoning'.

The world system as envisioned by Wallerstein consists of three types of regions: core, semi-periphery and periphery. These do not need to entail the entire world as there can also be regions external to the world system. The global division of labour is arranged along this hierarchy: the core consists of strong states focused on high-skilled and capital-intensive production, and accumulates most of the surplus from the world economy. The dominant mode of labour in the core is wage labour and self-employment. The periphery consists of weak states focused on low-skilled and labour-intensive production based on the extraction of resources. Slavery and servitude are common forms of labour coercion in the periphery. The semi-periphery, as one would expect, is somewhere in between those categories. For the system to operate, and the global division of labour to function, there needs to be a continuous flow of essential goods that are low profit and highly competitive from the periphery, in exchange for high-profit and quasi-monopolized goods from the core.

Wallerstein suggests that the world system arose in the long sixteenth century, and that the core consisted of the countries in northwestern Europe. Sweden and Prussia were part of the semi-periphery, while the periphery constituted the regions in the Americas. Still external to the system were the Indian Ocean areas, the Far East, the Ottoman Empire and Russia. Over the course of the late eighteenth and nineteenth centuries, all other parts of the world became incorporated in this one system. For most of the early modern period, Asia and Africa thus remain outside of the world system, and global trade in these areas was not able to bring about any changes in economic relations in these regions, as this trade was only in luxuries.

Thus, the world system is dynamic, and states can shift in their status: among core states there is the struggle to become the hegemon, semi-peripheral states can become part of the core, or decline in status to a periphery, and external areas can become incorporated in the world system.

For placing Europe at the heart of this world system, and giving little room for indigenous agency in other parts of the world, Wallerstein has been accused of Eurocentrism. Andre Gunder Frank, in his later work *ReOrient* (1998), suggests that the world system was not headed by Europe, but rather by Asia (at least until the nineteenth century). The timing of the world system has also been contested. Some suggest that around the year 1000, inter-regional contact began to shape the development of societies in the East and West (Northrup 2005; Stearns 2010). Janet Abu-Lughod (1989) suggested that in the century between 1250 and 1350 there was not one world system, but multiple world systems that existed simultaneously. The least developed of these was the western European system (consisting of Flanders, northern France, Genoa and Venice) while the other (more developed) systems were Middle Eastern (Constantinople, Baghdad and north-eastern Africa) and Asian (containing parts of China, India and Southeast Asia). Andre Gunder Frank, together with Barry Gills (1993), argues that the world system was much older: at least 5,000 years. Long-distance trade relations, structured between core and periphery, are also at the heart of this world system.

Frank in his earlier work, was one of the leading scholars of the dependency school, whose central thesis is very similar to that of the world systems school. Frank suggested that it is precisely the manner of incorporation of the Global South into the global capitalist world system that has caused its underdevelopment (1978, 1979). Different countries entered into the world system in different ways and the process of unequal exchange meant that some (the core) benefitted more than others (the periphery). Capital was accumulated in Western Europe, a process to which the countries in the Global South contributed. The more such a country was engaged in the global capitalist system, the more it became underdeveloped. Related is the thesis by Eric Williams (1944), who suggested that it was mainly the profits accrued in the slave trade that were invested in the English manufacturing industries and thus that slavery and the slave trade were crucial for the start of the Industrial Revolution.

What these views have in common is that the current income distribution is influenced by the patterns of global interaction somewhere in the past. At some point a global division of labour came into existence which pushed Western Europe on the path to industrialization and high standards of living, while the 'periphery' was driven towards primary production and low levels of per capita incomes. Present-day poverty in some parts of the world can be attributed to their peripheral status in the world economy (in the past, as well as now), while the wealth of the West was at some point accumulated through these countries' core position and by exploiting the logistics of the capitalist world system at the expense of the periphery.

Dismissing Early Globalization

Such accounts of the world economy have attracted a fair deal of critique. Starting in the 1980s, economic historians have pointed out that global interaction could not have had the impact ascribed to it by world systems theorists as quantitatively these interactions amounted to very little. Three interrelated points have been made: (1) intercontinental trade was too small a sector, and profits were not high enough, to bring about any instrumental economic changes and a global division of labour. Therefore, it played no part in the rise of Europe; (2) global trade in the early modern era did not cause a decline in the 'periphery', for similar reasons, and because no decline took place there before 1800; and (3) international trade was inefficient and shipping technology stagnant in the early modern period.

One line of criticism of the world system approach has been that it overestimates the impact that long-distance overseas trade had on European economic development. Patrick O'Brien developed this critique most clearly in a number of papers, and he memorably concluded that 'for the economic growth of the core, the periphery was peripheral' (1982, p. 9). O'Brien made three related statements, namely that intercontinental commerce until 1750 was on a small scale; that it did not generate supernormal profits; and that it generated no externalities that were decisive for the economic growth of Europe. O'Brien gives a figure of 1 per cent as an upper-bound estimate of the total contribution of intercontinental trade to Western European GNP. Profits in international commerce were not higher than in other sectors of the economy and thus played no special role in capital accumulation.

Finally, while intercontinental trade did stimulate shipbuilding, shipping, banking and insurance sectors, as well as the food processing and textile manufacturing industries, these industries were also relatively small as a percentage of the total economy even by 1841. The iron and coal industries were more important. David Eltis and Stanley Engerman (2000) specifically focused on the slave-based plantation economies and the slave trade and came to similar conclusions: the contribution to the British economy was small, and there were no special spill-over effects.

Second, there are those scholars who claimed, like Frank (1998) cited above, that Europe and Asia were on the same level of development until the late eighteenth century (e.g. Wong 1997; Pomeranz 2000; Parthasarathi 2011). Intercontinental trading patterns could not have led to divergence between the 'core' and 'periphery' before 1800, simply because no divergence had taken place by that time. As measured by a variety of economic indicators, it is claimed, Europe and Asia were on a similar level of development: 'it seems likely that average incomes in Japan, China and parts of Southeast Asia were comparable to (or higher than) those in Western Europe, even in the late eighteenth century' (Pomeranz 2000, p. 26). Prasannan Parthasarathi (1998; 2011) made similar claims regarding incomes in India. Living standards, technological development and institutions in Asia were not noticeably inferior to those in Europe before 1800. Only after that did divergence take place, primarily as a result of favourably located coal and access to land in the New World that relieved Western Europe of important resource constraints (Pomeranz 2000). Global trade began to matter only after the eighteenth century. Studies that have appeared over the past years have both disputed and refuted the separate claims made by these revisionist scholars, collectively known as the 'California School', referring to their – in some cases, past – associations with the University of California (for an overview, see Vries 2013).

Third, both previous views gained further strength by studies demonstrating the limited impact of international maritime transport and the persistence of monopolies and other barriers to trade. Several studies have argued that there was little technological progress in the shipping sector and that, as a consequence, transport costs failed to decline. Freight rates, when properly deflated, did not decline on most intercontinental trade routes until the nineteenth century (Menard

1991; Harley 1988). As a result of this, and monopolies and tariffs, international commodity prices failed to converge over the early modern period. This meant that trade volumes continued to be relatively small and focused on non-competing luxury goods. Trade was thus unable to lead to shifts in domestic production and therefore did not influence economic development. Only from the nineteenth century onwards did technological progress and changing market institutions allow interaction at such a scale that it influenced economic development across the globe (O'Rourke and Williamson 2002a, 2002b). Subsequently, a global division of labour came into place, as the cheap importation of grains from the New World allowed a part of the workforce to move from agriculture into manufacturing, opening the path to the Industrial Revolution in Europe.

Such views have attained considerable influence and the nineteenth century is generally viewed as the first age of globalization. We believe that such views overlook many crucial aspects of global interaction in the early modern era; over this period, the world economy was radically restructured and global interaction played a role in this.

Transformation of the Global Economy

The world in 1800 was in many ways unrecognizable from what it had been before the voyages of Christopher Columbus and Vasco da Gama. Before 1500, the great empires in the world were situated in the Middle East and Asia. Around 1500, there was no great empire in Europe. The Holy Roman Empire, or Germany, had some 12 million inhabitants, but was ruled by many different princes; the emperor held very little real power. England, France and Spain did steadily become stronger, more centralized, states, and stretched across roughly the same territory they still do today, but at that time were inhabited by roughly 3, 15 and 7 million people respectively (Clio-Infra 2015). Especially compared with those in Asia, these were small polities (see Table 1.1).

In the Americas, at the beginning of the sixteenth century, the Aztec and Inca empires may have ruled over empires containing perhaps as much as one-fifth of the world population. The other truly big political entities were found in the 'Golden Band' stretching from the Eastern Mediterranean to China, the traditional centre of gravity of the Eurasian economy that was connected via caravan routes such as the famous silk route. The fifteenth and sixteenth centuries saw a consolidation of political

Table 1.1. *Estimates of total population and current size of countries*

		1500	1600	1700	1800	1820	Size in 1,000 km²
Europe	England/ Britain	2.8	6.2	8.6	10.6	21.2	242
	France	15.0	18.5	21.5	29.0	31.3	550
	Germany	12.0	16.0	15.0	18.0	24.9	349
	Netherlands	1.0	1.5	1.9	2.0	2.3	34
	Portugal	1.0	1.1	2.0	2.8	3.3	91
	Spain	6.8	8.2	8.8	11.5	12.2	499
Asia	China	103.0	160.0	140.0	330.0	381.0	9326
	India	110.0	142.0	164.0	207.0		2973
	Indonesia	10.7	11.7	13.1		17.9	1812
	Japan	15.4	18.5	27.0	28.0	31.0	364
	Turkey	6.3	7.9	8.4		10.1	770
Americas	Mexico	17.2	3.0	2.8	5.1	6.6	1944
	Peru & Bolivia	3.4	1.6	1.2	2.2	2.4	2363
	United States	5.0	3.5	2.3	5.9	10.1	9148

Sources: Population: All European countries except England/Britain: Clio-Infra (2015); England to 1600 & Britain 1700–1800: Broadberry et al. (2015); Great Britain 1820: Clio-Infra (2015); India 1500: Clio-Infra (2015); India 1600–1800: Broadberry, Custodis and Gupta (2015); Indonesia: Maddison (2007); Japan: Clio-Infra (2015). Mexico 1500: Newson (2005); Mexico 1600–1800: Arroyo Abad and Van Zanden (2016); Mexico 1820: Clio-Infra (2015); Peru and Bolivia 1500 & 1820: Clio-Infra (2015); Peru and Bolivia 1600–1800: Arroyo Abad and van Zanden (2016); United States: Haines and Steckel (2000). N.B. including Native North American population (interpolated for 1600 and 1700); 5 million in 1500, 600,000 in 1800 and 471,000 in 1820. No estimates for Africa shown because of widely ranging estimates (see Chapter 4). Size: current-day country size in 1,000 square km http://world.bymap.org/LandArea.html: N.B. Some of these countries expanded or retracted in size over this period, others did not yet exist as countries.

power at the western end of this Golden Band. The Ottoman Empire had control over a large part of western Asia and in 1517 took control of Syria and Egypt. Under Suleiman the Magnificent (r. 1520–1566) the empire extended into the Balkans and Hungary and attempted the capture of Vienna – capital of the Habsburg Empire – for the first time

in 1529, and, as late as 1683, the Ottomans attempted another siege of
the city. In Persia, the Safavids under Shah Abbas the Great (r. 1588–
1629) ruled a territory stretching from eastern Turkey to southern
Pakistan. Its capital, Tabriz, was inhabited by some 230,000 people.
In India, the Hindu Vijayanagara Empire ruled over most of the Southern
Peninsula and its capital (Vijayanagara) boasted about a half million
inhabitants (over twice the size of Paris and the second largest city only
after Beijing). In northern India, the great Delhi Sultanate, which had
ruled over most of the northern part of the subcontinent for 300 years,
was succeeded by the even greater Mughal Empire in the sixteenth century. The entire population of India may have been between 150 and 160
million (Moosvi 1987a). Further east, despite being past its prime of the
tenth to twelfth centuries, the Ming Chinese emperor ruled over a relatively prosperous, commercialized and unified territory inhabited by perhaps 125 million people (Frank 1998, p. 109). And, after demographic,
agricultural and commercial expansion from the fourteenth century, the
Japanese shogun Tokugawa Ieyasu (r. 1603–1605) ruled over a unified
Japan including a population of 18.5 million (Clio-Infra 2015). While
population figures deep into the past are obviously subject to a large margin of error, considering the magnitude of the differences the main point is
undisputed: the demographic and economic power wielded by the major
Asian sovereigns exceeded that of the European rulers by a large degree.

Maritime commerce flourished across the Indian Ocean and South
China Sea and was incomparable to the commercial networks in the
West; the Strait of Malacca was probably the busiest waterway in the
world (Morris 2010, p. 408). Large populations and cities were sustained by highly productive rice agriculture. Scientifically and tech-
nologically, the Middle East and China were arguably (still) more
advanced than Western Europe in the first centuries of the first millennium. The Muslim world around the year 1000 was pioneering in the
fields of cartography, medicine, philosophy, mathematics and optics
(Ferguson 2011). Gunpowder, the compass and the printing press were
all invented in China. Chinese and Indian naval innovations in rigging
and navigation, via the Arabs, also transferred to the West in the late
twelfth century (Morris 2010, p. 396). Already by the twelfth century,
shipbuilding and navigation in China had reached a level that would
have allowed Chinese ships to sail to the Americas.

Map 1.1 shows the world with all cities with 100,000 or more inhabitants in 1500 (Buringh 2016; Chandler and Fox 1974). Most of these

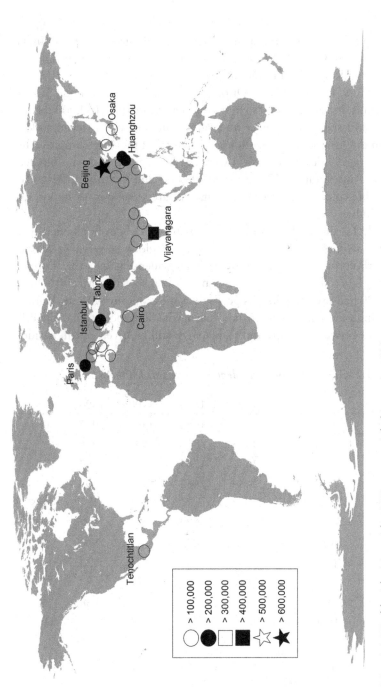

Map 1.1 World with cities with 100K or more inhabitants in 1500
Sources: Buringh (2016) and Chandler and Fox (1974).

Legend:

- ○ > 100,000
- ● > 200,000
- □ > 300,000
- ■ > 400,000
- ☆ > 500,000
- ★ > 600,000

City labels: Tenochtitlan, Paris, Istanbul, Tabriz, Cairo, Vijayanagara, Beijing, Huanghzou, Osaka

(13) were situated in Asia, with seven in China (Beijing, Chang'an, Chengdu, Hangzhou, Guangzhou, Nanjing and Suzhou), four in India (Ahmedabad, Cuttack, Gaur and Vijayanagara), one in Japan (Osaka) and one in Korea (Seoul). Of all cities in the world with above 100,000 inhabitants, five were Arab/Ottoman: Cairo, Edirne, Istanbul, Tabriz and Tunis. In Europe, a mere four cities had more than 100,000 inhabitants: Milan, Napoli, Venice and Paris. Only one city reached such a size in the Americas: Tenochtitlan, the capital of the Aztec Empire. The three largest cities of the world were in Asia: Beijing had an estimated 678,000 inhabitants, Vijayanagara 498,000 and Hangzhou 250,000. These big cities were either the capitals of great empires, or important trade hubs.

Table 1.2 shows the most recent estimates of the development of per capita incomes (GDP per capita) across the globe between 1500 and 1820 (Bolt and Van Zanden 2014). This evidence shows that Europe already had a slight advantage over most other societies in 1500. China by 1500 had probably lost its position as the economy with the highest per capita incomes, which it had during the Song period, but the differences between Europe and China were still relatively small. Besides

Table 1.2. *GDP per capita in selected countries, 1500–1820*

		1500	1600	1700	1800	1820
Europe	England	1114	1082	1563	2097	2074
	Germany	1146	807	939	986	
	Italy	1533	1363	1476	1363	1511
	Holland	1454	2662	2105	2609	
Africa	Egypt	680				475
Asia	China	1127	977	841	597	600
	India		682	622	569	520
	Japan	554*	596	610	732	
	Turkey	660		700		740
Americas	Mexico				836	627
	United States		587**	900	1296	1361

*Japan 1500 = 1450 **United States 1600 = 1650
Sources: Bolt and Van Zanden (2014); Bassino et al. (2015); Broadberry, Custodis and Gupta (2015).

this, there were few indications that the divided Europe would dominate the global economy for centuries to come.

By 1800, however, a 'reversal of fortune' had occurred: Western Europeans were in control of the entire Americas, Southern Africa, a string of territories and forts along the African coast, as well as parts of India and Southeast Asia. The Ottoman Empire had entered a long period of decline, and its trading interests in Asia had been taken over by Europeans. While real incomes in England had doubled, GDP per capita in China was perhaps only half of what it had been three centuries before. Furthermore, one of the richest societies was now to be found in the New World. Inhabitants of the newly formed United States earned an average income of almost 1,300$ in 1800 (Table 1.2). In terms of real wages, their lead was more evident: workers in Philadelphia, Maryland and Boston earned wages significantly above those in London around 1800, earning between four to six times subsistence level (Allen et al. 2012). At the same time, real wages in Asia had declined to subsistence level (Allen et al. 2011).

A shift in patterns of urbanization and the location of large cities had also taken place. While Europe was more urbanized than Asia already in 1500, this trend continued into the eighteenth and nineteenth centuries (Bosker et al. 2013). The urbanization rate of the Netherlands doubled from around 15 to about 30 per cent, while that in England and Wales increased dramatically from 3 to 20 per cent. At the same time, urbanization rates in China probably declined between 1500 and 1800 (Yi et al. 2015), while those in Japan had increased to some 13 per cent in that same period. The number of large cities in China, Japan and India was still very impressive and had grown considerably (29), but of the cities with more than 100,000 inhabitants in the world, now 19 were situated in Europe (Map 1.2). Of the 11 large cities in India, most were under British control around 1800: Benares, Bombay, Delhi, Calcutta, Dhaka, Madras, Murshidabad and Patna. Only Lucknow and Hyderabad were still ruled by independent *Nawabs* (the title of the ruler of an Indian region), while Bijapur was controlled by the Hindu Maratha dynasty of central India. Makassar, besides the Burmese capital of Amarapura the only city in Southeast Asia with over 100,000 inhabitants, was controlled by the Dutch. One could further add the two large cities in Mexico, then still part of New Spain, to the list of European-controlled cities.

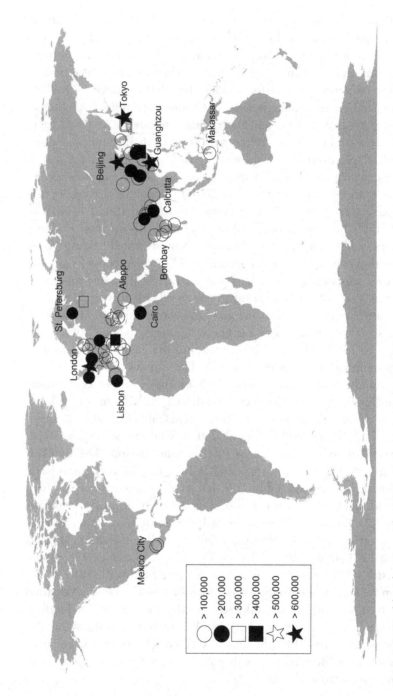

Map 1.2 World with cities with 100K or more inhabitants in 1800
Sources: Buringh (2016) and Chandler and Fox (1974).

Thus, in these three centuries, an important shift had taken place in the world's economic centre of gravity towards the West. Only in recent decades has this trend started to reverse.[4]

The Revival of Early Globalization

This 'reversal of fortune', which occurred at the global level but which was also very pronounced within Europe itself, where the North Sea area emerged as the engine of European economic growth at the expense of the Mediterranean, we argue, cannot be properly understood without taking early modern globalization into account. At the same time that Western Europe became the centre of the global economy, it came to dominate the world's sea lanes, controlled the global trading network and had begun to colonize substantial pieces of the world's landmass. While correlation does not mean causation, a causal link between these developments is likely, although perhaps difficult to demonstrate considering the multitude of developments taking place over these three centuries.

Both the patterns of urbanization observed in Maps 1.1 and 1.2 as well as the estimates of GDP are, we argue in this book, related to the trends in world commerce. The contrasting development of the North Sea region (England and the Low Countries) on the one hand, and the Yangtze river delta in China on the other, that form the heart of the 'Great Divergence' debate, is illustrative for the role of international trade. The Song period (960–1279) reflects a high point of economic development in Chinese history. The economy remained strong after the Song dynasty lost control over the northern part of their empire in conflict with the Jin dynasty; they moved their capital to Hangzhou, south of the Yangtze river. From the Yangtze delta, the Song exported porcelain, silk and other manufactures to Southeast Asia in exchange for primary produce like spices. This lucrative commerce was continued under the Yuan dynasty (1271–1368), which reopened overland commerce to Europe and the Middle East on the Silk Road, allowing Marco Polo to use this route to China in the thirteenth century, and the Plague to spread both east- and westwards in the fourteenth century. Under the Ming (1368–1644), international commerce was initially continued. The new capital city of Nanjing also had the largest shipyard in the world as the Yongle emperor (r. 1402–1424) ordered the construction of large treasure ships (four to five times the size of

Columbus' flagship the *Santa Maria*), which, under the command of
Admiral Zheng He, travelled to ports in the Middle East and along
the coast of eastern Africa. Hundreds of vessels carried almost 30,000
men to those shores. Yet in 1421, the Yongle emperor moved the
government seat from Nanjing to Beijing. Due to internal political
considerations (Schottenhammer 2012), Yongle's successors quickly
lost all interest in overseas trade. Instead, China started to expand
inland, and its territory (and population) increased dramatically over
the subsequent centuries (see Chapter 8). The voyages were immediately suspended. Only one last Indian Ocean expedition took place
in 1432–1433, as in 1433, with the death of Admiral Zheng He, the
expensive treasure missions that had brought thousands of men crossing the Indian Ocean were ended for good by the Xuande emperor
(r. 1425–1435). Not long after that, private maritime trade was
declared illegal and no more investments were made in the Chinese
fleet, which consequently rotted away. From 1500, building an ocean-
going vessel with more than two masts was a capital offense (Ferguson
2011, p. 32). Around the same time, da Gama's ships appeared in the
waters of the Indian Ocean.

Da Gama's voyage broke the monopoly over the sale of Southeast
Asian spices in Europe held by the Venetians. Venice, at that moment,
was the wealthiest city in Europe and its wealth was based to a large
extent on its commerce. In the words of the Venetian ambassador
to Cairo at the time of da Gama, the opening of the Cape route
was a 'causa de grande ruina del Stato Veneto' (cited in Findlay
and O'Rourke 2007, p. 204). As shall be discussed in Chapter 6,
the Portuguese were unable to firmly control their monopoly on
the spice trade in the Indian ocean, and the overland route was
continued in the sixteenth century, putting off the immediate ruin
of Venice for another century. The Venetian downfall would be at
the hands of the Dutch and English who gained the upper hand in
global trade in the seventeenth and eighteenth centuries. In congru-
ence with these shifts in the economic centre of gravity, the highest incomes per capita changed from Italy to, first, the Netherlands
and then England. At the same time, London became Europe's
largest city, with Amsterdam in fourth place, Lisbon in fifth and
Venice, having fallen from third place (together with Milan) in
1500, in seventh place in 1800 (Buringh 2016). We argue in this
book that the trends of economic growth and decline before the

1800s were clearly related to trends in international commerce. In subsequent chapters, we will provide an analysis of trends in incomes and urbanization in relation to patterns of trade for all major regions of the newly created world economy.

We are not alone in our restating of the importance of global trade in shaping the global economy in the early modern era. In an introductory book on the history of globalization, Jurgen Osterhammel and Niels Petersson (2005, p. 146) note that:

if there is indeed a turning point at which globalization becomes a central feature of history and of many human experiences, then it occurred in the early modern period of discovery, slave trade and 'ecological imperialism', not in the late twentieth century.

And, as we noted above, Flynn and Giraldez (2002a, 2004, 2008) emphasize the foundation of Manila in 1571 as the start of globalization. They show evidence of several phases where silver prices converged (in the 1640s and around 1750), on the basis of which they argue that a highly integrated global economy, based around silver, emerged in the late sixteenth century.

Perhaps even more important for our argument are studies that investigated the effects of global interaction. Recent works by Daron Acemoglu et al. (2005), Robert Allen (2003, 2009b), De Vries (2008), have stressed the direct and indirect effects of the rise in international trade on the growth of Western Europe in this period. Kenneth Pomeranz (2000) and Parthasarathi (2011) also put forward New World colonies and intercontinental competition as central to the 'Rise of Europe', albeit in a later period than we discuss here. As regards the decline of 'the Rest', recent econometric work by e.g. Acemoglu et al. (2001; 2002), Melissa Dell (2010) and Nathan Nunn (2008) demonstrated the long-term economic effects of European colonialism and the Atlantic slave trades in the Americas, Africa and Asia. This literature, inspired by new institutional economics,[5] stresses the path dependency of institutions that were imposed by European colonizers and their (slave-trading) allies. In certain respects, it is a 'modern' version of Wallerstein's world systems approach which also argued that there was continuity between the division of labour that emerged in the sixteenth century, and global inequality in the nineteenth and twentieth centuries. The approach developed by Daron Acemoglu and James Robinson in their *Why Nations Fail* (2012) stresses a similar continuity in global inequality induced by the institutions Europeans introduced in various parts of the world. Partially drawing on the arguments set forth in such works and partially developing new arguments on the basis of the most recent evidence on global trade and economic developments, we construct our claim on the diverse forms and effects of early modern globalization.

What Drove Early Globalization?

What drove globalization in the early modern era? One of the misconceptions about the process of globalization we wish to set straight is that it was, and is, solely driven by technological advances. Surely technological advances have played a major part in the shrinking of the globe, but it was by no means the only force driving it. We put forward four main carriers of globalization (1) the European competitive state system; (2) technological and institutional innovations; (3) European surplus income and demand; and (4) American silver and gold deposits. This is not to say that non-Europeans played no role in shaping the process of globalization. On the contrary, the shape and consequences of globalization were very much affected by the interaction with local conditions and the agency of inhabitants in all different parts of the globe. Particularly in connections with the large land empires of Ming/Qing China, Mughal India, Ottoman Turkey, Tsarist Russia and Safavid Persia, Europeans played only a small role in their development paths. Maritime trade was generally marginal in these large agricultural economies and of this, the trade with Europeans was only a part – and often only a small part. Nonetheless, it is clear that as long-distance trade and interaction across continents was carried out almost entirely on European ships (Vries 2017), largely manned by European shippers,[6] and managed by European entrepreneurs and/or state officials (O'Brien 2005, p. 29), the process was to a large extent fuelled by Europeans.

A first factor influencing globalization was the European competitive state system. A glance at the European political map around 1500 shows a continent dotted with a large number of states that, in order to safeguard their position in the European state system were in constant competition with their neighbours. Between 1500 and 1800, the European powers spent between 50 and 80 per cent of their time fighting foreign enemies. Wars had to be financed, and the countries situated on the seaboard were eager to explore the globe and thereby benefit from the profits earned through international trade. Thus, Isabella of Castile sponsored Columbus' 1492 voyage to find a western route to India. Henry VII sent Giovanni Caboto to find an alternative northern route to India in 1497. Manuel I, king of Portugal, sponsored da Gama's travels to India via the Cape in 1498 and Pedro Alvares Cabral's attempt to find an alternative route to the East Indies in 1500, when he instead stumbled on the coast of Brazil. The aim was to control the world's supply of spices – mainly mace, nutmeg, cloves and cinnamon – that grew in confined areas – cinnamon only in Ceylon and the other three only in the Moluccas. In the early sixteenth century, Tomé Pires (1515), first Portuguese governor of Malacca, the city controlling the sea lanes to the Spice Islands, noted that 'whoever is lord of Malacca, has his hand on the throat of Venice' (cited in Findlay and O'Rourke 2007, p. 136).

Second, this competition among the European naval powers spurred technical and institutional innovations that allowed rising volumes of trade. Views that transport technology progressed little in the early modern period cannot be easily disregarded. Indeed, as we will discuss in the next chapter, the evidence for progress in naval transport is mixed. Trade grew despite the possible stagnation in shipping technology. In order to accumulate capital, conduct trade efficiently and trump their competition, Europeans started to set up joint-stock companies. This was probably the most important innovation in the organization of trade in the early modern period. The English East India Company (EIC), created in 1600, and the Dutch East India Company (VOC), created in 1602, were the first joint-stock companies in the world. The VOC was the first to finance its operations entirely via the stock market; while the EIC issued its first stocks only in 1613. Companies like the Royal Africa Company, the Dutch West India Company and the French, Danish, Swedish and Ostend companies were all modelled after these. These companies, by their charters, attained the monopoly right to sell exotic goods in their domestic markets, as well as gained quasi-sovereign powers in Asia and Africa. In return for this monopoly the companies were supposed to support the state in its military and economic ventures; the VOC had to fight the enemy (Spain, Portugal) and do as much harm as possible to its trade and military.

Whether these companies (due to their monopolistic nature) hindered or (due to their ability to accumulate capital) stimulated globalization is the subject of discussion. De Vries (2010) suggests that if the companies had not benefitted from their monopoly power in Europe and state-like powers in Asia, they would have had more pressure to reduce shipping and overhead costs. Instead, they remained focused on expanding their access to markets under favourable conditions. He cites the success of French and American private traders in the Asian trade in this regard. Another clue may be that the Atlantic trade – where monopolies played no – or a less important – role, grew much faster than trade with Asia. At the same time, the joint-stock companies did enable the pooling of large sums of capital and without them trade with Asia, may not have been lucrative at all before the nineteenth century.

Competition among European powers led to advances in military technology. Europeans perfected gunpowder technology, the military tactics applying it and the related defence strategies (such as the *trace italienne* fortifications) as a result of almost continuous warfare in late medieval and early modern Europe (Parker 1988; Hoffman 2015). This also led to the greater fiscal capacity of European states, which was necessary to erect the new defensive fortifications, and to pay for the well-trained standing armies (Dincecco and Prado 2012). Furthermore, Europeans usually fought to capture land and kill people, while in most other areas of the world, that were generally population scarce and land abundant, fighting techniques were focused on capturing rather than killing people. In Northern America, the Indians' fighting 'was farre lesse bloudy and devouring than the cruell warres of Europe'.[7] The two large empires in the Americas yielded quickly to only a small number of *conquistadores* in the first half of the sixteenth century. The Aztec Empire collapsed between 1519 and 1521 to Hernán Cortés' force of some 2,000 Spaniards, while the Incan Empire yielded to Francisco Pizarro's 168 Europeans a decade later. These *conquistadores* were, of course, greatly aided not only by many indigenous allies that were eager to get out from the yoke of Tenochtitlan and Cuzco, but also by the infectious diseases the Europeans brought with them. On the water, large 'man-of-war' warships allowed Europeans to gain an upper hand in relations with sovereigns in other parts of the world. Along the coasts of Africa, South and Southeast Asia, where they gained a foothold, Europeans erected impenetrable fortifications; very few of these ever fell to a native siege and only the Chinese and Japanese states at times successfully evicted

European merchants and their armies. Nonetheless, European military dominance was far from absolute before the nineteenth century. The Ottoman, Mughal, Ming and Tokugawa empires were able to withstand European military might longer, until the late eighteenth and nineteenth centuries. Still, European military superiority would define relations between Europe and most of the rest of the world in the centuries following the Columbus and da Gama voyages.

While Europe constituted only about 8 per cent of the world's landmass by 1800, Europeans had extended their control to over 35 per cent of the total and, further helped by industrialization, this figure had increased to 84 per cent by 1914 (Hoffman 2015, pp. 2–3). This allowed the Europeans to conduct trade abroad on their own terms and organize the world system according to their rules, which allowed them to reap most of the benefits of this global trade. As the infamous VOC governor-general of the East Indies, Jan Pieterszoen Coen, wrote in 1614:

You gentlemen ought to know from experience that trade in Asia should be conducted and maintained under the protection and with the aid of your own weapons, and that those weapons must be wielded with the profits gained by the trade. So trade cannot be maintained without war, nor war without trade (cited in Parker 1988, p. 132).

Third, European income surplus and luxury demand were also vital factors. The search for alternative routes to Eastern exotic luxuries would not have commenced if there had been no consumers in Europe to buy these at high prices. As noted above, per capita incomes, as measured by GDP per head, were already relatively high in Europe in 1500. In fact, evidence of real wages suggests relatively high north-western European incomes since the Black Death (1346–1353) (Allen 2001). This meant that they had money to spare to make life somewhat more pleasant by spicing up their meals, and drinking some coffee and tea with sugar. Higher incomes not only spurred the demand for exotic luxuries; the availability of these luxuries in turn stimulated Europeans to work additional hours in order to be able to buy them (De Vries 2008). This ensured increased demand for these commodities, even if wages were stagnant. Kevin O'Rourke and Jeffrey Williamson (2002b) estimate that in the seventeenth century all growth in international trade was driven by European demand. The European desire for exotic goods eventually led to the rise of industries in Europe that could imitate these luxuries (see Berg 2005).

Finally, one of the factors that had held back intercontinental trade before the 1500s was the lack of demand for European goods. India and China had generally no interest in the goods that the Europeans offered them (while Europeans, on the other hand, had great demand for the full range of goods offered by Asians). The silver and gold found in the America's relieved this bottleneck and allowed Europeans to purchase Asian luxuries. China's and India's manufacturing industries were dominant in the early modern period. As we shall see, only in the late eighteenth and early nineteenth centuries did India's position as the 'workshop of the world' decline. This lack of interest in European goods becomes clear from the following letter by the Qianlong emperor – who ruled over China for most of the eighteenth century – to King George III of Great Britain in 1793:

Our dynasty's majestic virtue has penetrated unto every country under Heaven, and Kings of all nations have offered their costly tribute by land and sea. As your Ambassador can see for himself, we possess all things. I set no value on objects strange or ingenious, and have no use for your country's manufactures (cited in Woodruff 1981, p. 102).

However, as we will see in Chapter 8, the Emperor greatly underestimated the dependence of China on the silver that it consequently imported.

The Consequences of Early Globalization

Our argument on the consequences of globalization is less straightforward than previous accounts. Rather than a simple dichotomy between winners and losers of this process – the rise of the West and the decline of the East as a result – we emphasize variations in the interactions between global trade and local development. The consequences of global trade were shaped by both the different forms of globalization, and local conditions and reactions to the process. As noted above, the question is also who benefits at the local level. The interests of indigenous (and colonial) elites were often not aligned with the majority of the population, nor were short-term gains aligned with long-term consequences.

Early modern globalization was, to an extent, driven by the European desire for bullion, exotic commodities and monopoly profits, and this determined the consequences of that process. These goals interacted with three local factors (1) geographical conditions (disease environment, crop suitability); (2) factor endowments (availability of land and labour); and (3) levels of state centralization, which played an important role in shaping globalization's form as well as its consequences (Engerman and Sokoloff 2000). Not only was the process itself affected by these forces, but also the distribution of the benefits of globalization.

Three different roles for geography can be distinguished. First is the presence of exotic spices and the spread of their cultivation. Europeans discovered the routes to the Americas and the East Indies in search of spices like cinnamon, cloves, ginger, mace, nutmeg and pepper. In Asia, colonization, finding new homes for Europeans overseas, was not the goal (not from the beginning at least). Because administration and military control over large areas far from Europe entailed large costs, Europeans often tried to avoid it. Only when it was thought that the profits from such endeavours would outweigh the costs was it attempted in Asia. This was only the case for the famous four spices – cinnamon, cloves, mace and nutmeg – that were cultivated in confined areas: cinnamon grew only on Ceylon, cloves on Ambon and mace and nutmeg on the tiny Banda Islands. Pepper cultivation was too widespread over South and Southeast Asia, so that monopolization of pepper and effective price control through limitation of production was 'out of the question at any time' (Kathirithamby-Wells 1977, p. 180). In the areas that produced the monopolized spices, the whole system of production was transformed by the Europeans (the Dutch in this case) into a plantation system.

Second, the crop planted mattered for the system of production implemented by the Europeans. This is shown for the New World in order to explain the divergence between the North and the South (Engerman and Sokoloff 2000). Whereas the northern American colonies produced food grains that are associated with relatively small-scale production by independent proprietors, in Southern America and the Caribbean the soil and the climate were conducive to the growth of cash crops, like sugar, whose production benefitted from economies of scale in the form of large plantations using slave labour. The former system created a relatively egalitarian distribution of wealth, whereas the latter led to extremely unequal distributions of wealth and income. As we will show in the case of North America, the type of crop also interacted with migration patterns and labour market conditions in the metropole, as these influenced the relative scarcity of labour.

Third, geography influenced colonization via the disease environment. In some places in the world, until 1800 primarily in North America and South Africa, the Europeans settled in large numbers and began to farm the land themselves, whereas in most other places their numbers remained limited and they depended on (forced) native labour or imported (slave) labour to till the fields (Acemoglu et al. 2001). In those areas where the Europeans settled themselves, they installed political and legal systems that set the incentives favourably, distributed wealth fairly and ensured freedom for the majority of the population. As a result, these areas prospered. In regions where Europeans settled in relatively small numbers in response to the deadly environment, they implemented institutions (or continued and extended indigenous institutions) that had the purpose of extracting wealth and labour from non-European workers. Large-scale European settlement in most of Africa was out of the question before the nineteenth century, as the environment was highly dangerous for Europeans (Öberg and Rönnbäck 2016). Furthermore, Native Americans succumbed *en masse* to 'Old World' diseases, which led to a rise in demand for African slave labour in the Americas. Great wealth and income disparities, and the lack of political freedom and voice, hindered economic growth in the long run.

In addition, initial population densities and political institutions and levels of centralization also affected the consequences of globalization. Population densities were much higher in regions like China, India and parts of Southeast Asia than they were anywhere in the Americas, especially after the impact of military conquest and spread of diseases that may have reduced American populations by 90 per cent. As a result, state centralization was much stronger in these areas. In Asia and the Middle East, state formation in the Ottoman, Ming, Mughal, and Tokugawa empires was of a more lasting nature. In these areas, the Europeans were merely a group of merchants among many and had to abide by the rules of the market and/or by the constraints dictated by those strong states that were controlling the region. In these areas, where the additional money supply generated by this trade did not lead to inflation, the results could be positive (although often small as compared to the large size of these agricultural economies). Strong states in China and Japan could more or less decide when and how to profit from the new commercial opportunities offered by the growing integration of world markets. The other extreme is offered by polities – in the Moluccas or in the Americas – which were much less able to defend themselves and were conquered by European powers aimed at profiting from the natural resources or export products present there. Conquest by Europeans usually meant that the advantages of globalization were largely creamed off by the colonizers, although there are of course exceptions to this rule (as the complex story of Spanish America presented in Chapter 3 shows). Colonization meant that trade was not conducted on market terms, but on the terms of the colonizer. In the age of mercantilism, it was perceived to be in the colonizers' interests, to hinder the functioning of the free market, and instead buy and sell under monopsony and monopoly conditions. Negotiations about such conditions were between the European powers and the local elites, who perceived the agreed-upon contract to be in their best interests, even though it was probably not in the best interests of the majority of the local population. Local elites, even in regions that were colonized, thus had substantial agency and influenced who benefitted and who suffered from colonization. As shall also be discussed in Chapter 9, in Europe it mattered whether trade was organized under an absolutist or 'representative' political regime, with trade conducted under the latter generating more beneficial economic and institutional spill-overs (Acemoglu et al. 2005).

Book Outline

Our argument will unfold as follows. In the next chapter, we will start by giving an overview of the most important trends in global interaction taking place over the period 1500–1800, showing statistics for shipping, movements in bullion, commodity trade and migration. After that we will take the reader on a tour around the world following the journeys of the first European explorers, starting with the discussion of the changes taking place in Latin America, where almost the entire indigenous population succumbed to Old World diseases. Its consequent development was highly affected by the output of silver from the mines in Spanish America and by the emerging plantation system in Brazil and the Caribbean. We move on, in Chapter 4, to discuss the external slave trades and their far-reaching consequences for the African continent. Chapter 5 will discuss the economic development paths of the North American colonies; here we find a divergent development between the colonies in the North and those in the South and argue that these differences are the result of factor endowments, export trade and migration patterns. Chapter 6 will go on to describe the globalization process for South Asia; a story that is dominated by the export of textiles to Europe, Africa and Southeast Asia, and the import of bullion from Latin America and Japan. While the large domestic economy of India meant that global trade may not have had much impact on living standards and economic growth there, we do note a shift in political and economic power from inland to coastal regions. In Chapter 7 we will turn our attention to the 'Age of Commerce' in Southeast Asia. Spices from the region were an important catalyst of global trade, and the region itself also experienced sustained commercial growth as well as trends towards greater political centralization, but we also note that not everyone benefitted from these processes. Chapter 8 will review how even limited globalization may still have played a role in some of the economic developments that took place in the large and centralized states of East Asia. In the penultimate chapter, we will discuss why it was that Western Europe benefitted so much from globalization in the early modern era, and how it affected the push towards global economic primacy. Using the most recent data on trade volumes, GDP per capita, urbanization and wages, we analyse the changes that resulted from global interaction, thereby uncovering globalization's many faces. The concluding chapter brings together some of the main trends of the era and demonstrates the important impact that long-distance overseas trade had on them.

Suggested Reading

Acemoglu, Daron, Simon Johnson and James A. Robinson (2005). 'The Rise of Europe: Atlantic Trade, Institutional Change, and Economic Growth', *American Economic Review* 95, pp. 546–579.

De Vries, Jan (2010). 'The Limits of Globalisation in the Early Modern World', *Economic History Review* 63, pp. 710–733.

Findlay, Ronald, and Kevin H. O'Rourke (2007). *Power and Plenty. Trade, War, and the World Economy in the Second Millennium.* Princeton, NJ: Princeton University Press.

Flynn, Dennis O. and Arturo Giraldez (2004). 'Path Dependence, Time Lags and the Birth of Globalisation: A Critique of O'Rourke and Williamson', *European Review of Economic History* 8, pp. 81–108.

Parker, Charles (2010). *Global Interactions in the Early Modern Age, 1400–1800.* Cambridge: Cambridge University Press.

O'Brien, Patrick K. (1982). 'European Economic Development: The Contribution of the Periphery', *Economic History Review* 35, pp. 1–18.

O'Rourke, Kevin H., and Jeffrey G. Williamson (2002a). 'When Did Globalisation Begin?' *European Review of Economic History* 6, pp. 23–50.

Wallerstein, Immanuel (2011). *The Modern-World System*, 3 vols. UC. Berkeley [3rd edition; original 1974–1989].

2 | Global Connections: Ships, Commodities and People

Introduction

The voyages of Columbus and da Gama in the late fifteenth century were crucial events in the history of global trade. They inaugurated a period of unprecedented global flows of ships, commodities and people. As noted in Chapter 1, there has been a debate on the question of whether these flows were significant enough for this period to be viewed as the first age of globalization. In this chapter, we will sketch the key trends in the global connections of the early modern era: shipping and transport costs, flows of silver, commodity trade, price convergence and global migrations. These figures will be reviewed in terms of how big these were relative to the size of the various economies and populations engaged in global trade and migrations. These trends form the background against which the effects of globalization for the different components of the world economy can be analysed in subsequent chapters.

Shipping and Transport Costs

By today's standards, early modern shipping was dangerous and slow. Volumes were low: one modern container ship carries a similar volume of goods as some 70 East Indiamen in the eighteenth century (De Vries 2010). The rhythm of trade on the high seas was determined by shifts in winds and currents: the monsoon wind on the Indian Ocean, for example, blew from the south-west in summer, but reversed in winter. Sailing from Amsterdam and Batavia (now Jakarta) took some eight months (Bruijn 1980). Intercontinental transportation was, and remained, extraordinarily expensive: freight rates were so high that many bulk goods could not be shipped profitably to Europe. Pirates and privateers, as well as storms, endangered those engaged in overseas trading. Poor hygienic conditions and limited availability of fresh food aboard the ships further added to the perils of seafaring folk. Nonetheless, overseas transport was generally more efficient than transport over land, as ships were faster and could carry more goods at lower costs.

Ships and Companies

Overseas trade grew substantially over the period between 1500 and 1800, even if overland trade initially survived the discovery of the Cape route and substantial amounts of pepper continued to reach Europe through the Caravan route in the sixteenth century (Steensgaard 1973, p. 178). After the first decades of 1600s, however, the Caravan trade was in decline and most goods were carried aboard the various East India Companies' ships. The Cape route between Asia and Europe was dominated by Portuguese ships in the sixteenth century, starting with 150 ships sailing to the east in the first decade. However, their numbers rapidly declined to 50 ships per decade in the remainder of the century. From the end of the sixteenth century onwards, the numbers of Dutch, British, French and Scandinavian ships sailing to Asia swelled from about 100 in the early 1600s to almost 1,200 in the 1780s (De Vries, 2003). In the seventeenth and eighteenth centuries it were the Dutch, with their VOC, who came to dominate Asian shipping until 1800: 49 per cent of all ships in the Eurasian trade between 1600 and 1800 were Dutch (Bruijn and Gaastra 1993).

The main reason for the decline of the Portuguese and the rise of the northern European East India companies was that they were more adequately funded. Whereas the *Casa da India* was consistently in financial difficulties from the beginning, the various companies (*voor-compagnieën*) that were merged into the VOC in 1602 created a concern with a starting capital of 6.4 million guilders (Gelderblom, de Jong and Jonker 2013). The VOC and the English EIC were joint-stock companies, which, by their charters, held exclusive rights on the wholesale trade of East Indian goods in their home countries. The French, Danish and Swedish companies that were established later were modelled after the VOC and EIC. In Asia, these private companies held state-like power: they could wage wars, construct fortresses and engage in diplomacy with local potentates. The companies were administered by a board of directors that was held accountable by the shareholders. This combination of military might and the hunt for profit fundamentally influenced the directors' decision-making and the companies' activities in the East.

These companies were not without their problems, however. The EIC was reorganized three times, and the French and Danish companies were dissolved and restarted. The VOC went defunct in 1799, while the EIC would remain in business until the later nineteenth century, but mostly as a result of its transformation into a colonial power in India and its consequent access to substantial tax revenues. High costs associated with controlling large territories, long-term declines in profit margins, smuggling and corruption constituted some of the difficulties faced by the companies.

While in the Americas there were also companies with rights to trade with specific territories, like the Hudson's Bay Company (which is still in business), the Virginia Company, and the Dutch West India Company, much shipping in the Atlantic trade was carried out by many smaller private traders. It is therefore unfeasible to compute the total amount of ships sailing in the Atlantic, but their numbers must have been a large multiple of those sailing in the Asian trade. Not only were overall trading volumes in the Atlantic larger, the Atlantic ships were generally smaller than East Indiamen (250 tons vs some 800 tons) (Davis 1962). Ships employed in the Atlantic slave trade were generally smaller than normal trading ships: whereas the average West Indiaman was 261 tons in the late eighteenth century, an average slaver was about 127 tons in the same period (Klein 2010, pp. 145–46). Figure 2.1 shows a Dutch East Indiaman and two smaller warships.

Transportation Costs

Whether this increase in trade and shipping relates to a decline in transport costs is still the subject of much debate. Transport costs may decline as a result of growing labour productivity on ships, better organization of the shipping trade and a more efficient use of ships; for example, due to increased knowledge of currents and winds.

A number of recent studies have emphasized greater shipping productivity resulting from increased speed of ships. There is evidence of increasing shipping speeds on English East India Company ships (Solar and Hens 2015) and the ships of the Royal Navy (O'Grada and Kelly 2014). Most of the increased shipping speed occurred only at the end

Figure 2.1 *Two Warships and a Dutch East Indiaman*. East Indiamen were relatively large ships compared with those sailing on other routes. Etching by Wenceslaus Hollar, 1647. Courtesy of the Thomas Fisher Rare Book Library, University of Toronto

of the eighteenth century, however. Peter Solar (2013) found that the average duration of the trips by English East India Company ships sailing to Asia fell by about a third between the early 1770s and the 1820s. He attributes this increase to a late eighteenth-century innovation: the copper sheathing of ships. This innovation was not adopted by the largest company sailing in the Asian trade, the VOC, until the 1790s, and the speed of Dutch ships did not increase in the eighteenth century (O'Grada and Kelly 2014). The average length of the journey of VOC ships from the Dutch Republic to Batavia was 239 days in both the seventeenth and the eighteenth century, but the return trip took almost three weeks longer in the eighteenth century (Bruijn 1980). Dutch East Indiamen were generally slower than those from other companies.[1] English ships, in particular, were significantly faster: in the early 1770s they were able to make the trip to Batavia in just 173 days (Solar 2013, pp. 636–637), but French and Danish ships also seem to have been slightly faster (Gøbel 1993; Solar 2013).

Costs may also have been reduced by quicker loading and offloading of ships, reducing the time between voyages. It seems that VOC ships were being used less intensively over time: the frequency of voyages declined over the seventeenth and eighteenth centuries,[2] which meant that they were making longer voyages, or more and longer stops, on average in the eighteenth century. In addition, the total number of return trips that VOC ships made also declined (De Zwart 2016a). This could have increased capital costs and may explain the paradox of rising labour productivity yet stable freight rates in Dutch-Asiatic shipping. We have no comparable data for the other companies for this period. Only at the end of the eighteenth century is there evidence of an increase in the frequency of voyages of EIC ships (Solar 2013). In addition, the total number of voyages made by EIC ships increased in this same period and copper sheathing played an important part in this.

Shipping costs per ton may also have declined as a result of the growth of tonnage. The average Portuguese ship sailing to India in the first decade of the sixteenth century had a carrying capacity of some 280 tons; but this had increased to 1,000 tons at the end of that century (De Vries 2003, p. 46). Between the early seventeenth century and the 1790s, the average amount of goods transported by a VOC ship roughly doubled from about 400 to more than 800 tons per ship (with some ships even carrying some 1,000 tons in the 1770s) (Bruijn, Gaastra and Schöffer 1987, pp. 177–178) which could have reduced transportation costs per ton. Scandinavian ships (of the Danish and Swedish Companies) may have been slightly bigger, but British ships were generally smaller than those of the VOC. French ships were roughly of similar size (Koninckx 1993, p. 132). Yet, in all cases, ships grew in size in the early modern period.

The increase in tonnage aboard Dutch ships was not matched by a similar growth of personnel. This meant that the ton–man ratio on ships also increased, from some 4–6 tons per man in the first half of the seventeenth century to roughly 8–10 tons per man in the last decades of the eighteenth century (Gaastra and Bruijn 1993, p. 198). This should have led to a decline in labour costs involved in Dutch shipping. Ton–man ratios on EIC ships remained stable (at around 5 tons per man) between 1670 and 1760 (Chaudhuri 1993, pp. 75–76), but increased thereafter to almost 8 tons in the period 1783–1792. Labour productivity also increased on Danish ships as ton–man rates increased from 3.5 in the 1730s to 8 in the 1790s (Gøbel 1993). This confirms suggestions of increased labour productivity in ocean shipping starting already from the end of the Middle Ages (Lucassen and Unger 2000). Recently, this increase in labour productivity in the eighteenth century is observed for ships from a variety of countries and it has been suggested that this growth resulted from increased human capital of sailors (Van Lottum and Van Zanden 2014).

Did shipping also become safer over time? Notwithstanding spectacular stories of piracy and shipwrecks, shipping in general was in fact remarkably safe: of all the VOC voyages from the Dutch Republic to the East Indies, just over 2.5 per cent ended in shipwreck (Bruijn 1980). For the VOC, the evidence does not show improvement in the eighteenth century over the seventeenth century: while in the seventeenth century a total of 2.7 per cent of all voyages ended in disaster (due to capture or shipwreck); this increased to 3.2 per cent in the eighteenth century (De Zwart 2016b). Evidence from the Danish Company, on the other hand, suggests a strong decrease in numbers of ships lost over the course of the eighteenth century (Gøbel 1993). Some scholars have suggested a decrease in piracy and privateering over the eighteenth century, which would have allowed a decline in labour and capital costs (for soldiers and armaments) (Ronnback 2012). Piracy in the Asian trade certainly existed, but was limited: of a total of over 8,000 journeys made by the VOC, only 36 ships to, and 24 ships from, the East Indies were raided. Between 1674 and 1781 not a single VOC returning ship was attacked east of the Cape of Good Hope (Van Goor 1994, p. 50).

These are indirect indicators of shipping costs related to different factors that may have influenced those costs. Several scholars have attempted a direct estimate of transportation costs by computing freight rates. J.R. Bruijn (1990) found that VOC freight rates per ton remained relatively stable (on average 286 guilders per ton) over most of the eighteenth century, only briefly increasing during the Fourth Anglo-Dutch War. It is therefore unclear whether costs in the eighteenth century were lower relative to the seventeenth century. EIC freight rates declined from some £30–32 per ton to £16–23 per ton in the first half of the seventeenth century (Steensgaard 1965, pp. 148, 152). Yet, over the period 1676 to 1760, freight rates increased slightly (Chaudhuri 1993, pp. 79–80), also when correcting for inflation (using data from Allen 2001). A decline in EIC shipping costs may then have occurred again only at the end of the eighteenth century, resulting from copper sheathing. As far as we know, there are no estimates of freight rates in the shipping of the other European companies.

Thus, evidence on the development of transport costs in the Eurasian trade over time is mixed. What about the transportation across the

Atlantic? Studies from the 1960s and 1970s suggested increases in shipping productivity and declining freight rates on the Atlantic routes from 1600 on, resulting to a large extent from better market organization and reduced risk associated with declining piracy and privateering. Several studies have found empirical evidence of increasing tonnage-per-gun ratios on a variety of routes in the early modern era (see Rönnbäck 2012). This could have reduced capital and insurance costs in trade.

Average tonnage per ship increased in the trades between London on the one hand and New York, Virginia and Jamaica on the other (French 1987). There was also an increase in the tons per man between the late seventeenth and late eighteenth centuries for a variety of other routes (Walton 1967). This concerns the smaller colonial trading vessels, but the size of crews on larger ships (250 tons) sailing on the North Atlantic route declined by half from over 30 in 1600 to about 15 in 1800 (North 1968, p. 962). The decline in crew sizes also decreased victualling costs by a similar degree. The average port time of ships transporting tobacco both in the North American colonies (Chesapeake) and the West Indies (Barbados) halved between the late seventeenth and late eighteenth centuries: from 100 to 50 days in the Chesapeake and from 50 to 25 days in Barbados (North 1968, p. 963). Furthermore, there is evidence of increased speed of ships in the Atlantic slave trade (Rönnbäck 2012), which, to a significant extent, was the result of the copper sheathing of slave ships (Solar and Rönnbäck 2015).

As a result of these productivity changes, freight rates declined by between 0.7 and 1 per cent annually in the bullion, oil, tobacco and sugar trades between the New and the Old Worlds in the seventeenth and eighteenth centuries (Walton 1970). Menard (1991) shows that freight costs on tobacco transported from Chesapeake to Britain declined by an impressive 1.4 per cent annually between 1619 and 1775, but emphasizes that this was only the result of more efficient packaging. All in all, it seems fair to suggest a decline in Atlantic transport costs between 1500 and 1800. In general, of course, shipping across the Atlantic was cheaper than on the routes to Asia, simply because the distance was much shorter. Declining shipping costs in the Atlantic were therefore probably less important in allowing a growth of trading volumes than in the trade with Asia.

The combined results of increased numbers of ships from an increasing number of countries and a steady growth of ship size allowed for the general growth of early modern trade discussed below.

The Flows of Silver

One of the most well-known dimensions of this new world economy that was emerging after 1500 concerns global silver flows. Silver was the principal lubricant that kept the global wheels of commerce rolling. As Flynn and Giraldez (1995, p. 201) note, '[m]ore than the market for any other commodity, the silver market explains the emergence of world trade'. The Americas were overwhelmingly the dominant production site of precious metals: 85 per cent of the total silver and 70 per cent of the total gold production in the world came from there (Barret 1990, p. 224).

Figure 2.2 shows estimates of the global silver flows between 1500 and 1800 in annual averages. These figures are incomplete and subject to large margins of error,[3] yet we can be fairly confident about the following general trends. The silver that was exported to Europe increased rapidly until the beginning of the seventeenth century; after a period of stagnation, exports rose again in the later part of that century. Some of the silver was exported by the Spanish directly across the Pacific Ocean to Manila. The size of Manila galleon flows are subject to discussion, as much of this trade was illicit; a high estimate suggests over 50 tons in both the seventeenth and eighteenth centuries, while a low estimate suggests somewhere between 15 and 17 tons annually (De Vries 2003, p. 81). Much of the silver transported to Manila ended up in China (Flynn and Giraldez 2002a), while even more Peruvian silver may have reached China in illicit trade via the ports of Buenos Aires and Sacramento (Flynn and Giraldez 1996, p. 65). A growing part of American silver was retained in the Americas in the eighteenth century, and the rise of the Caribbean plantation economies and the economic growth of the Thirteen Colonies may account for this.

The shares of silver, as well as the absolute amounts, that were retained in Europe were very high in the sixteenth century but declined somewhat in the seventeenth and eighteenth centuries. Despite such declines, the inflow of silver into Europe was substantial over a period

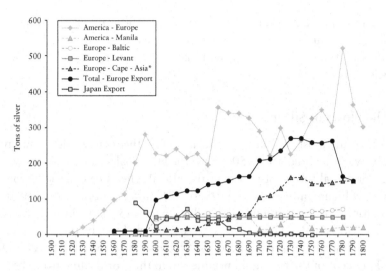

Figure 2.2 Average annual silver flows, 1500–1800
Note: *before 1581 Only to China
Sources: America–Europe: TePaske and Brown (2010); America : Flynn and
Giraldez (2000a); Europe–Baltic and Levant: Barrett (1990);
Europe–Cape–Asia: De Vries (2003). Japan export: Schreurs (2015).
Data collected by Jonathan Fink-Jensen.

of three centuries, which dramatically increased the silver stock. The
consequences of these inflows for prices and economic development
in Europe have been a subject of debate and are discussed at length in
Chapter 9.

Of the silver that was re-exported from Western Europe, a significant part went to the Baltic, which was important in supplying a number of basic necessities like grains, timber and furs. Ships travelling
to the Baltic had to go through the Sound, where the Danish levied
a customs duty: the Sound Toll. These tax registers have been well
preserved and we are thus relatively certain about the trade flows in
these waters. In the seventeenth and eighteenth centuries, on average,
some 53 tons of silver were exported to the Baltic region annually. We
are less certain about the European exports of silver to the Levant. De
Vries (2003, pp. 80–81) suggests an increase from 38 tons in the first
half of the seventeenth century to 60 tons a century later,[4] but notes
that these are most likely overestimates. Substantial amounts of silver
flowed through the Baltic and Levant to South and East Asia (Flynn

and Giraldez 2002b). Over the course of the seventeenth century, the eastward flows beyond the Ottoman Empire and beyond Russia may have diminished as China's silver prices declined and there is evidence that both these regions became more monetized over the course of the seventeenth and eighteenth centuries (De Vries 2003, p. 80).

Finally, a large chunk of American silver was re-exported from Europe to Asia through the Cape route on East India Company ships. As Figure 2.1 shows, this route remained minor until the second half of the seventeenth century. The amounts of silver transported to Asia were generally below 20 tons before the 1650s, but they increased after that. In the first half of the eighteenth century, the amount of silver reaching Asia through the Cape route was generally over 100 tons per year, but it declined somewhat in the second half of the eighteenth century as the British attained colonial power in India and started to use taxes to pay for the Asian commodities brought to Europe. De Vries (2010) estimated that, on average, 160 tons of silver may have reached Asia annually over the eighteenth century via this route.

Of the silver exported by the British the overwhelming majority was spent in India: around the turn of the eighteenth century some 87 per cent went to India, 12 per cent to China and less than 1 per cent ended up in Southeast Asia.[5] This was quite different for the silver transported by the Dutch, where some 55 per cent went to India, 19 per cent to China and 26 per cent to Southeast Asia.[6] While difficult to obtain precise numbers, it is likely that much of this silver eventually ended up in China as the world's 'silver sink'. Silver also came to China from the Iwami mines in Japan from the 1540s until the late seventeenth century. Japanese exports were very substantial in the late sixteenth and early seventeenth centuries, but after that these numbers dwindled as a result of the increasing regulation of trade via Nagasaki (on the island of Deshima) and trade restrictions on silver exports.

Many scholars have attributed great significance to the silver flows to India and especially China, which apparently had an insatiable desire for silver. At the same time, it is important to keep in mind that perhaps two-thirds of the world's population lived in Asia (especially India and China), so that the additional annual influx of silver was perhaps small relative to the total population (as suggested by De Vries 2010). Nonetheless, compounded over a long period of time, these flows had a lasting impact and significantly increased silver supplies in both Europe and Asia. Furthermore, as Flynn and Giraldez

(2002a) argue, these silver flows created an integrated global monetary system, as the value of silver converged globally (see pp. 44–45).

The Rise of Global Commodity Trade

These specie flows were exchanged for a variety of commodities. Finding an alternative route to the Asian spices in order to circumvent the Arab-Venetian spice monopoly was the immediate impulse for Vasco da Gama to sail to India via the Cape. Immediately following the voyage of da Gama, pepper and other spices formed, by far, the majority of goods imported from Asia in the sixteenth century.

In the early sixteenth century, over 80 per cent of the goods brought to Europe by the Portuguese consisted of pepper, while the remainder constituted other Asian spices (nutmeg, mace, cloves and cinnamon). As the Portuguese were unsuccessful in their attempts to monopolize the entire spice trade (discussed in Chapter 6 on South Asia), additional pepper found its way to European markets through the Middle East by Venetian hands: some 2,000 tons of pepper in the 1560s (Bulbeck et al. 1998). At the end of the sixteenth century, goods other than spices, namely textiles and indigo, came to be transported on Portuguese ships. This period thus saw a greater diversification of imports that characterized the remainder of the early modern period. When the Dutch came to dominate Asian trade in the seventeenth century, the importance of pepper gradually declined: from 26 per cent of total imports to some 12 per cent at the end of the eighteenth century. The fine spices (cinnamon, cloves, mace and nutmeg), on which the Dutch East India Company had a monopoly, continued to form an important part of the trade as it consistently constituted some 25 per cent of the total volume (De Zwart 2016b).

By far the most important products traded in the Dutch-Asiatic trade were the Indian textiles: good for an average 21 per cent in terms of total sales values for the entire period, and even over 50 per cent when expressed in Asian purchase prices (De Zwart 2016b). In the British trade from Asia, textiles took up 70 per cent of Asian values in the later seventeenth century, but declined thereafter to 60 per cent around 1750 and to 30 per cent at the end of the eighteenth century – mostly due to the rising tea share in EIC trade (Chaudhuri 1978; Bowen 2010). Besides markets throughout Europe, Indian textiles were exported to markets in Japan, Southeast Asia, Africa and even the Americas (Riello

2009). It is thus clear that in the early modern period, India really did 'cloth the world' (Riello and Roy 2009). This textile trade played an important role in the eventual industrialization of Britain at the end of the eighteenth century.

The importance of coffee and tea in global commerce increased drastically in the eighteenth century. The amount of tea imported by the VOC from China increased dramatically from 7 tons annually at the end of the seventeenth century to some 1,500 tons annually in the closing decades of the eighteenth century (De Zwart 2016b), which entails a growth rate of 5.5 per cent. British imports of tea increased even more spectacularly from 2.5 tons in the 1670s and 1680s, to 3,700 tons (Chaudhuri 1978; Bowen 2010) – an annual increase of 7.5 per cent! One-third of all tea imported from China in the eighteenth century was transported by the Danish and Swedish East India Companies, who imported on average some 2,000 tons of tea per annum in the late eighteenth century (Hodacs 2016, pp. 2, 73). All these companies competed with each other in buying teas from Canton (China).

The growth in the coffee trade was, most likely, even more spectacular, as it came to be imported from the Americas as well as Asia. Coffee originated in Yemen, where at the end of the seventeenth century a very competitive market existed and various European companies were trying to buy increasing quantities. High demand led to high prices, which pushed buyers to search for alternatives. In the early eighteenth century, the Dutch succeeded in smuggling coffee seedlings to Java and started the production of Java coffee. VOC coffee imports increased from 30 tons annually in the closing decade of the seventeenth century to 2,000 tons in the 1770s and 1780s (De Zwart 2016b). The French followed suit and started cultivating coffee on the Indian Ocean island of Réunion in 1715 (Topik 2003), while the EIC continued to import coffee from Yemen.

Even more coffee came from the Americas. Whereas coffee exports from eighteenth-century Java constituted about 2,000 tons per year, production in the main Dutch West Indies colony of Surinam was generally over 5,000 tons in the second half of the eighteenth century (Samper and Fernando 2003). Figures for coffee from Haiti are not abundantly available, yet numbers from the years for which we do have data suggest that it was one of the greatest coffee producers in the late eighteenth century, producing some 5,000 tons around 1750,

22,000 tons in 1775 and over 35,000 in the late 1780s, just before
the slave revolt (Samper and Fernando 2003). Exports from Jamaica
and Brazil further augmented coffee imports to Europe. The growth
of supply was matched by an equally strong growth of demand. As we
will discuss in Chapter 9, the increase in consumption of these goods
had more important effects than simply making life a bit more pleasant: it has been argued that it had important effects on, for example,
household decision making and living standards (see also Chapter 9).

In the colonies, at the same time, these goods were often produced
on plantations using slavery or other forms of coerced labour. In
the Priangan region in Java (south of Batavia), the local rulers (the
bupati) coerced peasants to cultivate coffee for the VOC. By the end
of the eighteenth century, forced coffee cultivation was directly super-
vised by Europeans (Jacobs 2006, pp. 260–275). In the Americas,
the export commodities were produced on large plantations worked
by African slaves, but owned by Europeans. Production methods of
the different export crops differed depending on local factor endowments as well as per crop. As we will see in subsequent chapters,
the economic systems associated with the production of these export
crops in the colonies had drastic consequences for long-term development. The production of textiles in India, on the other hand, seemed
to take place in more favourable conditions for manufacturers,
although even there the situation went into decline in the course of
the eighteenth century as the EIC increased its control in some areas
(Prakash 2009).

The trade crossing the Atlantic is harder to quantify, as it was not
dominated by a few chartered companies that entirely dominated the
trade for a long period. Next to coffee (and the treasure discussed
above), sugar, tobacco and cotton were the most important commodities exported from the Americas to Europe in the well-known triangular trade. In this trade, Europe transported manufactured goods to
the African coasts, where they purchased slaves that were transported
to the Americas. The slave trade is further discussed below in the section on forced migrations. While some sugar was imported from Asia
(mainly Java), the plantations of the West Indies and Brazil were the
main suppliers of sugar to the European markets. Total European
imports of sugar from the Americas can be estimated at 170,000
tons annually. Tobacco came predominantly from the American
colonies in the north: around the middle of the eighteenth century

the Chesapeake plantations exported perhaps some 25,000 tons per annum (Steensgaard 1995, pp. 11–12).

A final product that was a part of the triangular trade was cotton. It attained significance only late in the eighteenth century, however. Exports from the newly formed United States still amounted to only 86 tons in 1791, yet increased rapidly to over 10,000 tons per annum in the years immediately before 1812 (Findlay 1990). Raw cotton (so the argument goes) as the basic material for producing manufactured textiles was important in fuelling the Industrial Revolution in Britain. However, considering the late growth of exports in raw cotton, the link seems rather to be the other way around: British industrialization pushed the growth of cotton production (Eltis and Engerman 2000).

This section may be summarized by discussing the overall trends in trading volumes over these three centuries. The total volume of Euro-Asian trade can be reconstructed fairly accurately, as it was in the hands of a few trading organizations whose records have generally been preserved (except those of the *Casa da India*) (De Vries 2010, p. 716). De Vries estimated a growth of this trade of about 1.1 per cent per annum over this 300-year period. Based on more patchy data on the sugar, tobacco and slave trades, he suggests that the Atlantic trade grew by 2.2 per cent annually in the same period, except for the crisis decades in the first half of the seventeenth century. O'Rourke and Williamson (2002b) arrive at slightly lower figures: they suggest a growth of European trade with both the Americas and Asia of about 1.06 per cent between 1500 and 1800. They also note that the growth of trade was substantially slower in the seventeenth century (about half) than in the sixteenth and eighteenth centuries. The general crisis of the seventeenth century demonstrates that globalization was not a linear process. Just like in the early nineteenth and twentieth centuries, the early modern period also experienced periods of 'de-globalization'. Ebbs and flows of world trade were influenced by climate (Parker 2013), but also by deliberate attempts of governments to close themselves off from the global economy (as was the case in China and Japan, as we will discuss in Chapter 8). Despite such contractions it is clear that early modern trade growth was impressive compared with the growth of trade in the centuries before, and relative to developments of GDP and population. World GDP in the same period grew by only 0.4 per cent annually, while world population rose at a rate of

0.24 per cent. Trade as a share of world GDP, or the degree of 'openness', thus increased in this period (Estevadeordal et al. 2003).

We should not get over-excited though; even at the end of the eighteenth century the amount of Asian goods received was only about 0.5 kg in per capita terms (De Vries 2010, p. 718). Furthermore, while the commodity trade did become more diversified already in the seventeenth century, early modern trade remained, by and large, a trade in luxuries rather than necessities. Trade theory presupposes that it is the trade in basic necessities that has the most important effect on the restructuring of economies. Only for the 1770s is there evidence of significant quantities of grain being transported across the Atlantic from the American Colonies to Britain (Sharp and Weisdorf 2013) and from the Cape Colony to Amsterdam (Braudel 1982).

Previous works have noted that these luxuries were non-competing: coffee, pepper and nutmeg did not grow in Europe, after all. We suggest, on the other hand, that as consumers across the globe were faced with limited choices, because their incomes were limited, all goods were in fact competing. British worsted manufacturers faced increasing competition from the inflow of high-quality Indian cotton textiles. A British consumer could buy domestically produced woollen and linen clothes or purchase Indian cotton textiles. Eventually, the British managed to imitate Indian craftsmanship and then 'mechanized' the production process, leading to a process of import-substitution industrialization (Berg 2009; Broadberry and Gupta 2009; Riello 2009). Additionally, an Amsterdam dockworker could decide whether to spend his day's wages on locally brewed beer or American cultivated coffee. The rise of coffee and tea consumption in the seventeenth and eighteenth centuries occurred simultaneously alongside a dramatic decline of the Holland beer brewing industry (Unger 2001). As will be discussed in Chapter 9, the consumption of these exotic luxuries was, by the eighteenth century, not limited to the elite, but was also enjoyed by lower-income groups. Finally, we would argue, the global flows presented here had important spill-over effects that would alter economic organization across the globe and also affect patterns of urbanization and institutional change.

Creating a Global Market

According to Flynn and Giraldez (1995, 2002a, 2004) the founding of Manila in 1571 created one global market, as all major landmasses were in direct contact with each other from that date onwards. The global silver flows discussed above led to a 'highly integrated global economy' and they note several phases in which silver prices converged over the early modern period. Between the 1540s and 1640s, the unprecedented silver output from the mines in Spanish America and Japan flowed to a large extent to China as a result of the higher silver prices there (in terms of gold): in the early sixteenth century 1 ounce of gold could be bought with 6 ounces of silver, while in Europe it cost 12 ounces of silver (Flynn and Giraldez 2002a, p. 393). Over the course of this century, silver prices converged and by the 1640s the price of silver was the same in China as in the rest of world. Less silver then found its way to China for the remainder of the seventeenth century. At the beginning of the eighteenth century, the value of silver in China once more was above that in the rest of the world (a premium of 50 per cent), but converged in the first half-century and regained equilibrium around 1750. Were these trends in silver price convergence unique, or was there a unified global market for other commodities as well?

Commodity Price Convergence

O'Rourke and Williamson (2002a) dispute the existence of a global market, and thereby the beginning of 'globalization', prior to the nineteenth century. They define globalization as the integration of markets across regions, with commodity markets reflecting one important dimension of this phenomenon. In a theoretical, perfectly integrated world market prices would be the same across the globe. In reality, prices are never completely the same across markets, as transaction costs incurred in trade drive a gap between prices in export and import markets. These include transport costs and tariffs, the costs of administrating the trading firm and the acquisition of goods. Defined in this way, the process of globalization is driven by a decline in these costs and the diminishing of monopoly profits. This also allows for a growth of trade (as we have seen above), but since trade volumes may also increase as a result of population growth, capital accumulation, and/or other factors unrelated to market integration, the best evidence of globalization is the declining gap in prices between export and import markets (O'Rourke and Williamson 2002a, pp. 25–26).

O'Rourke and Williamson (2002a) found no evidence of convergence of prices in Euro-Asian trade before the 1820s and concluded that globalization started only after that. The issue has been re-investigated over the past years, and a number of recent studies have shown evidence of price convergence in both Atlantic and Asian trade. The gap between prices paid for sugar at the plantations in Brazil and the prices fetched in the European market place declined significantly between 1550 and the end of the eighteenth century (Rönnbäck 2009). Similarly, there is evidence of convergence in tobacco prices across the Atlantic in the eighteenth century, but the evidence for the other American plantation commodities is more ambiguous (ibid.). Grain prices between North America and Europe also converged in the eighteenth century (Dobado-Gonzalez et al. 2012), but much more so in the nineteenth century. In order to observe such convergence, grain prices were converted into a common currency: silver weight. Since only a limited amount of grain was transported across the Atlantic in the eighteenth century (Sharp and Weisdorf 2013), it is difficult to interpret these results: to what extent was this a convergence of grain prices or a convergence in the purchasing power of silver?

Significant evidence of price convergence can also be found for the trade between Europe and Asia. Of all the products transported by the VOC on this route, the majority show price convergence in the seventeenth and eighteenth centuries (De Zwart 2016a). Considering the limited evidence of declining transportation costs, this price convergence was mainly driven by the general growth of volumes and increased competition in international trade (discussed above).

The integration of markets was especially pronounced in free market conditions: in places where the European companies competed in the acquisition of commodities (for example in the cases of textiles in India and tea in China) prices were driven up, while at the same time the increased supply of these products to European markets pushed down prices there. Figure 2.3 shows the prices for tea, silk, textiles and saltpetre in Asia and Amsterdam, as well as the 'mark-up': the ratio of the selling to the purchasing price. The mark-up allows easy interpretation of price differentials: e.g. a mark-up of 10 implies that the price in the selling market was 10 times the price in the purchasing market, while a mark-up of 1 implies similar prices.[7] Figure 2.3 shows evidence of strong price convergence in goods acquired in competitive markets in India and China. Considering the fact that

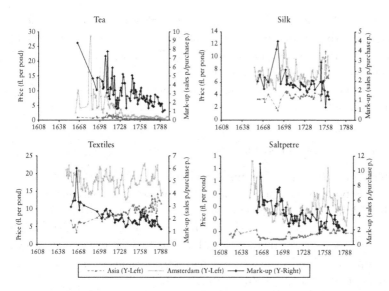

Figure 2.3 Prices and mark-ups for goods traded by the VOC between competitive markets, 1608-1800
Source: De Zwart (2016a).

the VOC had to cover all its costs by the difference between sales and purchase prices, these margins were certainly very small by the end of the eighteenth century.

This process was hindered if a European company employed its guns to influence market conditions. The VOC often used its firepower to force local potentates into signing contracts that gave them monopsony market power, thereby acquiring commodities at relatively low prices (for example in the case of pepper). Only in the case of the Moluccan[8] spices (cloves, mace and nutmeg) and cinnamon from Ceylon (present-day Sri Lanka), was the VOC the only seller on world markets and therefore able to set sales prices in Europe. As a result, the difference between prices in Europe and Asia was very big over the entire seventeenth and eighteenth centuries. In all other cases, such control over sales prices was limited by third-market competition (De Zwart 2016a).

Our conclusion for the early modern globalization process is that there was significant scope for prices to converge. There is the possibility that transportation costs declined slightly as a result of increasing ship speed, especially at the end of the eighteenth century. Mostly, it was the growing competition among Europeans active on the world's sea lanes that squeezed profit margins. The process was by no means automatic, however, and was fundamentally shaped by the extent to which the chartered companies could affect market conditions across the globe.

Relative Price Developments

Early modern consumers were probably not interested in the difference between prices across the globe: instead they were interested in their ability to purchase these exotic goods (De Vries 2010). How price convergence affected households in Europe is best studied by asking the question of whether these 'colonial groceries' became cheaper in Europe. They generally did, but here there are also significant differences between the different commodities.

Immediately following Vasco da Gama's opening of the Cape trade route, real prices of pepper, cinnamon, cloves and ginger declined in markets across Europe in the sixteenth century (O'Rourke and Williamson 2009). A large part of the real price decline happened in the second half of the sixteenth century, as the price revolution (driven by the large influx of silver from American mines) pushed up the prices for most commodities in Europe, while pepper prices remained stable. The entry of the English and Dutch companies into the Eurasian trade system further pushed the pepper price decline in the seventeenth century. Figure 2.4 shows the price of pepper deflated by the trends in a consumer price index as well as relative to builders' unskilled wages. These large price declines meant that pepper was a fairly common

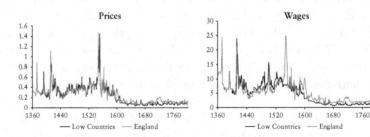

Figure 2.4 Real pepper prices: relative to prices and unskilled wages, 1360–1800
Sources: Allen (2001), Van Zanden (1999)

spice that was consumed by many people, and not only the very rich. Due to the monopoly policies of the VOC, no such decline could be found in prices of the fine spices, which remained incredibly expensive in the early modern period and only available for the very rich. For example, for much of the eighteenth century, one pound of cloves cost 3.75 guilders, while the daily wage of an unskilled building labourer was only about 1.25 guilders (Allen 2001). Three full days of work were needed to buy only a pound of cloves; while few consumers would purchase their cloves by the pound, it is clear that, under such circumstances, not a lot of people could afford to flavour their dinners with these spices. Shortages of pepper meant that prices no longer declined in the eighteenth century. Prices of sugar, coffee and tea, on the other hand, would continue to show a decline relative to consumer price indices over the seventeenth and eighteenth centuries. These price developments had enormous consequences for the consumer revolution in Europe (Chapter 9).

At the same time, the producers of these commodities in Asia and the Americas were interested not so much in the European price, but rather in the price for which they could sell their produce in their home countries. Figure 2.5 shows for four

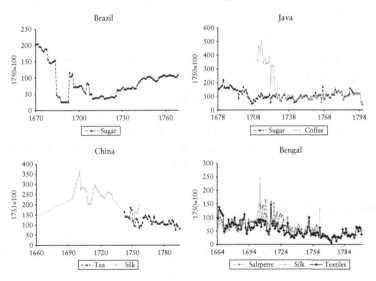

Figure 2.5 Real prices of export commodities in South America and Asia, 1660-1800
Source: De Zwart (2016a; 2016b); Levin, Arroyo Abad and Cuesta (2007).

major export-producing countries the price for the most important exports relative to the price of the main staple. These trends thus suggest the extent to which producers of these export crops were able to buy more or less food. It can be seen that, for all these major export items, the real price declined. In Brazil, the real price of sugar plummeted in the 1680s as a result of the strong increase in the price of cassava. In Java, the sugar price decreased, particularly in the later seventeenth century, most likely driven by increased production on the island. In the eighteenth century, real sugar prices in both Brazil and Java recovered somewhat although they did not reach their previous levels. The decline in the Java coffee price was entirely the result of VOC colonial policies. In China, real prices for silk and tea declined slightly over the eighteenth century. The strongest evidence is for Bengal, however, where in real terms the price of the main exports, saltpetre, silk and textiles, declined by a half to a third. In both cases, it seems that domestic forces (such as population growth) driving up the price of rice and wheat were stronger than the growing international demand for trade goods. In none of these cases, did prices, whether determined by the colonial power or by the market, move in favour of export-commodity producers.

People on the Move

The growth of trade previously discussed was matched by flows of people, both to organize this trade and production, but also as workers producing these global commodities. In terms of the global migrations in the early modern era we distinguish between two types of flows: voluntary migrations and forced migrations. The first concerns mainly the movement of Europeans to the colonies in Asia and the New World, while the second includes the Atlantic slave trade.

Voluntary Migrations

On its voyage back to Spain in December 1492, the *Santa Maria*, Columbus' flagship, hit a coral reef off the coast of Haiti. Its crew, left behind by Columbus due to lack of space on the two remaining caravels, may be considered the first transatlantic colonizers (although in this case not entirely by choice). The ship wreck was used to build a fort and

shelter for them. They did not fare well, however, and when Columbus
returned a few months later, this first American colonial outpost was
burned to the ground and the men had been killed (Sanchez-Albornoz
1994). Over the course of the next three centuries, these unlucky pio-
neers were to be followed by many more.

   In their footsteps arrived 243,000 of their fellow Spaniards in the
sixteenth century, and another 300,000 in the seventeenth and around
200,000 in the eighteenth century (Lucassen 2016).[9] A first group of
Spaniards that moved to the Americas were military men, the *conquistadores*, who vanquished the native societies and took over their lands.
They were followed by a variety of settlers: artisans, priests, adminis-
trators, merchants, etc., who built up the Spanish Empire that arose
from the ashes of the native states (Sánchez-Albornoz 1994, p. 27).
Most of these migrants were young males: in the early sixteenth century only 6.2 per cent of the migrants were female. While the number
of females increased over the remainder of the sixteenth century, their
share remained below a third of the total (ibid., p. 30). A consequence
of this gender imbalance was, of course, that the Spaniards mixed with
the indigenous population and had children of combined European and
Amerindian descent: *mestizos*. In the later seventeenth and eighteenth
centuries, soldiers continued to constitute a major group of migrants
going to the Americas, but the Spanish government also sponsored the
migration of peasants and merchants from densely populated areas in
the metropole to build up the empire's economy.

   The other Iberians, the Portuguese, constituted the largest group of
Europeans settling in the Americas, mainly in Brazil. About 1.5 million
Portuguese, mostly men, left for the Americas between 1493 and 1820
(Lucassen 2016). As a result of the discovery and exploitation of gold
and diamond mines in Brazil, half a million Portuguese migrated in the
first half of the eighteenth century alone. These figures are especially
spectacular considering the small size of the country; in 1700, the
Portuguese population was only 2.3 million (Palma and Reis 2014).
Like the Spaniards, these Portuguese men blended with the native
populace and had *mestizo* offspring. In addition, the Iberians came
generally from the middle classes in the urban areas of the peninsula
(or the Canary Islands), and in the Americas they founded cities (and
lived in them) (Sánchez-Albornoz 1994). Spanish America was highly
urbanized (see Chapter 3).

A small number of Dutchmen also migrated to Brazil in the seventeenth century, while Englishmen settled in the Caribbean. However, most northern Europeans, mainly from the British Isles, but to a lesser extent from France, Germany and the Dutch Republic, went to the northern American mainland (Lucassen 2016). The northern Europeans came generally in much smaller numbers than the Iberians. In the seventeenth century, this figure totalled some 400,000 and an overwhelming majority of these were from the British Isles. This figure increased to a total of 600,000 migrants between 1750 and 1820 and while most of them again came from Britain, other groups, like the French, Germans and Dutch, became more prominent among these flows. Many British settled in the Thirteen Colonies, whose population increased to 2.5 million settlers in 1775, as a result of both immigration and natural increase.

While the northern Europeans did not arrive in completely empty lands, the indigenous societies of North America were generally less developed than those in the South. Settlement patterns in North America were more rural, and many settlers acquired large tracts of land or came to America to work and live on these farms as indentured servants (more than 50 per cent between 1600 and 1800) (Lucassen 2016). Many of these people came from the lower ranks of English society and a significant part of the remaining 'free' migrants established themselves as artisans, planters or traders in the colonies.

Another major settlement area for Europeans was the Cape Colony at the southern tip of Africa.[10] It was founded in 1652 as a victualling station for Dutch East India Company ships on their way to the Indies. In the first decades of its existence, immigration from Europe was actively stimulated (as the VOC paid for immigrants' voyage), and land was made available to the settlers on a first come, first served basis. After 1717, however, immigration was no longer encouraged and population growth relied on high fertility rates among the settlers: the white population grew from 1,300 in 1700 to around 22,000 by the end of the century (De Zwart 2013).

In order to organize trade with Asia, there was also European migration to the East as the chartered trading companies sent almost two million Europeans to Asia over the course of these centuries. A large proportion of these returned, but a share of these Europeans stayed in Asia. That is, if they survived the trip and the tropical climate conditions. Due to high mortality, their total numbers were never very big; '[i]t has been estimated that in any one year between 1600 and 1740 there were not more than fifty thousand Europeans to be found in the whole of Asia' (Giraldez 2013, p. 266). The Portuguese were the first to settle in significant numbers in Asia. They established a substantial presence in Goa, Ceylon and Malacca, and they were followed by Spaniards, who built up their presence in the Philippines. About one million Europeans went to Asia aboard the ships of the VOC, which included, besides many Dutchmen, also significant numbers of Germans and Scandinavians. English and French migration to Asia was limited until the end of the eighteenth century.

More significant in number were the Chinese migrants living across Southeast Asia. The Philippines, Java and Thailand all came to boast over a 100,000 Chinese peoples 'and perhaps as many as 1 million were scattered across Southeast Asia' (Parker 2010, p. 137; see also Chapter 7). Chinese migrants also reached the Americas – Lima and Mexico City had Asian populations (Hoerder 2015, p. 21), though numbers are unknown. Migrants from other Asian countries were less abundant and there were only minor Indian and Japanese trading communities across Southeast Asia.

Finally, a large number of Chinese were on the move overland as a result of the expansion of the Qing Empire.[11] Between 1600 and 1800, almost 20 million Chinese moved towards the frontiers of the empire and to sparsely populated, inland mountain areas (McKeown 2014, p. 286). This colonization of Asia's interior could be compared to the Russian migration across northern Asia (Siberia), though the absolute numbers of those movements were smaller.[12] Both Russian and Chinese migrations were, in their overland nature, different from the Western European migration in the early modern era (McKeown 2011, p. 318). But one could also argue that it was the building of empires that spurred large-scale migration and that only Western Europeans built their empires across the high seas. Thus it is important to keep in mind that not all migration in this period was overseas: large numbers of people moved within the borders of overland empires. Our focus, however, has been on trans-continental overseas migration.

Forced Migrations

The figures of voluntary migrations were more than matched by those of involuntary migrations in this period. Three times as many slaves as European settlers landed in the Americas before 1820 (Richardson 2011). The transatlantic slave trade was the largest forced maritime migration in the history of mankind. As a result of a large international research endeavour that started in the 1960s, there is nowadays a huge amount of evidence available online.[13] In total, until the 1860s, about 12.5 million slaves were transported, but at the end of the eighteenth century this figure already stood at some 8.6 million. The Portuguese and Spanish started to transport Africans to the Americas in the sixteenth century, but the intensity of the slave trade clearly increased over time: rising from almost 3,000 slaves annually in the sixteenth century to almost 19,000 per annum in the seventeenth century, and almost 70,000 annually in the eighteenth century.

The Middle Passage, as the crossing of the Atlantic is known, was a notoriously dangerous journey. The average mortality rate over the period 1590 to 1867 was 12.4 per cent. Conditions under which the slaves were transported were horrendous. Ships of about 250 tons provided only about 0.5 square meter of room per slave (Klein 2010, p. 135) (see also the famous depiction of the British slave ship *Brookes* in Figure 2.6). At the height of the trade, around 1800, slave ships carried 1.5 to 2.5 slaves per ton and, depending also on ship size, carried between 350 and 450 slaves per voyage (ibid., p. 146). Most deaths were caused by illness, but some mortality may have been the result of the cruelty of slave traders. A particularly gruesome event from 1781, where the captain of the slave ship *Zong* ordered 133 slaves to be thrown overboard in order to collect insurance money, has been immortalized by the British painter J.M.W. Turner in *The Slave Ship* (1840). In general, however, it was not in the slave traders' interest to diminish the value of their cargo.

The transatlantic slave trade was by no means the only forced migration flow. Other involuntary migrations in the early modern period are much less covered, but were by no means negligible: the total numbers of these add up to almost 8 million in 1800 (Richardson 2011, p. 570). The data on which such an estimate relies are much scarcer and should therefore be taken with a grain of salt. Many of these other migratory

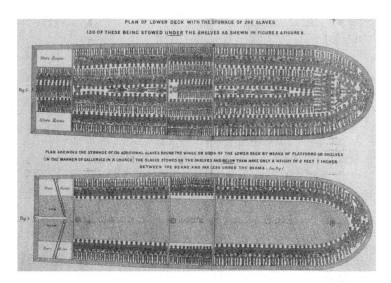

Figure 2.6 *Stowage of the British slave ship* Brookes *under the regulated Slave Trade Act of 1788.* This famous image was used by abolitionists to sketch the atrocious conditions aboard slave ships. Library of Congress, Broadside Port. 282, no. 43

flows were regional, rather than global. The most well-known example is the Islamic slave trade through the Sahara and via the Red Sea and Indian Ocean, in which over the course of three centuries another three million Africans were exported from Sub-Saharan Africa. The total numbers exported across these routes steadily increased over the period 1500–1800, with by far the most going through the Sahara (almost two million) (Lovejoy 2011) – which will be discussed at greater length in Chapter 4. At the same time, slaves were imported into the Cape Colony, Mauritius and Réunion, from other parts of Africa, but also from South and Southeast Asia (Allen 2008). The Mediterranean Sea was the raiding area of pirates from the North African coast, the Barbary corsairs, and between 1500 and 1800 an estimated 1.3 million Christians were captured and sold in the ports of Algiers and Tunis (Richardson 2011). Europeans also participated in this slave raiding and a similar number of Muslims and Africans were captured and put to work as slaves in the Italian and Iberian peninsulas (Lucassen 2016).

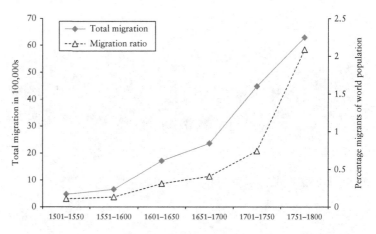

Figure 2.7 Total intercontinental migration and migration ratio, 1500–1800
Sources: Lucassen (2016); Richardson (2011); De Vries (2003); Eltis et al. (2013) and see text.

Summary: Migration vs Total Population

By way of concluding this section on migration, we may construct migration ratios – the number of people moving against the total population. We use the figures above in combination with total world population estimates. Figure 2.7 shows the results: as global migration increased from almost half a million in the first half of the sixteenth century, to two million a century later and over six million in the last half of the eighteenth century, the percentage of all people moving also increased. From 0.1 per cent in the sixteenth century, to between 0.3 and 0.4 per cent in the seventeenth century and reaching 2 per cent in the late eighteenth century. These percentages may not be impressive compared with the number of people on the move in the nineteenth century, but they show that global migration did increase, not only absolutely but also relative to the slower-growing population, which can also be seen as a indication of globalization with, as we argue, profound consequences.

Conclusion

In this first substantive chapter we have laid down the groundwork for our subsequent analysis of globalization's effects for its different regional components. We have reviewed the evidence of the most important flows of ships, precious metals, commodities and people in the three centuries following da Gama's and Columbus' travels.

In these centuries, the trade in silver and commodities generally grew faster than world population and GDP. In both per capita terms and as a part of the total economy, international trade thus increased in importance. Trade was also much more voluminous and grew faster than in all the centuries before the 1500s. At the same time, as a share of total GDP and in terms of the net increased amounts of goods or silver per capita, the flows of ships, precious metals and commodities were not very large. However, over the course of these centuries, such increases would amount to significant figures. A similar argument could be made with regard to Asia, where the net inflow of silver constituted only 0.32 grams per person per annum (De Vries 2010), which was less than 10 per cent of a daily unskilled wage of about 0.1 silver *tael* of 37 grams (Allen et al. 2011). It is for this reason that several studies have argued that the quantitative significance of these global flows was negligible before the nineteenth century (O'Brien 1982, O'Rourke and Williamson 2002a, De Vries 2010). We will show, however, that the effects of such increases in bullion, sustained over a long period, were important, especially in the case of China and Europe.

Additionally, the flows of bullion, ships and commodities had important spill-overs. In Europe, these spill-overs were mainly positive; they stimulated the work ethic, raised wages, increased living standards and improved institutions. In parts of Asia, Africa and America, global trade was associated with systems of forced labour and exploitation. There were many exceptions and variations to this, however, often depending on the interaction between trade and the local context. Therefore, we will analyse this aspect for the various continents separately in the following chapters.

The migratory flows were quantitatively substantial and the demographic results of these migrations were dramatic, especially for the Americas and Africa. In the areas of large-scale immigration, i.e. the Americas, the impact on native populations was disastrous: as a consequence of violence and diseases (like influenza and the bubonic plague) brought by the Europeans, most of them perished; some estimates suggest that by 1650 the native population may have declined by as much as 90 per cent. As a result of the huge influx of slaves in the economies of Latin America, slavery became a building block of modern society in many regions and the large degrees of inequality between population groups associated with this would hinder economic development in the long run (Engerman and Sokoloff 2000). Similarly, extreme degrees of inequality, and the problems associated with this, characterize South African society up until today.   •

The effects of emigration were especially noticeable in Africa, and, according to some, they explain Africa's long-term poverty (Rodney 1972). We will discuss these consequences in more detail in the remainder of the book, beginning with Latin America, a region that was transformed completely as a result of the inflow of both free Europeans and forced Africans, while the production of its silver mines in Mexico and Potosí played an indispensable role in lubricating the wheels of global commerce.

Suggested Reading

De Vries, Jan (2003). 'Connecting Europe and Asia: a quantitative analysis of the Cape-route trade, 1497–1795', in: D. O. Flynn, A. Giraldez, and R. von Glahn (eds), *Global Connections and Monetary History, 1470–1800*. Aldershot, pp. 35–106.

De Zwart, P. (2016a), 'Globalization in the Early Modern Era: New Evidence from the Dutch-Asiatic Trade, 1600–1800', *Journal of Economic History* 76, pp. 520–558.

Flynn, D.O., and A Giraldez (2002a). 'Cycles of Silver: Global Economic Unity through the Mid-Eighteenth Century', *Journal of World History* 13, pp. 391–427.

Lucassen, Leo (2016). 'Connecting the World. Migration and globalization in the second millennium', in C.A. Antunes and K.J. Fatah-Black (eds), *Explorations in History and Globalization*. London: Routledge, pp. 19–46.

O'Rourke, Kevin H., and Jeffrey G. Williamson (2002b). 'After Columbus: Explaining Europe's Overseas Trade Boom, 1500–1800', *Journal of Economic History* 62, pp. 417–456.

Richardson, David (2011). 'Involuntary migration in the early modern world, 1500–1800', in: D. Eltis and Stanley Engerman (eds), *The Cambridge World History of Slavery*, vol. 3, pp. 563–593.

Rönnbäck, K. (2009). 'Integration of Global Commodity Markets in the Early Modern Era', *European Review of Economic History* 13, pp. 95–120.

Solar, Peter M. (2013). 'Opening to the East: Shipping between Europe and Asia, 1770–1830', *Journal of Economic History* 73, pp. 625–661.

3 | Consequences of Conquest in Latin America

Introduction

The Genoese explorer Christopher Columbus famously set sail from the southern Spanish port of Palos de la Frontera on 3 August 1492, with three caravels – the *Santa Maria* (Columbus' flagship), the *Pinta* and the *Niña* – containing a total of only 87 men – in hopes of reaching 'the Indies' (Elliot 1984, p. 160). 'Land! Land!', shouted Juan Rodríguez Bermejo, the lookout on the *Pinta*, just over two months later when he saw 'a white stretch of land' as the three ships approached one of the islands of the Bahamas, which Columbus named San Salvador (Thomas 2003, p. 96). On Christmas Eve 1492, after further explorations across the Bahaman archipelago and Cuba (which Columbus initially thought was Japan), the *Santa Maria* was wrecked off the coast of Haiti. This forced Columbus to leave the first 39 'colonists' behind, using the ship wreckage to build a small fort, as he himself – still convinced he had visited Asia – set sail for Europe in order to tell the stories of his exploits and gather new ships and men to start the conquest of the America's in earnest.

The arrival of Columbus in the Caribbean in a sense inaugurated early modern globalization. Latin America[1] is therefore the logical place to start this history. The effects of early globalization were dramatic: no part of the world (with the possible exception of North America) was so dramatically altered by European attempts to create a world market. Almost no aspect of the political, social, religious, cultural and economic life of this part of the world was left untouched by the Spanish and Portuguese conquest and its long-term consequences. It is, in a way, the best proof of how hard 'soft globalization' could be.

The consequences of Latin America's incorporation into the global economy for its further rise were enormous as Latin America produced the gold and, in particular, the silver that would enlarge the monetary basis of the world economy and smooth international exchange. The big waves of economic expansion (1500–1650, 1750–1820) and contraction (1650–1750) that are so typical of the early modern world economy were at least to some extent the result of the inflationary and deflationary impulses emanating from the silver mines of Bolivia and Mexico. It is no coincidence that we find these waves in those large parts of the world that were most strongly integrated in the world economy – in Europe, China, India and Southeast Asia. It was, moreover, silver that tied the world economy together – supplying Europeans with the means to buy Indian, Indonesian and Chinese goods. In a way, the heart of the early modern world economy was beating in Potosí, almost constantly pushing new purchasing power into its veins and thereby ensuring that these complex international networks would remain vibrant. If one wants to understand why this post-1492 world economy was fundamentally different from the 'Medieval' one, we not only have to look at Columbus and da Gama but also, and perhaps more so, to these silver strings that tied the world market together.

Latin America is usually seen as the classic example of an early victim of globalization, which already at an early stage fell prey to the aggressive imperialism of Western Europe. Frank (1969, 1970) has written extensively about the underdevelopment of Latin America as a result of its incorporation into the capitalist world economy and as the metropole expropriated all surpluses: the closer its ties with Europe, the more underdeveloped a country became.[2] This is also the role it played in Wallerstein's model – the typical example of a periphery dominated by coerced labour – and it arguably does still figure as such. Furthermore, it is used as the archetypical example of path dependency in the New Institutional Economics literature. In fact, as John H. Coatsworth (2005, p. 239) noted: '[f]or more than two centuries, travellers, politicians, historians, and economists have argued that Spanish and Portuguese colonial institutions inhibited economic growth'. Rather than the identity of the colonizer, Stanley Engerman and Kenneth Sokoloff (2000) have famously argued that the specific geography and factor endowments of Latin America – its favourable climate to grow tropical plantation crops, the widespread reserves of precious metals and its abundance of land relative to labour – led to greater concentrations of wealth, which became entrenched in the development of economic and political institutions, causing long-run underdevelopment. In their 'Reversal of Fortune' article, Daron

Acemoglu and his co-authors (2002) suggest that it was especially in those areas most urbanized around 1500, i.e. Central Mexico and Peru, that the Europeans introduced 'extractive institutions', causing underdevelopment in the long run. Was Latin America truly the main victim of early modern globalization? Or is the story more nuanced?

Spanish America offers a solid case for the crucial importance of globalization for economic development between 1500 and 1800. The plantation economies of the Caribbean and Brazil are possibly even a stronger case in point – these economies were fully dependent on the international market forces that created them. In this chapter, we review the long-run development of both parts of the world economy, analysing more in detail how dependent both parts of Latin America were on international market forces – but also how they helped to shape the world market in return.

The Conquest and its Impact

On the return of Columbus' first expedition in 1493, the Spanish monarchs, Ferdinand and Isabella, petitioned the pope for a line of demarcation confirming their right to the newly found lands. A year later, the Portuguese successfully negotiated the shifting of this line further west in the Treaty of Tordesillas, allowing them to claim Brazil – which would only be 'discovered' in 1500.

The purpose of Columbus' second expedition, of 17 ships containing 1,200 men, was to conquer and colonize; besides a great number of soldiers, there were artisans and agricultural workers among these men (Elliott 1984, p. 161). They first settled on Hispaniola (present-day Haiti/Dominican Republic), where they found that the initial settlement had been destroyed and the first settlers killed. This was possibly done by aggressive peoples ('cannibals'), who lived alongside the 'affectionate and generous'[3] *Tainos* who resided in the Antilles. The Spanish *conquistadores* would encounter more highly developed societies in Mesoamerica and the Andes. In April 1519, Hernán Cortés and some 600 men landed near present-day Veracruz on the Mexican coast, with the goal of toppling the Aztec Triple Alliance headed by Moctezuma II. Cortés cunningly exploited the divisions among the different groups that inhabited Mexico. Forging an alliance with some of these, Cortés soon marched to the great city of Tenochtitlan with an army of some 200,000 Indians eager to cast off the yoke of Alliance

Figure 3.1 Views of Tenochtitlan and Cuzco by George Braun. The *conquistadores* were marvelled by the sight of these extraordinary cities. *Mexico, regia et celebris hispaniae novae civitas, Cusco, regni Peru in novo orbe caput*, 1570 (MC80). George T. Abell Map Collection, Special Collections, Mary Courts Burnett Library, Texas Christian University

rule. The *conquistadores* were amazed by Tenochtitlan (Figure 3.1), which, according to some accounts, was larger than Paris – the biggest city in Europe at that time. In *The True History of the Conquest of New Spain*, 'one of its conquerors', Bernal Diaz del Castillo, wrote:

When we arrived at the great market place, called Tlaltelolco, we were astounded at the number of people and the quantity of merchandise that it contained, and at the good order and control that was maintained, for we had never seen such a thing before (written in 1572, cited in Hirth 2016, p. 3).

This meant that some level of market specialization was happening – with specialized cash crop farming and highly skilled craftsmen as typical features of Tenochtitlan. Yet, private property in land did not exist, and only rather 'primitive' forms of money (such as cocoa beans) were used to equalize transactions which were usually based on barter.

Francisco Pizarro needed even less men than Cortés to overwhelm the (even larger) Incan Empire in the Andes, as he left Panama in 1531 with only 168 men. He lost none of them in the capture and murder of the Inca emperor (*Sapa Inca*) Atahualpa and the initial seizure of the

capital, Cuzco (Mann 2005)(Figure 3.1). Like Cortés, Pizarro benefitted from superior fighting power, resulting from guns, military organization and horses, which were unknown to the Incas and Aztecs. The
Incas had ruled a vast territory stretching from the north of current-
day Ecuador, all the way south to central Chile. The Inca economic
system was characterized by central planning and labour services
for the state and knew almost no market exchange, and no money;
exchange and surplus extraction were entirely organized socially, via
mechanisms of redistribution and reciprocity. All land was officially
owned by the king, who claimed in return a large share of the crop,
and this 'taxation' was stored in and redistributed from central storage facilities (Storey and Widmer 2005, p. 87). Despite the lack of
markets, the Incan economy produced significant surpluses as is evidenced by the 'overflowing' state storage facilities that the *conquistadores* encountered (Mann 2005, p. 74). Such surpluses are all the more
impressive, as they were generated in difficult geographical conditions:
much of the empire was positioned at high altitudes in rugged terrain
with very steep slopes; Cuzco is located at a staggering 3.4 km above
sea level. The specific features of this terrain, with large differences
in altitude and climate, also meant that specialization did occur – as
fish from coastal areas were exchanged for cotton and beans from the
valleys, maize from the hills, or llama and alpaca wool and meat from
the highlands. Some villages concentrated on the making of textiles
for the court, while others specialized in mining and metallurgy. Yet all
of this was centrally planned and organized (Mann 2005; Storey and
Widner 2005).

The Conquest came as an extreme shock to the indigenous population. Belief systems were suddenly shaken by the brutal force of the
Spanish. Warfare caused many casualities: the siege of Tenochtitlan,
for example, resulted in the death of some 100,000 people according
to some estimates (Mann 2005, p. 129). After the capture of Cuzco,
the Incas continued to fight the Spanish *conquistadores* for more than
40 years, but lacking the military technology and tactics to withstand
Spanish firepower and cavalry, they always lost. As J.H. Elliott (1984,
p. 182) notes, however, 'The conquest of America was a conquest by
microbes as well as by men, sometimes running ahead of the main
Spanish contingents, at others following in their wake.' These microbes
were part of what Alfred W. Crosby (1972) famously dubbed the
'Columbian exchange'; the ecological integration of the New and Old

Worlds. As the native population had no immunity against Old World diseases (e.g. smallpox, measles, influenza, malaria), the human losses of integration were dramatic: the first smallpox epidemic in 1518 killed about a third of the inhabitants of Hispaniola, while in 1530 a contemporary estimated a population decline in Hispaniola from half a million to 20,000 (Reinhard 2015, p. 874). One of the main effects of the Conquest and the Columbian exchange was therefore a dramatic demographic collapse: whereas it was estimated that in 1492 the native population of Spanish America, Brazil and the Caribbean had been roughly 50 million (according to the latest estimates), the number of indigenous peoples had fallen to around five to six million in the middle of the seventeenth century (Newson 2005, p. 143).[4] As Coatsworth (2004, p. 41) formulates it: 'Globalization killed more than 90 per cent of the inhabitants in the Americas.' It is also important to note that such a decline was not limited to the centres of state formation and urbanization in the Andes and Mexico (where possibly some 60 per cent of the pre-Columbian population lived); recent evidence suggests that in Amazonia, population levels (and degrees of economic sophistication) also fell dramatically. Both in Amazonia and in North America, complex societies disappeared without leaving much evidence – it required recent archaeological research to dig up their settlements.

The Transition Economies of Spanish America

Soon after the Conquest an extensive royal administrative apparatus was set up. The highest governing institutions in Spanish America were the Viceroyalties of New Spain and Peru – complemented in the eighteenth century by those of New Granada and Rio de la Plata (see Map 3.1 below) (Elliott 2006, p. 125). In the king's permanent absence, the viceroys were his representatives. Additional layers of government consisted of the *adiencias*, high courts which combined administrative and judicial functions, governorships and many more local governing institutions (Elliott 1984, p. 293). On paper the crown's power was absolute, yet as the king was far away, the various layers of government – which often competed over control – attained considerable autonomy. Over time, local elites would enhance their position against the central government in Madrid, yet in the sixteenth and early seventeenth centuries, especially compared with

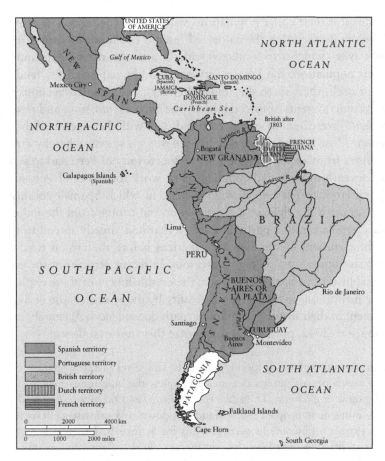

Map 3.1 Colonial Latin America
Source: McNeill and Pomeranz (2015, p. 528).

many other colonies, 'Spain's government of the Indies could only have looked like a triumphant assertion of the obedience properly due to kings' (Elliot 2006, p. 130).

Thus, within a few decades after initial contact the Spaniards established colonial states aimed at exploiting Latin America's endowments, making use of indigenous institutions of forced labour and hierarchical coordination. In view of the demographic collapse, the Spanish crown tried to limit the degree to which local populations were exploited. The experiences of the Antilles – the first islands conquered and colonized – had shown that fully enslaving the Indians led to disaster: most islands lost their entire populations within a few decades. The crown therefore decided that the colonized Indians could not be turned into full slaves – which also conflicted with the aim of christening the indigenous population. But labour services could be requested (in 'feudal' Spain itself, these were not unusual either), and adapted versions of indigenous systems of forced labour (the *encomienda*, *mita* and *repartimiento*) were used to supply elite and state with the necessary labour power. Most infamous is probably the *mita*, a system whereby communities from a specific region in the Viceroyalty of Peru had to send one-seventh of their male population to work the mines of Potosí as forced labour.[5] The *encomienda* system, in which Spanish colonists were granted the right to extract labour and tribute from the indigenous population of a particular area – that had already spread to the farthest corners of the Spanish Americas before the crown tried to limit its abuses – was equally notorious. In recent versions of the economic history of Spanish America, the establishment of these exploitative institutions in the sixteenth century by the Spanish is the decisive moment in their history – the rest is 'path dependency'. Acemoglu and Robinson (2012, pp. 18–19) summarize this view as follows:

After an initial phase of looting, and gold and silver lust, the Spanish created a web of institutions designed to exploit the indigenous people. The full gamut of *encomienda*, *mita*, *repartimiento*, and *trajin* was designed to force indigenous people's living standards down to a subsistence level and thus extract all income in excess of this for Spaniards. This was achieved by expropriating their land, forcing them to work, offering low wages for labour services, imposing high taxes, and charging high prices for goods that were not even voluntarily bought. Though these institutions generated a lot of wealth for the Spanish crown and made the conquistadores and their descendants very rich, they also turned Latin America into the most unequal continent in the world and sapped much of its economic potential.

It is the classic tale of underdevelopment brought about by the establishment of colonial 'extractive institutions' – a story that is not that different from the one told by Wallerstein (and authors from the *dependencia* school such as Frank) that the roots of the underdevelopment of the region are to be found in the 'world system' that emerged in the sixteenth century. The history of Spanish America offers, however, more than the *dependencia* fashionable in the 1970s or the path dependency that is more trendy at present.

We suggest an alternative interpretation, stressing institutional change brought about by globalization, resulting in the transition from economies in which markets were absent or marginal to societies fundamentally reshaped by market forces, a process that took centuries to be completed. In other words, Spanish American societies can best be understood as early examples of 'transition economies': as symbolic for this stage of globalization as the East European formerly planned economies after the fall of communism in 1989 were for the globalization wave of the final decades of the twentieth century. They too were exposed to a massive blow to their complex institutional structures, in which elites largely acquired a surplus via 'coerced' labour and complex forms of redistribution. Where pre-existing structures were relatively advanced, the Iberian colonial powers sought to leave indigenous institutions in place and rule indirectly. As a consequence, labour markets initially retained their pre-Columbian elements of coercion, while commodity trade was monopolized. But the organization of factor and commodity markets did change over time, as we will now show.

Labour Supply and Real Wages

We will start with the crucial issue of how to organize the labour supply.[6] Many scholars have emphasized that one of the main long-run effects of the Iberian colonial expansion in Latin America was achieved through the development and organization of labour systems (Monteiro 2005). What actually happened from the 1550s onwards was that labour scarcity became increasingly problematic, due to the dramatic decline of population levels, and the Spanish crown and local authorities reacted to this by trying to use 'free' wage labour as an alternative. The crown stopped issuing new *encomiendas*. In the absence of wage labour, the *encomienda* was initially an important instrument to extract labour and tribute from the native population. Depopulation meant a decline in the numbers of natives participating in the system. In Mexico, the number of *encomiendas* declined quickly from 537 in 1550 to 126 in 1560 (Zavala 1935). The system was officially terminated in 1601 for all sectors except mining, although it may in practice have persisted for some decades in the seventeenth century. The system was replaced by the *repartimiento* system, which was similarly characterized by a degree of coercion, although the labourers were paid wages. This system was gradually transformed into a free wage labour system and, by the 1630s, the *repartimiento* no longer had a purpose and was abolished (Allen et al. 2012; Monteiro 2005).

Cities increasingly turned to, possibly more efficient, wage labour as it became more difficult to acquire coerced labourers. Even in Potosí, where labour for the mines was drafted via the *mita* system, wage labour became increasingly important. Research suggests that between 50 and 70 per cent of the labour force in the mines in Peru and Mexico was free labour (Bakewell 1984; Tandeter 1993). One can even argue that the main innovation introduced by the Spanish conquerors was not so much labour coercion (which had existed on a large scale in pre-Columbian societies), but a labour market with paid wage labour. This new institution took time to fully develop and labour coercion remained important until the early seventeenth century (in Mexico) or even later (in Peru). We might see a certain path dependency here again, as the Aztecs were much more familiar with market exchange than the Incas. Moreover, even forced labour was not without costs. As stipulated by the many laws on the forced labour system, labourers were entitled to compensation for their services. Even in the allegedly most injurious *mita* (see e.g. Dell 2010), wages were regularly paid in cash, and workers were only set to work during part of the year. The workers could then sell their labour at higher free market wages during half or one-third of their stay. In addition, they were sometimes compensated for travel time and other costs (Bakewell 1984). In New Spain, miners were free agents working voluntarily (Brading 1971). In the Guadalajara region in Mexico, free rural labour accounted for the bulk of the supply in the seventeenth century (Van Young 1981). In Chile, the boom of the mining sector required more labour than the *encomienda* could provide. As a result, *mestizos* and free Indians migrated to the northern region lured by high wages (Carmagnani 1963). From the reforms of the early seventeenth century onwards, free wage labour became the norm in large parts of Latin America, but it was often mixed with elements of coercion. The term 'peonage' has been introduced to describe this: quite often labourers were bonded by the credit they owed from their employer, the *haciendados* or the owner of a mine. The degree of debt-bondage varied from region to region and from period to period, but this continued to play a role well into the nineteenth and even the early twentieth century.[7]

Wage labour was obviously embedded in the very unequal socio-political relationships of the period, but that was the case elsewhere as well. At the same time, wage labour responded to market forces: the increased scarcity of labour resulted in a strong increase in wage levels. This can be seen in Table 3.1, which shows the development of Latin American real wages expressed as 'subsistence ratios': this is the level of wages relative to the prices of a basic consumption basket reflecting the minimum for survival (also taking into account the consumption of three other family members) (see Allen 2001; Allen et al. 2011). During the mining boom of the 1580–1640 period, nominal (silver) wages of free labourers in Potosí were the highest in the whole world economy, and their purchasing power was also quite high (3–6 times the subsistence basket); but *mita*-labourers also earned a wage that was above subsistence (Arroyo Abad et al. 2012). The trend in real wages in Mexico closely follows the increasing and, after 1750, decreasing scarcity of labour, rising at first from about subsistence in the sixteenth century to a level which was not much below that earned by London labourers in the seventeenth century, only to decline again to half that level after 1800. The decline of real wages clearly reflected the turnaround of demographic development during the eighteenth century, when the population began to grow again (Table 3.1).

Real wages in Mexico, with its freer labour markets, were higher than in most other places in Latin America. Real wages for *mita* workers fluctuated between 1 and 2 for most of the period under discussion, yet wages for free mining labourers, the *mingas*, were two to three times higher than that. Free mining labourers in Chile earned somewhat lower wages, as the mining activities there were more limited and therefore did not put the same upward pressure on wages. Real wages in Colombia were on roughly similar levels, while those in Bolivia were initially somewhat above those earned in Chile. Extremely high real wages were earned in Argentina, mostly by immigrants from Western Europe who profited from the labour scarcity and the almost free supply of land here, which drove up wages. Subsistence ratios were therefore much higher even than in London. The abundance of land also led to low prices of wheat and meat. Living standards for all free labourers in Latin America were above the levels in most parts of Europe, as shown by the comparison with Leipzig.

This evidence on trends in real wages is corroborated by data on heights and human capital formation. Jörg Baten and Matthias Blum

Table 3.1. *Real wages (expressed as subsistence ratios) in Spanish America and Europe, 1525–1820*

	Argentina	Bolivia	Chile	Colombia	Mexico	Peru	London	Leipzig
1525–1574					0.76		3.22	1.89
1575–1624					1.20	1.10	2.67	1.64
1625–1674					2.36		3.02	1.76
1675–1724		2.95	1.46	1.80	3.03	1.18	3.86	1.48
1725–1774		2.95	1.45	1.78	2.99	1.18	3.84	1.29
1775–1820	9.47	2.20	2.40	1.58	1.86	1.48	3.31	0.71

Sources: Spanish America: Arroyo Abad et al. (2012); London and Leipzig: Allen (2001) and Allen et al. (2011)

(2014) suggest that Argentinians were very tall, around 170 cm, even compared with most Europeans, in the early nineteenth century; meat was very cheap there, as the main export product was cattle hides, and meat consumption was extremely high in Buenos Aires. Peruvians and Bolivians were shorter, about 163–165 cm in the same period, which is roughly comparable to European levels. Consistent with the decline in real wages, Mexican heights declined from around 165 cm in the 1740s to 162 cm around 1800 and declined even further in the decades after that (Challú 2010). Finally, the development of human capital formation also showed similar trends as the decades for which we have data – levels of numeracy increased over most of the seventeenth and eighteenth centuries in Argentina, Brazil, Mexico and Peru (Manzel et al. 2012).

Transition to a Market Economy

The emergence of labour markets in Spanish America was one aspect of a much broader transition process towards a more-or-less market-based economy. Commodity markets had hardly existed at all before 1500, but within decades the Spanish managed to get a form of money economy going – a process which is still not well understood. This transition was arguably more dramatic, if not more traumatic, than the transition which the centrally planned economies of Eastern Europe experienced after 1989 – the latter economies already knew well-developed markets (and money) before. But the coming of the market has not been studied and is therefore clouded in mist.

What is clear is that early on, from the 1530s or 1540s, the Spanish occupiers managed to use the market to cater for their needs, first in Mexico – where this transition was facilitated by greater familiarity with markets – and later in the Andean region. At the same time, the Spanish introduced a wide range of new crops and livestock that formed the core of their diet: wheat, olive oil, wine, and cattle, pigs, sheep and poultry – all previously unknown to the native population. In the middle decades of the sixteenth century, the prices of these 'Spanish' products on Mexican markets were declining (whereas other prices rose), indicating their increased supply. Native producers may have stepped in, but were handicapped by colonial regulations and a lack of capital. The gradual growth of the *hacienda* system, in which

Spanish farmers made use of partly dependent labour specialized in catering for these markets, was probably largely responsible for the growth of supply. Consumer and producer patterns of the indigenous population changed as well, due to the influx of new crops and livestock. Sheep reproduced on a large scale, and woollen textiles became generally used, whereas the luxury textiles of the Andean, made from alpaca wool, declined as the demand for them collapsed with the disappearance of indigenous elites. Before the Conquest, the Indian population had consumed only very small quantities of meat – in the absence of major meat producers in the agricultural system and possibly because of the high population density in core areas. This changed dramatically in the sixteenth and seventeenth centuries: pigs, cattle and poultry were integrated into agriculture, and the land/man ratio became much more favourable (due to depopulation). In general the food supply per capita improved a lot, benefitting the population of both cities and countryside. Latin America became a relatively large consumer of meat; in the southern cone (Argentina, Uruguay) this was due to the large surplus of meat, as only the hides of cattle could be exported. But very low meat prices were a phenomenon of the region as a whole, and, in a city like Mexico, meat consumption per capita was at 150 kg in 1767 – well above European levels, where meat consumption had declined dramatically since the late Middle Ages (Van Zanden 1999).

What greatly facilitated the transition towards a money-based economy was the rapid expansion of silver mining in the two core regions of the Spanish American Empire, Mexico and Peru/Bolivia. Silver and to a lesser extent, also gold production (first coming from Spanish America and after 1550 increasingly from Brazil), were the fundamental contributions of the region to the booming world market of the early modern period. Silver production moved to an entirely different level during the sixteenth century, as Figure 3.2 demonstrates. Before 1540, global silver output was less than 50,000 kg per year, and concentrated in Central Europe and Japan. Scarcity of money was a regular phenomenon – both in Western Europe, that had deficits with almost all surrounding regions and was in danger of being constantly drained of money, and in China, that after bold adventures with paper money, was under the Ming switching back to silver as the main basis of money, especially for large-scale transactions (and

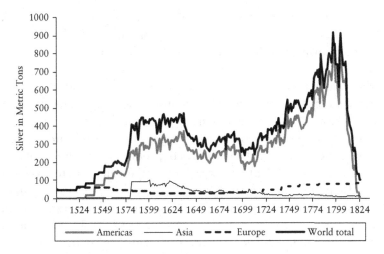

Figure 3.2 World silver production per region, 1500–1825
Sources: Brown and Tepaske (2010); Schreurs (2015); Attwell (1982), Munro
(2003); Von Glahn (1996a)

tax payments). But due to the rapid expansion of silver mining , especially in Potosí (which dominated the industry in the late sixteenth
century), global silver production soared to levels unknown before:
in the 1550s, American production surpassed the 100,000 kg level, in
1577 it broke the 200,000 kg threshold, and between 1600 and 1640
it was on average far above the 300,000 kg level (Figure 3.2) (see:
Brown and Tepaske 2010; Tandeter 1993, 2005).

What was impact of the mining sector on the transition process
that was characteristic for Spanish America? The industry had strong
backward and forward linkages, through which silver, money and thus
purchasing power were pumped into the economy. Potosí and other
centres of mining were, for example, deficient in foodstuffs and needed
the agricultural surpluses of other regions to feed the rapidly growing
population of coerced and free labourers. Potosí's 160,000 inhabitants
(between 1600 and 1650), who were usually paid in silver *reals* (and
well paid by international standards – as suggested above), greatly
stimulated interregional trade far into Chile and Peru. Important
inputs into the mining business – such as the indispensable mercury –
were mined at large distances from the silver mines, or imported from

Europe. Merchants profited from these trades, from the exploitation of the mines (which were usually leased from the colonial state), and from the transport of the silver to far-off destinations.

Mexico became the most important supply for global silver flows in the eighteenth century (Garner 1988, pp. 934–935). In the seventeenth century silver production stagnated in Mexico as a result of the scarcity of mercury – necessary in the production process. Increases in mercury provision allowed for the growth of production in the eighteenth century. By 1800, Mexico produced two-thirds of the global silver output. With the expansion of the mining sector, Mexico entered a period of economic growth as a result of positive linkages that were created between the mining sector and the agricultural, manufacturing, finance and transportation sectors. Recent studies confirm this picture. Carlos Alejandro Ponzio (2005) provides a very optimistic account, suggesting that 'Mexico experienced rapid economic growth' as a result of silver exports. Rafael Dobado-Gonzales and Gustavo A. Marrero (2011) similarly highlight the importance of the mining sector in spurring economic growth in eighteenth-century Mexico. Success in mining therefore helped the development of the market economy.

Finally, it is important to note that the mining sector was not only important for the Spanish American economy, but also for the newly created global economy as a whole. Silver was minted in *reals* and *pesos*, which became the standard currencies for large parts of the world economy in the early modern period. This meant that fluctuations in the global economy were, to a large extent, dictated by the up- and downswings of American silver mining: with expansion in the periods 1500–1650 and 1750–1820 and contraction between 1650 and 1750.

Cities and Commodity Markets

Silver mines were not the only source of demand and market exchange. Cities played a central role in the governance structure of the Spanish colonies. Again, this was a combination of Spanish and indigenous influences. The *conquistadores* were urban citizens who saw cities as the logical places to control and exploit the countryside – this was similar to the structure of Spanish state. Both the Aztec and the Inca states had been dominated by large capital cities; Tenochtitlan and

Cuzco, respectively, were centres of religion and administration (Katz 1978, Greenfield 1984), which, as typical 'consumer cities' exploited the countryside without supplying services and goods in return (see Bosker et al. 2013 for a discussion of this concept). But in the north and the south, cities collapsed due to the Conquest and because the many diseases imported by the Spanish struck there first and probably most violently. De-urbanization was, however, followed by renewed urban expansion between 1550 and 1650 as the colonial states became consolidated while the overall population of the colonies continued to decline (albeit at a rate which was slowing down). The net effect was that Spanish America became a relatively highly urbanized part of the world economy, with, in its core regions (Peru/Bolivia and Mexico), 12 to perhaps as much as 20 per cent of the population living in cities with more than 10,000 inhabitants – this was, at times, more urban than the metropole (Spain) itself (Table 3.2). These cities flourished as a result of taxes levied in the surrounding countryside, allowed by the surpluses generated by the agricultural sector. In turn, these cities stimulated market exchange and created market outlets for farmers and peasants in the surrounding areas. The growth of cities implied increasing commercialization and the development of local markets.

The cities of Spanish America were key players in the political economy of the region. Not only was the total level of urbanization high, the urbanization was concentrated in only a few urban centres. These cities were consequently extremely large. Mexico City had some 168,000 inhabitants in 1800, representing 20–30 per cent of the total Mexican urban population. Potosí had roughly a similar number of inhabitants in the early seventeenth century, which entailed even 50–60 per cent of the urban population in Peru/Bolivia. Cycles in urbanization and de-urbanization were driven by trends in the economy, as well as colonial policies. The *mita* gave rise to urbanization, as natives tried to avoid compulsory labour services by moving to cities. Furthermore, rises and declines in silver production are related to the urbanization movements. The population of Potosí was at its highest during the boom in silver production in the seventeenth century, but declined during stagnation in the eighteenth century (see Arroyo Abad and Van Zanden 2016).

The growth of cities and their consolidation after 1550 occurred within a context of slowly changing power relationships within the Spanish colonial Empire. Colonial elites gradually strengthened their

Table 3.2. *Total population and urbanization rates in Mexico, Peru and Spain, 1550–1800.*

	1550	1600	1650	1700	1750	1800
Mexico						
Total population (in millions)	6.6	3.0	2.3	2.8	3.8	5.1
Urban population (in thousands)	116	194	220	338	435	744
Urbanization rate	1.8%	6.5%	9.8%	12.0%	11.5%	14.6%
Peru[a]						
Total population (in millions)	2.1	1.6	1.5	1.2	1.4	2.2
Urban population (in thousands)	63	193	212	237	212	271
Urbanization rate	3.0%	12.1%	14.1%	20.0%	15.9%	12.6%
Spain						
Total population (in millions)	5.4	6.9	7.2	7.5	9.3	11.9
Urban population* (in thousands)	604	972	900	833	1,256	2,210
Urbanization rate	11.2%	14.2%	12.5%	11.1%	13.5%	18.6%

[a] As noted earlier, these figures include Bolivia.
* Adjusted urbanization rate – excludes 'agro' towns.
Source: see Arroyo Abad and Van Zanden (2016).

position *vis-á-vis* Madrid, as is for example clear from estimates of the degree to which income transfers to Spain burdened the colonial economy. The best proxy for this is the colonial remittances to the Treasury in Spain, which were dramatically high during the sixteenth century, but declined sharply in the seventeenth century (Figure 3.3), first from Mexico, and later on also from Peru. From the

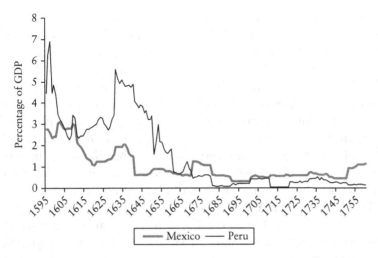

Figure 3.3 Public revenues remitted to Spain (as percentage of GDP),
1595–1755
Source: Arroyo Abad and Van Zanden (2016).

1670s onwards they were less than 1 per cent of the GDP of the two
core regions involved – sizeable by any standard (compare current
attempts to achieve a 0.7 per cent of GDP target for development
aid), but much less than during the pre-1650 period. These figures
are in line with studies by Regina Grafe and Alejandra Irigoin (2006;
2012), who show low eighteenth-century remittances. The declining
outflow of remittances reflected changes in power balances between
Spain and its colonies. Gradually, colonial elites established themselves, learned to better understand and defend their interests and
those of the Indians they governed, and increasingly managed to
spend the funds raised in the colonies themselves, instead of sending
money off to the Treasury in Madrid. These shifts ultimately resulted
in the independence that would follow after 1810.

The sharp decline of colonial exploitation is also noticeable from
the degree to which Spain was able to control and monopolize the
international trade of the colonies via the *Casa de Contratación*. In the
sixteenth century this control was near total, but smuggling and the
rise of independent commercial elites in the main port cities gradually
undermined the ability of Spain, and their partners (until 1640) the
Portuguese, to fully dominate the international trade of the empire
(Marquez 2005). Moreover, Spanish power at sea gradually waned,

and competitors such as France, the Netherlands and Britain became increasingly aggressive. In 1702 France acquired the *Asiento*, the permission granted by the Spanish crown to sell slaves to the Spanish colonies, while 11 years later the *Asiento* was obtained by Great Britain. The circulation of the *Asiento* among different European naval powers marked the opening of Spanish American markets to outside competition. The liberal reforms of the Bourbons in 1765 officially ended the Spanish system whereby only four Latin American port cities were allowed to participate in international trade. Liberalization of international trade completed the transition process towards a market economy that had begun in the first half of the sixteenth century.

The woollen textile industry organized in large workshops (*obrajes*), operating with up to 100 workers, was the principal victim of liberalization of the eighteenth century. In Mexico and the Quito region, this textile industry had emerged in the second half of the sixteenth century, making use of the internal supply of wool. As the mining towns and cities were the most important market for these cloths, the fate of the industry was closely linked to trends in mining. Thus, with the growth of mining in Potosí, the industry expanded rapidly during the seventeenth century but after 1690 the decline set in (Gomez-Galvarriato 2005, pp. 379–381). This was to an extent the result of globalization: increased international competition resulted in falling prices, both in the Quito region (which mainly produced for Lima and the silver mines) and in Mexico (Dobado-Gonzalez et al. 2008; Gómez-Galvarriato 2005). In the eighteenth century, total production fell by 50–75 per cent in the Quito region, while in Mexico textile output by 1812 was insignificant (Gómez-Galvarriato 2005, p. 381). The fate of the woollen industry in the eighteenth century foreshadowed what would happen on a much larger scale after 1800, deindustrialization in the 'periphery' due to aggressive competition from the British textile industry worldwide (Williamson 2011). In Mexico, where Puebla developed into a dynamic producer of cottons, the growth of the cotton industry could initially compensate for the collapse of woollen manufacture (see Dobado Gonzales et al. 2008).

The market for textiles is one of the few examples which point at 'hard' globalization in this period: in Europe prices of textiles were falling as well, but much less rapidly than in Latin America, indicating a certain degree of price convergence between these parts of the world.

The positive relationship between silver output and British cottons exported to the West Indies, and the negative association between silver output and *obraja* production in the eighteenth century (Gómez-Galvarriato 2005), also testifies to the relationship between global trade and domestic economic development. For other markets, there is much less evidence for pre-1800 market integration. The much-studied international markets for grains – wheat in particular – show increased integration between North America and Western Europe during the eighteenth century, accompanied by increased integration within both regions, but as Dobado Gonzalez et al. (2012) have demonstrated, Latin American markets remained outside this process. In that sense, the region knew no 'hard' globalization fitting the definition of O'Rourke and Williamson (2002a). As we argue in this book, this by no means suggests that globalization did not have any effects on the Latin American economies. In contrast, few societies were as radically transformed by the global forces as those in Latin America.

Economic Growth

How dynamic were these 'transition economies'. Tentative attempts to estimate the development of GDP per capita of Mexico and Peru show relatively productive economies growing rapidly between the middle of the sixteenth and the middle of the seventeenth centuries. By that time, 'per capita GDP in the Americas was raised to levels well above the most advanced pre-Columbian societies' (Coatsworth 2008, p. 549).

This growth spurt was the result of urbanization, the rapid growth of silver mining and the increase in real wages (reflecting the growing labour scarcity). Initial productivity increases were made possible by technological transfers from Europe. This included the wheel, the sailing ship, and iron and steel making. Particularly important for the mining sector was the transmission of deep shaft mining and ore processing technology. Especially in areas that had higher population densities in the fifteenth century, the decline in the population resulted in higher per capita agricultural productivity as the less productive lands were abandoned and only the most fertile lands were used (Coatsworth 2004, p. 38). Before the Columbian exchange, the only large domesticated animals in the Andes and Mesoamerica were llamas and alpacas. The introduction of new domesticated animals raised the productivity of agriculture – especially under the new conditions of labour scarcity in the sixteenth century, as animal farming needs less labour, but more land, to produce similar amounts of nutrients as arable farming. Animals also provided an important source of protein. Whereas pre-Columbian Mesoamericans had suffered from protein shortages, in the middle of the eighteenth century, Mexicans ate more meat than most Europeans. Around the same time, central Mexicans were also slightly taller than southern Spaniards (Challú 2010, p. 23).

While earlier estimates of Mexican GDP have suggested expansion over the eighteenth century (Maddison 2003), the most recent estimates instead show stagnation (Arroyo Abad and Van Zanden 2016). These numbers show that after the initial import of these technologies and animals, Latin America seemed unable to generate further innovation. Productivity stagnated and the growth of the population led to diminishing per capita income gains. Consequently, as can be seen from Figure 3.4, the early eighteenth century was a period of stagnation for both these economies, but the second half of the eighteenth century was another phase of growth, leading to a peak in the 1770s. Both Mexico and Peru started to decline from about 1780.

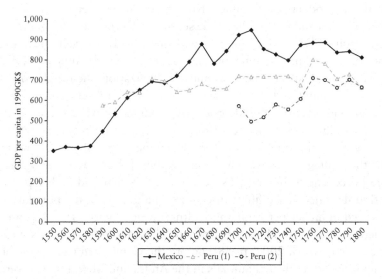

Figure 3.4 GDP per capita in Mexico and Peru, 1550–1800
Sources: Arroyo Abad and Van Zanden (2016).

These incomes were surprisingly high in comparison with GDP estimates from Spain. Real incomes in Mexico were on a par with those in Spain between 1650 and 1800. There were episodes when incomes were higher than in the metropole (Arroyo Abad and Van Zanden 2016). Incomes in Peru were somewhat lower, but also there, during years of high Peruvian performance, GDP per head was about 90 per cent of Spanish levels. This is consistent with our observations above that markets were more developed in Mexico and wages there were higher. Rough estimates suggest that Cuba, around 1700, and Argentina and Cuba, around 1800, may have had even higher GDP per capita (Coatsworth 1998, p. 26) – the Argentinian estimate is corroborated by the evidence on real wages shown above. According to Coatsworth (1998, p. 33) such high levels of GDP were driven by specialized export production. Compared with English GDP, these colonies lagged behind already in the sixteenth century, however, as income per head there increased from around 1,000 to over 2,000GK$ between 1500 and 1800.[8]

For what they are worth, these estimates, in combination with the evidence on real wages shown above, illustrate that it is too simple to see Spanish America simply as a victim of early modern globalization – the hostage of the institutions established there in the sixteenth century. It was a region most dramatically restructured by the forces of globalization – for better and for worse – which experienced institutional changes that would increasingly open it to market forces. The large swings in labour scarcity, which increased during the first 100–150 years of Spanish dominance, but declined during the eighteenth century, resulted in equally large fluctuations in real wages – a clear sign that to some extent labour markets were working. Furthermore, as noted above, the decline of monopolization and increased international competition had dramatic consequences for the indigenous textile industry. The institutions adapted by the Spanish to exploit the labour force, *encomienda, mita, repartimiento,* were gradually replaced by more market-oriented ways of recruiting labour. However, the fortunes of the Spanish colonial economies were closely related to the booms and busts of the mining sector. The Engerman and Sokoloff thesis, that the given geographic conditions and factor endowments resulted in high levels of inequality and limited incentives for human capital formation, is still to the point as, in particular, the fate of the plantation economies illustrates.

Plantation Economies in the Caribbean and Brazil

Despite population growth over the eighteenth century, Latin America remained sparsely populated. In 1820 its population was about 22 million, somewhat more than 2 per cent of the total population of the world; heavyweight China alone counted 380 million inhabitants, 17 times the Latin American total. The region on which we focus in this section, the Caribbean, had a total population of less than 3 million, or 0.3% of global population. If we include Brazil here, we may add another 4.5 million, but the share of the global total remains small. Of course, some European states, like the Dutch Republic and Portugal, had only small populations in the early modern period (1–3 million), but Western Europe as a whole boasted 133 million by 1820 (Maddison 2007).

Between 1500 and 1800 this part of the world had a large impact on international trade and development because a very specific set of institutions – the plantation economy – achieved its 'highest stage of development' here. Already on his second voyage in 1493, Columbus brought sugarcane with him, as he had realized immediately that the geography and climate of the island were ideal for sugar production (Gomez-Galvarriato 2005, p. 360). The model of a plantation economy – a highly capital-intensive, market-oriented economy based on slave labour – had been developed already during the Middle Ages in the Mediterranean by Venice (on Crete and Cyprus, mainly growing sugar), after which Portugal and Spain had copied the example in the Canary Islands and Madeira (again, mainly focused on sugar). These systems not only exploited their labour power intensely, but often also led to rapid environmental degradation (for example because they used up all forest resources as it needed firewood for sugar refining), making it necessary to constantly find new lands to expand into. Brazil was the obvious next candidate; in particular during the Dutch interregnum (1630–1654) the slave-based model expanded rapidly in what is now the north-eastern part of the country, thanks to the rapid growth of the supply of slaves (and the access to the dynamic Amsterdam market). The Dutch also modernized production processes and their organization of the Brazilian plantations became a new model for expansion of this 'mode of production' into the Caribbean after 1654.

From the middle of the seventeenth century onwards, the plantation economy of the Caribbean (and increasingly, the southern part of the North American colonies, which will be dealt with in Chapter 5), arguably became the richest part of the world economy – a position it would continue to claim until the British abolition of the slave trade in

1808. Exports of sugar, coffee, tobacco and cotton expanded dramatically. Under its influence, prices on world markets collapsed (helped to some extent by the growing efficiency of Atlantic trade and transport – as noted in Chapter 2). In particular, the export of sugar expanded dramatically. Brazil was initially the world's most important producer in the sixteenth century, and still accounted for about one-third of all the sugar produced in the Americas in 1730, after which its production was overtaken by the British West Indies and St Domingue. The share of Brazil had declined to less than 10 per cent in the later decades of the eighteenth century. Instead, the British West Indies became more important producers over time; whereas they produced 4,000 tons per annum in the 1650s, this increased to 25,000 in 1700 and further to 125,000 tons in 1800. From 1697, the French gained a foothold in the western part of Hispaniola (renamed St Domingue – present-day Haiti); sugar exports there also grew over the eighteenth century, with some 60,000 tons exported in the second half of the eighteenth century (Gómez-Galvarriato 2005, pp. 366–368). Figure 3.5 shows a seventeenth-century depiction of slaves in a variety of occupations on a plantation in the French West Indies.

Most plantation economies initially started as ventures by free settler farmers who mainly produced with their own labour and that of white, indentured servants. Until the 1640s, Barbados was such a settler society, attracting large numbers of immigrants from Great Britain (there were only 800 black slaves in a population of 30,000 in 1644). However, access to cheap slave labour and significant economies of scale in sugar cultivation and processing caused a gradual shift from small-scale farming to large-scale plantation agriculture with dozens, if not hundreds, of slaves and a tiny minority of staff, owners and overseers. In Barbados it took 60 years for this transformation to materialize; in 1700 the number of blacks (50,000) far outnumbered the European population (of about 15,000) (McCusker and Menard 1985, p. 151). Barbados was the most extreme example of a plantation economy, but Dutch and French colonies developed along similar lines (Van Stipriaan 1993; Burnard and Garrigus 2016).

By the end of the eighteenth century the 'West Indies' were the origin of about a quarter of imports and the destination of a similar share of exports from Great Britain, the leading trading nation. Their share of Dutch international trade was smaller, 10 per cent, and for France, the third commercial power, it lay probably in between both

Figure 3.5 Sugar plantation, French West Indies, seventeenth century
Source: Pierre Pomet, *A complete history of drugs. Written in French by monsieur Pomet.* London, 1748, p. 57 [Original: 1667]. Image as shown on www.slaveryimages.org, compiled by Jerome Handler and Michael Tuite and sponsored by the Virginia Foundation for the Humanities.

estimates. The sharp decline of these colonial prices stimulated the growth of demand, which responded dramatically to these changes. Sugar, which had been an extreme luxury before 1500, became an object of mass consumption, as did coffee and tobacco (see Chapter 9 for the 'consumer revolution' of the seventeenth and eighteenth centuries). The Caribbean islands that profited most from these changes were among the wealthiest parts of the world economy. Per capita product in Barbados was estimated by David Eltis (1995) to have been between one- and two-thirds higher than in England and Wales. This made Barbados the country with probably the highest GDP per capita during much of the late seventeenth and early eighteenth centuries. After that, the centre of gravity of sugar production moved to Jamaica and Santo Domingo.

This high level of productivity and GDP per capita did not reflect high levels of welfare, because these societies were extremely unequal – more than 90 per cent of the population of Barbados consisted of slaves – and a large share of income was transferred abroad to investors in Britain (and other colonial powers). The high productivity of the labour force was the result of many influences: slave labourers could be driven to very hard work, but their life expectancy was low; it was often considered cheaper to push slaves to maximum effort and to replace them by new slaves after 10 or 20 years. The resulting population structure was highly skewed – dominated by young men, and with many fewer children, women and elderly than would have been the case in a self-reproducing ('sustainable') demographic system. This skewed population structure blew up GDP per capita; in a more sustainable age pyramid the actual population would have been much larger, probably at least twice the actual population number. For another slave-based society, the Cape Colony, it was established that a sustainable population would have been 1.5 to almost 2 times as large as the actual population – in the Caribbean, which was even more dependent on slave imports, this ratio was probably much higher (Fourie and Van Zanden 2013).

The high productivity of labour in plantation economies was also a real phenomenon (Eltis et al. 2005). Sugar needs to be processed immediately after harvest. Labour costs were relatively high, creating incentives to save on labour by investing in large-scale equipment: mills, processing plants, etc. necessary for the processing. Sugar production became a highly capital-intensive activity, characterized by large economies of scale, which led to the concentration of production in large plantations. Productivity and efficiency were also enhanced by the complete dependence on markets: all output was exported (mainly to Western Europe), inputs – including foodstuffs for the slaves – were also often imported from abroad. The plantations were often owned by merchant families living abroad, and the whole system was dependent on large-scale imports of slaves from Africa. As such, the European-owned sugar plantations in the Caribbean can perhaps be seen as the '[t]he first truly "global" economic enterprise', worked by African slaves producing an 'Asian crop in the American tropics for the export to European consumers' (Coatsworth 2004, p. 39).

It is puzzling that in the debate on early globalization the plantation economy of the Americas has not figured more prominently. Perhaps because it is so obvious that these parts of the world were fully integrated into the world economy that nobody cared to make the point.

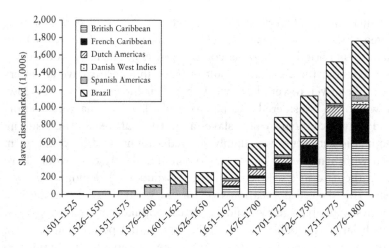

Figure 3.6 Slaves disembarked in Latin America, 1500–1800
Source: Eltis et al. (2013).

Whereas the debate about globalization in the nineteenth century has focused very much on the Atlantic economy – on the interactions between Europe and North America – the discussion of the pre-1820 world economy has centred on market integration (or the absence thereof) between Asia and Europe (O'Rourke and Williamson 2002a; Flynn and Giraldez 2004; De Vries 2010). This is remarkable as the growth of trade in the Atlantic was more spectacular than the rise of Eurasian trade (De Vries 2010).

The best proxy of the expansion of the plantation system is probably the growth of the Atlantic slave trade between 1500 and 1800 (Figure 3.6). As we will see in Chapter 4, the slave trade grew rapidly, especially in the eighteenth century; between 1776 and 1800 the slave trade was at its all-time high, as almost 1.8 million slaves disembarked in the Caribbean and Brazil. In the sixteenth century, Spanish America was the main destination for these slaves, but in the early seventeenth century Brazil surpassed the Spanish Americas as the most important destination and it continued to be so for the remainder of the period; over the period 1500–1800 an astounding 38 per cent of all slaves ended up there. Besides the sugar plantations, slaves in Brazil were put to work in the Minas Gerais gold mines from the end of the seventeenth century on (Monteiro 2005, p. 210). Over the seventeenth and eighteenth centuries, the British Caribbean, mainly Jamaica and Barbados, also took up considerable numbers of slaves, suggesting their increasing prominence in world sugar production (as discussed above).

One of the forces behind the dynamic spatial expansion of the seventeenth- and eighteenth-century plantation economy was that it used large amounts of environmental resources – firewood and timber in the first place – which led to degradation of the plantation islands after one or two generations. The centre of gravity had the tendency to move constantly: from Brazil to Barbados, to Jamaica and Santo Domingo, and later on to Cuba. The rapid growth during the eighteenth century also resulted in increased scarcity of slaves in the ports of Africa – supply simply could not keep up with the enormous demand from across the Atlantic. Slave prices went up on both sides of the trade, which had important consequences for plantation economies (Figure 3.5). It became more economical to take good care of the slaves, feed and clothe them better, try to maintain their good health and even encourage them to procreate.[9] In Surinam, the booming plantation economy of the Dutch in the Guyanas, slaves were stimulated to grow their own food crops, and gradually they developed their own subsistence strategy and a small-scale cash economy. The plantation economy should therefore not be viewed as a completely static system. Some slaves acquired skills in plantation management, and were in a few cases able to buy their freedom. In the margin of the plantation economy, a small group of free blacks emerged. But for the vast majority of slaves, the system meant extreme inequality and an almost complete absence of free choice about the most important decisions in life.

Figure 3.7 also shows that the ratio of slave prices in America to those in Africa declined over the course of the eighteenth century, which can be seen as evidence that the huge numbers of slaves being transported resulted in price convergence, an indication of the integration of Atlantic slave markets.

Plantation economies were changing – moving to other islands, becoming somewhat less dependent on imported slaves – but continued to be highly profitable and dynamic parts of the world economy. The frontal attack on the slave trade and slavery in general, that began in Britain in 1783, was not induced by the decline of the system (as has been suggested in older literature), but was entirely inspired by old and

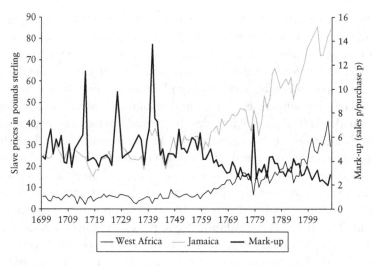

Figure 3.7 Prices for slaves in Africa and the Caribbean, 1699–1807
Sources: Eltis et al. (2010); Eltis et al. (2013); Richardson (1991)

new ideas from radical Christians, such as the Quakers, and enlightenment philosophers who believed in the equality of all men before God.
They criticized the corrupting effect slavery had on the slave owners
and slave society. The plantation economy was ultimately based on
force, on the use of systematic violence to strip the slaves of their freedom and have them work as intensely as possible for their owner. This
led to a society in which various forms of violence were much more
normal than in the European societies from which the slave owners
originated (and the African societies from which the slaves came).
This was, arguably, a feature of colonial society in general – in the
Moluccas or the Cape Colony, the VOC, for example, did not hesitate
to impose its will through force. It not only injured the slaves and the
other 'subjects', but also eroded the values of slave owners who often
returned to their home country – all unchecked power corrupts. One
of the reasons for criticizing the slave trade and the slave system in
general was this backlash of the relatively 'egalitarian' societies that
had emerged in north-western Europe, which already in the Middle
Ages had abolished domestic slavery (Drescher 2009).

The abolition movement achieved successes quite quickly. As slavery was inconsistent with French revolutionary values of 'freedom,

equality and brotherhood', the new French constitution of 1793 abolished it. This development was also helped by the slave revolt in Haiti that had started in 1791. In 1808 the British movement managed to abolish the slave trade, and in order to prevent 'unfair' competition, the British started to suppress slave trading worldwide. The Congress of Vienna supplied them with the legitimacy to do this on a global scale. The worldwide ban on slave trading (issued by the European nations gathered in Vienna in 1815) was, in a way, the first attempt by a European power to reform the institutions of the world – a first step towards the development of a global set of institutions that would not only govern relationships between states, but also the relationships between states and their citizens. In this respect, its importance is comparable with the Universal Declaration of Human Rights adopted by the United Nations (UN) in 1948.

For most Caribbean plantation economies, the abolishment of the slave trade was an almost mortal blow – the watershed between dynamic growth during the eighteenth century and long-term stagnation in the nineteenth century. These economies were unable to make the transition to an economy based on the reproduction of the slaves themselves, as was done successfully in the American south. Whereas Barbados in the seventeenth century had perhaps been the place with the highest GDP per capita in the world, it became – like almost all other plantation economies – a poor backwater of the world economy after 1800.

Conclusion

Latin America played a disproportionate role in the world economy between 1500 and 1800. Latin America produced the silver that kept the wheels of commerce spinning. Production was organized initially with a considerable degree of coercion – as we would expect on the basis of Wallerstein's world systems theory, where labour in the capitalist core is free and remunerated with wages, while labour in the periphery is coerced. Already in the sixteenth century, however, labour in Spanish America was increasingly being paid in wages. In the plantation economies of the Caribbean, labour was, of course, mainly performed by African slaves. But slave labour was not cheap, and its price increased over the eighteenth century as the integration of the world economy gathered pace. This meant that it became more economical to take better care of slaves, to increase their productivity and longevity. Furthermore, labour productivity was increased by the input of significant amounts of capital with large investments in the equipment of mills and processing plants.

Both regions were heavily affected by the soft and hard powers of globalization. Not only did the entire population change, with the native Americas succumbing *en masse* to European violence and diseases, but Latin America was repopulated by Europeans, Africans and, later, Asians. Furthermore, these societies, which had known (almost) no money or market exchange previously, were being transformed into capitalist market economies. As we have seen, the Caribbean is another example of a region that was thoroughly restructured by world market forces during the early modern period, and whose history would from then on be determined to a large extent by the economic and sociopolitical institutions that were (almost literally) implanted there by the forces of globalization. Commercialization of the Americas, based on the exploitation of African labour and driven by European demand for bullion and luxuries, further fuelled underdevelopment in Africa and development in Europe. To this we will now turn.

Suggested Reading

Arroyo Abad, Leticia, and Jan Luiten van Zanden (2016). 'Growth under Extractive Institutions? Latin American Per Capita GDP in Colonial Times', *Journal of Economic History* 76, pp. 1182–1215.

Bakewell, Peter, and Jacqueline Holler (2010). *A History of Latin America to 1825* (3rd ed.). Oxford: Wiley-Blackwell.

Bulmer-Thomas, V. J. Coatsworth and Robert Cortes-Conde (eds) (2005). *Cambridge Economic History of Latin America. Vol. 1: Colonial Era.* Cambridge: Cambridge University Press.

Coatsworth, John (2008). 'Inequality, Institutions and Economic Growth in Latin America', *Journal of Latin American Studies* 40, pp. 545–569.

Dobado Gonzáles, Rafael, A. Gómez Galvarriato and J.G. Williamson (2008). 'Mexican Exceptionalism: Globalization and De-Industrialization, 1750–1877', *Journal of Economic History* 68, pp. 758–811.

Elliott, J.H. (2006). *Empires of the Atlantic World. Britain and Spain in America 1492–1830.* New Haven and London: Yale University Press.

Eltis, David, Frank Lewis and David Richardson (2005). 'Slave Prices, the African Slave Trade, and Productivity in the Caribbean, 1674–1807', *Economic History Review* 58, pp. 673–700.

Engerman, Stanley L. and K.L. Sokoloff (2000). 'History Lessons. Institutions, Factor Endowments, and Paths of Development in the New World', *Journal of Economic Perspectives* 14, pp. 217–232.

Grafe, Regina and Alejandra Irigoin (2012). 'A Stakeholder Empire: The Political Economy of Spanish Imperial Rule in America', *Economic History Review* 65, pp. 609–651.

4 | Africa and the Slave Trades

Introduction

Decades before the Portuguese discovered the sea-route to Asia, they landed on different parts of the African coast. A crucial role in this process was played by Henry the Navigator. In August 1415, the young Prince Henry was aboard a large armada led by his father King Joao I of Portugal to conquer Ceuta on the Moroccan coast. Ceuta had since long been a base for North African pirates, the Barbary corsairs, that raided villages on the Portuguese coast, thereby capturing inhabitants for the Arab slave market. Ceuta fell within the day, and the Portuguese claimed they had captured 'the gateway and key to all Africa' (Meredith 2014, p. 144). While Ceuta would remain a small Portuguese enclave surrounded by Arab enemies, expeditions along the African coast continued. Henry spurred developments in navigation and shipbuilding. In search for the land of Prester John and, especially, Africa's gold deposits, Portuguese ships sailed further south, passed the Canary Islands, and reached the mouth of the Senegal river in 1445 (ibid., p. 146). Thinking they had found the River of Gold, about which merchants in Ceuta had spoken, they called it *Rio d'Oro* (Meredith 2014, p. 146). By the time of Henry's death in 1460 the Portuguese had reached Sierra Leone. His death temporarily delayed further explorations and it took until 1471 before they finally reached the Gold Coast, calling it *El Mina* ('the mine') (Fage 1997, p. 223). In 1484, the Portuguese reached Angola, which would become the most important region for exporting slaves in the following centuries. Four years after that, the explorations of the West African coast were concluded as Bartolomeo Dias reached the Cape of Good Hope (initially aptly calling it the *Cabo das Tormentas* – where over the years thousands of ships perished). Da Gama explored the coast of eastern Africa, visiting Mozambique, Mombasa and Malindi on his way to India in 1498.

The Portuguese explorations were followed by raiding and trading missions that were, from the outset, at least partially focused on capturing and trading slaves. Already in 1441, a young Portuguese captain captured a couple of inhabitants on the coast of the western Sahara, to be brought back to Portugal in order to please Prince Henry (Iliffe 1995, p. 127). In subsequent years, many more slave trading missions would follow. Slavery and slave trading were already familiar to many African societies, and the Portuguese encountered many active slave markets where predominantly Arab traders were willing to sell slaves in return for guns and other European manufactures. At the same time, sugar plantations, which already existed in the Mediterranean in places like Cyprus, Sicily and Andalusia, spread westward to Madeira, the Canary Islands and then to the Cape Verde Islands, 'discovered' by the Portuguese in 1456. It was, however, on the island of Sao Tomé, off the coast of Gabon, that the Atlantic sugar plantation system attained its characteristic form of European-owned plantations worked by large numbers of African slaves (Schwartz 1985, p. 14). Similar plantations would eventually be set up in Brazil and the Caribbean. These were the beginnings of the Atlantic slave trade that would continue deep into the nineteenth century, with coerced labour being transported from the African continent to plantation islands. The Atlantic slave trade constitutes the largest overseas migration flow up to that time and the consequences of the African slave trade for both the development of the world economy and the relative underdevelopment of the African continent have been widely discussed.

According to Wallerstein (1989, p. 129), as a result of intensified slave trading West Africa became incorporated in the European capitalist world economy from the middle of the eighteenth century. He notes:

Incorporation means fundamentally that at least some significant production processes in a given geographic location become integral to various of the commodity chains that constitute the ongoing divisioning of labor of the capitalist world-economy.

Incorporation thus entails that local production processes respond to the dynamics of the world market. Wallerstein suggests that the increasing intensity of the slave trade in the eighteenth century, in response to rising slave prices, is a sign of the incorporation of West

Africa. Slave raiding expanded significantly in the eighteenth century, while prior to that time global dynamics did not influence 'production' in Africa: Europeans tapped into the existing market. Furthermore, Wallerstein (1989, p. 145) notes that the proportion of profits, whatever their size, from the slave trade was West Africa's main contribution to global capital accumulation.

Such views build on the argument put forward by Eric Williams in *Capitalism and Slavery* (well known as the Williams thesis), who notes that a crucial contribution was made to the development of the world economy by 'Negro slavery and the slave trade in providing the capital which financed the Industrial Revolution in England' (Williams 1944, p. v). As slavery meant an elastic supply of cheap labour, the slave trade and the slave plantation system yielded higher rates of profit than domestic industries and thereby spurred new investments in Europe. More recent research, however, questions whether profits in slavery were really much higher than in other industries, and, if so, whether the slave sector was large enough to bring about industrialization (Eltis and Engerman 2000).[1] Joseph Inikori (2002, 2007) goes beyond profits and argued that the goods produced by Africans were crucial in the creation of the modern world economy, the transformation of the Americas as well as the British Industrial Revolution. Another strand of research has focused on the consequences of the slave trades – which, besides the Atlantic, include the trades across the Sahara and the Red Sea – on African societies. In this chapter, we will review the most recent evidence on global trade: the slave trades as well as the commodity trade (in early modern Africa) and discuss the immediate and long-term consequences for African societies. The effects of the plantation system and the slave trade on economic growth in Europe are discussed in Chapter 9, while the role of slavery for the economic and social transformation of the Americas is discussed in Chapters 3 and 5.

Africa in the Global Economy

Before we delve into an analysis of the consequences of the slave trades, we need to get a picture of what these trades entailed, where the slaves came from, where they were transported to and what goods they were exchanged for. While the general picture is well-known: in the triangular trade, Europe exported manufactures (mainly textiles and guns) to Africa to exchange for slaves and gold. The former were sent to the Americas, where they formed the backbone of the plantation systems that put out sugar, cotton, coffee and tobacco for the European market. Lesser known are the regional differences across Africa. In this chapter, we will briefly discuss these as well as the trends over time. The Trans-Atlantic Slave Trade Database (Eltis et al. 2013) allows for detailed study of the export of slaves from different regions between 1501 and 1800 (shown in Figure 4.1).[2] Map 4.1 shows where these regions are in West and West Central Africa.

While the slave trade across the Atlantic began with the arrival of the Portuguese in the fifteenth century, Africa's slave trades traversing the Sahara, the Red Sea and the Indian Ocean were much older and continued after the Atlantic trade had been suppressed in the nineteenth century. The only external contact of sub-Saharan Africa prior to the arrival of the Europeans was through the Islamic world, where pagan slaves were in demand. The figures on these early trades are patchy, but Paul Lovejoy (2011, pp. 25–27) suggests that between 800 and 1600, some 1,000 slaves left Africa via East African ports annually, double that figure left via Red Sea ports, and between 3,000 and 8,000 left from across the Sahara. Regarding the societies where the slaves came from, most historians seem to agree that the impact of the early trades was limited (Klein 2010, p. 9). Slavery had certainly existed in early

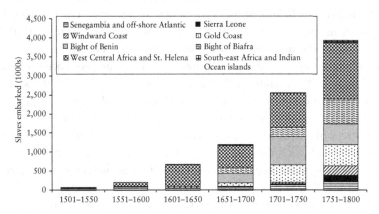

Figure 4.1 Exports of slaves, totals per region of embarkation, 1500-1800
Source: Eltis et al. (2013).

African societies, but it was not central – as Lovejoy (2011, p. 13) noted: 'these were not slave societies'. In parts of Africa, this was to change as a result of global interactions in the early modern period and we suggest that the rise of the Atlantic slave trade presented a significant watershed in Africa's history.

Exports

Until 1600 the total number of slaves exported via the Atlantic seaboard represented only a quarter of all slaves leaving Africa (Klein 2010, p. 58), but the Atlantic trade grew significantly over time. In the fifteenth century the Atlantic slave trade was limited to some 800 to 2,000 slaves annually, and they went mainly to Portugal and the above-mentioned islands of Madeira and Sao Tomé. The figures increased somewhat in the sixteenth century as shipments to the Americas began: over 1,200 annually in the first half and 4,200 per annum in the second half of that century.[3] Most of these went to plantations in Brazil. Yet even in the period up to 1600, the Atlantic slave trade was still small and its impact on the already existing African slave markets was limited (Klein 2010, p. 58). In this period, the Atlantic slave trade, as well as the trade with Africa in general, remained an exclusively Iberian affair. In the seventeenth century, the slave trade accelerated as British, Dutch and French traders joined the competition: the number of slaves exported increased to 19,000 per annum. The height of the trade was reached in the late eighteenth century: in the second half of the eighteenth century almost 80,000 Africans were embarked on slave ships annually. The annual growth rate in slave exports between the first decade of the sixteenth and the last decade of the eighteenth century was over 2.1 per cent, which was far above the natural increase of the population. The strong demand for slaves in the eighteenth century began to exceed supply, and prices of slaves began to increase across Africa (Eltis et al. 2010). The total value of exports therefore increased even more strongly than the growth in the number of slaves. This growing intensification of the trade meant that African societies were increasingly affected by it: whereas in the fifteenth and sixteenth centuries, the Atlantic trade merely 'tapped into the traditional internal slave markets of Africa' (Klein 2010, p. 72),[4] by the eighteenth century the rising demand from the Americas spurred developments in Africa as it became a part of the global economy.

Map 4.1 Western Africa in the early modern era
Source: Klein (2010, p. xi).

Yet there were significant variations in the regional distribution of slave exports. The Senegambia, by the Senegal and Gambia rivers, was one of the first regions where the Portuguese traded slaves for plantations in Madeira and the nearby Cape Verde Islands. After an initial period of Portuguese monopsony, British and French traders visited the region regularly from the late sixteenth century onwards. Up to 1800, some 650,000 slaves were exported from this region, representing 8 per cent of total slave exports. Further south-east were Sierra Leone and the Windward Coast, which, especially in the eighteenth century, were important regions of slave exports. The Gold Coast was the most attractive region for trade, as it not only exported slaves but was also rich in gold and developed commercial agriculture. Both the British and the Dutch established the headquarters of their African activities on the Gold Coast. On both sides of the Niger River Delta were the Bights of Benin (west) and Biafra (east). The former exported so many slaves (1.1 million up to 1800) that it came to be known as the Slave Coast, and it was the second-largest slave-exporting region.

The Biafran coast exported relatively few slaves until the 1730s, yet grew
to be the biggest slave-exporting region by the later eighteenth century.
Yet, by far the most important exporting region was West Central Africa:
Angola, Gabon and the Congo. Up to 1800, this region exported over 3.5
million slaves, or 42 per cent of the total. This region was very large, however, and the Dutch were active in the northern regions (Loango-Congo-
Brazzavile), while the Portuguese were more active in the southern region
(Angola) and penetrated relatively deep into the interior. About half of
all Africans transported from this region left on Portuguese ships. A final
region of slave exports from Africa was Mozambique and Madagascar. As
a result of the larger distance from the American colonies, the slave trade
in this region attained significance rather late (when the prices of slaves
became high enough to make it profitable to transport them across these
larger distances) and as a result the region was good for only 1 per cent of
the total. This regional differentiation meant that the consequences of the
slave trades differed significantly across Africa.

As noted above, the Atlantic route was not the only way by which
slaves were exported from western Africa. The numbers of slaves that
were exported in the Islamic slave trade across the Sahara and Red Sea
and East coasts also increased, yet at a much slower pace. Due to the
much greater increase in the Atlantic slave trade, the other external
slave trades constituted less than a fifth of the total exports by the
eighteenth century.

Besides slaves, the international export trade of Africa also consisted of gold and goods trade. It were Africa's gold deposits that
initially lured the Europeans to the continent, not captives, and it
seems that only after 1700 slaves exceeded the total value of the
other exports. Gold, and, to a lesser extent, ivory and other products
still made up over 50 per cent of the exports until the late seventeenth century (Eltis 1989, 1994).[5] A century later, this was radically
different and slaves made up over 90 per cent of the total value
of African exports (Eltis 1989). This means that a very important
shift took place in the composition of Africa's export trades over
the eighteenth century. It also shows that while the slave trade was
clearly important, it certainly did not constitute the only interaction of Africa with the global economy (at least until the eighteenth
century).

Finally, it should be noted that despite the increase in international
trade, it remained a relatively small sector of the African economy

(Klein 2010, p. 74). David Eltis and Lawrence Jennings (1988, p. 956) estimated that even at the height of the slave trade in the 1780s, the average value of intercontinental overseas trade per person in West Africa was £0.10 per annum, compared with £2.30 in Britain and even £5.70 in the British West Indies. This figure would be even lower if we accept Patrick Manning's (2014) new population estimates (discussed on pp. 104–105). The effects of these exports go beyond such figures, of course, as slaves were not just a commodity but also an important source of labour, and their capture and enslavement went hand in hand with conflict and great social, political and economic costs.

Imports

In exchange for these exports, West Africa mainly imported currencies, iron, textiles and firearms. Table 4.1 shows the changing composition of imports into West Africa. In order to sketch some of the developments over time, we combined data from a variety of sources to calculate averages per decade for four different regions. Such figures are, of course, based on a limited amount of observations and one may question the representativeness of such data. For now, these seem to be the best available data and it is important to see what story they tell.

Textiles and currencies (beads and cowrie shells) dominated African imports. On the basis of the data on the Bights of Benin and Biafra, Inikori (2011) noted the rise of textile imports and the decline of currency imports between the seventeenth and late eighteenth centuries. Taking the average of West Africa data series, we cannot see a similar rise in textile imports, although there is a decline in currency imports after 1720. Inikori (2011) argues that the shift away from currencies is a sign of the adverse impact that the slave trade had on commercialization. The data for Kongo-Angola are based only on Portuguese figures (and for 1680 based on a small sample, see Eltis 1989), but if these figures are roughly representative for the entire trade in the region, they also show a declining share of currencies. Textile imports, however, also declined, and the import of weapons and alcohol became more important. Gareth Austin (2013, pp. 254–255) doubts whether the relative decline in currency imports is evidence of a contraction in commercial activity: if the volume of imports surpassed the quantity of currency that was lost, the money supply would still grow. Nonetheless it is

Table 4.1. *African imports, shares (%), 1660–1780*

	Year	Textiles	Currencies	Weaponry	Iron & other metals	Alcohol	Tobacco	Other
'West Africa'/Gold Coast	1680	50.8	10.0	4.7	14.5			20.0
	1700	47.2	11.2	11.9	3.3	4.3		22.2
	1710	50.5	10.5	12.6	1.3	4.1		21.0
	1720	51.1	11.3	12.0	1.3	5.3		18.9
	1780	63.3	2.5	9.0	3.7	6.3	3.0	12.2
Bight of Benin	1680	35.6	55.8		5.5			6.0
	1690	32.0	38.6	3.3	13.7			12.4
	1700	38.0	20.5	9.6	1.8			30.1
	1720	66.1	22.1	8.9				2.9
	1780	13.0	0.5	1.9	0.8	1.3	80.0	2.5

	Year							
Bight of Biafra	1660	1.6	68.5	6.8	9.6			13.6
	1680	4.3	49.1		41.2			7.0
	1690	12.7	33.2		30.5			23.8
	1700	9.3	29.9	3.2	35.5			22.1
	1720	30.3	33.2	7.6				28.9
	1790	42.3	4.6	33.4	6.4			13.5
Kongo-Angola	1680	66.6	5.4	1.0		4.3		22.7
	1780	49.6	0.0	3.3	1.1	21.4	0.6	24.0

Sources: 'West Africa' 1680: British figures from Eltis (1989); 1700–1720: Dutch imports from Den Heijer (1997); 1780: unweighted mean British, French, and 'Other' figures from Eltis (1989); Bight of Benin 1680–1720: British data from Inikori (2011); 1780: Portuguese imports North of Equator from Eltis (1989); Bight of Biafra 1660–1790: British data from Inikori (2011); Angola 1680–1780: Portuguese imports south of equator from Eltis (1989). All of this concerns European export values.

clear that, with the intensification of the slave trade in the eighteenth century, substantial shifts took place in the composition of exports which most likely had adverse consequences for economic developments in West and West Central Africa.

Despite being such an important slave-exporting region, Kongo-Angola imported relatively few weapons. For the entire region of West Africa, Inikori (1977) estimated that in the second half of the eighteenth century between 283,000 and 394,000 guns per annum were imported, or between 14 and 20 million guns in total.[6] In the first half of the eighteenth century, this figure was probably below 180,000 per year (Richards 1980, p. 51). The second half of the eighteenth century was clearly the height of gun importation, as can also be seen by the increased share of imports to the Bight of Biafra. In the Gold Coast, in the period before the mid-seventeenth century, when trade was still dominated by gold rather than slave exports, guns were hardly imported (Inikori 2011, p. 671). Some research suggests that the rise in gun imports may have already started in the second half of the seventeenth century (Richards 1980). There were differences in the distribution of these firearms over the region. In the second half of the eighteenth century, a very large part of the guns went to the Bight of Biafra where they were mainly exchanged for slaves. The spread of European firearms in Africa had two important effects. First, it meant that the Europeans had no advantage in the use of violence, besides on the coasts, even if the quality of firearms imported into West Africa was relatively low (Inikori 1977, p. 362). In combination with the disease environment, this meant that, after a few early ventures, generally no European expeditions were undertaken in the African interior or attempts made to monopolize specific legs of the trade by conquest. The Portuguese in their campaigns in the interior of Angola were dependent on African allies (Thornton 1992, pp. 100–116). Second, it had consequences for the process of state formation: the rise and fall of states, as will be discussed below.

The change in trade from the exports of gold and ivory in exchange for currencies, iron and textiles, to exports of captives for mainly weaponry, textiles, alcohol and tobacco, meant that whereas this trade initially could have had a beneficial impact on African economies, spurring commercialization and vent-for-surplus growth, this changed in the seventeenth and eighteenth centuries when trade had mainly negative consequences – leading to conflict and population loss.

Functioning and Organization of the Slave Trade

Why did Africans engage in a trade that had such a negative impact on their societies? Were global, i.e. European, or local forces fundamental in driving the slave trade, or both? How was this trade organized and where did the slaves come from?

Some scholars, like Walter Rodney (1972), but also Acemoglu et al. (2001, 2002) and Nunn (2008) suggest that Europeans had some sort of advantage over Africans which allowed them to determine the organization of trade and implement 'extractive institutions'. Such accounts provide too little room for African agency. By the time the Portuguese arrived in Africa, it was politically, socially and economically well developed (Klein 2010, p. 49). The continent boasted some large states, like the Songhai Empire and the Kongo Kingdom. Slavery, and slave markets, had existed in Africa many years before the start of the Atlantic trade. When Europeans came to Africa they merely became additional buyers in those pre-existing markets. Thornton (1992, p. 125) notes that Europeans lacked the economic and military means to force African leaders to sell slaves. Thus, when the states of Benin and Kongo in the sixteenth century disengaged from the slave trades, Europeans simply had to buy slaves elsewhere – these states could not be pressed to continue slave trading (ibid., p. 111). Africans entered the Atlantic trade at their own initiative and on an equal footing with the Europeans – African elites were often active and willing participators in the slave trades as it brought them economic and/or political gains (Jerven 2016).

Of course, African rulers tried to reduce the economic and social costs of exporting slaves by shifting the burden to their neighbours. They also tried to protect their own subjects from enslavement, while capturing and selling inhabitants of rival rulers (Austin 2008a, p. 1005). Most of the slaves were captured in wars and state-sponsored large-scale raids, which explains the relationship between the slave trade and the incidence of wars. People could also be captured in small raids or be enslaved through a judicial process (ibid.): in response to the Atlantic slave trade, more and more crimes were being punished by enslavement as laws were changed or judges distorted the law to provide more slaves. Some people ended up in slavery as a result of outstanding debts. Slave exports peaked during famines, suggesting that people sold themselves into slavery in return for food. Rulers raiding their own subjects also occurred, however, as for example in seventeenth-century Kongo (Iliffe 1995, p. 133). At the start of the slave trade densely populated coastal regions could supply most of the slaves, but as demand for slaves increased in the eighteenth century, many slaves came from areas in the interior, far from the coasts. They could change ownership many times before they reached the coasts where traders made the final sale to Europeans (ibid., p. 134). These Europeans were dependent on, usually African, middlemen and had to adapt to local trading practices.

In this process Europeans, as well as some Africans, benefitted: the rulers, the slave raiders and the middlemen extended their wealth and power. Exporting urban centres along the coast also profited from increased commerce, and in their immediate surroundings agricultural areas produced the foodstuffs for slave ships (Inikori and Engerman 1992).[7] The costs of the slave trade were borne by the hinterlands, which were troubled by enduring political and social conflicts.[8]

Demographic Impact

The slave trades affected African societies in various ways. First, and most obviously, the trades had demographic effects, which were especially negative as Africa was already a labour-scarce continent before the rise of the Atlantic slave trade. As a result of the paucity of historical population evidence, total population estimates are based on projections rather than historical data. Such figures may not be ideal and are subject to large margins of error, yet it is still important to see the broader picture they sketch.

Manning (2014) and his team have recently computed decennial population estimates for the eighteenth century for various African regions. These numbers challenge earlier figures. Whereas there was a rough consensus that the population of West Africa numbered some 25 million in 1700 (Klein 2010, p. 128), Manning (2014) estimates a total population of some 50 million in that year and a further 20 million in Central Africa. These figures also show a decline in the population in the eighteenth century: between 1700 and 1800, West Africa's population went from over 50 million to 46 million and even further declined to 42 million in 1900 and started growing only after that. Central Africa's (including the Loango-Kongo-Angola region) population declined from 20 million in 1700 to 17 million in 1800, but recovered after that, increasing to 19 million in 1900. If we accept these estimates, this means that the African domestic economy was even larger than previously assumed and international trade played an even smaller role (as noted above). Despite this, the enslavement of many Africans still had a significant negative effect on the growth of the population. This was not only the direct effect of the export of people, but also the effect of the conflict and warfare related to the capture of people for the slave trade. While we have no good estimates on on the magnitude of these effects, the statement of David Livingstone that for every slave exported from East Central Africa ten other human beings lost their lives in the mid-nineteenth century is telling (Fage 1997, p. 260). Although Manning suggests that his new estimates may call for a revision of the consensus view of pre-colonial Africa as a labour-scarce continent, we think that even such a large upward revision puts no doubts on this view (see also Jerven 2016). This becomes clear when comparing population densities across continents: even a large upward revision of the population would still only increase the average number of persons per square km from some 2.7 to 5.4 in 1750, while in Europe, India and China these figures stood at 26.9, 24.1 and 22.1, respectively (Herbst 2014, p. 16). Multiple studies have confirmed the land abundance thesis for various regions in Africa (see Austin 2008b). At the same time, the upward revision makes it more likely that pockets of high population density existed, especially in West Africa, the most populous part of the continent. Densities in the Niger Bend (the northern part of the Niger river) were possibly even above 60 persons per square km in the fifteenth and sixteenth centuries (Inikori 2014). Finally, there were seasonal fluctuations in the demand for work and therefore its scarcity/abundancy – allowing, for example, labour-intensive handicraft production outside the agricultural season (Austin 2008a, p. 1006).

Older estimates suggest smaller absolute decreases in the population of West Africa, from 25 million to 23 million between 1700 and 1850. Detailed studies on local levels have confirmed population losses, especially in regions like the Bight of Benin, which exported, relatively, far more slaves. In more conservative estimates, the population of West Africa remains stagnant. Yet without the slave trades, this population would have grown between 1600 and 1850 by some 14 million (Klein 2010, p. 129). So, even with these estimates, there is in that sense a loss of population of 14 million people! In addition, most of the slaves – about

64 per cent – in the Atlantic trade were male (Lovejoy 1989, p. 381), which affected the age and gender distribution of the populations of the main exporting regions. In Angola in the late eighteenth century, women outnumbered men by two to one (Lovejoy 2011, p. 64). On the one hand, this may have limited the long-term effects on population growth, as women are more important for demographic growth than men. The fact that young people (of a reproductive age) were taken aggravated the demographic consequences. At the same time, polygyny[9] became more widespread and persisted: across larger regions there is a relationship between the prevalence of polygany today and exposure to the slave trade (Dalton and Leung 2014). Matrilineality decreased and the spousal age gap increased, as men married later, which may have diminished the position of women in African societies (Manning 1990, p. 133). At the same time, the shifting sex ratios also changed the role of women on the labour market; they must have taken over work that had initially been in the hands of men (Thornton 1980). In areas where women were already involved in agriculture, they came to dominate agricultural labour – e.g. in Central Africa, the Bight of Biafra and the Gold Coast (Manning 1990). In areas where they were traditionally not much involved in agriculture, women turned to commerce; a recent study has shown that higher exposure to the slave trade is related to higher female labour market participation today (Teso 2014).

Thus, we may conclude that, even taking the most conservative stance, the slave trade had a negative impact on Africa's long-term economic development as it diminished the long-term growth rate of the population of an already labour-scarce continent and may have had a negative impact on gender relations. Again, we should emphasize, the impact differed markedly across the different regions of West Africa.

Markets, Commercialization and Living Standards

The functioning of markets in pre-colonial Africa has long been a central debate in African economic history. In the 1960s, it was in fact generally assumed that markets, other than those for slaves, did not exist in pre-colonial Africa. Such views were most famously expressed by Karl Polanyi, who in his classic 1944 book *The Great Transformation* wrote a powerful critique of market liberalism, emphasizing the embeddedness of the 'economy' within society and culture. In 1966, a book by Polanyi was posthumously published, in which he noted that despite international trade and the spread of money in the form of cowrie shells, a market economy in Dahomey did not exist as all exchange was monopolized by the state. Such views have been discredited since. Anthony Hopkins (1973) argued that markets, and even the lack thereof, could be completely explained by economics, rather than by arguments related to customs and traditions. Commodity markets were often functioning according to supply and demand dynamics in pre-colonial Africa. There was sustained price inflation, suggesting the operation of markets in eighteenth-century Dahomey (Law 1992). Similarly, prices were not fixed in the commercial centres of nineteenth-century Sokoto Caliphate and Asante (Jerven 2016, p. 23). African states, although they certainly tried, simply failed to monopolize trade entirely (Thornton 1992, p. 66).

Functioning capitalist commodity markets coexisted with more pre-capitalistic markets for the factors of production. The size of the free labour market was limited, but it was not entirely absent: there existed pockets where wage labour was available in urban centres, as has been shown for Elmina on the Gold Coast (Rönnbäck 2014). In general, however, most of the agricultural production relied on family labour, or labour obtained with coercion, through corvée and slavery (Austin 2009). In addition, cultivable land was so abundant that anyone could simply clear and start cultivating land 'belonging to the household, clan or chief without paying more than token sums in rent' (ibid., p. 33). Evidence of a functioning land market, where land was bought and sold according to market principles, is therefore scarce. Only in the nineteenth century, with the rise of commercial cash crop production, did such land markets come into existence. There was a capital market where interest rates were seemingly very high; Austin (2009) cites a rate of 33.3 per cent per 40 days in the early nineteenth century. Yet all lending seemed to be constrained to two-party interactions: institutions were limited and there were no networks of intermediaries linking borrowers to lenders across larger distances.

Did the Atlantic trade help the development of capitalist markets? Inikori (2011, p. 662) argues that in the first two centuries of the European trade with Africa, it 'provided an additional stimulus to the preceding ongoing development of markets and the market economy in West Africa'. As trade in this early period was still characterized by the exports of African-produced goods, it led to the growth of markets and allowed vent-for-surplus growth. However, with the intensification of the slave trade in the late seventeenth and eighteenth centuries, such developments were reversed. With the trade by that time almost entirely dominated by the sale of human captives, it no longer stimulated export growth and stopped pre-existing trends in the commercialization of agriculture. As slaves were captured, as opposed to traded, no market exchange took place in the areas of capture – often in the interior. Along the coast, and the immediate hinterlands, however, slaves were exchanged by middlemen for European manufactures (Inikori 2007, p. 84). This may have led to diverging developments between coastal areas and the interior. Furthermore, Inikori (2011) suggests that the shift in import composition towards more textiles and guns, and less intermediate goods and currencies, had a negative impact on African craft production. John Iliffe (1995, p. 145) notes, however, that considering the limited size of international trade vis-à-vis the domestic economy, there were few areas with intensive trading where imported cloth did damage indigenous textile production. In most places the local market absorbed the increased imported goods in combination with locally produced products (Eltis and Jennings 1988).

The most important agricultural export from West Africa in the Atlantic trade was food for the slave ships (Iliffe 1995). In a recent paper, Angus Dalrymple-Smith and Pieter Woltjer (2016) show that, in the trade on the Biafran coast, over the eighteenth century and first decade of the nineteenth century, there was an increase in both the volume and prices of African commodity exports (in relative as well as absolute terms). The share of commodities in eighteenth-century British exports from Africa increased from 3 per cent in the 1740s to 8 per cent in the early nineteenth century. This suggests increasing agricultural opportunities. But while the share of commodities was increasing, it was still very far below the shares in the first centuries of the slave trade, when over half of the goods exported consisted of ivory and gold.

One of the positive effects of the Atlantic trade was the introduction of new American crops which allowed increases in agricultural productivity to occur. Cassava and maize were introduced to Africa in the early period of the slave trade. Cassava was ideal for forest cultivation, while maize became an important food crop on the savanna (Klein 2010, p. 64). Together with sweet potatoes, these New World crops augmented

African diets and may have spurred population growth. Cash crops, like tobacco, cacao and peanuts would become important only in the nineteenth century.

As a result of the slave trades, Africa bestowed on America the relative advantages of cheap labour in combination with cheap land. As a result, it was America, rather than Africa, which produced tropical commodities for the world market. The colonies in the Americas were consequently transformed into thriving market societies. Furthermore, as productivity in African agriculture was also dependent on bringing more workers into the fields, the export of many young men further inhibited agricultural productivity growth in Africa. Without the export of slaves, the comparative advantage in cash crop production would have rested with Africa.

Apparently African labour was so much more productive in the Americas that it was more profitable to ship slaves and put them to work there, despite high transportation costs and casualties along the way, rather than to put them to work within Africa. Austin (2008b) notes that African agricultural productivity was limited due to the tsetse fly – which spread sleeping sickness that is deadly to many large animals and thus hindered the use of animal-drawn ploughs and caused a lack of manure to use as cheap fertilizer – the rapid erosion of thin African soil and an overall lack of capital. The latter constraint could have been reduced by the import of European capital, yet when in 1726 King Agaja of Dahomey suggested to the Europeans that they should set up plantations in his kingdom – he would even supply the slaves – he received no response (Iliffe 1995, p. 146). Inikori (2002, p. 389) notes the opposition of European planters in the Americas who feared competition and who had significant political influence. Yet, Europeans did experiment with establishing plantations in West Africa. Law (2013) notes that these were failures due to incompetent management, insecurity, lack of secure land tenure, lower soil productivity and the higher risk of runaway slaves. Another probable factor is that few Europeans, needed for supervision, were willing to live in tropical Africa for longer time periods because of the extremely high risk of dying there (Öberg and Rönnback 2016).

According to Inikori (2007, 2011), without the slave trades, Africa's commercialization, agricultural commodity production and market institutions would have been much more developed in the nineteenth and twentieth centuries. One indication of the growth of commercialization is the growth of cities, which depends on a market of surplus food. The percentage of people in cities of 10,000 or more inhabitants (using data from Buringh 2016) remained roughly stable with 1.3–2.6 per cent in 1700 and 1.4–2.8 per cent in 1800. These ranges are dependent on the population estimates discussed in the previous section, where the low figure is based on Manning's (2014) recent estimates of the total population, while the high estimate uses more conservative population estimates (half of Manning's population). Two features stand out. First, from a comparative perspective, both estimates suggest low rates of urbanization in the same period: in Europe and Asia the percentage of the population in urban environments was between 5 and 10 per cent. This was not only the result of the slave trade of course, as urbanization rates were presumably low already before the seventeenth and eighteenth centuries. Second, at least over the eighteenth century, the trend in urbanization was roughly stable, and, considering the substantial margins of error attached to these figures, allows for little interpretation. Looking at the figures for only West Africa, the urbanization rate possibly increased slightly from 1.2–2.3 per cent in 1700 to 1.8–3.6 per cent in 1800. Still, this growth is unremarkable compared with the growth of urbanization in the same period in Europe. Clearly, in Africa, intercontinental trade did little to push up levels of urbanization.

What do we know about developments in living standards in precolonial Africa? We completely lack estimates of developments in GDP per capita (except for the Cape Colony in South Africa, discussed below) before the twentieth century. Rönnback (2014) recently showed the decline in real wages (computed as subsistence ratios, comparable with those shown in other chapters) on the eighteenth-century Gold Coast. His evidence for free unskilled labourers, the canoemen, shows that wages were below the level needed to sustain a family consisting of six people. Yet this could be resolved by the fact that, as discussed above, African women also made significant contributions to family incomes. Prices, besides a drop in the 1720s, were roughly stable between 1699 and 1759, so that the decline was driven by a fall in wages in the early eighteenth century. This decline in real wages is in correspondence with the evidence of wage and price trends in eighteenth-century Dahomey (Law 1992). There, however, the wages of porters remained stable from the late seventeenth (in Whydah, overtaken by Dahomey in the early eighteenth century) to the mid-nineteenth century. Prices of foodstuffs at the same time increased between the later seventeenth and middle of the eighteenth century, leading to a decline in purchasing power. Declining real wages during a period when the slave trades increased may support the view that the slave trades in the eighteenth century had negative effects on African economies. Possibly, real wages in Africa were higher during the early decades of contact with the Europeans. However, the evidence is still very thin and the precise channels of causation that led to declining real wages should be further explored. Furthermore, these figures refer to only a few coastal West African ports, and it may be questioned whether they say much about developments in other areas as, due to transportation constraints, food markets (and thus prices) were 'highly localized' (Austin 2013, p. 257).

State Formation and Fragmentation

It is generally assumed that pre-colonial Africa lagged behind Eurasia in terms of state formation (Acemoglu and Robinson 2010). Large states were, however, not unknown to Africa. Thornton (1992, p. 104) notes that the size of some African states, like the Songhai Empire, were in the range of 0.5 to 1 million square km and thereby similar in size to France (550,000 square km) and Spain (1 million square km). West Africa also had medium-sized states, like the Oyo Empire in Nigeria, which was roughly the same size as England and Portugal (between 50,000 and 150,000 square km). Yet, most parts of West Africa's landmass, around 70 per cent, were occupied by small polities. Over half of West Africa's population lived in tiny states that covered only 500–1,000 square km. In thinly populated areas, such states may have been inhabited by as few as 3,000–5,000 people, yet along more densely populated coasts such an area could contain between 20,000 and 30,000 people (Thornton 1992, p. 105). At the same time, in 1500, European kingdoms like Spain and France boasted about seven million and 15 million souls, respectively (Van Zanden et al. 2016).

Rulers of African states claimed absolute power. Dahomey was the property of the king: the king owned the land and everything on it. Consequently, as noted by a British contemporary in the 1770s, the inhabitants of Dahomey were 'all slaves to the king' (cited in Law 1992, p. 71). Despite their claims to absolute power, African rulers often lacked the means to project their influence over large territories and large amounts of people. Because land was abundant, it was not highly valued. Furthermore, this abundance of land led peasants to depend on rain-fed extensive agriculture, meaning that little investment was made in farmland (Herbst 2014, pp. 38–39). Famously, the plough, needed for intensive agriculture, was not adopted by African societies. This also meant that it was usually not worthwhile defending such lands, nor was it necessary to acquire large territories, which were difficult to control without adequate infrastructure. Rulers found it hard to tie people to the land, making it hard to tax them. Power, instead, rested with control over people and wars were often fought for obtaining people and booty, rather than land. The slave trades only strengthened already existing notions linking power to control over people.

In Kongo, the king, supported by a standing army, engaged in slave raiding on his own population next to extracting numerous taxes from his subjects (Iliffe 1995, p. 143). Under such conditions, there were few incentives for private parties to make investments in agriculture or production. Instead, Kongolese villagers moved away from roads in order to reduce taxation from their rulers and avoid capture by slave raiders. Dahomey and Kongo also provide good examples of how the interests of the elites differed from those of the general population, and how, accordingly, the benefits and detriments of intercontinental commerce diverged. Whereas the king and the slave raiders increased their wealth and power, large parts of the population suffered as a result.

While it is generally accepted that the growth of the slave trade went hand in hand with the increase in warfare, it is not clear whether it contributed overall to greater state fragmentation or, in contrast, more political centralization. As mentioned before, many scholars have argued that warfare in early modern Europe drove state formation there. In Africa, a similar process could have remained absent, as there was no private property in land which meant that wars were not fought over territory, but over people. This may therefore have reduced the need to build extensive fortifications to defend such lands, which was an important feature of the war–state formation relationship in early modern Europe. Some authors have suggested that the slave trade further caused the fragmentation of states in West Africa (e.g. Rodney 1972; Nunn 2008). The Kingdom of Kongo, which collapsed in the late seventeenth century, is put forward as an example where extensive slave trading and raiding led to the collapse of the state (Nunn 2008, p. 143). The slave trades stimulated corruption in the legal system (as noted on p. 103, an increasing variety of offenses were being punished by enslavement). Nunn (2008, p. 166) shows that those areas with a relatively high level of slave exports had low levels of state development in the nineteenth century. Yet there is a possible problem of reversed causality here, as we would expect more slaves to be exported from areas with low initial levels of political centralization (Austin 2008a, p. 1005). A higher level of political centralization would have reduced incentives to prey on neighbouring populations to feed the slave trade. In fact, there is little evidence to suggest that the average size of states decreased during the period of the slave trades (Austin 2008a). In contrast, Austin notes that maps of West Africa from historical atlases hint at a trend towards larger states, but acknowledges that this may also be the result of increasingly better information on states over time, rather than the actual increase in large states. Military historians of Africa have noted that fortifications were in fact used in African warfare (Thornton 1992) and that the positive link between warfare and state formation also existed in Africa (Reid 2012).

In any case, it is clear that states both rose (e.g. Oyo, Dahomey and Asante) and fell (e.g. Kongo) over the period of the Atlantic slave trade, depending on which region one looks at. One consequence of the rise of the Atlantic trade was that it merged political and commercial power: either states became heavily involved in the Atlantic trade, or Atlantic traders gained political power (Ilife 1995, p. 139). This is related to the broad pattern of decline in land-based agricultural empires and the rise of mercantile naval kingdoms in West Africa, which is to an important extent related to the rise of the Atlantic trade. In particular, the import of European firearms allowed relatively small minorities with access to these weapons to subdue larger populations without such access. Jeffrey Herbst (2014) notes that guns reinforced the centralization of power as they could be stored until they were needed, while bows and arrows were available to everyone. Furthermore, the lack of gun manufacturing in Africa also boosted the power of mercantile states who controlled transactions with the Europeans.

The rise of Oyo in the seventeenth century was strongly related to the rising export of slaves. The empire established itself in the hinterland of the Bight of Benin and between 1690 and 1740 a significant part of the slaves sold there were the results of Oyo's conquest (Acemoglu and Robinson 2010, p. 30). Similarly, Dahomey became a dominant local power in the same area, conquering two neighbouring kingdoms in the 1720s by building a large army and specializing in warfare and slave raiding. Down south, in Angola, the Ndongo used a similar strategy to build a slave-raiding state in the sixteenth and seventeenth centuries (Iliffe 1995, pp. 144–145). In the eighteenth century, the rise of Asante on the Gold Coast was also related to Atlantic commerce, though not necessarily the slave trade. Instead, some people of the Gold Coast became rich in the seventeenth century as a result of exporting gold. In the early seventeenth century, Asante became the most important state in the area because of its agricultural success, which was built on a combination of forest and savannah produce. It used gold exports to purchase firearms for defence against slave-raiding enemies and bought slaves to work in agriculture. Only with the rise of slave prices in the eighteenth century did Asante become a net slave exporter (Iliffe 1995, p. 144).

The Legacy of the Slave Trades

In 1807, the British banned the slave trade. This did not end the external slave trade from Africa entirely, as the Portuguese and Spanish continued to export African slaves until the 1860s. In fact, in the nineteenth century, almost four million people were exported in the Atlantic slave trade (Eltis et al. 2013). Nonetheless, the abolition of the trade by the British, and subsequently the Dutch in 1814 and French in 1818, did significantly reduce the external demand from the early decades of the nineteenth century.

It did not, however, end slavery in Africa. In contrast, reduced demand in the nineteenth century pushed down slave prices and increased slavery and slave trading within Africa (Klein 2010, pp. 130–131). There are estimates suggesting that at the height of the Atlantic slave trade, in the later eighteenth century, there were an equal number of slaves in Africa as in the Americas: between three and five million. These numbers increased in the first half of the nineteenth century to some ten million by 1850 (ibid.). The slave trade gave way to so-called 'legitimate commerce'; the export of tropical produce like palm oil, peanuts, ivory, rubber and cocoa. Slave labour was crucial for the production of commodities for 'legitimate commerce' and increasing commercialization went together with the growth of coerced labour within Africa. As a result of overall labour scarcity, it was hard to find free labour for commercial agriculture at a competitive price, but as a result of the already widespread existence of slavery and a tradition of slave raiding, a more extensive use of slave labour within Africa provided a solution to this problem. With the decline of slave prices, opportunity costs for employing slaves domestically declined. The continuation of slavery and slave trading served the interests of the ruling classes of many African states, who resisted abolition; many political leaders resorted to violence in order to safeguard their position and armed conflict rose as a result (Fenske and Kala 2014). In Angola, for example, the decline of the external slave trade in the nineteenth century caused political disintegration (Iliffe 1995, p. 152).

As a result, slavery persisted for a long time in Africa. In 1900 the Sokoto Caliphate, located around present-day Nigeria, had a slave population of between 1 to 2.5 million people (Lovejoy and Hogendorn 1993), or about a quarter of the total population. Similarly, in the early twentieth century, there were almost 1.2 million slaves in a total population of 5.1 million in French Western Sudan (Lovejoy 1989, pp. 391–392). While no precise figures are available, it is clear that, in Dahomey slaves were labouring on large palm oil plantations, whereas in Asante they were put to work in gold and kola-nut production (Acemoglu and Robinson 2010, p. 31). In Sierra Leone, slavery was abolished as late as 1928 (ibid.) and even today, forms of slavery have not been completely eradicated from the continent (Global Slavery Index 2016). Children and adults are kidnapped and forced to provide labour. In Central Africa thousands of abducted children are serving in armed conflicts as soldiers.

Nineteenth-century British campaigns to eliminate the slave trade increased British interference in African politics, which would eventually lead to the European partition of Africa (Austin 2008a). There is thus a relationship between the Atlantic slave trade, the subsequent period of intensified slavery in Africa and colonialism. The consequences of colonialism for African development are outside the scope of this book, but are discussed extensively in recent literature.[10]

Nunn (2008) has statistically demonstrated that the slave trades not only had immediate effects, but in fact played a role in Africa's current underdevelopment. He finds a strong and robust relationship between the number of slaves exported from each country (an extension and reworking of the regional differentiation shown in Figure 4.1) and the level of economic development (as measured by GDP per capita) nowadays. The slave trades increased ethnic fractionalization and this, in turn, had a negative effect on the provision of public goods, which is important for economic growth in the long run. Additionally, he associates the slave trades with lower levels of political centralization, although the direction of the relationship is not entirely clear yet (as discussed on pp. 111–114). While some have criticized Nunn's data and findings, the notion that the slave trades had significant long-run negative effects has been influential in recent economic historical literature.

Southern and Eastern Africa

The discussion thus far has focused on developments in West Africa, as it was at the centre of the Atlantic slave trade. In this section, we will briefly review developments in East and South Africa.

In comparison with West Africa, population densities were certainly lower in East Africa. A string of commercial towns along the East African coast had long since been in constant engagement with the Indian Ocean trade. Mozambique and Zimbabwe had been exporting ivory and gold to different parts of Asia for many centuries. Slave exports from the region remained relatively small between 800 and 1700: about 1,000 per annum. These slaves were often intended for harems or domestic work in the Middle East and the share of women and children among them was therefore much higher than in the Atlantic trade. In exchange, East Africa received textiles, weapons and porcelain (Barendse 2000, p. 176). Not long after da Gama first explored the eastern coasts in 1498, the Portuguese would violently enforce control over East Africa's coasts in an attempt to claim their share of commerce. Zanzibar was forced into submission in 1503 and two years later the Portuguese first razed the Islamic port of Kilwa (in present-day Tanzania), which had been the centre of East African trade, and then established themselves in Sofala (Mozambique) – a port with access to inland ivory and gold deposits – and Mozambique Island (Alpers 1975). They allied themselves with the rulers of Malindi

(Kenya) and in 1591 captured Mombasa. Due to Portuguese intrusion in long-established trading patterns, commerce along Africa's eastern coast was depressed as many Arab merchants diverted trade elsewhere.

While the Portuguese continued to hold a substantial degree of influence on politics and economics on the coast over the seventeenth century, their power, as elsewhere in the Indian Ocean, would start to wane at this time. As their control and financial position weakened, the Portuguese tried to stimulate trade in order to reap tax benefits, so the seventeenth century may have seen trade growth (Alpers 1977, p. 531). The Omani, who had recently cast off Portuguese occupation, established themselves as a substantial power along the East African coast from the late seventeenth century onwards, capturing Mombasa in 1698. While the early eighteenth century was a period of some unrest and depressed commerce, trade grew in the second half of the eighteenth century. As the Omani capital of Muscat gained prominence as a trading centre in Indian Ocean commerce, slave exports increased to some 4,000 annually (Lovejoy 2011). French entry into East African trade also spurred slave exports in the eighteenth century and many would also be sent to Réunion and Mauritius. Ivory replaced gold as the most important article of commerce and Indian, rather than Arab, merchants became its main traders. Prices for ivory rose in the eighteenth century, evidencing the growth in international demand (Alpers 1975, p. 97). Growing trade also intensified relations with the interior towards the end of the eighteenth century; there is evidence that luxury commodities obtained in international trade began to penetrate inland kingdoms like Buganda, which had been largely closed off from the rest of the world until then (Fage 1997, p. 297).

Edward Alpers (1975, pp. 264–267) argues that international exchange in the early modern era was harmful to East Africa as the goods received in no way matched the value of the labour power exported and '[t]he multiplier effects of this trade did nothing to promote either economic development or social equality in African societies.' Similar views are expressed by Abdul Sheriff (1987). But international trade was definitely less developed than in West Africa and the effects on demographic and economic development in East Africa were most likely limited until the nineteenth century. Portuguese control was very limited and attempts to monopolize trade failed (Pearson 1998, p. 154).

South Africa experienced quite a different development in this period as it was the only region in Africa with significant numbers of European settlers already in the early modern era. The Cape Colony was founded in 1652 by the VOC as a refreshment station for ships sailing between Europe and the East Indies.[11] After failed attempts to secure provisions by trading with the indigenous Khoesan, a number of VOC employees were released from their contracts in order to become free burghers and farmers at the Cape in 1657. These farmers soon switched to extensive agriculture, which required expansion into new territories. Between 1679 and 1717 this type of production was supported by the VOC. Immigration from Europe was actively stimulated (as the VOC paid for immigrants' voyages), and land was made available to the settlers on a first come, first served basis. After 1717, however, population growth relied on high fertility rates among the settlers: the white population grew from 1,300 in 1700 to around 22,000 at the end of the century. Labour was supplied predominantly by imported slaves from the shores of the Indian Ocean (Keegan 1996, p. 15), as well as by indentured Khoesan. Cape Town, though not the only town, was the sole port and main market for agricultural products. Wine and wheat farms, worked by slaves, dominated the area surrounding Cape Town, while further into the interior, pastoral livestock farmers occupied an ever-expanding territory (Van Duin and Ross 1987, p. 2). A study by Boshoff and Fourie (2010), has shown that passing ships (and thus the external trade controlled by the VOC) did have a considerable positive economic impact on the Cape Colony, which they demonstrate via a statistically significant relationship between ship traffic and agricultural production.

Fourie and Van Zanden (2013) have shown high estimates of GDP per capita for the Cape Colony: Europeans in Southern Africa earned incomes as high as those in Holland, one of the wealthiest regions of the world. Such high incomes were attained at the expense of many slaves: over half of the population of the eighteenth-century Cape Colony consisted of slaves. A similar picture emerged from the development of purchasing power. Real wages of European wage labourers in the Cape Colony were relatively high and very stable, about twice the subsistence level in the period 1652–1800 (De Zwart 2013). We have no evidence about the welfare of the indigenous Khoesan. It is clear, however, that in the long run, the South African economic system gave rise to greater inequality among different population groups (see De Zwart 2011).

Conclusion

This chapter has dealt with one of the most horrible events in human history: the trade in millions of Africans over the course of many centuries – arguably the worst excess of globalization ever, linking the fates of the Americas and Africa. While both slavery and the trade in slaves had existed in Africa many centuries prior to the arrival of the Europeans, the scale would increase tremendously as a result of their involvement. We have provided an account, based on the most recent data and literature, of these trades and their effects on African societies. In the fifteenth and sixteenth centuries, and even large parts of the seventeenth century, the total number of slaves exported across the Atlantic was limited and did little to alter developments in Africa. Large shares of the Atlantic trade were dominated by the export of gold and ivory, which had, if any, positive effects on commercialization along the African coast. From the later seventeenth century onwards, however, the slave trade intensified, the share of exports shifted to almost entirely human captives and the trade as a whole increased dramatically. Although, as a percentage of the total domestic economy, international trade may have been small, the nature of the 'commodity' exported – human beings that could have otherwise performed productive labour – as well as the nature of the 'production process' – warfare and kidnappings – meant that the consequences could be destructive and bear no relation to the value of exports as expressed in any currency. Furthermore, the notion that the trade was small compared with the West African domestic economy does not take into account the large differences between regions. For example, the Angola region and the Bight of Biafra exported a disproportionate number of slaves. In these areas, the Atlantic slave trade almost certainly led to an absolute decline of the population. In heavily affected areas, the atlantic slave trade also changed gender relations, retarded commercial development and gave rise to violent conflict. As the Europeans did not have the means to force Africans into this trade, African elites and slave traders entered on their own account as they sought out political and economic benefits. Coastal centres benefitted, while hinterlands bore the costs and regional inequality increased. Recent econometric studies have shown how various negative effects of the slave trades may have persisted in current times. Future research will have to trace such developments over time in order to be more certain about the causal mechanisms. Nonetheless, it is clear that Africa's contribution to the construction of the global economy by providing labour for American plantations was made at the cost of those enslaved, as well as many of those left behind. It demonstrates that even Africa – the continent which was probably least commercialized of all world regions – was fundamentally affected by the forces of globalization.

Suggested Reading

Akyeampong, Emmanuel, Robert H. Bates, Nathan Nunn and James A. Robinson (eds) (2014), *Africa's Development in Historical Perspective*, Cambridge: Cambridge University Press.

Austin, Gareth (2008b). 'Resources, Techniques and Strategies South of the Sahara: Revising the Factor Endowments Perspective on African Economic Development, 1500–2000', *Economic History Review* 61, pp. 587–624.

Boshoff, W. and J. Fourie (2010). 'The Significance of the Cape Trade Route to Economic Activity in the Cape Colony: A Medium-Term Business Cycle Analysis', *European Review of Economic History* 14, pp. 469–503.

Iliffe, John (1995). *Africans: The History of a Continent.* Cambridge: Cambridge University Press.

Inikori, Joseph E. (2007). 'Africa and the Globalization Process: Western Africa, 1450–1850', *Journal of Global History* 2, pp. 63–86.

Jerven, M. (2016). 'Capitalism in Pre-Colonial Africa: A Review', *AEHN Working Paper* No. 27.

Klein, Herbert S. (2010). *The Atlantic Slave Trade.* (2nd ed.). Cambridge: Cambridge University Press.

Lovejoy, Paul E. (2011). *Transformations in Slavery. A history of slavery in Africa.* (3rd ed.). Cambridge: Cambridge University Press.

Nunn, Nathan (2008). 'The Long-Term Effects of Africa's Slave Trades', *Quarterly Journal of Economics* 123, pp. 139–176.

5 | Export-Led Development in North America

Introduction

Viking *sagas* suggest that there have been several expeditions to North America. In one of these, around the year 1000, the Vikings established a settlement in the north of Newfoundland, but conditions turned out to be unsuitable for building a long-term settlement and it was soon abandoned (Black 2011, p. 22). Many centuries would pass until a Venetian in English service, Giovanni Caboto, sailed to North America again in the late fifteenthth century and over a century later, in 1607, Jamestown (Virginia) was established as the first British colonial settlement. Jamestown was initially a failure and its population faced significant hardship: shortages of food and fresh water caused widespread illness and staggering death rates: of the original 105 colonists, 67 had died within the first year. Attacks by hostile Native Americans added to the perils of the young colony; by 1623 the average life expectancy of settlers arriving in Jamestown was two years (Walton and Rockoff 1998, pp. 29–30).

At this time, north-eastern America had few attractions for Europeans; there were no indications that there was any gold or silver, and with a temperate climate similar to that in Europe there was little exotic flora which produced the kind of commodities that could be sold for high prices back home (Vickers 1996, p. 210). As Susan Lee and Peter Passell (1979, p. 19) note '[i]n 1640 the American colonies were a collection of farming villages barely self-sufficient in the essentials of life, and heavily dependent on Britain for protection against a hostile environment'. What allowed these colonies, apparently placed in such difficult conditions and where seemingly no valuable resources were to be found, to become, in a very short amount of time, the richest societies on the globe?

Trade is an important part of the story. In fact, it seems hardly necessary to make the point that the development of the economy and

121

society of North America – and in particular the settler economies that emerged there in the seventeenth and eighteenth centuries – was closely aligned to the world market. The seminal book by John McCusker and Russell Menard (1985) entitled *The economy of British America, 1607–1789* analyses its development in the light of the 'staples approach'. This is the argument that new settlements such as those in the Americas, required successful export products to sell at international markets. Moreover, often a single product came to dominate these new colonies, and the characteristics of the production process of these products shaped the social and economic realities of the colonies concerned. To give an example, the large-scale production of sugar resulted in a plantation economy with low-skilled slave labour, whereas the different requirements of growing wheat were consistent with family farms (see e.g. Engerman and Sokoloff 2000). Yet, as we will see, the story is more complicated than that; tobacco, for example, was produced by family farms in the seventeenth century, but in the eighteenth century slave labour came to dominate the cultivation of this crop as well. Nonetheless, as a first approach pointing out the importance of links to world markets for the development of the new settler societies, this 'staples approach' is useful. It follows from this approach that without successful new products which can compete at world markets, these new settlements stagnate, or, in other words, the growth of these settler economies is dependent on the growth of their exports. Growth is limited by the capacity of the metropole – Western Europe – to absorb more products, and by the ability of the settlers to develop new markets. In the long run, however, the development of internal markets, diversification and urbanization will change this, and result in endogenous growth. It is, though, a clear feature of North American economic development that diversification and urbanization came late; only towards the end of the eighteenth century did the cities on the East Coast begin to expand quickly. Until the final decades of the eighteenth century growth was extensive – involving the expansion of settlement inland and the growth of rural populations – rather than intensive. As a result of the generous availability of land fit for cultivation, incomes and living standards for colonists were high over much of the seventeenth and eighteenth centuries.

We will suggest that the dependence of North American settlements on world markets was even higher than the staples approach – with its focus on producing an export commodity – implies. For the supply of labour, capital and skills, international markets were again fundamental – and this supply, or the lack of it, further influenced paths of development. Given the almost unlimited supply of land, labour was usually in short supply and had to be recruited in Western Europe (mainly in England), often in the form of indentured labour. Alternatively, following the plantation economies that had emerged in the Caribbean, slaves from Africa were imported on a large scale, especially in the Southern colonies. As a result of imported labour from both Europe and Africa, as well as large family sizes, population numbers rose dramatically over the seventeenth and eighteenth centuries. This expansion 'was without parallel in history' according to Thomas Malthus, who used his observation of the colonies for his famous suggestion that, when unchecked by limits in available land, population would expand geometrically (Galenson 1996, p. 169). In the eighteenth century, population growth in the colonies was between 2.4 and 2.9 per cent annually – which was six to seven times the rate of population growth in Western Europe (Lindert and Williamson 2016, p. 54).

In this chapter, we will discuss the role of the global market in allowing the expansion of this population without any serious declines in living standards (discussed below). Following the literature on colonial America, we will group the 13 colonies into four regions for the analysis: New England (Connecticut, Massachusetts, New Hampshire and Rhode Island), the Middle Colonies (New Jersey, New York and Pennsylvania), the Upper South (Delaware, Maryland and Virginia) and the Lower South (North and South Carolina and Georgia). Map 5.1 shows the 13 American colonies, as well as the 'proclamation line' that separated the lands of the colonists from the lands west of the Appalachians granted to Native Americas after the Seven Years' War (1756–63). We will begin the investigation by providing an overview of the trading patterns of the colonies, and then, delving deeper into the consequences of this trade, deal with the differences between the regions.

Export Trade and Development

One of the main elements of the story of trade and development in the North American colonies is that there was a marked difference between the packages of goods exported between the various regions.

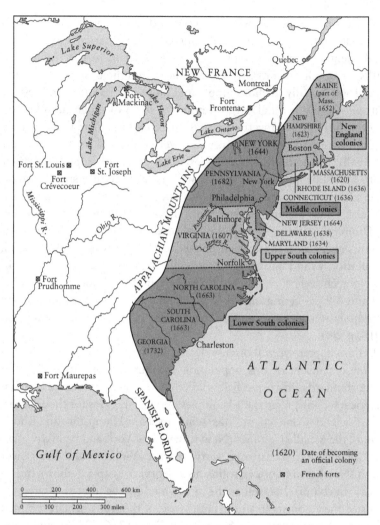

Map 5.1 North America in the eighteenth century.
Source: Grant (2012).

As we shall discuss below, such differences would have profound effects on average incomes as well as institutional developments.

As a result of research on the colonial export trade in the late eighteenth century by James Shepherd and Gary Walton (1972), we have information on exports from the Northern American colonies for the years 1768–1772, just before the American Revolutionary War. These figures (shown in Table 5.1) show that the Canadian regions were mainly exporting fish, while the Middle Colonies specialized in grain

Table 5.1. *Shares of the values of commodity exports from the different North American regions, 1768–1772*

	Canada[1]	New England	Middle Cols.	Upper South	Lower South
Deerskins	8%				7%
Fish	73%	35%			
Flaxseed			7%		
Grains, grain products	9%	5%	72%	19%	2%
Indigo					20%
Iron			5%	3%	
Livestock, beef, pork		20%	4%		2%
Naval stores					6%
Postash		5%	2%		
Rice					55%
Rum		4%			
Tobacco				72%	
Whale products	9%	14%			
Wood products		15%	6%	2%	5%
Other	2%	2%	4%	4%	3%

Source: McCusker and Menard (1985).

production, the Upper South in the export of tobacco and the Lower South's in the production of rice and indigo. New England's exports were much more diversified and show a combination of fish, whale and wood products, and livestock. While it is uncertain whether these shares were similar further back in history, there are some suggestions that this was the case. The respective shares of the goods exported from Virginia in 1733 (McCusker and Menard 1985, p. 132), were similar to the relative shares of exports from the Upper South period 1768–1772: in both cases tobacco dominated with over 70 per cent of all exports, a specialization that started early in the seventeenth century. McCusker and Menard (1985, p. 85) also note that the more diversified exports of New

England were remarked upon by contemporaries already in the seventeenth century. At the same time, the growth of grain exports from
the Middle Colonies may have been a primarily eighteenth-century
phenomenon, resulting from the growth of the West Indies plantation
economies that needed to be supplied with foodstuffs.

There are no overall long-term figures on the entire export and
import trade from the colonies. What we do have are data on the
value of trade between the colonies and the metropole (England and
Wales) between 1693 and 1791. While this exchange was probably
the most important for all the colonies combined, it was by no means
the only trade, and for some colonies it was much more important
than for others, as becomes clear from late-eighteenth century figures
(Shepherd and Walton 1972). The South exported over 70 per cent of
its commodities to Britain, while the Middle and Northern Colonies
only between 13 and 19 per cent (Table 5.2). For the latter, the export
trade to southern Europe and the West Indies was much more important (at least by the end of the eighteenth century). In terms of imports,
England was the most important trading partner for all colonies, as
between 66 and 95 per cent of all imports came from Britain. Only

Table 5.2. *North America: shares of export and import values to and
from different destinations, 1768–1772*

	Canada[2]	New England	Middle Cols.	Upper South	Lower South
Exports					
Great Britain	19	18	13	79	71
Ireland	3	0	10	3	0
S. Europe	72	15	35	9	10
West Indies	6	63	42	9	18
Africa	0	4	0	0	0
Imports					
Great Britain	95	66	76	89	86
S. Europe	2	2	3	1	1
West Indies	3	32	21	10	13

Source: Shepherd and Walton (1972) and McCusker and Menard (1985)

New England and the Middle Colonies also imported a substantial amount of goods from the West Indies (mostly rum and molasses).

Earlier studies have suggested a decline in per capita trade values for the colonies over the eighteenth century (e.g. Davis et al. 1972, pp. 554–555). Such conclusions were based on the trade with Britain, yet especially for Canada, New England and the Middle Colonies this concerns only a small proportion of all trade and, according to McCusker and Menard (1985, p. 86), the 'other trades grew more rapidly than that with Britain'. Any trends based on the trade with England thus underestimate growth of trade over time. In addition, such estimates were based on prices set in 1690, while in reality prices for North American exports increased over the eighteenth century, as evidenced by the improving terms of trade for the colonies up to the Revolution (Lindert and Williamson 2016, p. 63). This means that the declining trend observed in export values must have been less dramatic than that based on 1690 prices. New estimates by Peter Mancall et al. (2006, 2008) show slight increases in the value of per capita exports for the Lower South until the middle of the eighteenth century and for the Middle Colonies until the Revolution. They do find a substantially reduced level of trade in the final decade of the eighteenth century caused by the wars. In light of the very high population growth rates, relatively stable trade figures per person were quite impressive and allowed the colonists to maintain high living standards (discussed on pp. 139–144). We will now take a closer look at some of these trades and their consequences.

The North: Furs, Fish and Whales

There were many ways in which regions were integrated into world markets in the early modern era. One way was by the outright exploitation of the natural resources of that region: by hunting its game and by depleting its fish stocks. In the period between 1500 and 1800 this direct exploitation of the resources of nature increased dramatically and became a truly global business. Of course, men and women had always exploited the environment in a systematic way, making use of all the potential supplies on offer – for food, shelter, clothing and all other needs. What changed between 1500 and 1800 was the scale on which this happened and the degree to which this was done for production for the market, which made it qualitatively different from home consumption by hunter gatherers and agriculturalists that had lived there for centuries. The trappers who harvested beaver furs, whalers who hunted down bowhead and right whales, and cod fishermen near Newfoundland, were all integrated into complex markets; they produced for distant consumers and acquired their capital from European sources. Both whale and cod fishing became highly capital-intensive industries, copying the example of North Sea herring fishing that had evolved in that direction from the late Medieval period.

The exploration of the North Atlantic gave an important stimulus to these developments, as it opened up largely unexploited natural resources – of cod near Newfoundland for example, or of beaver populations in inland America – which could be exploited at great profit. Moreover, local communities (of Native Americans and Inuit) were integrated into the same networks as local suppliers of furs and foodstuffs, and were often soon facing the consequences of their more intense contacts with Europeans (see e.g. Carlos and Lewis 2001; Salisbury 1996). The expansion of European settlement in North America can therefore not be understood without taking into account this history of direct exploitation of natural resources. It is crucial for understanding the growing links between North America and the world markets, but it is a history not exclusive to this region. The integration of Siberia in trading networks, or the exploitation of the rich natural resources of South Africa – including the slaughtering of its populations of elephants to satisfy the European demand for ivory – are other examples of the history of this 'unending frontier', as John Richards (2003) in his brilliant synthesis of the environmental history of this period saw it. North American whaling, cod fishing and fur hunting are perhaps the most extreme and 'successful' examples of direct resource exploitation in this period, but this happened on a more limited scale almost everywhere, except in the most urbanized parts of the world economy, where no nature had survived that could be exploited (and even in highly urbanized Holland, local fisheries and fowl hunting remained important elements of the economy).

From the perspective of the processes of globalization and economic change that are the topic of this book, the growth of these new activities in the North Atlantic added to the economic dynamism of the European economy (on which more in Chapter 9) and facilitated the integration of North America into the world economy. In a way, it started with cod. Already in the 1490s fishermen from the Basque region in Spain, and the first English and Portuguese explorers, crossed the North Atlantic in search of the cod fish that were found in the coastal waters near Newfoundland (Roberts 2007, pp. 33–35; Richards 2003, p. 547). Soon, they were followed by dozens of fishing boats from mainly France and Spain, who preyed upon the very large stocks that were available there. Fish was in high demand in Europe as an alternative to meat, which a good Catholic was not supposed to consume on Fridays and during the fasting season before Easter. Initially each ship made a return trip to the Newfoundland shores, but soon a division of labour emerged in which fishermen settled for the season on shore. They focused on the fishing itself, making use of small boats; processing and drying occurred locally and large transport ships were used to transport the catch back home (Richards 2003, p. 554). In time, some fishermen stayed behind during the winter, starting the process of settlement. In the seventeenth century the English arrived on the scene as competitors of the French (who had dominated initially), and an intense competition for fish stocks – both coastal and inland – began that would shape the history of European colonization in the next century or so. At the same time, new fishery grounds in the south – near New England – developed that contributed to the expansion of the local economy. In fact, fishing became, and remained, the main export activity of New England until the final decades of the eighteenth century: about 50 per cent of total exports from New England and over 80 per cent from the Atlantic Canadian regions were centred around the export of fish and whale products (Table 5.1 above, and McCusker and Menard 1985, pp. 108, 115).

Basques also played an important role in the initial development of the whaling industry. They had developed the technique of whale hunting locally, in the Bay of Biscay, and already, in around 1500, expanded their reach to Iceland and Labrador, developing large-scale and capital-intensive technologies (ships) in the process (Roberts 2007, pp. 86–88; Richards 2003, pp. 585–586). In the seventeenth century, the Dutch took over the industry, making use of the Basques' skills to learn the trade. They established a large chartered company for this purpose (the *Noordsche Compagnie*), but the most spectacular growth occurred after the dissolution of this company in 1642. In their footsteps, the Danish, German and English became involved in whale hunting. In the seventeenth century the main catchment area was near Spitsbergen, where the Dutch set up a processing station, but whale stocks in that region declined (or whales chose other migratory routes) as a result of which most activity moved to Greenland. Whaling became an important source of income for the north-eastern coast of the Americas, with the small island of Nantucket as its legendary centre. In 1768–1772, whale products were the most important export from New England to Britain, and held fourth place in total export volumes (Table 5.1 above, McCusker and Menard 1985, p. 108).

The activity that had a huge impact on the process of colonization of North America was fur hunting. From the start, Native Americans were involved and their fate sometimes oscillated with the ups and downs of their coalition with fur traders and their commercial and military allies (Salisbury 1996). As stocks of beavers, martins, otters, deer and other fur-producing animals in the coastal areas declined due to overexploitation (Carlos and Lewis 1993), fur trappers moved more deeply inland, following major rivers, and prepared the way for settlers who profited indirectly from the trade. Whereas the fishing industry had required large capital-intensive ships and equipment, the fur trade demanded (only) skilled labour, a small amount of capital, and good commercial relationships with local populations who often produced most of the furs. As in the cod fisheries, competition between the English and the French became intense, both parties trying to develop profitable coalitions with local Indian groups (and fighting with them on other occasions). In Europe, meanwhile, competition between the French and the English also meant that prices for fur hats in London and Paris moved in similar directions (Carlos and Lewis 2010, pp. 28–33). English expansion in the seventeenth century led to an encircling of the French sphere of influence radiating from the Saint Lawrence River region (Richards 2003, p. 486). It also led to bitter conflicts in which Indian groups were forced to choose sides. Endemic conflict combined with the spread of Eurasian diseases caused the Native American populations to dwindle (Salisbury 1996).

In the meantime, Native American groups responded to the new opportunities offered by the high European demand for furs – and, consequently, high prices offered – and they increased their work efforts (Carlos and Lewis 2001). As fur trappers moved further inland, increasingly large areas were covered by their activities. Estimated numbers of furs that were 'produced' continued to increase from 410,000 per year in the 1700–1763 period to 904,000 in 1780–1799

(Richards 2003, p. 511). While the fur trade in New England became unimportant around 1650, the trade continued to be important in the Middle Colonies (Vickers, 1996, p. 214). These frontier dynamics continued over the course of the nineteenth century, when trappers moved further and further inland to obtain their furs.

In Newfoundland, the cold climate greatly limited farming opportunities and its small population remained entirely focused on maritime activities. Moving southward, economies became more diversified and fishing and whaling were two occupations among many. In New England, while wheat and barley did not grow well, its population was preoccupied with the cultivation of rye and Indian corn, and many depended significantly on livestock farming (Vickers 1996, p. 219). The key export products of the more prosperous Middle Colonies – in between the Chesapeake and New England – were grain and related agricultural products from the 'temperate zone', as well as flax and livestock. Farms were typically somewhat larger in the Middle Colonies and could support the costs of indentured servants and slaves as well as family labour, whereas in New England most farms were solely dependent on family labour. In these regions, the socio-economic structure that emerged most closely resembled those of the countries from which the settlers originated – most came from Britain and Ireland, but there were migrants from the Low Countries as well (until 1664 New York was a Dutch colony, called New Amsterdam), as well as from Germany and Scandinavia. In order to attract these workers, wages were set at relatively high rates that were above almost all those in Western Europe (Allen et al. 2012).

While most farm production continued to be for domestic consumption, both regions developed a flourishing commercial economy. This included a substantial non-agricultural sector in the towns, where there were shipbuilding and craft industries, banks and merchants. As a result of the growth of New York and Philadelphia (which overtook Boston as the largest town in the second half of the eighteenth century), the Middle Colonies became the commercial heart of the region in the eighteenth century.

The South: New Plantation Economies

Furs, whales and cod determined the history of settlement in the northern colonies of New England and the Middle Colonies, as well as the integration of that part of the Americas into world trade. In the Upper

South, around the Chesapeake (Virginia and Maryland), however, it was the cultivation of tobacco that dominated. It was first introduced in 1616 when Virginia was considered a near failure (as noted above), after ten years of rather fruitless investment by the Virginia Company. The introduction of tobacco, on the other hand, was an immediate success: output exploded, and prices on the British market consequently declined by more than 90 per cent (McCusker and Menard 1985, p. 121), demonstrating the strong effect of Virginia production on global markets. Within a generation, the region became the world leader in tobacco production. George Alsop, who had been an indentured servant, wrote already in 1666 that, 'Tobacco is the only solid Staple Commodity' which was 'generally made by all the Inhabitants' (cited in Menard 1996, p. 261). These declining prices helped to create a mass market for tobacco in Western Europe. Although local varieties of tobacco were grown in the area before, it was the import of superior varieties from the Caribbean (where the Spanish had begun to suppress tobacco cultivation) that started the dramatic spread of the crop. From the 1660s onwards, however, the industry was depressed by extremely low export prices due to overproduction. Part of the decline in prices can be attributed to the decline in costs, as the output of tobacco per worker more than doubled between the 1620s and 1670s, from 710 lbs to 1600 lbs per annum (Kulikoff 1986, p. 31), yet prices declined even more: from between 20 and 30 pennies per lb in the 1620s to 1 penny in the 1670s (Menard 1973; 1976). Prices remained low until the 1720s and there were no further cost reductions.

A second boom in tobacco cultivation occurred in the second half of the eighteenth century, when prices were on the rise again and output doubled. The period of low prices and stagnating output did, however, result in a major restructuring of the economy. In the seventeenth century, family farms of limited size making use of indentured labourers were the norm (Menard 1996, p. 264). Yet, in the second half of the seventeenth century, the supply of this kind of labour declined, as the total population of England fell slightly after 1650, and real wages increased until 1700 (see p. 140). Moreover, once indentured labourers had finished their contract they could set up their own farms, as land was still cheap and their contracts included a bonus payment at the end which allowed them to set up their own household. Therefore, farmers increasingly turned to imported black slave labour. Whereas in 1660 less than 4 per cent of the population of the region consisted

Table 5.3. *Percentage of African Americans in the total population of the United States, 1660–1790*

Year	New England	Middle Colonies	Upper South	Lower South
1660	1.7	11.5	3.6	2.0
1700	1.8	6.8	13.1	17.6
1740	2.9	7.5	28.3	46.5
1750	3.1	7.1	40.0	42.3
1780	2.0	5.9	38.6	41.2
1790	1.7	6.2	37.6	32.6

Sources: McCusker and Menard (1985) and Walsh (2000, p. 193).

of people from African descent, this share had risen to almost 40 per cent by the last decades of the eighteenth century (see Table 5.3). The move from family farming to a plantation economy based on slave labour was accompanied by greater disparities in wealth and a growing polarization of the social and political structure (the rise of the Chesapeake gentry) (see e.g. Kulikoff 1986). The Upper South is the best example of a colony almost entirely based on one staple product – tobacco – which grew extensively during almost the entire 1620–1800 period.

From the 1690s, commercial cultivation of rice began in South Carolina. Work in the rice fields was seen as highly oppressive and therefore failed to attract European migrants: according to an account from 1775, 'the cultivation of it is dreadful' and a 'horrible employment ... not far short of digging in Potosí' (cited in Menard 1996, p. 277). The unhealthy environment and, consequently, higher mortality rates further reduced the pool of potential white migrants (Galenson 1996, pp. 174–182). This explains part of the shift to black slave labour. Rice production also demanded significant capital and labour input in order to build flooding systems with dikes, which meant that producers could benefit from scale economies. As exports increased from a mere 4.5 tons in 1695 to almost 20,000 tons in 1740, the demand for labour increased dramatically (Menard 1996, p. 275). This led to large increases in the demand for slave labour and, similar to the Upper South, to growing numbers of African Americans in the total population of the Lower South (Table 5.3). Therefore, in the view of the proponents of the 'staples approach': 'Rice, in short, turned a farm colony into a plantation colony and produced, in the process, a region more similar to the Caribbean Islands than to the other continental colonies', and 'rice brought the demographic regime of the sugar islands to South Carolina' (McCusker and Menard 1985, pp. 181–183).

These differences in exports also created different patterns of urbanization. Whereas New England and the Middle Colonies saw the gradual emergence of cities such as Boston, New York and Philadelphia with between 25,000 and 80,000 inhabitants – with diversification and industries focused on internal markets – Maryland and Virginia remained almost entirely rural with only a few small urban concentrations (Baltimore and Norfolk each had about 6,000 citizens in 1800) (McCusker and Menard 1985, p. 131). Charleston (South Carolina) was the only Southern city with over 5,000 inhabitants in 1750. In Canada after 1750 urbanization rates were high, because the total population was small so that once cities like Montreal and Quebec City reached the 5,000 benchmark they immediately took up a relatively large part of the total. The Thirteen Colonies in the eighteenth century were among the least urbanized regions in the world. Urbanization rates were clearly much below those in England (Table 5.4).

Table 5.4. *Urbanization in North America: percentage of total population in cities with 5,000 or more inhabitants, 1700–1800*

	1700	1750	1800
Canada	0.0	21.1	26.0
New England	11.9	4.4	6.0
Middle Colonies	0.0	8.1	12.9
Upper South	0.0	0.0	3.9
Lower South	0.0	3.5	2.9
Thirteen Colonies	4.2	4.9	8.2
England	16.9	23.2	28.6

NB: Due to small cities in North America, urbanization is here shown as the percentage living in cities of 5,000 inhabitants or more, in contrast to the 10,000 shown in the other chapters.
Sources: Urban Population in North America: Buringh (2016); Total Population North America: McCusker and Menard (1985);[3] Urbanization England: Allen (2000).

Exports and Institutional Development

British control over the colonies in North America was less absolute than was the case for the Spanish in South America, partly as a result of English civil strife in the early period of colonization and partly because representation was an aspect of British political culture that was consequently transplanted to America (Elliott 2006). This led to the establishment of local assemblies and juries which limited the degree of imperial control and gave the British American colonies considerable independence. As political and administrative institutions were built up from below, this allowed for variations in institutional development across the different British American colonies.

Acemoglu and Robinson (2012, pp. 25–27) have suggested that the colonization of Virginia and Maryland only became successful once the companies that organized the new settlements had given up the Spanish model of colonization – which was based on the extraction of surplus produce from the indigenous population – and had moved to an 'inclusive' set of institutions that allowed the new settlers to profit from the economic opportunities of the region. Attempts to reinstate some kind of feudal hierarchy in the new environment were doomed to fail, as settlers were not keen on being exploited by companies and their rulers (such as Lord Baltimore, who had acquired the right to set up the colony of Maryland from the British crown). Only once they moved to institutional arrangements that were attractive to new settlers – political representation and clear rights to the newly acquired land – did these colonies 'take off'. The success story of tobacco, in their view, is the result of this change towards more inclusive institutions. The irony of this is, however, that the dramatic success of the new crop, and changing labour market conditions in Great Britain, would dramatically undermine these inclusive institutions. The spread of slavery led to the rise of large plantations, at the expense of the family farms that dominated the region in the mid-seventeenth century. The 'democratic' institutions of the colonies had to be adapted to the existence of large-scale slavery: already in the 1640s new rules were issued that stipulated that 'negroes' were supposed to be enslaved for life, and that the status of children would be determined by that of their mothers (meaning that children born of a white father and a black mother would also be lifelong slaves) (Walsh 2010, pp. 138–139). In a series of steps, black women and men were stripped of their citizen rights and the institutional basis of a slave economy was laid down. This coincided with the concentration of political power at the top of the social pyramid: the concentration of wealth went together with the rise of political dynasties that controlled the key political positions in the colonies. According to Alan Kulikoff (1986, p. 7) this also had consequences for power relations at the household level: 'among whites, patriarchal families replaced relatively egalitarian families'.

These strong statements about the long-term effects of crops have been nuanced, if not contradicted, by more recent research. Why would the production of rice lead to plantations in this particular context, whereas in other parts of the world, Monsoon Asia for example, it was mainly grown as a crop on small family farms. Tobacco could successfully be grown on small plots – as the European experience also demonstrated (see e.g. Roessingh 1976); why did its cultivation in the Chesapeake result in dramatic changes in agrarian structures and the political economy? The inherent characteristics of the cultivation of certain crops are therefore not an entirely satisfactory explanation of the variation in socio-economic structures that emerged. Why did slavery come to dominate the South and family farming the North? Labour supply seems to have played a large role, as we saw in the Chesapeake case. The north–south gradient runs parallel with what Acemoglu, Johnson and Robinson (2002) have called 'settler mortality', or the prevalence of diseases which lower the life expectancy of immigrants from Europe. This disease gradient was to some extent the result of climate and other environmental conditions (the quality of water for example), but partly also endogenous, as J.R. McNeil (2010) has demonstrated. People from Africa were more resistant to the illnesses that became characteristic for the South. In certain respects, slavery was a self-reinforcing process, as alternative supplies of labour (such as indentured labourers) were at a 'biological' disadvantage. McNeil (2010, p. 46) writes about this: 'It is among Atlantic history's crueler ironies that in their bodies slaves brought new infections to the Americas – yellow fever, falciparum malaria, and hookworm among them – to which they also carried (inherited or acquired) resistance of immunity, which in turn raised the value of slaves and the slave trade.' The relative advantage of using imported black labour was therefore much greater in the South. In the North, by contrast, life expectancy and the rate of natural increase of the European population were relatively favourable. The European Marriage Pattern that regulated demographic strategies at home was adapted radically, resulting in a strong decline in the age of marriage of women (who were, particularly at the beginning of the colonization process, quite scarce). This led to a high natural increase of the population, which meant that internal sources of supply of labour became increasingly important. The northern regions managed to maintain their relatively inclusive institutions, which disappeared in the South under the pressure of the growth of slavery and related hierarchical (and patriarchal) institutions.

The effect of the type of crop on institutional development is thus clearly dependent on the wider conditions of factor endowments. Tobacco was only transformed into a plantation crop worked by slaves once the migration from England declined, which forced planters to look for other sources of labour. Rice was usually not a plantation crop in the labour-abundant areas of Asia, yet as a result of the disease environment, the Lower South attracted few workers voluntarily and therefore became dependent on imported slave labour. Patterns of international migration further influenced long-run institutional development.

Native Americans and the Frontier

Native Americans were increasingly affected by the changes sketched so far. Gradually, the frontier of European settlement and influence moved from the shores of the Atlantic to the west, driven by the appetite for land of the settlers. At the frontier, two fundamentally different societies and sets of institutions met and dramatic differences in customs and values – concerning commerce, for example – meant that it was a place of high uncertainty where violence was often the ultimate arbiter of conflict. Native Americans sought to profit from exchange – furs against European manufactured goods, preferably weapons – and to defend the integrity of their existence. Their ranks were at times decimated by imported diseases, and they often tried to survive by concluding alliances with European settlers. The Dutch in New Amsterdam, for example, developed strong ties with the Iroquois, and the French in the Lawrence River Delta allied themselves with the Hurons (Salisbury 1996, p. 18). In return for favourable prices for their furs, the European settlers supported them with weapons and help against enemies. Cooperation and conflict took turns: the frontier was an explosive combination of conflicts between native clans – sometimes deadly enemies for many generations – conflicts between European settlers – French, English and Dutch were similarly competing for power, land and access to the most profitable trade routes – and conflicts between Europeans and native clans.

But the frontier was not static; it was moving west due to population growth and expansion of the agricultural area. Already, after one or two generations, the supply of furs at the coastal strip dried up due to the decline of wildlife, and hunters began to move inland in search for fresh sources of supply. Squatters followed in their footsteps, and political authorities tried to drive the natives from their land to organize profitable settlement schemes. The eviction of one clan led to more pressure on the land of other clans, and might cause a cascade of population movement and conflict over land.

The frontier was not a subsistence area: new settlers needed agricultural implements, cattle, seed and household utensils, and the cash to pay for these purchases, in order to start farming and set up a household (Vickers 1996). Neither were the Native Americans isolated from the impact of markets and trade. Imported diseases (smallpox, influenza, malaria, yellow fever) had wiped out large parts of the indigenous population and weakened their socio-political structures. The sophisticated Mississippi culture, characterized by sedentary agriculture and larger concentrations of population, which had flowered in the twelfth and thirteenth centuries, had already declined when Columbus set foot on American soil (Salisbury 1996, p. 10). Similar, but somewhat less spectacular, sedentary societies had not survived the onslaught of the post-Columbian epidemics. In the seventeenth century, life in the Great Plains was changed drastically due to the spread of the horse. Fur trapping moved rapidly inland, involving increasingly large areas – the Hudson river, the Ohio river, the Great Lakes – forming large networks of native and European trappers and merchants. In this way, the world market penetrated deep into the interior of even this continent.

How did the Native Americans fare under these pressures? Historical anthropological research, analysing the features of skeletons, has been able to reconstruct aspects of the standard of living of the indigenous population. One pioneering study reconstructs the impact of the agricultural transition and of European contact on the height of men and women in the Georgia Bight (on the coast in the Lower South). It demonstrates that the rise of agriculture (after 1150) led to a decline in

stature (pointing to a reduction in nutritional intake and/or a deterioration of the disease environment), and that during the first century of
contact (1550–1680) this trend continued. Only after 1680 did some
recovery set in, which brought heights to about the level before contact
with Europeans (Larsen et al. 2002). This probably reflects a more general pattern, in which the biological standard of living is declining with
the spread of agriculture (now a generally and well-established result
of this kind of research). Native Americans – perhaps with the exception of the clans living in the Great Plains – also experienced a further
decline in well-being as a result of the many unfavourable effects of
European influence, as noted by C.S. Larsen et al. (2002, p. 435):

It turns out that being invaded by Europeans, though they be soldiers, traders, missionaries, or simply settlers, was pretty much a disaster for native
Americans. The newcomers might or might not be genocidal in intent, but
they worked the aborigines hard, interfered with their food production,
and – above all – brought with them the communicable diseases of Eurasia
and Africa.

Real Wages, Income and its Distribution

How successful were these new settler societies in generating high levels of income? There has been considerable debate about the question of when (colonial) North America grew rich. One interpretation,
based on the research by Angus Maddison, is that only between 1870
and 1910 did the US overtake Britain in terms of GDP per capita. This
was part of a fundamental shift in the world economy: before 1870
the 'first industrial nation', Great Britain, was the 'productivity leader'
of the world, but towards the end of the nineteenth century this leading role was taken over by the US (Maddison 2001, pp. 246–249).

Recent research has started to cast doubt on this interpretation. To
begin with, there is the simple fact that a large number of Europeans –
and in the eighteenth century mainly inhabitants of the British Isles –
voluntarily migrated to North America. Why would they do this if the
standard of living there was below that of Britain itself? From early
on in the seventeenth century, it was noted that wages in the colonies
were very high: a contemporary in Maine noted that 'workmen in this
Country ar very deare' and that he could not 'Conceave which way
their masters can pay yt, but yf yt Continue this rates the servants will

be masters & the masters servants' (cited in Galenson 1996, p. 137). A man in Pennsylvania wrote to his English family, 'it is a great deal better living here than in England for working people, poor working people doth live as well here, as landed men doth live with you' (cited in Galenson 1996, p. 138). As an indentured servant in Pennsylvania, William Moraley (1699–1762), concluded in his autobiography, 'In short, it is the best poor Man's Country in the World' (Moraley 2005 [original: 1743], p. 53).

Investigating this development of wages systematically, Allen et al. (2012) reconstructed the evolution of real wages of unskilled labourers in the new settler economies in the seventeenth and eighteenth centuries in a way that is directly comparable with real wages in England (London and Oxford). Figure 5.1 presents these results which show that until the 1770s, real wages in London and Boston moved more or less in tandem, but that London wage levels were clearly somewhat higher than those in New England. But London wages were the highest in England and may not have been entirely representative for overall standards of living. Therefore, we have added real wages in Oxford to the comparison. These show that Boston wages were on

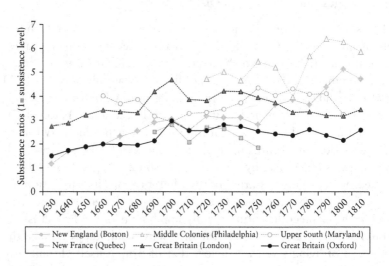

Figure 5.1 Wages expressed as subsistence ratios in North America and Great Britain, 1630–1810
Sources: US colonies: Allen et al. (2012); New France: Geloso (2016); London and Oxford: Allen (2001).[4]

a par, or even higher than those in one of England's smaller towns. This confirms the picture presented by Peter Lindert and Jeffrey Williamson (2016, p. 69) showing a divergence of wages for farm labour in southern England compared with New England in the eighteenth century. Only after 1750 were wages in the colonies generally higher than those prevalent in London. On the wage scale between the different colonies, it can be seen that New England generally had the lowest wages and that those in the Middle Colonies, represented by Philadelphia, were overall significantly higher. The study by Allen et al. (2012) suggests that wage labourers in Maryland earned wages generally slightly above those in Boston, but below those in Philadelphia. However, both the New England and Middle Colonies series are based on urban unskilled wages in cities, whereas those for Maryland were computed using models estimating rural small farmers' incomes. Similarly, the subsistence ratios for Quebec, that reflect the lower end of the colonies' wage scale, were computed based on wages earned on rural estates near Quebec City and wages were somewhat higher within the city (Geloso 2016, p. 69). Yet, Vincent Geloso (2016, p. 135) also compared GDP per capita in North America and found that New France lagged behind.

Wage labourers were only one group within these colonies, and they were neither the richest nor the largest group. Around 1774, whereas almost 30 per cent of the population of New England may have consisted of 'menial labourers', this figure was only 13 per cent in the Middle Colonies and even less than 2 per cent in the South (Lindert and Williamson 2016, p. 34). Therefore it makes sense to discuss colonial income and its distribution.

In an important recent study, Lindert and Williamson (2016) have estimated both long-run income trends and the specific distribution of income between and within the different colonies. They find that regional inequality between the different colonies was quite high. They show that income levels in the South were much higher than in the North; in 1774 per capita total incomes in the South Atlantic were 70 per cent higher than in New England; the difference between the Middle Atlantic and New England was much smaller (about 20 per cent) (Lindert and Williamson 2016, p. 28). We think slavery is part of the explanation for the high real incomes in the South: slave populations have, to begin with, a very unbalanced structure, with few children and a very large share of relatively young men and women.

The ratio between the active labour force and the total population is much higher, also because women are fully involved in the production process. Finally, slaves are usually coerced to work hard and for many hours. These factors, and the generally rather capital-intensive nature of most plantation economies, inflate the productivity of such economies, explaining a large part of the high level of GDP per capita of slave societies (as we have also seen for the Caribbean). In a case study of the income structure of Cape Colony in the eighteenth century it was, for example, concluded that the biased, 'unsustainable' structure of the slave population explained a large part of its high real income; correction for this (by assuming a more balanced population able to reproduce itself), reduced GDP per capita by about 30–40 per cent (Fourie and Van Zanden 2013).

Lindert and Williamson (2016, p. 40) also systematically compare the income distribution between England and the colonies around 1774, the year for which they have ample data, and conclude that income in the colonies was more equally distributed. Whereas the top 1 per cent of households in the colonies had some 8.5 per cent of all incomes (or 7.6 per cent not including slaves), this figure stood at 17.5 per cent in Great Britain in 1759. Besides the richest 1–5 per cent, incomes of all other colonists were higher than those in England. Perhaps most surprisingly (and provocatively), they show even that the income level of slaves in the American south was higher than that of English labourers.

Whether the early American economies showed growth or stagnation has been a topic of debate. Whereas much of the work until the early 2000s suggests relatively high growth rates in the Thirteen Colonies (e.g. Egnal 1998; McCusker and Menard 1985;) of about 0.6 per cent per annum, more recent investigations have questioned this picture and instead suggest slow rates of growth and even stagnation and decline for some regions (Mancall, Rosenbloom and Weiss 2006, 2008; Rosenbloom and Weiss 2014).

Following Lindert and Williamson (2016) who have combined the most recent estimates for the various colonies, the different trajectories can be easily discerned. As shown in Figure 5.2, real per capita incomes grew in New England, stagnated in the Middle Colonies (although at a slower pace), and declined in both the Upper and Lower South. The

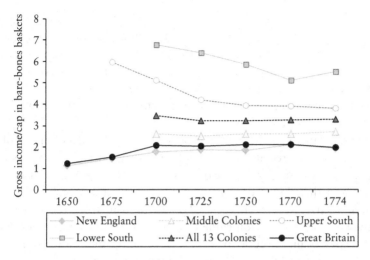

Figure 5.2 Gross income per capita in bare-bones baskets in North America, 1650–1774
Source: Lindert and Williamson (2016, pp. 62–63).

per capita trends and levels in the South also include slaves, a group that grew rapidly over the eighteenth century. While the overall distribution remained the same in the period under discussion, with the Lower South as the richest region and New England as the poorest, we can thus see a trend of convergence in incomes between the different regions up until the Revolution.

The economic development of these settler economies was characterized by two factors which, in combination, determined what happened with GDP per capita. One force was extensive growth, in particular of the agricultural sector that expanded inland: there was a very rapid increase in population and the area under cultivation, driven by the almost free availability of land (Vickers 1996, p. 227). Infrastructure and more general capital accumulation tended to lag behind, and distances to market outlets and export markets increased, which produced the tendency of real incomes to decline with expansion inland. The other driving forces were processes of specialization and urbanization in the coastal areas, where commodity streams to export markets grew with the expansion inland. The latter probably produced a tendency of income to grow more rapidly than population (in the coastal areas and the connected river systems). As the northern colonies were more diversified and had more employment in the coastal region (e.g. in the service sector), rather than extensive agriculture, they suffered less from diminishing returns in the interior than those economies in the South. This explains the converging growth paths. Settler societies, such as those of North America, grew rapidly in size and income, but real income per capita did not necessarily rise. In fact, maintaining such high incomes in the face of rapid population growth is impressive in itself.

Consequently, real incomes in North America declined dramatically up to 1800 as a result of the Revolutionary Wars and the post-war depression resulting from wartime damages. Rampaging armies left farms and their lands destroyed, and livestock stolen or killed, and caused many farming families to go on the run from the violence, while trade and migration came to a standstill due to blockades and embargoes (Kulikoff 2000, p. 256). The economy did not recover easily after the war. Hyperinflation and financial problems played their part, as did declining rates of migration, which increased labour shortages. Trade, both internationally and domestically, was highly reduced (Lindert and Williamson 2016, pp. 82–89). Yet, whereas the exports of New England and the Middle Colonies between the late 1760s and the early 1790s rose slightly, by, respectively, 1.2 and 9.9 per cent, exports in the Upper and Lower South declined dramatically, by, respectively, 39.1 and 49.7 per cent (ibid., p. 88). After that, a North American 'reversal of fortunes' took place as the two southern regions dropped from being the richest to the poorest somewhere in the early nineteenth century. By 1840, the South had per capita incomes 23 per cent below the national average, while the Middle Colonies had incomes 9 per cent above the national average and New England, previously the poorest region, had become the richest region with per capita incomes 18 per cent above the colonial average (Lindert and Williamson 2016, p. 91). The Revolutionary War and its aftermath played a part in this story, as the South was more negatively affected by the war than the North.

Conclusion

The staple approach to American colonial economic history emphasizes the role of commodity exports as the driver of long-term economic growth. It suggests that the specific commodity exported influenced regional differences in social structures and institutions. Thus, furs, fish and whales were important in the development of Canada and New England; grain production in the Middle Colonies; and the cultivation of tobacco and rice characterized development in the Upper and Lower South. Whereas the northern colonies consequently had thriving towns and a large middle class, the South remained overwhelmingly rural, with large plantations and greater disparities in wealth and income (Egnal 1998, p. 5).

This view has been criticized in a series of recent studies by Mancall et al. (2006, 2008) who have suggested that the export economy was too small a part of the total economy to have had far-reaching consequences. As exports grew at similar rates as the population, they suggest it was a 'reflection of extensive growth, rather than a driver of economic development' (2008, p. 18). Instead, they find Malthusian dynamics more important for the development paths of the American economies as they see 'the impact of resource abundance and labor and capital scarcity as the defining characteristics of colonial economic growth' (ibid., p. 19). McCusker and Menard (1985, p. 3) would counter that, 'A discovery that the major staple of a region contributed only a small and declining share to total income would not in itself dictate abandonment of an export-led growth model. Indeed, successful development around the export base would progressively reduce the proportion of income earned by staple production.'

In this chapter, we propose a combination of these views. We have shown that there is no reason to assume that the cultivation of rice and tobacco would automatically lead to large-scale plantation production employing slaves, or that grain production would always be done on small-scale family farms. Instead, the reduced pool of migrant labour from Europe available for the South, due to conditions in Europe and the unhealthy environment, in combination with the possibilities for higher returns to scale for rice and tobacco, shaped the development of the South.

The differences between the colonies in terms of trade and migration patterns eventually led to a reversal of fortunes between the North and the South in the nineteenth century. First, the South's decline relative to the North after the Revolution may be directly linked to the particularities of the export trade. As could be seen from the figures shown on p. 126, the South was much more dependent on trade with Britain than the North and it took the southern colonies until the first decades of the nineteenth century to recover from the collapse of this trade: South Carolina was exporting more rice in the early 1770s than was produced in the 1820s! Second, it seems that variations in social structure and institutions, which resulted from a particular combination of commodities exported and relative factor endowments, played a part in this story. In the early nineteenth century, when industrial technologies became available, the North's institutions and social structures were much better suited to take advantage of the opportunities to industrialize as a result of its diverse and skilled workforce, as well as more developed trade and financial institutions. As investment opportunities in export crops were more limited there, capital was fruitfully redirected towards new industries.

Suggested Reading

Allen, Robert C., Tommy E. Murphy and Eric B. Schneider (2012). 'The Colonial Origins of the Divergence in the Americas: A Labor Market Approach', *Journal of Economic History* 72, pp. 863–894.

Carlos, Ann M. and Frank D. Lewis (2010). *Commerce by a Frozen Sea. Native Americans and the European Fur Trade*. Philadelphia, PA: University of Pennsylvania Press.

Egnal, Marc (1998). *New World Economies: The Growth of the Thirteen Colonies and Early Canada*. Cary: Oxford University Press.

Engerman, Stanley and Robert E. Gallman (eds) (1996). *Cambridge Economic History of the United States. Vol. 1: The Colonial Era*. Cambridge: Cambridge University Press.

Lindert, Peter H. and Jeffrey G. Williamson (2016). *Unequal Gains. American Growth and Inequality since 1700*. Princeton, NJ: Princeton University Press.

McCusker, John J., and Russell Menard (1985). *The Economy of British America, 1607–1789. Needs and Opportunities for Study*. Chapel Hill, NC: University of North Carolina Press.

Rosenbloom, J.L. and Thomas Weiss (2014). 'Economic Growth in the Mid-Atlantic Region: Conjectural estimates for 1720 and 1800', *Explorations in Economic History* 51, pp. 41–59.

Shepherd, James F. and Gary M. Walton (1972). *Shipping, Maritime Trade, and the Economic Development of Colonial North America*. Cambridge: Cambridge University Press.

6 | Global Trade and Economic Decline in South Asia

Introduction

With a long coast line and convenient location between the Arabian Sea and the Bay of Bengal, South Asia had been a major trading hub connecting the Mediterranean and Middle East with Southeast Asia and China since antiquity (Hall 1985, pp. 26–28). There are records of South Indian trading communities in southern Chinese ports as early as the sixth century. In the tenth century, Tamil merchants, from the Chola dynasty of southern India, became important players in the trade with Southeast Asia (Wade 2009, pp. 235–237). Gujarati merchants from north-western India had a permanent presence in the Malay peninsula and the Indonesian archipelago by the fifteenth century or earlier (Abu-Lughod 1989, p. 302). With the Indians focused on the trade to the east, Arabs specialized in the trade connecting the Mediterranean with western India through the Arabian Sea. Therefore they set up trading colonies along the Indian west coast and by the mid-thirteenth century, Calicut had become the most important of these (Abu-Lughod 1989, p. 267).

On 20 May 1498, the Portuguese seafarer Vasco da Gama and his crew arrived in Calicut. This event inaugurated a new era of Euro–Asian interaction (Prakash 1998, p. 23). In the three centuries that followed, South Asia played an instrumental role in the 'global trade carrousel' (Frank 1998). Together with China, it was one of the main receiving regions of American bullion that was transported via Europe to Asia. Large amounts of copper flowed to the subcontinent from Japan (Shimada 2006). Furthermore, it was an important market for Southeast Asian sugar (Nadri 2008a) and spices: cloves, mace and nutmegs (Bulbeck et al. 1998; Jacobs 2006). In return, South Asia produced cotton and silk textiles, diamonds, pepper, saltpetre, opium, cinnamon, as well as a few commodities of lesser importance, for the global market. The significance of the South Asian economies for the rise

147

of world trade is hardly in dispute. In particular, the production of textiles had a large impact on the global economy: 'Indian cloth was one of the agents lubricating the wheels of commerce in the early modern world, and forging closer economic, social and cultural contact between Europe, Africa, and Asia' (Riello and Roy 2009, p. 10). The competitive pressure of the Indian textile manufacturing sector was an important factor in British industrialization (Parthasarathi 2011).

The local effects of South Asia's engagement with the world economy have long been an important subject in the historiography of early modern (and modern) India. Scholars have questioned the impact of maritime trade in the littoral on developments in the vast interior. And, if global trade had an impact, they debated whether its effects were beneficial or detrimental to India's economic development. In nationalist Indian historiography (e.g. Chandra 1992; Habib 1975, 1985), global trade (as well as the associated British colonialism) has long been seen as a major cause of stagnation and deindustrialization in the eighteenth and nineteenth centuries. Tirthankar Roy (2002) questions these interpretations, while others have put forward theses emphasizing the benign effects of European trade, at least in the seventeenth and eighteenth centuries (Chaudhuri 1978; Prakash 1985, 1998).

In fact, there is significant discussion on the overall performance of the Indian economy and the level of Indian living standards in the early modern period in general. In terms of comparative performance in the light of the Great Divergence debate, studies have offered radically opposing views: some have suggested that living standards in South Asia were similar to those in the most advanced parts of Europe in 1800 (Parthasarathi 1998; 2011; Sivramkrishna 2009), whereas others have put forward data showing much lower incomes already in the seventeenth century (Allen 2007; Broadberry and Gupta 2006; Roy 2010; De Zwart 2012). Furthermore, there is still some discussion on which periods are to be considered periods of growth and which of stagnation. In much of the literature, the eighteenth century has been portrayed as an 'epoch of decay, chaos, greed and violence' (Washbrook 2001, p. 372), yet a few recent studies have argued that there was economic development in various parts of India over the eighteenth century (Bayly 1983; Mukherjee 2011; Nadri 2008b). Deindustrialization may, or may not, already have started in the eighteenth century, and there is much discussion about its timing and causes (Clingingsmith and Williamson 2008). In any case, nineteenth- and twentieth-century economic decline may have had early modern roots.

In this chapter, we will address these issues. We will relate South Asia's economic development trajectory to developments in global trade. We will assess the various periods of economic growth and decline by looking at the most recent evidence for a number of economic indicators. In addition, we will discuss the classic topics of the role of Indian merchants and competition with European companies, the dynamics of textile manufacturing, the trade in spices, as well as the process of state formation and the rise of colonialism. An important element of the discussion is to what extent Indian fortunes were driven by domestic developments, or by the forces of the world economy. We suggest that, quantitatively, global trade flows were minor relative to the large Indian domestic economy. Yet, as the export sector was more dynamic and had effects on institutional change and the rise of the Indian coastal areas vis-à-vis the interior, the spill-overs were larger than one would expect based merely on its share in the total economy.

South Asia in the World Economy

For Wallerstein (1986), India (like the rest of Asia) remained outside of the Europe-dominated capitalist world economy until the later eighteenth century. Wallerstein emphasizes the role of British colonialism, from 1757 on, as a political structure that was necessary to facilitate changes in the economic and social structure of India to incorporate it in the world economy. He cites India's deindustrialization and the rise of indigo plantations in the nineteenth century as evidence that its 'productive structures' were getting in line with the global division of labour. We believe that the stage for these developments was set in the period 1500–1800. In this section, we give an overview of the most important trends in South Asia's global trade, after which we will discuss the consequences of these flows for the various South Asian economies.

The Portuguese Century?

Following da Gama's expedition, the Portuguese were the first Europeans to play a role in the Indian economy, as well as in the

Indian Ocean trade. Da Gama's initial voyage was commercially not very successful, which was attributed to the hostile attitude of the local Muslim merchants (Roy 2012, p. 82). With the Muslims seen as a potential hindrance to their trading ventures in Asia, subsequent Portuguese endeavours quickly acquired a violent character and the aim became to create colonies rather than to conduct trade via diplomatic means. In the second expedition to Calicut, the Portuguese captured and burned a number of local ships and even bombarded Calicut, killing 500 people. The expedition led to gruesome stories; da Gama also captured an approaching merchant fleet that brought rice from the Coromandel coast, and, according to the contemporary Portuguese historian, Gaspar Correia:

> Then the captain-major commanded them to cut off the hands and ears and noses of all the crews and put all into one of the small vessels, into which he ordered them to put the friar, also without ears, or nose, or hands, which he ordered strung round his neck, with a pal leave for the King, on which he told him to have a curry made to eat of what his friar brought him. When all the Indians had been thus executed, he ordered their feet to be tied together, as they had no hands with which to untie them: and in order that they should not untie them with their teeth, he ordered them to strike upon their teeth with staves, and they knocked them down their throats.[1]

The Portuguese employed this level of force in order to monopolize the Cape route trade between Europe and Asia until the second half of the sixteenth century. While the Portuguese also ventured into Southeast Asia, where they occupied Malacca in 1511, India was at the heart of the Portuguese trade in this period. Portuguese ventures were spurred by the quest for spices – the principal article shipped by the Portuguese *Carreira da India* was pepper, most of which was acquired on the Malabar coast and later the Kanara coast, in south-western India. In the first half of the sixteenth century almost the entire Portuguese return cargo consisted of pepper, while only 5 to 10 per cent consisted of Moluccan fine spices and a similar percentage of ginger and cinnamon. Only in the second half of the sixteenth and early seventeenth centuries did textiles and indigo become part of the return cargos (Prakash 1998). Including estimates on the cargo of private trade (that is, non-Company trade) would raise the importance of textiles in this period, as these occupied a larger share of private traders' cargoes (Boyajian 1993, p. 44). Thus, already in

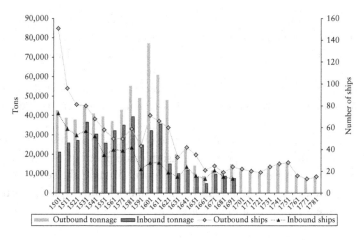

Figure 6.1 Portuguese shipping and tonnage to Asia, 1501–1790
Source: Prakash (1998).

the sixteenth century Indian textiles started to play a role in Asian trade. In return for these goods, the Portuguese paid mainly in copper as well as smaller amounts of silver and gold (Prakash 1998, p. 30). Later in the sixteenth century, silver became more prominent and accounted for between 60 and 80 per cent of outbound values (Steensgaard 1973, p. 87).

Looking at trends in Portuguese–Asian trade over time, Figure 6.1 shows the tons of goods departing to Asia from Europe, and those returning from Asia in the fifteenth and sixteenth centuries.[2] The number of inbound and outbound Portuguese ships fell continuously right from the start of the sixteenth century. This decline was initially offset by the increase in the size of ships, allowing outbound volumes of trade to increase towards the end of the sixteenth century. In the seventeenth century, the decline was absolute, however, and after the 1620s outbound tonnages were generally below 20,000. This decline was to a large extent the result of the crown's inability to put trade on a sound financial footing. It led the Portuguese state in India (*Estado da India*) to grant rights to participate in this trade to private traders and to try to extract revenue from the Asian trade network via the *cartaz* system. In this system, all Asian ships were obliged to buy a pass at a Portuguese-controlled port, and had to pay customs duties there before they could proceed and finish their trade (Prakash 1998,

p. 44). But problems in the system soon arose. The Portuguese lacked the means for effective patrolling of the Red Sea and abandoned it by the late 1560s. By the end of the sixteenth century the Red Sea route brought more pepper to the European market than Portuguese trade via the Cape (ibid., p. 46). In 1622, the Portuguese also lost the town of Hormuz and were no longer able to control trade in the Persian Gulf.

The immediate decline of Portuguese outbound and inbound ships and their failure to monopolize the Asian trade prompts the idea that if northern Europeans had not arrived in full force in the seventeenth century, European incursion into the Indian trading system would have been a short-term and minor event.

Northern European Rivalry

Portuguese difficulties were aggravated by the arrival of the northern European joint-stock companies in Asian trade in the early seventeenth century (see also Chapter 2). Whereas the Portuguese operated primarily in south-western India (Goa, Calicut and Cochin) and Ceylon, in addition to a few stations in the north-west, the Dutch, English and French were scattered throughout the whole of India, and had a greater presence on India's eastern seaboard (see Map 6.1). Roy (2012, p. 8) suggests that whereas Indian international trade remained a story of the Arabian Seas and the Bay of Bengal in the sixteenth century, it was in the seventeenth and eighteenth centuries that India became fully integrated in the trade that connected the Atlantic Ocean with the Indian and Pacific Oceans.

The Portuguese suffered most from the onslaught by the Dutch, who took over their positions in Cochin and Ceylon and established trading posts in Surat (in Gujarat, north-western India), across the Coromandel coast (south-eastern India) and in Bengal (north-eastern India). The Portuguese were able to hold on to their position in Goa (until 1961). Until the late seventeenth century, the Dutch constituted the most important foreign trading group and they would remain prominent until the end of the eighteenth century. It was, however, the British who were to become the dominant presence in India: by the mid-eighteenth century they sent roughly two-thirds of the total exports by all European companies (Roy 2013, p. 81). The British focused their presence around three areas: Madras, Bombay

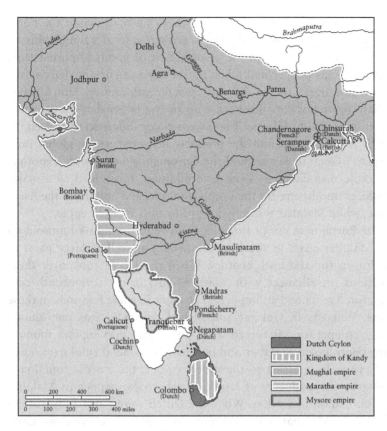

Map 6.1 South Asia in the early eighteenth century.

and Calcutta (see Map 6.1). In the second half of the eighteenth century, starting in Bengal, the English Company ascended from being merely one of the traders in India to *de facto* ruler of the province. The consequences of this are discussed on pp. 169–172. In the later seventeenth century, the French and Danish companies joined in the competition. The French were building up a significant enterprise, even if the French share remained substantially behind that of the British and Dutch (Prakash 1998, p. 266). In the eighteenth century, the Ostend, Swedish and other companies also conducted trading missions to India: 'quantitatively speaking, however, the trading activities of all these enterprises almost certainly added up to very little' (Prakash 1998, p. 81).

As a result of the entry of the northern Europeans into the Euro-Asian trade, there was an impressive growth in total trading volumes. There was also a shift in the composition of goods imported from Asia. Whereas pepper had taken up the most important share in the Portuguese trade and in the early seventeenth-century Dutch trade, Indian cotton textiles came to take up an ever larger share of the package transported to Europe. There were major differences between the South Asian regions and the products delivered to the global marketplace: Gujarat, Bengal and the Coromandel coast were exporters of textile manufactures. Bengal, in addition, functioned as a major producer of saltpetre for the European trade, and opium for the Asian trade, while Malabar was a major production area of pepper.

The Portuguese use of force had allowed it to gain a foothold on the Malabar coast in south-western India as well as large parts of Ceylon in the sixteenth century. When the Dutch took over these positions (in alliances with South Asians) in the seventeenth century, force remained an important element in trade relations in these areas. Whereas in Gujarat and Bengal the VOC was one among many competitors, it forced local potentates into signing monopsony contracts in Malabar and became the colonial ruler over much of Ceylon. In contrast to the other regions, these areas functioned primarily as producers of tropical cash crops: pepper in Malabar and cinnamon in Ceylon. While the Dutch were never fully able to control the Malabar coast and, as a result, pepper deliveries were seldom 'on time or in the promised quantity' (Prakash 1998, p. 205), in the eighteenth century pepper exported from Malabar still averaged almost 600 tons per annum, making it the second largest pepper-producing region in Asia (after Banten and the Lampung region in Indonesia) (Jacobs 2006).

A well-known indicator of the scale of trade is the total value of trade relative to the size of the entire economy (GDP): the openness ratio. Roy (2013, pp. 75–77) puts forward a range of plausible numbers depending on different assumptions. As there are only relatively accurate estimates of the European companies' trade with Europe, but almost no figures of European and Indian private intra-Asian and overland trade, such numbers remain speculative. Combined with a number of different estimates of GDP, Roy figures out a percentage of foreign trade to GDP ranging between 0.9 and 3.8 per cent at around 1750. The real figure is most likely closer to the lower bound estimate.[3] In an important exporting region like Bengal, this figure was around

4 per cent higher than for the whole of India. This suggests that the scale of foreign trade in early modern India was quantitatively negligible by modern standards, although locally it may have been important in determining incomes and power balances.

Bullion for Goods

As we have already seen in the case of Portuguese trade, the defining characteristic of Euro-Indian trade (as well as Euro-Asian trade in general) in this period is that it was an exchange of 'bullion for goods' (Prakash 2004). This was both a result of the lack of Indian interest in European goods (at least at the uncompetitive prices offered by the Europeans), and because silver had greater value in India than in Europe, which meant that European companies could buy more goods with the same amount of silver in Asia than they could in Europe. Some three-quarters of the total value of EIC and *Compagnie des Indes* exports to Asia consisted of precious metals, while over 90 per cent of the value of VOC exports to Asia consisted of gold and silver (Bruijn et al. 1979–1987, pp. 183 and 187).

Whereas the Portuguese exported only 7 tons of silver to Asia annually in the later sixteenth century, at its high point in the mid-eighteenth century the VOC and EIC combined poured almost 200 tons of silver into Asia. There are no exact figures for the entire period of what part of this went to India, but we know that for the EIC this share was over 70 per cent in the mid-eighteenth century (Datta 1999, pp. 346–348), and probably slightly less than that in the late eighteenth and early nineteenth centuries (Bowen 2010).[4] In the case of the VOC, which conducted almost all of its trade via its *entrepôt* in Batavia, we are not sure about the precise share of this received by India in the seventeenth century.[5] Considering the fact that over 55 per cent of the total value of goods sold by the VOC in the Dutch Republic was Indian (all cotton textiles and saltpetre, part of the silk and pepper, also see Chapter 2), and because Indian textiles played an important role in purchasing spices in Southeast Asia (discussed on pp. 188–190), it can be safely assumed that already between a half and two-thirds of this treasure was initially spent in India. For the eighteenth century, we are on firmer ground: for the years for which we have data, on average 85 per cent of the treasure was exported to India (and by far most of it to Bengal).[6] We do not know what part of this silver consequently flowed into China.

EIC imports of bullion stopped after 1765, as the Company completed the conquest of Bengal and started to use colonial land revenues to pay for Indian exports.[7] According to some scholars, this limited the inflow of bullion and ended the relationship of trade and income, output and employment benefits for Indian producers (Ghosh 2015, p. 1616). At the same time, however, British private traders, who became more important as the eighteenth century progressed, continued to export substantial amounts of bullion to India over this period: some 7 tonnes of silver per year in the 1760s, rising to almost 20 tonnes of silver annually by the end of the eighteenth century (Bowen 2010, p. 465). In the sixteenth and seventeenth centuries, the bullion entering the Mughal Empire from across the Persian Gulf, the Red Sea and via overland routes was more voluminous (three quarters of the total) than that imported by the Dutch and English via the Cape route (one quarter) (Haider 1996).

What were the consequences of the inflow of bullion? There has been significant discussion about this among Indian historians. Following the conventional quantity theory of money,[8] increases in the money supply may have led to inflation, if the volume of transactions (T) and the velocity of circulation (V) were constant. According to Irfan Habib (1982) it led to a 'price revolution' in seventeenth- and eighteenth-century India, not unlike that experienced in Europe in the sixteenth century, and he suggests that the sustained inflation was an 'unsettling factor' in the Indian economy. K.N. Chaudhuri (1978, p. 462), on the other hand, hails the 'huge influx of bullion' as driving the growth of income and employment in coastal India. Om Prakash (1998, p. 335) put forward similar sentiments, suggesting that there was an absence of inflation (no change in P) as the increase in output and population growth (increases in V and/or T) absorbed the increased supply of money (M) and argues that it therefore had positive effects on income, output and employment.[9] Shireen Moosvi (1987b) suggests there was no inflation in the seventeenth century and that the influx of bullion from the companies in the seventeenth century was not substantial compared with treasure imported through other channels.

Figure 6.2 shows the long-run price developments in Bengal and the Coromandel. The inflationary trends could have been fuelled by the cumulative effect of the inflow of bullion (increasing the total money stock) over a long period of time, especially in those areas where a lot of the bullion was imported. Prices are, of course, not only determined

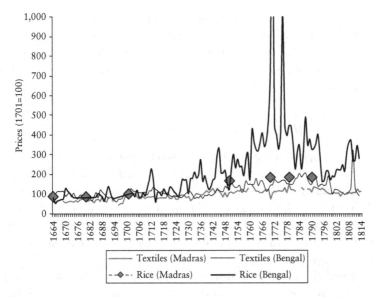

Figure 6.2 Prices of textiles and rice in Bengal and Coromandel, 1664–1814.
Sources: Textiles: Chaudhuri (1978) and Bowen (2010); rice: Allen and Studer (2009).

by the influx of bullion. In a functioning market, prices are determined by the forces of supply and demand and prices could be influenced by internal and/or external developments. In order to assess which one of these was more important, it may be hypothesized that if prices were predominantly determined by the growing influx of bullion, inflation would foremost manifest itself in products that were purchased with this bullion (i.e. textiles). Yet if prices were principally shaped by internal factors (local demand and production), inflation would be stronger in products for local consumption (i.e. rice). Figure 6.2 also shows developments in textile prices vis-à-vis developments in rice prices. It becomes immediately clear that in Bengal the rice price increased much more over the period 1664–1814 than the price of textiles: whereas the former rose by about 1.2 per cent annually, the latter increased by only 0.4 per cent per annum.[10] Even when excluding the peaks of 1771 and 1776, the increasing trend in rice prices was more significant than that in textile prices. The data for rice prices in Coromandel are less abundant, but the available figures lead to the same, though less strong, conclusion: rice prices increased faster than those for textiles: by 0.7

and 0.5 per cent annually. Thus, local dynamics were more important than global bullion influx in determining price developments, even in an outward-oriented region like Bengal. Because India was so large and populous, we should not overestimate the direct effects of this global trade for the economy.

South Asia in the Intra-Asian Trade

While earning profits in the trade between Europe and Asia was the main business rationale of the Portuguese, Dutch and English companies, the intra-Asian trade quickly became a very important component of their, and more importantly, of European private traders, trading ventures. India played two important roles in intra-Asian trade: (1) as an exporter of textiles and (2) as an importer of Japanese silver and copper and Southeast Asian spices.

First and foremost, Indian textiles were used to purchase spices in Southeast Asia: already before the arrival of the Europeans, Indian textiles were the main medium of exchange in Southeast Asia. Whereas the Portuguese and English left most of the intra-Asian trade to private traders, for the VOC the intra-Asian trade became an important element in its overall trading strategy. Figures from the early eighteenth century show that the VOC's intra-Asian trade in textiles was sizable: about three-quarters of the value of the textile trade back to Europe (Riello 2013, p. 95). The VOC had opened factories in the early seventeenth century on the Coromandel coast and Surat specifically to cater for the Southeast Asian need for textiles. Jan Pietersz. Coen (VOC Governor-General between 1618 and 1623, and 1627–1629) was the main architect of the VOC intra-Asian trading network. In 1619 he sketched the system to the VOC Directors (the Gentlemen Seventeen): cloth from Gujarat could be traded against pepper and gold in Sumatra and cloth from Coromandel was used to buy pepper at Banten (Prakash 1998, p. 92). By the mid-seventeenth century, the VOC was the most important player in the intra-Asian trade network and had established trading factories from Mocha in Yemen to Nagasaki in Japan. It was even hoped that proceeds from intra-Asian trade could be used to finance all exports to Europe, but that was never achieved and the VOC continued to pour specie into Asia.

At the same time as total textile exports to Europe increased impressively from the 1660s to the 1770s (Riello 2013; Berg 2015), the export of Indian textiles to Southeast Asia may have

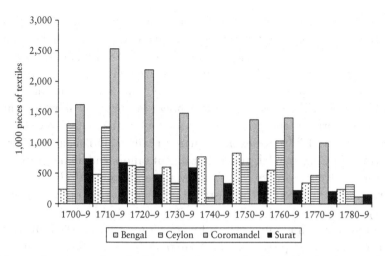

Figure 6.3 Exports of textiles from India by VOC, totals per decade, 1700–1789[a]
[a] Missing years were interpolated by computing annual averages per decade and multiplying those by 10 to arrive at totals for each decade.
Source: Bookkeeper-General Database.

started to decline (Reid 2009). This is confirmed by Figure 6.3, which shows declining VOC textile exports from the different Indian regions in the eighteenth century. As the imports into Amsterdam were stable in the eighteenth century (De Zwart 2016b), this would mean a decline in the VOC intra-Asian textile trade. These figures do not include the private trade by Asians and Europeans to other parts of Asia. This trade was still very large by the later eighteenth century (see Chaudhury 1999) and there is evidence that private textile trade to Southeast Asia increased over this period (discussed in Chapter 7). It seems that the growth of the international trade in textiles was complementary to – rather than a substitute for – the intra-Asian flow of textiles. Figure 6.5 (on p. 167) also shows trends in export by EIC of textiles in the eighteenth century, which increased at the cost of stagnating Dutch exports.

Foodstuffs were also important in intra-Asian trade. Rice and wheat were transported between surplus and deficit areas. For example, as there were continual shortages of rice in the coastal areas of Ceylon, rice was imported there from Coromandel and Bengal by both the VOC and Indian shippers. The quantities brought in by private ships could be quite substantial: in 1700, some 108 vessels arrived in the ports of Colombo and Galle which carried on board a total of 2,651 tons of rice (Arasaratnam 1988). Starting in the 1650s, VOC ships brought 500 tons of rice to Ceylon per annum, which then increased to between 1,500 and 1,800 tons annually in succeeding decades. Ceylon became so dependent on these rice imports that serious shortages and price rises resulted when the rice ships did not arrive. In the 1780s, for example, harvest failures in Bengal, political turmoil in Coromandel, and a shortage of sailors and higher priority given to rice exports to Surat and Malabar, meant a decline in rice imports that caused the highest rice prices in Ceylon in over a century (De Zwart 2012).

India was an important market for copper from Japan. The VOC had such an important position in the Asian trade because, besides a monopoly over fine Moluccan spices, it also held the exclusive right to trade with Japan via the artificial island of Deshima, in Nagasaki. Japan provided the VOC with precious metals, silver (until 1668) and gold, that were used to make purchases in India and China. Between the late 1630s and the 1670s, these precious metal flows from Japan were larger than those from Europe to Asia (Prakash 1998, p. 102). Additionally, copper was exported from Japan in large quantities and the influx of copper from Japan may well have had more important economic effects than the flows of silver. In terms of volumes, these flows were greater than the silver flows noted above (Shimada 2006). Recent research on monetization has suggested that smaller denomination (i.e. copper) coins were much more important than silver or gold coins in everyday transactions; copper pice and dams, rather than silver rupees, were used to pay for daily wages and, consequently, for the purchase of consumer goods in local bazaars (De Zwart and Lucassen 2015). There is abundant evidence for the high degree of commercialization and monetization of the Indian economy (Datta 1999; Lucassen 2016; Mukherjee 2011) and Japanese copper played an important role in facilitating these local market transactions (Nadri 2008b, p. 104; Prakash 2007).

India also obtained its luxuries from intra-Asian trade. Substantial amounts of spices and sugar from Southeast Asia were imported into the various Indian regions. Ghulam Nadri (2008b) suggests that the increase in sugar and spice imports he observed for eighteenth-century Surat provides clues regarding the dynamism of the region in the second half of the eighteenth century. Jos Gommans (2015) also

notes that, in concert with the European experience, the early modern era saw a rise of luxury consumption in India, that resulted from
the growth of global trade and rising incomes of those groups most
engaged in this commerce.

European private traders and Asian merchants were actually more
important in these Asian connections than the companies. There was
some private trade on the Eurasian routes, such as by Portuguese private traders after the crown opened up the Eurasian trade to competition in 1570, or by EIC servants in goods that the Company had
no real interest in. Most of the European private traders were active
in the intra-Asian trade. After the Portuguese crown withdrew from
intra-Asian trade, also around 1570, Portuguese private trade grew
rapidly. This trade in fact became so substantial that in 1630, private Portuguese intra-Asian trade was worth about 80 tons of silver:
15 times the value of the Portuguese sales by the crown in Lisbon
(Prakash 1998, p. 49).[11]

The VOC did not allow private trade on its Asian routes until the
1740s. Yet, illegal trading by Company employees acquired dramatic
proportions. The contraband trade in opium between Bengal and
Batavia thrived at this time: in 1676 the opium reaching Batavia ille-
gally was many times that imported officially by the Company (Prakash
1998, pp. 230–231). Since it was thought impossible to stop this
clandestine trade, the VOC chose to benefit from it through customs
duties: it was decided to partially open intra-Asian trade to private
traders in 1743. Yet this legal Dutch private shipping in all probability
remained insignificant in terms of total volumes. In contrast to the
VOC's intra-Asian trade, the EIC's participation in intra-Asian trade
was a disappointment and in 1661 it withdrew from it altogether. Yet,
in order to stimulate a continuation of English presence across Asia,
the EIC legalized the intra-Asian trade of Company servants and free
merchants. The volume of English private trade would swell considerably over the course of the eighteenth century. The French were active
in intra-Asian trade only between the 1720s and the 1740s (Prakash
1998, pp. 256–260).

Indian Merchants

The volume of trade handled by Asians may have been a large multiple of that carried aboard ships of the European companies, certainly

in the sixteenth century.[12] Due to India's geographic position it held centre stage in the trade between West Asian and African ports like Hormuz, Aden and Kilwa, and with Malacca and Banten in Southeast Asia. Through these connections Indian goods reached both China and Europe. Arab-owned ships dominated the Western part of this trade, while Indian-owned ships covered most of the trade with Southeast Asia. At the time of da Gama's first visit to Calicut, various Indian merchant groups hailing from different port towns were important for (parts of) these routes. Gujarati Muslims from Cambay were the most important by the fifteenth century, but there were also Mappila Muslim traders in Calicut, Hindu merchants from Pulicat and Negapatnam on the Coromandel coast, as well as Bengalis who sailed mainly from the port of Chittagong (Roy 2012, pp. 79–80). Following Ashin Das Gupta (1982, pp. 417–419) the Indian merchants may be subdivided into three groups: there were the large merchants, who had substantial amounts of capital and owned their own ships. Besides these larger ship-owning merchants, there were merchants who served as agents of the former and there were small traders who were just passengers on the bigger merchants' ships and who carried a small load of trade goods aboard with them. In addition to these Indian trading groups, there were Arab, Persian, Javanese and Malay merchants active in the Indian Ocean trade. The main Indian export articles of these groups were textiles and foodstuffs, as well as sugar and silk from Bengal and pepper from Malabar, while the main imports were bullion, horses, African ivory and Southeast Asian fine spices. This trade was generally conducted without much government intervention, as the large Indian empires – the Mughal and Vijayanagar – had little interest in overseas trade. Lack of sources consequently prevents us from sketching the sizes of these trade flows, but many scholars have suggested that they were substantially larger than those handled by the Europeans.

What changed in Asian trade after European entry? In terms of ports, some would rise at the expense of others: Surat would replace Cambay, Goa and Cochin would overshadow Calicut, while in the east Masulipatnam on the northern Coromandel Coast and Hooghly in Bengal would rise to prominence. In the eighteenth century, the British-controlled ports of Bombay, Calcutta and Madras would become the most important. Das Gupta (1982, p. 418) notes that especially larger Indian merchants from Gujarat suffered initially from the Portuguese entry in the first decades of the sixteenth century, but the disruptions were only temporary and their trade quickly revived after the third decade of that same century. The mass of Asian trade continued to be in Indian hands in the sixteenth century. A further challenge to Indian shipping was posed by the entry of the Dutch and their monopolization of the Southeast Asian spice trade in the early seventeenth century. As a result, Indian merchants abandoned voyages to Indonesia and focused on trade in the Red Sea, the Persian Gulf and Eastern Africa (see e.g. Alpers 1976; Machado 2009). Yet the later seventeenth century is seen as the 'Golden Period' of the Indian maritime and textile trade, in which, next to the Gujarati trade, the trade from Bengal and Coromandel boomed. This growth eventually resulted in glutted markets and declining profits in the early eighteenth century. Problems were then aggravated by the political collapse of both Mughal India and Safavid Persia, and a civil war in Yemen. Local rulers increased tax on trade in order to fund their military campaigns. The Indian merchant fleet at Surat declined from 112 ships in 1701 to about 20 in 1750 (Das Gupta 1982, p. 433). With the break-up of the Empire, many of the wealthy Indian merchants moved from Mughal ports, like Surat and Hooghly, to British-controlled Bombay and Calcutta (Roy 2013, p. 83).

There were also Indian traders who profited from the arrival of the Europeans; new merchants appeared who benefitted from additional European capital and the growth of Euro-Indian trade which increased the need for local and regional transportation (Roy 2013). While the Europeans came to dominate long-distance connections to Europe, most intra-Indian and intra-Asian trade remained in the hands of Indian merchants. Part of the vitality of Indian shipping is accredited to the lower freight rates charged by Indian compared with European merchants. European ships were, however, larger, more sturdy, better armed and (therefore) dominant in long-distance trade. Yet a wide variety of goods was transported between the various Indian regions and among these were not only high-priced luxuries, but also basic foodstuffs and, often lower-quality, textile goods. Much of this trade was via river and coastal transport, but trade was also carried overland (Raychaudhuri 1982). The vitality of Indian trade is also evidenced by research conducted by Sushil Chaudhury (1995, 1999), who argues that even by the middle of the eighteenth century the scale of Indian trade was substantially larger than that of European overseas trade. For example, of the total textile exports from Dhaka in Bengal in

1747, two-thirds were carried by Asian traders, and only one-third by Europeans, including private traders (Chaudhury 1999, p. 310). In silk textiles and raw silk, Asian traders were also firmly leading. Whether this was also the case for other goods, years and routes is unclear, but it is important to keep in mind that trade carried by Asians was substantial, even if this trade was in decline in the eighteenth century, at least in part, as a result of the Mughal collapse, increased warfare and the rise of British colonialism (discussed on pp. 169–172). Additionally, Indian merchants played an important role as agents and middlemen for the Europeans in India (Roy 2012, p. 97). Portuguese private trade, for example, was to a large extent funded by Indians. These merchants directly gained from the European rise in Asian trade. All of this meant that Indians in all parts of trade remained dominant actors and there was clearly no dominance of Europeans in intra-Asian trade until the late eighteenth century.

For the purposes of this book, we are mostly interested in the long-distance overseas trade and we therefore discuss European trade more extensively. Quantitative evidence on the trade carried out by Asian merchants is almost non-existent and therefore most studies are biased towards European activities. Nonetheless, it is important to keep in mind that there were many Indian and other Asian merchants active in Asian trade and that they continued their involvement on a large scale over the early modern period.

Global vis-à-vis Asian Interactions

As a result of the data left to us by European companies, which are biased towards intercontinental trade, Euro-Asian company trade has received most attention in the literature. Yet in terms of effects on the Indian economy, intra-Asian and private trade were of equal or greater importance. While it will be difficult to come to a definite quantitative assessment of such trade flows, compared with the size of the domestic economy, external trade including these flows would still be only a small part of the Indian economy. What did happen as a result of both Euro-Asian, intra-Asian, Company and private trade was that the unequal distribution of bullion across different groups and regions in this period meant a strengthening of merchant classes vis-à-vis feudal elements in society and a movement of state power from the interior to the coast (see Roy 2012; 2013).

Indian Deindustrialization

In the early modern period, India became the main textile manufacturer in the world. Exports rose over the seventeenth century and probably reached a high point during the late seventeenth and early eighteenth century, when both the trade across the Indian Ocean and to Europe was thriving (Riello and Roy 2009). India 'clothed the world' as it exported its textiles to Africa, Europe and Southeast Asia. Figure 6.4 presents a nice illustration of early globalization as it was produced in India and depicts two Chinese and two European figures, in addition to, strangely enough, two dancing monkeys. In these centuries, India was leading the world's total manufacturing output, but this leadership had clearly disappeared by 1900.[13] Already in the early nineteenth century, Britain had become the most important cotton textile manufacturer and India became a net importer of textiles. When did the decline set in, and was India's deindustrialization related to its ties with the global economy?

There is no consensus on the precise timing of India's deindustrialization. Some scholars suggest that India's decline started as early as the seventeenth century (in the case of southern India) (Ramaswamy 1985; see also Wendt 2009); others find a decline starting in the first half of the eighteenth century (Mukherjee 1994); or only after 1800 and even later (Bagchi 1976).[14] In order to assess when deindustrialization

Figure 6.4 Globalization in a piece of textile: an Indian chintz depicting two Chinese men (one swimming and the other fishing) and a European man and woman watching two monkeys dancing, made *c*.1700–*c*.1750
Courtesy of Rijksmuseum, Amsterdam.

began, let us first determine what 'deindustrialization' is. Following David Clingingsmith and Jeffrey Williamson (2008), deindustrialization can be defined in two ways: as a decline in the absolute number of workers engaged in manufacturing (*strong deindustrialization*) or as a decline in the share of industry in total employment (*weak deindustrialization*). An important distinction is to be made between employment and output in the international export sector, for which we have good data, and employment and output in the domestic sector, which was much larger, but for which we have no data. Furthermore, the degree and timing of deindustrialization may have varied depending on the different regions of South Asia (Frank 1998; Wendt 2009). The figures on VOC- and EIC-exported textiles provide a mixed picture: whereas VOC exports from the Coromandel declined from over 2.5 million pieces exported in the 1710s to less than 0.5 million in the 1780s, EIC exports from Madras (on the Coromandel coast) increased from one to four million over the course of the eighteenth century. The rise of Madras, at least in terms of export output, does not really support earlier deindustrialization in the south.

The most comprehensive set of data addressing the issue comes from a study by Stephen Broadberry, Johann Custodis and Bishnupriya Gupta (2015). Their recent study yields a number of important conclusions. First, they show slow, but steady increases in domestic textile production from the early seventeenth century to the end of the eighteenth century. There was stagnation, or even a small decline, in the domestic output between 1800 and 1830 and subsequent increases in domestic production until the 1860s. Second, textile production for overseas export increased rapidly between 1600 and 1800 (an increase in output of 300 per cent), but showed an even sharper decline after that: between 1800 and 1850, export manufacturing output was reduced by 90 per cent. After that export output rose again. Third, while the export manufacturing sector was much smaller than the domestic industry (0.7 vis-à-vis 21.5 per cent in 1871, although this difference was smaller around 1800), its decline was so dramatic between 1800 and 1830 that it drove an absolute decline in the total manufacturing sector. Broadberry et al. concluded that there was strong deindustrialization only in the first three decades of the nineteenth century, and weak deindustrialization thereafter.[15] Their work did not touch upon the causes of deindustrialization, nor did they address regional variation within India.

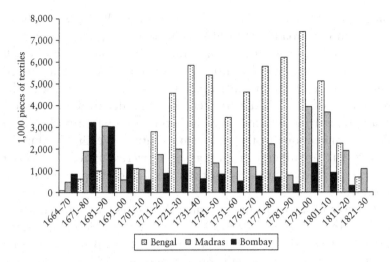

Figure 6.5 Exports of textiles from India by EIC, totals per decade, 1664–1830
Sources: Chaudhuri (1978) and Bowen (2010).

The EIC data show different trends in the export of textiles (in 1,000 pieces) for their three main trading centres in India (Figure 6.5). Whereas Bombay exports were declining from the late seventeenth century onwards, those from Bengal reached their peak in the last decade of the eighteenth century. Madras' exports first declined from the late seventeenth century to the middle of the eighteenth and then increased again towards the end of the century. The rise of Bengal was a consequence of the advantages it had in terms of low food prices, and rivers that allowed cheap transportation to areas with saltpetre, opium and indigo (Roy 2012, p. 94). The trends in EIC exports also differed markedly from those exported by the VOC. Figure 6.3 (on p. 159) showed all VOC exports from the different South Asian regions to both Europe and other parts of Asia. For the Dutch, the Coromandel coast was the most important textile-producing area, but total exports were continuously declining from the early eighteenth century. A similar decline could be observed in the Dutch data for the other regions. French East India Company textile imports reached their high point in the 1730s and early 1740s and declined thereafter (Gottmann 2016, p. 175). Broadberry et al. (2015) based their conclusions regarding the export sector solely on British figures, making assumptions on the basis of the seventeenth-century British share in total exports; the earlier Dutch decline is thus not captured by their analysis. Furthermore, Broadberry et al.'s study does not take into account private trade, nor the intra-Asian trade of Asian merchants, which may have moved in quite different directions. We have discussed above that trade by Indian merchants was at a high point at the beginning of the eighteenth century, and declined afterwards. Trade to Europe became more important compared with Indian Ocean connections in the eighteenth century. We should thus be aware that Broadberry et al. may have overestimated the rise of the export manufacturing sector in the seventeenth and eighteenth centuries.

We may now proceed to examine the causes of deindustrialization: were these global or local?[16] A first explanation emphasized the role of global trade, colonial policies and the British Industrial Revolution. Declining freight rates promoted an increase in trade and facilitated the workings of comparative advantage and specialization. As large productivity gains and consequent comparative cost advantages of the British textile industry took hold from the later eighteenth century, the Indian textile industry lost its competitive edge. Colonialism further added to India's problems, as the British market was protected against Indian exports, while India was open to imports from Britain (Broadberry et al. 2015, p. 60). In addition, eighteenth-century price developments in the world market, also resulting from increasing British productivity in textile manufacturing, meant that the terms of trade moved against textile manufactures in favour of exporting agricultural commodities (e.g. raw cotton, tea, opium), drawing economic resources away from the manufacturing sector (Clingingsmith and Williamson 2008, p. 210).

An alternative explanation for deindustrialization emphasizes local supply-side, rather than global demand, forces. This view stresses that economic difficulties resulting from the political fragmentation after Mughal disintegration, combined with adverse climate conditions which led to declining agricultural productivity and rises in grain prices. This consequently led to increases in nominal wages in Indian manufacturing and therefore to its declining competitiveness and subsequent demise. Clingingsmith and Williamson (2008) suggest that in the period between 1760 and

1810 it was the latter explanation that drove deindustrialization, while only in the period 1810–1860 it was the downward pressure on world textile prices driven by the British Industrial Revolution that further pushed deindustrialization.

Clingingsmith and Williamson (2008) make a compelling case for adverse domestic conditions in the eighteenth century.[17] There was a greater frequency of droughts in the period between 1735 and 1813 and these adverse effects may indeed have hindered the growth of agricultural production to match increases in population: as we have also seen above, rice prices increased against those for textiles. Yet, if we believe Broadberry et al. (2015), there was hardly any strong deindustrialization in the eighteenth century, but only in the first decades of the nineteenth century, and therefore it seems that the effects of the decline in foreign exports form a larger part of the story than adverse domestic conditions. Domestic conditions, on the other hand, were more important drivers of developments in living standards, as we will discuss below.

Mughal Collapse and Colonialism

The early modern period in South Asia was a period of, first, growing state formation and political centralization with the rise of the Mughal Empire, a subsequent period of fragmentation in the eighteenth century as Mughal power collapsed and various successor states arose from the empire's ashes, and the beginning of a colonial period in which the EIC increased its hold over the subcontinent.

The Mughal Empire is often viewed as a highly extractive state that expropriated a substantial proportion of surplus agricultural production. The emperor controlled (and expanded) his territory by giving grants over land revenues over a certain territory to military commanders (*jagirdars*) in exchange for their military assistance. These commanders often had little contact with the regions concerned and relied on local landlords (*zamindars*) who collected the land taxes from the peasantry. According to Roy (2013, pp. 14–15) the Mughal state functioned well when the interests of these different groups were aligned, but tensions rose when one (or more) of these groups tried to increase their share of the pie (at the expense of the others). The growth of maritime trade in the seventeenth and eighteenth centuries opened up increasing sources of cash to finance wars and increased the power of rulers in the coastal regions, shaking the delicate balance of power. Shortly after the death of the sixth Mughal emperor, Aurangzeb (r. 1658–1707), the empire collapsed. Continuous warfare under Aurangzeb had put too much pressure on the revenue system, causing a fiscal crisis and new power struggles. Various Mughal provinces (like Bengal) emerged as independent states as the Mughal governors, the *Nawabs*, steadily loosened their ties with Delhi. The Hindu Marathas rose to power in the Deccan (in central India) and challenged Mughal power in the north. In the west and south, local warlords also extended their authority (Roy 2013). None of the newly formed states managed to combine military with economic success, as the growth of power remained essentially based on continuous warfare and the exploitation of the agricultural economy.

It was the British East India Company that successfully combined the rise of military power with economic growth. As the Dutch VOC came to dominate the spice trade in Southeast Asia, the British focused their efforts on India. The EIC was a mercantilist organization that was in pursuit of high profits gained by exploiting monopolies, and it had initially refrained from expanding inland out of fear of high costs and a drain on profits. This changed as a result of the Mughal collapse and rivalries with the French Company. The EIC fought successful battles against the French that had been triggered by two wars in Europe (the War of the Austrian Succession of 1740–1748 and the Seven Years' War 1756–1763), which consequently had global repercussions. In Bengal, as the *Nawab* lost power at the hands of Maratha raids, the EIC stepped into the vacuum. In 1764, the Company successfully defeated a combined Indian army of the *Nawab* and his allies and was recognized as the *de facto* ruler of Bengal. Bengal was an agriculturally productive region favourably located on the coast, guaranteeing the EIC a significant stream of revenue. In addition, the English pushed important economic reforms that were crucial for their subsequent success in subduing the remainder of the subcontinent. They ended the dependence on the military power of the tax collectors; a land market was created and property rights over land were separated from obligations related to military service and tax collection (as had been the case under the Mughals). The EIC collected its own taxes and used the revenues to pay for a standing army. In addition, it implemented legislature and established courts of law to protect the interests of business (Roy 2013).

Southern India differed from the north in that its powerful empire, Vijayanagar, had collapsed already in the early seventeenth century, and from its ashes rose a number of smaller kingdoms. While the British would impose colonial rule over many parts of South India only in the early nineteenth century, the larger number of regional kingdoms in the seventeenth and eighteenth centuries in the south led to different market conditions than in the north. While the Mughal Empire did not distinguish between different Europeans, the companies were more involved in Indian politics in the south – making alliances with one king or the other in order to obtain trading privileges (Jacobs 2006).

In Ceylon, the process of colonization had started earlier. In the sixteenth century, the Portuguese achieved direct rule over large chunks of the island at the cost of the indigenous kingdoms of Kotte and Jaffna (De Silva 1981). In the first half of the seventeenth century, the Portuguese were ousted by the Dutch, a process that was concluded with the capture of Colombo in 1658 (De Zwart 2012; 2016b). The VOC controlled an extensive territorial area, the Maritime Provinces, including the former kingdom of Jaffanapatnam in the north and the cinnamon-rich lowlands around Colombo and Galle in the southwest, which was inhabited by at least 800,000 people at the end of the eighteenth century. The island's interior, together with some strips of coast on the eastern and western shores of the island, formed the Kingdom of Kandy that was to be annexed by the British in the nineteenth century. The VOC used its power to monopolize trade and production in cinnamon and, as a feudal lord, could order its inhabitants to perform labour services, the nature of which depended on their caste (the *rājākariya* system). Coerced labour played a more important role in Ceylon as the region was relatively labour scarce. From the outset, European ventures in the south were characterized by their colonial nature, setting it apart from the northern regions of South Asia.

British rule over India would expand over the remainder of the eighteenth and the beginning of the nineteenth centuries (when they also took power over Ceylon from the Dutch). The early modern era brought the Europeans to South Asia first as traders and then (with the timing depending on the region) as colonial rulers. An important body of literature suggests that this colonialism was consequently responsible for both the aforementioned deindustrialization, as well as the decline in economic fortunes and living standards that took place somewhere between 1500 and the present.

Declining Economic Fortunes

Both the trends in living standards over the early modern period as well as the comparative levels in standards of living have been subject to debate in Indian historiography. A large part of this discussion is concerned with real wages, one of the few indicators about which we have some data. Revisionists like Parthasarathi (1998, 2011) and Sivramkrishna (2010), have put forward wage evidence from as late as the eighteenth century, that represents a standard of living on a par with, or even higher than, that in Europe. Others, like Allen (2007) and Broadberry and Gupta (2006), show data suggesting otherwise. In this section we will show some of the evidence on living standards that has been put on the table to date. Because an important part of this debate concerns differences between silver, grain and real wages, we show all three measures for three benchmark years. These data all pertain to unskilled wages, though the exact occupations may differ slightly: they pertain to peons, coolies, weavers and unskilled building labourers.[18]

The first observations stem from the late sixteenth and early seventeenth centuries. For northern India, this was during the reign of Akbar, which is generally viewed as the peak era of Indian living standards. Such views are generally based on the amount of grain a daily wage could buy. Indeed, Table 6.1 shows relatively high grain wages in 1600 for northern India, when a day wage provided a worker with over 3 kg of rice and over 5 kg of wheat. For western and southern India, grain wages also reached their high point in 1600, with 3 kg wheat and almost 6 kg rice, respectively. Looking at the subsistence ratios (which include costs on other basic necessities besides the staple), it becomes clear that even in the areas with relatively high grain wages, these ratios are relatively low, suggesting the low price of the staple relative to other necessities (like clothing, lighting etc.).[19] From 1600 to 1800 we can see a decline in both grain wages and subsistence ratios in all regions of South Asia. This decline is despite increases in silver wages, which means that prices of basic necessities increased faster than wage rates. The subsistence ratios suggest that wages declined towards levels below subsistence in almost all regions of South Asia. Families could

Table 6.1. *Unskilled daily wages in South Asia in comparison with England, 1600–1800*

Region	Year	Silver wage	Grain wage		Subsistence ratio
	circa	grams silver	kg rice	kg wheat	
N. India	1600	0.7	3.1	5.2	1.4
(Lahore and Delhi)	1700				
	1800	1.2		4.7	0.8
W. India	1600	1.0	2.1	3.5	1.2
(Surat)	1700	1.4	2.1	2.8	0.9
	1800	2.4	2.0	2.7	1.1
E. India	1600				
(Chinsurah)	1700	0.8	4.1	2.9	1.1
	1800	1.3	2.4	2.7	0.7
S. India	1600	1.2	5.7		
(Golconda and Cuddalore)	1700	1.4	3.9		1.3
	1800	1.4	1.8		0.7
Ceylon	1600				
(Colombo)	1700	1.8	3.3		0.9
	1800	2.2	2.6		0.7

(cont.)

Table 6.1. (*cont.*)

Region	Year	Silver wage	Grain wage		Subsistence ratio
	circa	grams silver	kg rice	kg wheat	
S. England	1600	5.7		12.4	2.8
(London)	1700	10.6		18.4	4.4
	1800	16.3		11.6	3.1

Sources:

Wages: N. India: 1600: obs. 1595: (Broadberry and Gupta 2006), 1800: De Zwart and Lucassen (2015). W. India: 1600: obs. from 1616 and 1623 (Allen and Studer 2009); 1700: obs. from 1689 to 1693 (Habib 1982); 1800: obs. from 1790 to 1795 Nadri (2008b). E. India: Bengal 1700: 1699–1704; 1800: 1786–90, all incl. board series computed by De Zwart (2016b). S. India: 1600: obs. 1610–1613, 1700: obs. 1680, 1800: obs. 1790 (Broadberry and Gupta 2006); Ceylon: 1600–1800 from De Zwart (2016b); S. England: five-year averages around the years 1600, 1700 and 1800 employing London data from Allen (2001).

Prices: N. India: 1595, 1800 (Allen and Studer 2009): W. India: 1600: rice average price of 1615 and 1624: 0.49 grams silver per kg; wheat average price of 1619–23: 0.29 gr. silver per kg.; 1700: average p. of 1693–1694: 0.68 gr. silver per kg. rice, 0.51 gr. silver per kg wheat (Allen and Studer 2009); 1800: price Pune average 1790–1795: 0.89 gr. silver per kg wheat, 1.2 rice (Allen and Studer 2009); E. India: average price of rice in Chinsurah 1700–1705: 0.2 gr. silver per kg; wheat 0.29 gr. silver per kg (Allen and Studer 2009); 1800: average price of rice in Chinsurah 1786–1790: 0.54 gr. silver per kg; wheat 0.48 gr. silver per kg (Allen and Studer 2009); S. India: 1600: obs. 1610–13, 1700: obs. 1680, 1800: obs. 1790 (Broadberry and Gupta 2006); Ceylon: 1700: average 1698–1702: 0.54 gr. silver per kg rice; 1800: average 1785–1789 (De Zwart 2016b); S. England: five-year averages around the years 1600, 1700 and 1800 employing London data from Allen (2001): 0.46, 0.57, and 1.41 gr. silver respectively per kg wheat.

Subsistence ratios: All Indian wages multiplied by 250 to arrive at annual wage, divided by the family baskets computed by Allen and Studer (2009). Ceylon: 1700: average: 1698–1702; 1800: average 1785–1789: De Zwart (2016b); S. England: five-year averages around the years 1600, 1700 and 1800 employing London data from Allen (2001).

survive if women and children also made contributions to household incomes (De Zwart 2016b). In a comparison with England, the wages reported for India generally represent lower levels of income. The high grain wage, but low silver wages and subsistence ratios, suggests that overall Indian wage labourers remained relatively poor, but could, at times, benefit from low food prices in periods of good harvests. Broadberry and Gupta (2006) have shown that the price paid for skills was significantly above that in Europe: over 100 per cent in the seventeenth century, vis-à-vis some 50 per cent in north-western Europe (Van Zanden 2009), further signifying Europe's specialization in the higher-skilled sectors, and India's overwhelmingly rural and low-skilled economy.

New estimates on GDP per capita confirm the picture of relatively low and declining living standards over the seventeenth and eighteenth centuries (Broadberry et al. 2015). They show a decline of per capita real incomes of over 30 per cent in the period 1600 to the 1830s. Per capita GDP was around 60 per cent of the English level in 1600 and declined to only 20 per cent in 1850. These estimates not only pertain to the unskilled wage laborers discussed above, but should cover the whole economy. Such aggregates miss regional variations. Focusing on Bengal around 1763, Roy (2010) estimates a real income per head there that was only one-fifteenth of the income in England, suggesting that even one of the most highly commercialized regions of the subcontinent was by the late eighteenth century lagging behind severely. More research into the GDP of different Indian regions could shed more light on the causes of decline and the link with the global economy.

Trends in urbanization rates provide another clue regarding economic (and political) developments. Combining total population figures with the combined population in towns with above 10,000 inhabitants (see Table 6.2), we arrive at lower urbanization rates than are often presumed. Yet in the earlier estimates of Indian urbanization, smaller towns of 3,000–9,000 inhabitants were also included.[20] Focusing only on the larger cities, the picture is also more static than the view of de-urbanization over the early modern era: between 1700 and 1750 the urban share of the total population fell; for the remaining periods, urbanization was on the rise (if slowly). The reason for the relative stability of the urbanization rate is that the decline of the interior cities was compensated for by the growth of the coastal centres. Developments in urbanization correlate with both political and economic trends.

Table 6.2. *Urbanization in India: total population and percentage of total population in cities with 10,000 or more inhabitants, 1600–1850*

	Population (millions)	Urban population (millions)	Urbanization (%)
1600	142	5.6	3.9
1650	142	6.0	4.2
1700	164	7.4	4.5
1750	190	7.6	4.0
1800	207	8.8	4.3
1850	232	11.5	5.0

Source: total population: Broadberry et al. (2015); urban population: Buringh (2016). This includes the population of cities like Lahore and Dhaka that are now in Pakistan and Bangladesh respectively.

There is a broad consensus regarding the decline of the important trading and administrative centres of the Mughal Empire. Agra, Delhi and Lahore may have declined from some 400,000 inhabitants in the late seventeenth century to about 100,000 in the first decades of the nineteenth century (Roy 2013, pp. 108–109). As the empire fell into disarray these cities lost their access to resources in the surrounding areas, which resulted in strong population declines.

In the Mughal successor states, new cities of regional power emerged. Furthermore, in the eighteenth century, port cities, and particularly those controlled by the EIC like Bombay, Calcutta and Madras, grew rapidly in size. Already by 1760, Madras and Calcutta were the largest cities of the Indian subcontinent: the engagement with the world economy and relative security of these towns attracted labour and capital from other parts of the subcontinent, while British territorial conquests secured connections with the interior (Roy 2013, p. 114).

In Ceylon, a similar population movement from the interior to the coast may have taken place. While the data are admittedly subject to some margins of error, it seems that the population of interior Kandy declined over the course of the eighteenth century, while that of the Maritime Provinces rose in the same period (De Zwart 2012, p. 378). Furthermore, data for the commercial *entrepôt* Galle also show that population numbers swelled during the period of commercial flourishing of that port city, but declined in the second half of the eighteenth century when its importance in the VOC trading network was diminishing.

Most of the recent evidence on hard economic indicators (wages and GDP per capita) suggests that in the seventeenth century there was a gap in real incomes between South Asia and Europe, and that the gap only increased after that. It is unlikely that these trends were fundamentally influenced by globalization in this era: while trade was generally rising until the late eighteenth century, living standards stagnated or declined. Even in one of the most commercialized regions, Bengal, living standards (as measured by subsistence ratios and GDP per capita) were low and declining. At least before the onset of British imperialism, one would expect the export trade in textiles to have had a positive effect on output, employment and incomes. Yet, as a share of the total economy, trade simply mattered too little to influence living standards. In urbanization trends, where a shift from the interior to the coast took place, global connections played a stronger role, however.

Conclusion

In most of the sixteenth and seventeenth centuries, the Mughal Empire ruled over much of a subcontinent that was the world's leading producer of high-quality cotton manufactures. Around 1600, grain wages in the centre of the empire were still relatively high, while GDP per capita in the entire sub-continent was about 40 per cent below British levels. The expansion of the economy was helped by the influx of bullion, which spurred trends in monetization and commercialization. By the early nineteenth century, the situation was quite different. The Mughal Empire had disintegrated and the British had started to take direct control over an increasing part of the subcontinent. Real wages plummeted to below subsistence levels and GDP had declined to levels that were among the lowest in the world economy. Such a deterioration of economic performance, which took place over a period stretching 300 years, can hardly be attributed to a single cause. Political instability and a deterioration of climate conditions probably played a part in this. Trade may have aggravated the decline of the Mughal Empire. Rising revenues along the coasts first created instability through the rise of coastal power centres, and consequently allowed for the rise of British colonialism.

At the same time, compared with the large Indian population and economy, the scale of foreign trade was simply too small to bring about any decisive changes. Regarding Indian deindustrialization, only in the nineteenth century the decline of textile exports in the foreign sector was so dramatic that it partially drove strong deindustrialization. The effects of global interaction differed for the different regions and were of course more pronounced in coastal areas than in the interior. These interactions also had a different nature depending on area and time. Initially, in Surat (Gujarat) and Hooghly/Chinsurah (Bengal), which were ports of Mughal India, and in the different parts of the Coromandel coast, Europeans did not have power in matters of trade or otherwise until the middle of the eighteenth century; their trade generated an increase in economic activity (Prakash 1998). The absence of special privileges for Europeans, and the competition between different European companies and European and Indian private traders meant that producers received a fair (and rising) price for their goods. In Ceylon and on the Malabar coast, it is suggested that 'the Europeans' trade did not provide a positive stimulus to the economy at any point in time' (Prakash 1981, pp. 204–205), as trade was related to colonial control over resources from the beginning: here local producers and merchants did not receive a fair price and markets did not develop. Overall, it seems that rather than trade, the rise of political control by Europeans in South Asia and the variation therein between the Indian regions, was the most important effect of globalization on South Asia in this period.

Suggested Reading

Broadberry, S., J. Custodis and B. Gupta (2015). 'India and the Great Divergence: An Anglo-Indian Comparison of GDP Per Capita, 1600–1871', *Explorations in Economic History 55*, pp. 58–75.

Clingingsmith, D., and J.G. Williamson (2008). 'Deindustrialization in 18th and 19th Century India: Mughal Decline, Climate Shocks and British Industrial Ascent', *Explorations in Economic History 45*, pp. 209–234.

Parthasarathi, Prasannan (2011). *Why Europe Grew Rich and Asia Did Not. Global Economic Divergence, 1600–1850*. Cambridge: Cambridge University Press.

Prakash, O. (1998). *European Commercial Enterprise in Pre-Colonial India*. Cambridge: Cambridge University Press.

Richards, John F. (1997). 'Early Modern India and World History', *Journal of World History 8*, pp. 197–209.

Roy, Tirthankar (2013). *An Economic History of Early Modern India.* London and New York: Routledge.

Studer, Roman (2015). *The Great Divergence Reconsidered. Europe, India, and the Rise to Global Economic Power.* Cambridge: Cambridge Uiversity Press.

Washbrook, David (2007). 'India in the Early Modern World Economy: Modes of Production, Reproduction and Exchange', *Journal of Global History* 2, pp. 87–111.

7 | The 'Age of Commerce' In Southeast Asia

Introduction

Abu-Lughod (1989) suggests that Southeast Asia was part and parcel of the world system of the thirteenth and fourteenth centuries. Situated at the crossroads between the Indian and Pacific oceans, the region had long since been a central trade hub. Wade (2009) argues that the rise of global trade in Southeast Asia started even earlier. Between 900 and 1300 the growth of trade with China (resulting from Song economic expansion), as well as the connection with the burgeoning Islamic trade across the Indian Ocean, allowed the rise of ports and urban centres, population growth, the spread of Buddhism and Islam, and the emergence of ceramic and textile industries as well as the rise of commercial agriculture of rice and pepper. Impressed by Zheng He's trading missions in the service of the Ming Yongle emperor, Anthony Reid (1993a) suggests that, stimulated by Chinese population and wealth expansion, there was a clear take-off of Southeast Asian trade from 1400 onwards, inaugurating Southeast Asia's 'Age of Commerce'.

Thus, there was significant global interaction in Southeast Asia preceding the arrival of the Europeans. The arrival of Europeans in the region was a direct consequence of the region's export of these spices in the preceding centuries. In the late fourteenth century 9 tons of cloves and 2 tons of nutmeg arrived annually in Europe from Indonesia, and these figures increased significantly to 74 tons of cloves and 37 tons of nutmeg in the later fifteenth century (Reid, 1990). In this period, it was still the Venetians and Arabs who benefitted the most from this trade, which first led the Portuguese, and later the northern Atlantic trading powers, to sail to Southeast Asia themselves in an attempt to circumvent the Venetian-Arab monopoly.

There has been some debate regarding the changes resulting from the European arrival in Southeast Asia. Scholars like Jacob van Leur (1955) argued that the impact of the Portuguese and the Dutch on Southeast

Asian trade and society was minimal. Wallerstein was heavily influenced by Van Leur and suggested that Asia, and thus Southeast Asia, remained external to the world economy during most of the early modern period. Southeast Asia did not fulfil the conditions he set forth, which would suggest a shift from an external area to a periphery. Southeast Asia remained a supplier of luxuries, while a periphery provides the core with necessities. European influence on the region's economic, political and cultural organization was limited and involvement in the world system began only around the mid-eighteenth century or later (Wallerstein 1974). Reid, on the other hand, argued that the Europeans were responsible for ending Southeast Asia's 'Age of Commerce'.

In this chapter, we will argue that Southeast Asia played a pivotal role in the early modern global economy in the early modern era. Its famed spices were the main reason for the European voyages of the late fifteenth century. This quest for spices set in motion the wheels of commerce that connected the world: in search for these spices, the Europeans first encountered the Americas and consequently, American silver was exchanged for cotton cloth in India, which was subsequently used to buy the spices that were finally used to flavour European dishes. In Reid's words: 'Southeast Asia played its most central role in world history as a crucible for the birth of modernity and the unification of world markets' (2015, p. 74). While major parts of Southeast Asia may indeed have remained unaffected by these global interactions (just like the hinterlands of the other continents), the maritime areas stood in full contact with the global market and there are abundant indications that connections between the maritime ports and the hinterlands were important in bringing about crucial changes throughout the mainland and the archipelago.

We will show that, as a result of sustained global interaction, Southeast Asia between 1500 and 1800 went through a period of significant economic, social and political change. Reid (1993a) suggested that its 'Age of Commerce' between roughly 1400 and 1650 went hand-in-hand with a rise in wealth and living standards. Yet in the seventeenth century, adverse climate conditions, as well as European (especially Dutch) intrusion in Asian trading patterns led to a decline in Southeast Asian trade and welfare. In this chapter, we will investigate these claims on the basis of recent literature and new quantitative evidence and we suggest that many of the positive trends were sustained throughout the period 1500–1800.

An 'Age of Commerce' in Southeast Asia

From 1500 onwards, the commercial growth that had already started somewhere in the more distant past took a leap. Not only did the arrival of Europeans increase the total number of traders active in the area, the number of Indians and Chinese that had come to Southeast Asia for a long time grew significantly, and, from the early seventeenth century onwards, the Japanese also became engaged in Southeast Asian trade (Andaya 1993). Total trade grew impressively as a result. As Southeast Asia was the main producer of tropical luxuries that were in high demand in other parts of the globe, we start our discussion with the rise in export trade.

Exports

Figure 7.1 shows the values (in thousands of dollars) and the quantities (in metric tons) of four of the key exports of the region in the early modern period about which Bulbeck (et al. 1998) presented long series of data: cloves, pepper, sugar and coffee.[1] These were not the only products exported by the region. In fact, David Bulbeck et al. (1998, p. 6) estimated that in the 1630s, cloves, pepper and sugar represented

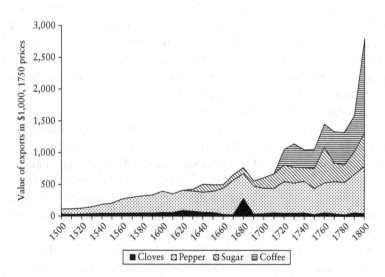

Figure 7.1 Value of Southeast Asian exports, 1500–1800
Source: Bulbeck et al. (1998, p. 12).

only a third of the exports originating from the region itself: other Southeast Asian products in this period were, among many others, benzoin, camphor, mace and nutmeg. Furthermore, the export of these four commodities reflected only 11 per cent of total exports of the region, because, situated at the crossroads between the Indian Ocean and the South China Sea, the majority of Southeast Asian exports consisted of re-exports from China. Lacking consistent estimates of the exports of these products for the period 1500–1800, some general conclusions about the growth of trade have to be based on the exports of those products shown in Figure 7.1.

Over the entire period 1500–1800, the value of exports in current prices of the region grew by over 1.1 per cent annually. This growth of trade was, as in the case of the world economy, faster than the growth in population as well as the growth of GDP (taking Maddison's estimates for Indonesia between 1500 and 1820). In per capita terms, exports increased by roughly 0.9 per cent annually between 1500 and 1800. This means that during this period the 'openness' of the region increased substantially. Looking at trends over this period, there is a rise in the total value of exports of pepper and cloves from 1500 until the 1680s. The consequent decline in the value of exports between 1650 and 1720 is in line with the contraction of the world economy (*c.*1650–*c.*1750) which we have also seen elsewhere, and which suggests a strong relationship with global developments. This decline was to a large extent driven by the decline in clove exports as a result of the effective monopolization of clove production and trade by the Dutch after 1656. In an attempt to raise world prices, the VOC reduced total production by concentrating production on Ambon and the neighbouring Lease Islands (Haruku, Saparua and Nusalaut) and wiping out all clove trees outside of those islands. Furthermore, whereas the VOC initially purchased cloves in markets where they competed with other companies and merchants which drove up prices in Asia, as a monopsony buyer after the 1650s it was able to stabilize purchase prices (De Zwart 2016a). Figure 7.1 shows exports in constant prices of 1750. The decline is more pronounced when using current prices, as argued by Reid (1993a) who puts forward such data as evidence for the end of the 'Age of Commerce'. Without information on general price trends, such current prices provide us with little information, however, and we therefore argue that constant prices are more informative about trends in export trade.

An increase in exports can be observed for the eighteenth century, which was to a great extent driven by the expansion of coffee and sugar production, as growth in pepper and clove exports was limited. Sugar cane was native to the Southeast Asian archipelago, but until the seventeenth century it largely grew in the wild and was consumed locally. Over the course of the seventeenth and eighteenth centuries, it became an important product both in Asian, and, after it was introduced to the Americas by the Spanish, global commerce. Coffee cultivation started in Java with the first harvest in 1711 and attained substantial proportions from 1724 onwards. Both sugar and coffee were important additions to the mix of exports from Southeast Asia and from the 1720s onwards the combined value of these products was generally greater than that of cloves and pepper.

Exports of nutmeg and mace (both harvested from the nutmeg tree, depicted in Figure 7.2)[2] to Europe also increased over the sixteenth century. The export of nutmeg increased from 16 tons per annum in the early sixteenth century to 200 tons a century later, and that of mace from 6 to 75 tons in the same period (Reid 1990, p. 7). After the Dutch monopolized the production and trade of nutmeg

Figure 7.2 Cinnamon, nutmeg, and cloves: Catalysts of global commerce in the early modern era. Etching by Romeyn de Hooghe, 1682
Source: Simon de Vries, *Curieuse aenmerckingen der bysonderste Oost en West-Indische verwonderens-waerdige dingen*, Pt.1. Utrecht: J. Ribbius, 1682. Courtesy of Rijksmuseum, Amsterdam.

and mace from the Banda Islands in the 1620s, exports to Europe would stagnate at levels somewhat below that: nutmeg at around 125 tons and mace just below 50 tons per year (ibid.). While some nutmeg and mace were sold in India, Ceylon and the Middle East, European exports dominated.

Of the remaining export products about which we have some data, sappanwood and tin were by far the most important. Data on VOC sales of sappanwood in Europe suggest a steady rise from 1650 to over 600 tons per annum in the 1720s and, apart from another peak in the 1750s, a decline afterwards. Company exports to other regions show a similar trend. Tin exports, from Melaka and Siam to Europe, averaged around 100 tons annually in the last decades of the seventeenth century, declined to 60 tons in the middle of the eighteenth century, and then increased to almost 300 tons in the period 1760–1790. China was a far more important market, however, as in the second half of the eighteenth century almost 1,000 tons were transported north annually by the VOC (also see Figure 7.4 below). For the remaining products of the regions, such as benzoin and camphor,

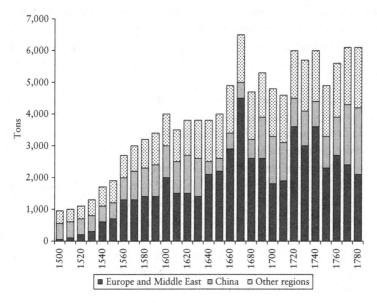

Figure 7.3 Pepper exports from Southeast Asia, average annual metric tonnage per decade, 1500–1800
Source: Bulbeck et al. (1998, p. 86).

the total quantities that were exported by the VOC to Europe and other parts of Asia are negligible (e.g. benzoin averaged around 10 tons annually in the eighteenth century).

It is, of course, not clear whether these VOC figures could be seen as representative for the entire trade in these goods: we know almost nothing about goods transported by Asian merchants (further discussed on pp.190–192). The demand served by these merchants may have shown different fluctuations. What we do know supports the notion of a significant rise in Southeast Asian exports between 1500 and 1800 and only a minor slump in the seventeenth century, if a slump at all.

To what extent was this boom driven by increased global – rather than regional, or continental – interactions? For pepper (Figure 7.3), European and Middle Eastern demand certainly became very important from the second half of the sixteenth century onwards, good for over 40 per cent of pepper exports on average. Chinese imports declined gradually, from over 50 per cent at the beginning of the fifteenth century to roughly 10 per cent in the middle of the seventeenth century, but increased somewhat to between 20 and 30 per cent in the eighteenth century. In absolute numbers, the amount of Chinese imports did not decline, however, suggesting that European demand supplemented rather than substituted Chinese imports. The 'Other regions' constitute a residual category including India, Japan and the Americas, and we know little about the distribution across these regions.

In the fifteenth century, still only a small part of total clove, nutmeg and mace exports went to Europe, as India constituted the largest market for Southeast Asian cloves (Bulbeck et al. 1998, p. 31). In the sixteenth century, India probably imported some 80 tons annually, and in the early seventeenth century this number had declined to 25–30 tons (ibid.). In the eighteenth century, over 50 tons went to India annually. At the same time, European imports of cloves increased from 75 tons annually at the end of the sixteenth century to 450 tons per year in the 1620s and somewhat less than that in the remainder of the seventeenth and eighteenth centuries. Europe accounted for over 70 per cent of all cloves, 80 per cent of all nutmeg, and about 90 per cent of all mace exports in the eighteenth century.[3]

Figure 7.4 provides an indication of the destinations of the other Southeast Asian exports as transported by the VOC. Of these sugar and coffee were the most important in the eighteenth century. For coffee,

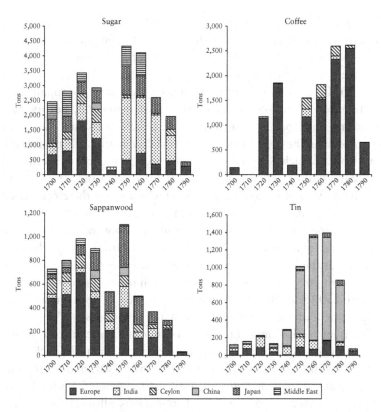

Figure 7.4 VOC exports from Batavia, various products, average annual metric tonnage per decade, 1700–1800
Source: Bookkeeper-General Database.

we again find that European demand was crucial in driving the rise in exports as almost 90 per cent was transported to Europe; the remaining coffee ended up either in Ceylon (8 per cent) or India (3 per cent). For sugar exports from Southeast Asia, European demand was less significant. Only during brief periods in the middle of the seventeenth century and around the 1720s did it amount to more than 35 per cent of total exports (Figure 7.4). The European market was flooded with sugar from the West Indies, which resulted in lower sales prices in Europe (Rönnback 2009; De Zwart 2016a). Because transport costs were lower in the intra-Asian trade network and as the VOC wished to pay for most Asian goods with the proceeds of sales from the intra-Asian trade, sugar was sold in large quantities to the Middle East

(Mocha and Persia), and especially, to north-western India (Surat). In other parts of India, such as Malabar and the Coromandel coast, there was no significant market for sugar from Southeast Asia as sugar was already imported from neighbouring Bengal (Nadri 2008a).

The VOC's eighteenth-century figures on the export of sappanwood and tin show a mix of destinations. For sappanwood, Europe was important, but Japan and Ceylon also received a fair share. The rising export of tin in the eighteenth century was driven primarily by demand from China, which received over 1,000 tons annually on average in the second half of that century. These figures reflect only the trade of one European trading company – the VOC – and are therefore biased towards the trade for Europe. Yet, as discussed below, most of the total trade remained dominated by Asian traders who were more active in local and regional networks. Nonetheless, it is hard to escape the conclusion that the increased European demand for Southeast Asian produce was of great importance for the growth of Southeast Asian trade between 1500 and 1800. In the next section, we will discuss the impact of the growth of export on Southeast Asian economies.

Finally, it is also important to note that a significant proportion of exports consisted of re-exports to and from China (Bulbeck et al. 1998, p. 6). It has been estimated that in the 1630s, of a total value of 8.6 million Spanish *reals* from all trade, about 5.7 million (or 66 per cent) were re-exports.[4] Such re-exports allowed the growth of certain commercial *entrepôts* and generated wealth for various merchant groups, but did not cause changes in the wider systems of production.

Imports

In exchange for these exports, Southeast Asia imported mainly silver and copper, ceramics, cloth and silk. The trade in silver was crucial in lubricating Southeast Asia's trade and stimulating the commercial expansion of maritime trading centres. Japanese silver dominated until the later 1660s, when silver exports were banned from the island (Reid, 1993a, p. 26). Another part of the silver came to Southeast Asia either from the mines in the Americas via Europe, or, from the 1570s onwards, directly across the Pacific through Manila (Flynn and Giraldez, 1995). While much of the silver was re-exported to China, as noted above, significant amounts remained in the region, especially as Europeans frequently had to pay for (for example) pepper with American bullion. Spanish silver coins (*reals*) became an important medium of exchange in the seventeenth century.

Indian textiles constituted another major import of the region. Reid (2009) finds that there was a significant growth in the import of these from a total value of 600,000 Spanish dollars at the beginning of the fifteenth century to 1,760,000 in 1641. There was a subsequent decline in imports after that to about a million Spanish dollars worth of textiles towards the end of the eighteenth century. Reid's analysis of the rise and decline of textile imports is based solely on VOC data. It is hard to come to any strong conclusions about the implications of this decline for the economy, as it also seems that the VOC started to increasingly pay for its goods in Southeast Asia using coins in the eighteenth century (Feenstra 2014). Wil O. Dijk (2002) discussed the trade in textiles by the VOC to Burma in the seventeenth century and suggested that the decline in the later decades of that century was not related to socio-economic developments in Burma, but was rather connected to the changing fortunes of the VOC. Gerrit Knaap and Heather Sutherland (2004) showed significant Asian and European private imports of Indian textiles to Makassar and found that private trade grew over the eighteenth century. The decline in VOC imports of textiles may thus have been partially compensated for by rising private trade. Also significant were imports of silk and ceramics from China, but we have no complete data on these flows. Finally, even if we follow Reid's thesis on the decline of textile imports, we are not wholly convinced about his entirely negative interpretation of this decline; Reid argues that it is a sign of economic decline, reflected in the decline of Southeast Asian purchasing power which, over the course of the seventeenth century, began to prevent them from buying the luxury textiles, having instead to spin and weave clothing themselves. Another interpretation, that is more often applied in other cases (e.g. in the cases of Africa and Europe), sees the rise of a domestic textile industry in response to increasing commercialization as a sign of economic development rather than stagnation.

A final important import involves European muskets and canon. The numbers from the VOC Bookkeeper-General Database show a total of 1,686 imported cannon to Batavia; accounting for the missing years in the data, this may have amounted to a maximum of some 3,000 cannon over the eighteenth century. The data suggest that almost 4,000 muskets were imported up to 1730. The absence of data for musket imports after this date suggests that no more muskets were imported afterwards. Yet, it is not the numbers that count in this case: as we shall discuss below, these, and other European imported cannon and muskets (about which we have no data at all), aided trends towards greater political centralization and therefore had an important impact in the development of the region in this period.

European and Asian Trade

Many of the figures shown above relate to Dutch trade, but there were also other European and Asian traders active in Southeast Asia. The rise in exports to Europe in the sixteenth century was driven by the arrival of the Portuguese after their capture of Melaka in 1511, and they dominated European markets in subsequent decades. Local trade was by no means disbanded in this period, and the Muslims also expanded their shipping to Europe in the second half of the sixteenth century. Many studies have argued that the Portuguese entry into this trade led to few significant changes in the structure of trade and societies in Southeast Asia (Van Leur 1955; Meilink-Roelofsz 1962; Steensgaard 1973).

It was only with the arrival of the Dutch, and, of lesser importance, the English, in the late sixteenth century, that things really started to change according to Reid. Dutch onslaughts on the Southeast Asian trading network, combined with unfavourable climate conditions, caused a reversal of trends in the seventeenth century – a decline in cash crop production, a return to subsistence agriculture and a retraction from the world economy, causing economic and cultural impoverishment: 'the positive interaction between international trade, scriptural religion, and expanding Southeast Asian monarchies was at an end – and with it the age of commerce' (Reid 1993a, p. 325).

There are good reasons to doubt the truth of such a drastic reversal, drawing on studies of both the Southeast Asian mainland and the archipelago. Victor Lieberman (1990, 1993, 1995, 2003) disputes whether such a displacement of trade took place on the mainland. First, he notes that European traders played a limited role, compared with Asian merchants, and that they were therefore in no position to fundamentally alter trading patterns there. Second, he suggests that if trade there did decline there in the seventeenth century, it was only for a brief period. Third, he argues that European attacks on archipelagic centres of trade such as Melaka, Makassar and Banten may have helped to divert Asian trade to safe mainland ports. Thus, he claims that European trade, if anything, may have contributed to the commercial development of the mainland. Besides these trends in commerce, Lieberman has argued that many of the other trends described by Reid, on cultural and political consolidation, continued throughout the early modern period, which we will discuss in the sections below.

Gerrit Knaap (1999, 2006, 2015) has shown, for a variety of cases in insular Southeast Asia, that indigenous and Chinese merchants were by no means driven out of business by the VOC in the eighteenth century, even in the Dutch-controlled parts. While trade in the articles of global commerce: pepper, coffee and cane sugar was indeed carried out almost entirely by VOC ships, trade in goods for the local and regional markets (rice, timber, salt, arrack, Javanese tobacco and cloths and palm sugar) was dominated by indigenous and Chinese merchants. In the 1770s, private traders dominated the ports along Dutch-controlled Java's north coast: in Semarang and Pekalongan over 90 per cent of total trade was in private hands; in Tegal and Cirebon some 70 per cent; about 60 per cent in Banten, and even almost 40 per cent of trade passed through private hands in Batavia, the VOC headquarters. The majority of the private traders were Javanese (45 per cent), yet in terms of volume and value of trade the Chinese skippers (30 per cent) were dominant as they had larger ships. Malay skippers were also active in this trade (10 per cent).

Records of trade in Makassar (in Sulawesi) show that the average number of private vessels calling in the eighteenth century, between 500 and 550, was similar to that before the conquest of the city by the Dutch in the 1660s. While there was a slight decline in total trade volume between 1725 and 1770, there was a major rise in trade from then to about 1790; over the entire period, trade grew by 0.6 per cent annually. Including VOC trade, total maritime commerce in Makassar increased by an impressive 2.7 per cent per annum in this period. Overall trading value by the end of the eighteenth century most likely exceeded that during the 'Age of Commerce'. In Makassar, Chinese merchants dominated the private trade, as about 50 per cent of goods were passing through their hands, but Malay and Sulawesi skippers also remained important throughout the eighteenth century (Knaap and Sutherland 2004).

In general, it seems that European trade complemented rather that substituted Southeast Asian trade. As Knaap (1999, p. 419) concluded: 'the idea [put forward by Reid] that the private sector had been entirely eliminated is the product of a narrow focus on a few long-distance trade items, such as spices, Indian textiles, and pepper'.

Conclusion: Wheels of Commerce

Based on this survey, we suggest that many of the trends observed by Reid for the fifteenth and sixteenth centuries continued in the seventeenth and eighteenth centuries and that there was a steady growth of commerce throughout the early modern era. Considering the relatively large growth rates of this trade (by early modern standards), this growth most likely exceeded that of other trends in Southeast Asian economies. The acceleration of the 'wheels of commerce' (Braudel 1982) between 1500 and 1800 had important effects on the economic, social, political and cultural development of the region. To this we will now turn.

Demographic and Economic Development

The extent to which the rise in global trade benefitted or burdened the Southeast Asian peoples is still the subject of much debate. Reid argued that in the period up to the 1620s, the rise in trade was positively correlated with the economic fortunes of the area. After this virtuous circle of expanding commerce and economic and political development, trade, now dominated by the Europeans, rather became a cause of underdevelopment of the region until the late twentieth century. In recent contributions, both Ronald Findlay and Kevin O'Rourke (2007) and Williamson (2015) have echoed Reid in arguing that European trade caused economic decline in the region.

In this section, we include developments in the Southeast Asian mainland (Lieberman 2009), as well as those in the archipelago. Furthermore, we stress that the distribution of the gains of trade was unequal and this is crucial in order to understand what happened. In general, all indicators show slow but steady growth over the period 1500–1800.

Demographic Growth and Urbanization

We will start this investigation by giving some figures on the total population and demographic trends. Depending on which estimates you take, the population of the entire region grew from somewhere around 18 million in 1500 to some 37 million by the end of the eighteenth century (Reid 1993b; Clio-Infra 2015, Maddison 2007). Over 40 per cent of these people lived in the Malay archipelago and some further 5 per cent in the Philippines; the remaining 50–55 per cent was spread across the mainland (Thailand, Burma and Indo-China). The population was unevenly distributed and large areas were virtually uninhabited, while in other areas population could be found concentrated in large trading cities.

Two features characterize early modern Southeast Asian demography: low population densities and relatively low growth rates (despite the abundance of land). Simply dividing the total land area in square km by the total population suggests an average population density of 5.5 persons per square km in 1600.[5] In comparison, this number was around 15 persons per square km in Europe in the eighteenth century, over 50 in China and even over 150 in Bengal in India (De Zwart 2016b). There were, of course, areas which had higher densities: Java was inhabited by over 30 people per square km and Bali by almost 80 (Reid, 1988, p. 14). Nonetheless, it is clear that most of Southeast Asia in this period consisted of jungle, untouched by humans, which had consequences for the process of early modern state formation (as discussed on pp. 203–206). Second, the population grew relatively slowly, some 0.22 per cent average annually, for over three centuries. In the same period, the population of Europe increased by 0.27 per cent and that of China by 0.41 per cent annually. While these differences in percentages seem small, the cumulative effects over 300 years were large, as Southeast Asia's population almost doubled, that of Europe more than doubled and that of China more than tripled (Maddison 2003). Cultural and religious factors may have led to smaller families, while warfare and disasters (e.g. earthquakes, tsunamis and volcano eruptions) also slowed demographic growth (Reid 1988, pp. 12–18).

Population growth was, to an extent, aided by the immigration of groups from China, Japan, India and Europe. While Chinese and Indians had been present in Southeast Asia since Antiquity, their presence increased impressively between 1500 and 1800. Though, in some cases, these immigrant groups consisted of substantial numbers, they almost always remained confined to urban commercial centres. Many southern Chinese settled in Manila, Batavia, Melaka and Ayutthaya (Andaya 1993, pp. 348–349). There was a large concentration of Chinese in Spanish Manila from the late sixteenth century onwards. In 1586, there were already 10,000 Chinese living there (in a total population of about 40,000–50,000), and their

numbers continued to swell to 15,000 in 1650 and even 40,000 in
1750 (Andaya 1993, pp. 348–349; Phelan 1959, p. 178). Batavia
and its immediate surroundings in Java were also an important destination for Chinese migrants. The Dutch initially actively encouraged settlement by the Chinese, as they were considered diligent
and skilled workers. Early in the seventeenth century (and possibly
earlier) Chinese migrants were an important source of free labour
in Java (Boomgaard 1990). Sugar cultivation became an important
industry dominated by the Chinese, as Chinese entrepreneurs owned
both plantations and sugar mills, which were worked by Chinese as
well as local labourers. However, tensions rose as the Chinese population quickly began to exceed the European presence by a large
margin: between 1670 and 1740 the Chinese population in Batavia
and its environs increased from some 2,700 to almost 15,000 (Ota
2014, pp. 196–197). In Manila, there were multiple anti-Chinese
riots over the seventeenth century, and in 1740 there was a massacre of Chinese in Batavia, where perhaps up to 10,000 were caught
in the onslaught (Blussé 1981, p. 177). Despite such atrocities, the
numbers of Chinese continued to grow; while in Batavia city itself
their numbers were reduced, in its environs the Chinese population
had returned to pre-massacre levels in the 1750s and continued to
increase thereafter (Ota 2014, p. 198). A third pocket of Chinese in
Southeast Asia could be found in the Siamese capital of Ayutthaya. As
a share of the total, their presence there was less impressive as there
were less than 16,000 Chinese in a total population of possibly over
200,000 in the late seventeenth century. But the Chinese were probably the largest foreign group, there and they not just merchants, but
also artisans, sailors and interpreters (Skinner 1957, p. 15).

While there was intensive trade between Japan and Southeast Asia
between 1600 and 1635, the Japanese never settled anywhere in
Southeast Asia in such large numbers. During this brief period, there
was an enclave consisting of some 1,000–1,500 Japanese in Ayutthaya
in the early seventeenth century, but this ended with the massacre
by the new Siamese ruler in 1632. Indians were another important
group present in Southeast Asia, but like the Japanese (and unlike the
Chinese), they did not settle in large numbers. Nonetheless, Indian
merchant communities, often Muslims (*Moors* in the sources), could
be found in various commercial centres such as Melaka, Batavia and
others.

The arrival and settlement of Europeans in the region was of course the major novel feature of the period 1500–1800. The Portuguese were the first to arrive and they established footholds at Melaka, Timor and the Moluccas, from where they both tried to reorganize Southeast Asian trade (though the effects of their efforts should not be overestimated) and to spread Christianity. Spanish presence was almost completely confined to the Philippines. In 1650 about 7,350 Spaniards lived in Manila and not many more in the rest of the archipelago (Phelan 1959, p. 178). In Manila, the Spanish connected trade from the Spanish Americas (silver) with China (silk and cotton textiles). Despite their small numbers, Spanish presence would have profound effects as they claimed authority over more than half a million Filipinos and converted them to Christianity (Phelan 1959, p. 11). By the late sixteenth century, northern Europeans joined the Iberians in the quest for Eastern riches. The English eagerly established a string of trading stations across Southeast Asia in the early seventeenth century, but quickly had to give way to the Dutch who came to dominate international trade in the later seventeenth century. Outside a handful of traders, the English presence was negligible. The Dutch East India Company not only opened trading posts across both the mainland and the entire archipelago (except the Philippines), it also became de facto ruler in the Moluccas in the seventeenth century and over much of Java in the eighteenth century.

Relative to the total population of Southeast Asia, the numbers of these migrants from other parts of Asia and Europe were not that impressive: a rough estimate on the basis of the above would be some 200,000, of which more than half were Chinese, in a total population of 28 million in the early eighteenth century. At the same time, the role these groups played in commercial, political and cultural developments in the region far exceeds what one would expect on the basis of such numbers. The fact that Southeast Asia attracted such highly skilled and commercially important immigrant groups suggests that the region itself lacked the financial and human capital to sustain the economic boom and therefore had to import it. Throughout the period, the region would remain scarce in capital and skills. Interest rates provide a clue with regard to the availability of capital and it seems that the lowest interest rates charged to indigenous Southeast Asians were somewhere between 25 and 35 per cent per year (Boomgaard 2009, p. 68). These rates were much higher than in Europe where interest rates around 5 per cent were closer to the norm. The price paid for skills (i.e. the difference between the wage of a skilled vis-à-vis an unskilled worker) provides information on the availability of human capital. Even in Batavia, with relatively more skilled immigrants as well as the presence of substantial numbers of artisan-slaves, the skill premium was very high – between 130 and 180 per cent in the eighteenth century. In India and China, this percentage was generally below 100 per cent, and often even lower; in Europe, it fluctuated around 50 per cent in the same period (De Zwart 2016b).

It was particularly in the urban centres that the population was most diverse and Chinese, Japanese, Indians, Europeans, as well as Southeast Asians filled the streets. Most Southeast Asian cities were located on the coast or large navigable rivers, which made it possible to supply them from distant places, and some of these port cities were dependent on overseas imports for more than half of their rice needs (see Map 7.1 and Reid, 1993b, p. 471). These port cities were

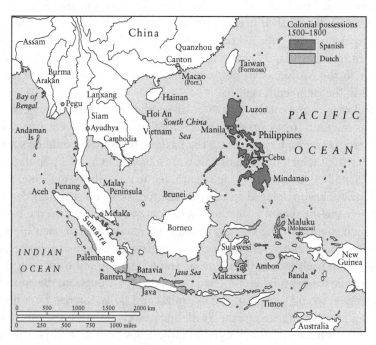

Map 7.1 Southeast Asia in the early modern era
Source: Bentley, Subrahmanyam and Wiesner-Hanks (2015, p. 377).

the nodes in the intra-Asian and intercontinental trading networks. The Chinese merchant communities of Batavia and Manila forged the links with China (mainly Canton – see also Chapter 8) and as direct trade between Japan and China was forbidden, the Japanese communities dotted across Southeast Asian cities (noted above) made it possible to conduct trade with Chinese traders there (Blussé 2008, p. 20).

While European-controlled maritime cities like Batavia and Manila were important in intercontinental trading networks, the largest cities were Asian cities like Ayutthaya and Thank-long (Hanoi). On the basis of new estimates (Buringh 2016), one can sketch the development of levels of urbanization across the early modern era. The figures show that there was a rise in urbanization in the sixteenth century, possibly resulting from the growth of trade, but a decline in subsequent centuries. In an international comparison (Table 7.1), the Southeast Asian urbanization rate in 1500 and 1600 was on a par with the rate in Western Europe and higher than other parts of Asia. By 1700 and 1800, however, as the urbanization ratio stagnated in Southeast Asia, and it continued to increase in Western Europe and Japan, the region clearly started to lag behind.

Monetization and Commercialization

An obvious result of the growth of commerce was the extensive influx of bullion that led to increasing monetization and commercialization. While monetization for commercial purposes may have started already in the twelfth century (Wicks 1986, 1992), the extent and scale

Table 7.1. *Urbanization in Southeast Asia: percentage of total population in cities with 10,000k or more inhabitants, 1500–1800*

	1500	1600	1700	1800
Southeast Asia	5.9	7.4	5.4	4.6
India		3.9	4.5	4.3
Western Europe	5.8	7.9	9.5	10.2
China	3.8	4.0		3.8
Japan	3.5	6.1	12.0	13.3

Sources: SEA and India: Buringh (2016); Western Europe and China: Maddison (2007); Japan: Bassino et al. (2015).

of monetization in the period 1500 to 1800 was unprecedented. The import of bullion led to the emergence of silver currencies, a reduction of barter and a slow but consistent change from in-kind to cash taxation of both trade and agriculture (Lieberman 1990, pp. 83–84).

Copper cash (*picis*) from China was the most important means of exchange in most parts of Southeast Asia in the fifteenth and early sixteenth centuries. These little coins had a small hole in the centre to allow the creation of strings of coins. After the Chinese imperial ban on trade to the south was lifted in 1567, Southeast Asia was flooded with Chinese copper cash. Nonetheless, occasional shortages of copper cash led to the spread of tin and lead coins, as those metals were more readily available in the region. Reid (1993a, p. 99) suggests that in the 1630s, around 800 million lead-tin *picis* were circulating among 10 million people in the archipelago, 'enough for most parts of society to become familiar with monetary transactions'. The degree of monetization was even higher in Cochin-China (southern Vietnam), an area with two million people where over 200 million coins were circulating (ibid., p. 100). The VOC preferred copper coinage and from the 1720s to the 1790s, it sent about 15 million copper coins to Java annually. Taking into account the re-export of these coins to other areas in the archipelago, wearing down, and Javanese demographic developments, the number of Dutch coins (*duiten*) per capita increased impressively in the second half of the eighteenth century from about 10 million in the 1730s to around 90 million in the 1790s (Feenstra 2014, p. 170).

These copper coins were crucial for smaller, everyday transactions and the growth of the supply of these coins hints at a growing degree of commercialization (as suggested by Feenstra 2014, p. 153), yet for larger international transactions, gold and silver were more important. Gold coins (*mas*) from Aceh and Makassar circulated in the early seventeenth century, but the inflow of silver from Japan and Spanish America after 1570 clearly led to the rise in importance of silver coins. It was the silver Spanish *real* that dominated as the main international currency in the seventeenth and eighteenth centuries. The amount of silver circulating increased threefold (or more) between the early 1590s and the late 1630s (Reid 1993a, p. 103). The influx of bullion may have been less spectacular from then until the early eighteenth century, but must have increased again, and reached even higher levels, with the rise of exports from the 1720s onwards (in line with silver exports from Latin America).

On the mainland, a similar trend of long-term monetization can be discerned. Lieberman (1993, pp. 502–504) provides telling figures of increased monetization in Burma. Records show that whereas in the fifteenth century, over 60 per cent of all sales of land were based on goods payments or a combination of goods and currency payments, between 1750 to 1830 almost all land sales were concluded in silver money. In addition, the percentage of tax paid in coin increased from just over 20 per cent in the period 1350–1550 to 70 per cent in the second half of the eighteenth century. In Ayutthaya, Reid notes the rise of coinage in the fifteenth century, and in Cambodia (Angkor) the minting of gold and silver coins in the early sixteenth century. In late seventeenth-century Ayutthaya, it had become possible for those eligible to perform *corvée* to pay off these obligations using cash (or goods) (Lieberman 2003, pp. 298–301). The eighteenth-century Nguyen government in Vietnam began to remunerate labour obligations and was 'accepting cash for certain in-kind taxes' (ibid., p. 417).

As will be discussed later, this monetization and commercialization also pushed political integration between 1500 and 1800.

Economic Growth and Living Standards

The increase in monetization and commercialization could have led to economic growth and rising standards of living (Feenstra 2014). Growth in the total export of cash crops had to be matched by a similar rise in the production, as well as a rise in the people engaged in the production, of these crops. Different commodities were associated with different modes of production and the production mode of one crop could change over time. In general, as labour was scarce in early modern Southeast Asia, some degree of coercion was often involved in the production of these cash crops. In addition, Reid (1993a) has argued that when new products were exported from Southeast Asia in the eighteenth century, most notably sugar and coffee, these were plantation crops and largely managed by Europeans and Chinese and that Southeast Asians benefitted little from the export of these products. We will briefly review the modes of production for the most important export crops before discussing trends in living standards.

Pepper was produced in Sumatra, Borneo and the Malaysian peninsula. Reid (1993b, p. 469) estimated that in these regions, around

10 per cent of the population may have been dependent on the production and sale of pepper for their livelihood – half of them in production and the other half as 'traders, port workers, city-dwellers and dependants of the merchants and officials who drew the largest profit from trade'. Pepper production in the interior of Sumatra was in the hands of 'free' pepper farmers who responded to price incentives (Jacobs 2006): lower pepper prices thus often also resulted in smaller supplies and rulers had little means of forcing farmers into production. In another labour-scarce environment, Banjarmasin (Southeast Borneo), on the other hand, pepper was generally cultivated by slaves (Reid 1993a, p. 35).

Cane sugar was a native crop in Southeast Asia and, as a result of the growth of commercial growth, became one of the major cash crops in southern Vietnam, Siam, Cambodia and Java in the seventeenth century (Reid 2015). The VOC came to rely solely on sugar produced in Java, predominantly in the area immediately south of Batavia. Here, the field work was partially done by Javanese seasonal (free) wage labourers (the so-called *bujangs*) and partially recruited labour by paying village heads a recruitment fee (Bosma 2013, p. 15). The refining of sugar had to be done immediately after harvesting, which was entirely in the hands of the Chinese. The sugar mills in Southeast Asia employed Chinese capital and methods of refining, as well as animal power, but also significant amounts of labour. It was estimated that a sugar plantation in Java employed some 200 people, some 140 Javanese in addition to 60 Chinese migrants. According to Nagtegaal (1996) many higher VOC officials had invested in the sugar industry in Java. Sugar production for the world market was thus a business that combined international capital and expertise with local unskilled labour. Sugar was to become the region's most important export crop in the nineteenth century (Reid 2015, p. 79).

Coffee production in Southeast Asia started in Java, in the Preanger region south of Batavia. The VOC left the production and transport of coffee to the local Javanese rulers (the *bupati*, or regents) who were paid a fixed price for the amounts of coffee delivered. The *bupati*, in turn, forced local farmers to plant the coffee. Whereas in the early eighteenth century the purchase price paid for coffee was considerable, this was drastically lowered in 1730: from 40 to 11.5 cents per Dutch *pond*. Over the course of the eighteenth century, the VOC increased their hold over coffee production and by the end of the eighteenth century, production was done by the Javanese with direct supervision of VOC servants.

Nutmeg trees, that produced both mace and nutmeg, grew only on the Banda Islands in the Moluccas. By 1621, the VOC had killed or expelled almost the entire indigenous population and transformed the Banda Islands into a plantation colony: the nutmeg trees were divided among 70 plantations that were leased to the plantation holders – former VOC servants who had served out their contract. These plantations were worked by 20 to 30 slaves from different parts of the Moluccas. In contrast, the production of cloves in Ambon was left to the indigenous population. Ambonese families planted cloves on their own plots of land, alongside their subsistence crops. Through village chiefs, the cloves were sold to the VOC and from the proceeds they could buy some luxuries like Indian cloth (Jacobs 2006). The different organization of production of these crops would have different consequences for the economic and social developments of these territories.

The growth of these exports may thus have increased the amount of both forced and free labour engaged in this production. As interest rates were high and capital markets thin (Boomgaard 2009, p. 68), generally little capital investment was made in modes of production and all the extra output had to be generated by increased amounts of land and labour. The growth of small denomination coinage may also indicate the growth of the free wage labour market (Lucassen 2007; Feenstra 2014). Population growth in this period may have increased the amount of labour per square mile, but even in relatively densely populated Java, labour remained scarce until at least the late nineteenth century (De Zwart and Van Zanden 2015). This growth of labour demand may have created a dual development in living standards: those peasants with subsistence plots liable to service obligations most likely saw their *corvée* duties increase at the expense of their own subsistence production or leisure, while those who were free to sell their labour or their crops on the market may have increased their monetary incomes (those with plots of land could, of course, also use these incomes to buy themselves out of their labour obligations).

How do these developments relate to what we know about trends in income and well-being in Southeast Asia in this period? According to Reid, Southeast Asians had a relatively high standard of well-being until 1600 as their 'lives were no more squalid, their health no more wretched and their physical stature no worse than those of eighteenth-century Europeans' (Reid 1993b, pp. 503–504). Southeast Asians were roughly as tall as Europeans, since travellers declared them as 'being of "average" height'. Reid furthermore stresses that he could not find any evidence of famine, starvation or misery in the accounts of early European travellers (as was the case for India and China), and gives examples of wages around 1600 that were on average 25 times the daily rice requirements of one person (Reid 1988, p. 130).[6] However, as a result of the seventeenth-century crisis, standards of well-being were declining over the early modern period. This is confirmed by Boomgaard (1990), who finds a declining trend in the real wages in Java between 1600 and 1780.

The first GDP estimates for Southeast Asia stem from 1820. There is a difference in levels between the various Southeast Asian regions. Insular Southeast Asia, mainly Malaysia and the Philippines, had the highest income per capita of around $600, while mainland Vietnam and Burma were on the lower end of the income scale, closer to $500 (Bolt and Van Zanden 2014). However, considering Lieberman's (1990, 2009) work on the mainland, suggesting relatively high agricultural productivity allowing higher levels of centralization (discussed in the next section), it may have been the case that per capita incomes there were in fact on a par with, or even higher than, those in the archipelago. Compared with Europe, per capita incomes in Southeast Asia were relatively low.

Such figures are, of course, tentative and should be combined with other indicators of economic development and well-being. All the more so, as the distribution of the gains from trade was highly skewed and favoured the elites (Williamson 2015). Spurred by the debate over the 'Great Divergence', some new evidence on other indicators has come to light. Recent work on real wages in Java confirms stagnation, or decline, in purchasing power in the later seventeenth and early eighteenth centuries, but finds a growth in the second half of the eighteenth century (De Zwart and Van Zanden 2015). Viewed in a global perspective, urban free labourers in Java had high real wages compared with those in China and India, even if they did not reach the high wage levels of north-western Europe.

Human heights can also be seen as an indicator of the well-being of people. Whereas Reid suggested that Southeast Asians and Europeans were of equal height during the age of commerce, a recent anthropometric study shows a significant gap at the end of the eighteenth century. Quantitative data on heights in Southeast Asia are available only for Indonesia and start in the 1770s, suggesting increases from an average height of 158.2 cm for men born in that decade to 160.3 cm for those born in 1840. For this decade, there are also estimates available for Cambodia, Malaysia and Vietnam (Baten and Blum 2014), suggesting heights in the range of 157–161.5 cm, which is significantly below those in north-western Europe and China.

That Javanese were shorter than the Chinese, while real wages there were higher, demonstrates the importance of using a variety of indicators to come to definite conclusions about living standards, as they measure different dimensions of the standard of living. They also reflect living standards of different social classes. The study on Indonesian heights used data on the adult heights of slaves in Batavia (Baten et al. 2013), while the study on real wages was concerned with 'free' wage labourers in the urban areas of Java; wage labourers probably had higher living standards than slaves. While both groups may have been minorities in Java, we would argue that the living standards of wage labourers are the more representative indicator, as wage labour provides a viable alternative to small-scale farming – the activity of the majority of the Javanese population – and slavery does not.

Reviewing this evidence of wages, heights and income in the light of the earlier sketched trends on global commerce, it is likely that there was a slight upward trend over the entire period. However, as the benefits of trade were unequally dispersed, and as the growth of trade outpaced the growth in well-being, it most likely increased inequality (Williamson 2015).

Political Centralization

The period between 1500 and 1800 was a period of political centralization in Southeast Asia, although more so on the mainland than in the archipelago. In the fifteenth century, the region as a whole was characterized by political fragmentation: on the mainland there were at least 15 independent kingdoms and empires (Lieberman 1990, p. 79), while there were even more in the archipelago: in north Sumatra alone there were eight kingdoms (Watson Andaya 1993, p. 403). By 1800, the number of kingdoms on the mainland had been reduced to three: Burma, Siam and Vietnam. The archipelago remained more fragmented until colonialism became an important unifying force in the nineteenth and twentieth centuries. These trends were, to an extent, driven by the rise of global trade and European intrusions (Lieberman 1990, 1993; Reid 1993a; Watson Andaya 1993).

Historically, state centralization in the region was hindered as a result of geographical factors (Watson Andaya 1993, pp. 402–407). The region consists of thousands of islands and is home to many dense and uncongenial swamps and jungles as well large mountain chains, which meant that people lived far apart from each other. Despite some pockets of high concentrations of people in the Red River Delta (in northern Vietnam), Java and Bali, the region was characterized by low population densities. Labour scarcity meant that political power was related to control over people rather than land. In order to build a centralized state system, a ruler needed income and manpower, yet if a king taxed his subjects too much, they would simply flee from his kingdom. As the ruler of Palembang noted in 1747: 'it is very easy for a subject to find a lord, but it is much more difficult for a lord to find a subject' (cited in Watson Andaya 1993, p. 441). This situation was not conducive to the rise of strong centralized states.

Nonetheless, over the period 1500–1800, there were trends towards greater territorial expansion and administrative centralization (Watson Andaya 1993, Lieberman 1993, 1995). For the mainland, the influence of European trade on these developments should not be overestimated. The resources wielded by mainland rulers were greater than those of the Europeans, who consequently refrained from employing military power. The potential gains of such risky ventures were limited, because there were no fine spices grown on the mainland. Trends towards territorial consolidation on the mainland were primarily driven by domestic factors: population growth, increased agricultural output and cultural integration (see discussion by Lieberman 1993). At the same time, Lieberman suggests that the rise of commerce and the European trading presence did contribute to these trends. States on the mainland benefitted from rising commerce as the growth of income from maritime trade enhanced their tax revenues. It was much easier for these early modern states to collect taxes on trade than to tap the agricultural resources that were scattered across the interior. Some of these states were also directly engaged in overseas trade (Lieberman 1990, pp. 82–84). The benefits thus reaped were employed for state building and military campaigns. The growing import of bullion aided the process of monetization and commercialization (discussed above),

which further enhanced state capacity as cash taxes are easier to collect and transport than bulk goods like rice. Trade also stimulated the
trends of population growth and growing agricultural production in
the hinterlands due to the growth of demand for certain goods (e.g.
rice, pepper, cotton and timber). Finally, the introduction of European
muskets, cannon and mercenaries in Southeast Asian warfare aided
state building. Just as has been argued for Europe (Tilly 1990; Parker
1988), these new weapons, as well as the defences needed against
them, were very expensive and thus advantaged strong states (with
large tax revenues) over smaller polities. Furthermore, as European
guns were superior to those produced in the region itself, coastal rulers
had an advantage over inland lords (Lieberman 1990, pp. 87–88).

While European involvement may not have done more than aid
trends towards administrative centralization and territorial expansion on the mainland, it was in the archipelago that the impact of
the European presence was most pronounced. Here, some areas came
under the direct control of Europeans: in the Malay peninsula, Melaka
was controlled first by the Portuguese (from 1511 to 1641) and then
by the Dutch (from 1641 to 1825), while in the archipelago the Dutch
came to control significant parts of Java, the Moluccas and Sulawesi,
and the Spanish started to colonize the Philippines in 1599 (see Map
7.1). Furthermore, the Dutch opened various lodges and were heavily
involved in local politics in the rest of the archipelago.

Trends towards political consolidation were less evident in the
archipelago. Geography may have played a role as scattered settlements over different smaller islands were more difficult to control than
the more concentrated settlements in the floodplains and river basins
of the mainland. European presence from the 1500s added to the fragmentation. Reid (1993a, pp. 303–319) argues that the archipelago saw
the same trends towards centralization as the mainland in the sixteenth and early seventeenth century, as demonstrated by the powerful sultanates of Aceh, Banten, Makassar and Mataram and he claims
that these trends were related to those in commerce as a result of the
connections laid out above. Yet with the 'Age of Commerce' brought
to an end by the Dutch (according to Reid), trends towards greater
centralization and the loss of trade incomes rendered these states incapable of running their expanded bureaucracies. Banten and Makassar
fell to the Dutch in the later seventeenth century, while Mataram was
split into two separate sultanates – Yogyakarta and Surakarta – which

became vassals of the Dutch in the mid-eighteenth century. Only Aceh would remain independent until the end of the nineteenth century. While this may have spelled the end of indigenous states, it was countered with the rise of Dutch and Spanish colonial states, which in terms of state consolidation may be compared with the mainland empires (Lieberman 1993, pp. 566–567).

Concluding, we find a process of expansion and consolidation of states in early modern Southeast Asia. As Barbara Watson Andaya (1993, p. 402) noted:

Whereas throughout Southeast Asia the 'states' at the beginning of the sixteenth century only generally approximate those we know today, three hundred years later the current shape of Southeast Asia is clearly discernible.

But this process was not linear and great dynasties and empires rose and fell over this period. Important sultanates in the archipelago fell in the seventeenth century, while the mainland saw major disruptions of state power in the later eighteenth century. Yet on the mainland, the trend towards centralization was already so powerful that they had recovered from fragmentation within decades: three large polities (Burma, Siam and Vietnam) were in firm control by the early nineteenth century. In the archipelago, state centralization took the form of early Dutch and Spanish colonialism in eighteenth-century Java, the Moluccas and the Philippines. In the nineteenth century, European (then including French and British) colonialism would spread across the remainder of Southeast Asia (except Siam) and would have major effects on the region in the nineteenth and twentieth centuries, yet the foundation for this was firmly laid out in the centuries before.

Conclusion

Between 1500 and 1800, Southeast Asia underwent a series of important changes and attained the basic form it would retain to this day. These transformations, we argue, were to an important extent shaped by global interactions. It was the spices of Southeast Asia that set the wheels of global commerce in motion, with important repercussions across the world. The development of Southeast Asia itself was fundamentally affected by this process: it experienced commercial growth and increasing cash crop production and trends towards greater political and cultural consolidation. In various pockets of the peninsula and the archipelago, European colonial powers began to increase their hold over land and labour. In some of these areas, production for the global market came to take place under coercion: through forced deliveries as well as slavery. It was these trends that would continue to characterize Southeast Asian history in the nineteenth and much of the twentieth centuries.

Suggested Reading

Boomgaard, Peter (2009). 'Labour, Land and Capital Markets in Early Modern Southeast Asia from the Fifteenth to the Nineteenth Century', *Continuity and Change* 24, pp. 55–78.
De Zwart, Pim and J.L. van Zanden, (2015). 'Labor, Wages and Living Standards in Java, 1680–1914', *European Review of Economic History* 19, pp. 215–234.
Jacobs, Els M. (2006). *Merchant in Asia: The Trade of the Dutch East India Company During the Eighteenth Century*. Leiden: CNWS Publications.
Knaap, Gerrit (2006). 'All About Money: Maritime Trade in Makassar and West Java around 1775', *Journal of the Economic and Social History of the Orient* 49, pp. 482–508.
Lieberman, Victor (2003–2009). *Strange Parallels. Southeast Asia in Global Context, c. 800–1830.* 2 vols. Cambridge: Cambridge University Press.
Reid, Anthony (1988–1993). *Southeast Asia in the Age of Commerce 1450–1680.* 2 vols. New Haven and London: Yale University Press.
Tarling Nicholas (ed.) (1993). *The Cambridge History of Southeast Asia Vol. 1: From Early Times to c.1800*. Cambridge: Cambridge University Press.

8 | East Asia and the Limits of Globalization

Introduction

China's external trade flourished under the Song dynasty (960–279). Trade was conducted overland via the Silk Road, but already since the tenth century, the focus came to be increasingly on maritime trade. While trade with Japan was particularly buoyant, merchant communities of Chinese were also established across Southeast Asia. Maritime trade provided an important source of revenue for the Song state. In this period, silver and copper flowed out of China in large amounts as a result of the maritime commerce (Wade 2009, 2015). It has been estimated that, by 1100, maritime trade amounted to 1.7 per cent of the total GDP in Song China (Von Glahn 2016, p. 272). The Yuan dynasty (1271–1368) also tried to benefit from growing maritime trade, but they were not equally successful. Foreign trade declined in the late thirteenth and early fouteenth centuries. Trade was further limited under the first Ming Hongwu emperor (r. 1368–1398), who banned private maritime trade. Only in the seventeenth century did China fully re-engage with the world economy.

Global research interest in the long-run development of the Chinese economy has surged in the past few decades. There are at least three relevant debates to deal with. One is about the role East Asia (or Asia in general) played in the world economy of the period. In Wallerstein's (1989) view, Asia was and remained outside the 'world system' that emerged in the 'long' sixteenth century. Trade with Western Europe barely touched the surface of the societies involved and did not fundamentally change the socio-economic structures involved. Only in the nineteenth century, as a result of the advance of modern industrialization with its dramatic consequences for indigenous industries of India and China, did the region become integrated into the world system. In his *ReOrient*, Frank (1998) has turned this picture on its head, by arguing that China was the core (or at least an important part) of an Asian 'world system' and that Europe was the backward, slowly growing part of the world economy: 'Europe did not expand to "incorporate" the rest of the world into its "European world-economy/system". Instead, Europe belatedly joined ... an already existing world economy and system' (Frank 1998, xxiii). He sets out to show that China and India (and other parts of Asia) 'were more active ... and more important parts of the world economy than Europe until about 1800', and that Europe only 'used its American money to buy a ticket on the Asian train' (ibid., xxv).

This leads to the (related) debate about the relative performance of East Asia in the world economy between 1500 and 1800: was China indeed the engine of an 'Asian train', maintaining a high level of prosperity until the early decades of the nineteenth century, as scholars of the California School, and, in even more radical terms, Frank have maintained? There clearly were periods of stability and growth. The 'silver century' between 1550 and 1630 saw the best years of the Ming dynasty; the eighteenth century has a similar reputation for the Qing dynasty. But were underlying trends 'up' or 'down'? And, more appropriate for the subject of this book: how did China interact with the world market in periods of growth and stability? Did it become more integrated into the world economy? Did commercial relations between Japan and China intensify? The optimistic interpretation of the California School, and in particular Pomeranz's seminal book on *The Great Divergence* (2000), has kick-started a debate about these long-term trends in the Chinese economy that has at least nuanced these views. Recent research that set out to quantify these trends suggests that China was not the intensely dynamic economy that, for example, Frank sketched so vividly.

A third, again related, debate is about the, arguably, most problematic link between the Chinese economy and the world market: the large-scale import of silver. China in this period has been described as a 'silver junk'. When silver was easily available such as in the period 1550–1630 – first from Japan, and after 1570 also from Spanish America – and again between about 1690 and 1800, the demand for money could be satisfied and the economy boomed. But when silver was in short supply – after 1630 and in particular after 1800 (when Spanish American silver production fell dramatically) – this resulted in intense economic problems, which had dramatic social and political repercussions. This 'silver connection' was the most important link between the world market and the Chinese economy. But what explains this dramatic weakness? Why did a sharp reduction in silver imports almost automatically result in economic depression and social unrest? And was this link so strong – was China indeed a 'silver junk', or is the story more nuanced?

The Chinese dependence on silver imports for its money supply illustrates that even the largest and arguably strongest economy in Asia developed very close ties with the world market, and became subject to some of the forces of early modern globalization. Japan is a different story, however, as we will see below. No country in the world managed to remain 'outside' the world market so successfully between the early 1600s and 1854, and no non-European country developed so dynamically in this period. But was this long-term success related to its policy of isolation? Before we delve into these discussions later in the chapter, we will provide some basic information on the histories of these states, as well as sketch the long-term evolution of both economies.

Centralized States

East Asia was in many ways different from many of the regions that we have visited so far. Strong, centralized states had emerged there, which were (on land) far stronger than the forces that could be mobilized by European states. China, Japan, as well as Korea, remained by and large independent from foreign influences and developed policies to keep the world market at arm's length. China had turned more inward looking and had restrained international trade after the great voyages of Admiral Zheng He, and only definitely lifted those policies at the end of the seventeenth century when the Qing dynasty was stabilized. But for Europeans, access to China remained largely confined to one port city, Guangzhou (known as Canton by the Europeans – which we use in the remainder of this text), in the south. Japan travelled the opposite road and became from almost entirely open to foreign trade and ideas in the sixteenth century to almost fully closed after the consolidation of the Tokugawa regime in the 1630s. Korea, under the Chosŏn dynasty, became similarly inward looking and isolated in trying to regain stability after the Japanese invasions of the late sixteenth century and the Chinese invasions in the first decades of the seventeenth century (Deuchler 1997). In this section we discuss these states and their fiscal system, as this crucially influenced their relation with the world market.

Since as early as the tenth century, much of China, and in particular the area often referred to as 'China proper' (the south-eastern part of China, below the Great Wall of China), has been under almost constant unified rule (Brandt et al. 2014, p. 62). While some have suggested that lack of competition may have played a part in China's long-term economic stagnation (e.g. Ferguson 2011), others have argued that the empire provided stability and an institutional framework in which private property was protected and markets functioned effectively (Pomeranz 2000; Ma 2012). In the period covered by this book, 1500–1800, China was ruled by two dynasties: the Ming and the Qing. Despite relative constancy in the rule over China over the early modern period, there was almost constant warfare: Debin Ma (2012) notes between 200 and 250 incidences of warfare in the sixteenth and seventeenth centuries. Nomadic hordes and other peoples beyond the Great Wall were a continuous source of instability. In 1644, after over two decades of fighting, one of these northern peoples, the Jurchen, or Manchus, conquered Beijing and established the last imperial dynasty of China: the Qing – which lasted until 1917.

The Chinese emperors, with their 'heavenly mandate to rule', commanded absolute power, which was limited only by the capacity of the bureaucracy to levy taxes, the emperor's limited ability to monitor the bureaucracy and the inclination of the population to rise up if they felt that their livelihoods were threatened by excessive taxation (which occurred regularly; Ma 2013). The bulk of the imperial revenue consisted of land taxes: at the end of the eighteenth century, some 70–90 per cent of the total. The remaining 10–30 per cent consisted of salt revenues, custom duties on both internal and external trade and a number of miscellaneous taxes (Vries 2015; Yuping 2016, p. 168). Under the Ming, most of these taxes had been in grain (Von Glahn 2016, p. 309), yet by the later eighteenth century the tax system had become highly monetized, as 80 per cent of the revenue was levied in silver, while the remainder consisted of grain tributes (Ma and Rubin 2016, p. 6). Tax rates were rather low – generally below 10 per cent of output (Wong 2012, p. 356) – and the Ming government was 'chronically underfunded' (Von Glahn 2016, p. 309). The situation did not improve after the Qing takeover, as, despite the large expansion of territory (see Map 8.1) and rapid growth of the population (see next

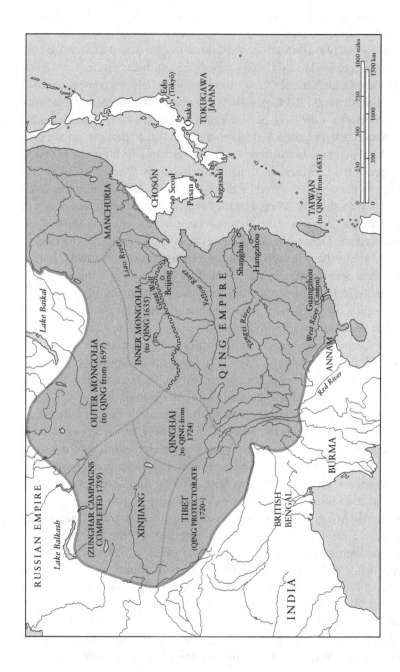

Map 8.1 East Asia in the seventeenth and eighteenth centuries
Source: Holcombe (2017, p. 182).

section), overall revenues were fairly stable over the seventeenth and eighteenth centuries. The tax rate per person expressed in grams of silver declined from 7 grams in the second half of the seventeenth century, to 4.2 grams a century later (Ma 2013, p. 489). To compare: in England and the Dutch Republic, the tax rate per person was 40 times that level; between 158 and 171 grams of silver in the late eighteenth century. This suggests an increasingly limited capacity of the Qing government to raise taxes, possibly as a result of rampant corruption at various levels of the bureaucracy. Even at its peak, the Qing government had about 70 million *taels* in its reserves, which was only about 3–5 per cent of total GDP (Ma and Rubin 2016, p. 11). Furthermore, most part of the revenue was generated by inelastic land taxes while a large part of expenditure was related to matters of security, which could be highly variable (rising sharply in the face of a large-scale rebellion). As we shall see below, this meant that Chinese imperial finances were vulnerable to crises resulting in such a sudden rise of expenditure, or an abrupt decline in silver income. The fortunes of the dynasty were therefore tied to the importation of silver and the ability to levy duties on external trade.

In 1600, Tokugawa Ieyasu won the Battle of Sekigahara and became de facto ruler over all of Japan (Hayami 2004, p. 2). This event and the consequent proclamation of Ieyasu as *shogun* in 1603 marked the end of a long period of violence known as the *Sengoku* – Warring States – era which lasted throughout the entire fifteenth century. Ieyasu and his successors would rule a unified Japan for 268 years, until the Meiji Restoration of 1868. Like in China, land taxes formed the bulk of government revenue of the *bakufu* (the Shogunate). While Japan was to some extent monetized, all land values were expressed, and taxes were generally levied, in *koku* of rice, which made it less dependent on silver. Revenue raised from foreign trade was probably limited as a result of the *sakoku* policy. The *sakoku* – 'closed country' – policy operated in Japan from the 1630s onwards, and was motivated by the Shogunate's desire to close off the island from unwanted external influences, most notably Christianity, and to limit the danger of the *daimyo* – feudal lords – receiving foreign support in case of rebellion (Francks 2016). Considering the long history of civil war, such a fear was not ungrounded.

While the Chinese state was, of course, much larger in absolute terms, a recent study has shown that the amount of tax revenue per person was significantly higher in Japan than in China (Sng and Moriguchi 2014). Official tax rates on agricultural production fluctuated at around 35 per cent of the total output (Oguchi 2004, p. 199). Expressed in kg of rice, the per capita annual tax around 1700 stood at 45 and 24 in Japan and China, respectively.[1] Due to the decline in Chinese per capita taxes (discussed above) this gap increased over time, whereas the amount of taxes in China was about half that of Japan in the late seventeenth century, they constituted one-third of the Japanese level around 1800 (Sng and Moriguchi 2014). Japan's greater stability – there were no more armed uprisings in Tokugawa Japan after the Shimabara until 1856[2] – meant that Japanese finances were in much better condition than those in China and therefore less vulnerable to outside forces (Sng and Moriguchi 2014). As Geoffrey Parker (2013, p. 497) observed: 'whereas Europe knew only four years of *peace* during the seventeenth century, China knew none, Tokugawa Japan knew only four years of war (and none at all after 1638).'

The Chosŏn dynasty in Korea was founded by Taejo (r. 1392–98) at the end of the fourteenth century and lasted over an impressive five centuries (until the annexation of the Korean empire by the Japanese in 1910) (Deuchler 1997, p. 299). Seong Ho Jun et al. (2008, p. 250) describe Chosŏn Korea as a *laissez-faire* state that 'provided infrastructure to support production, was quick to extend tax relief, and held dear, as the highest ideal of public good, a skilled and honest bureaucracy'. Yet its financial base was probably substantially thinner than both of its neighbours, although reliable overall estimates are lacking. Government revenue was initially highly dependent on tribute, while the land tax was the second most important source of income. The rate of the land tax was much lower than in Japan, and even lower than in China – between 5 and 7 per cent of output (Palais 1996, pp. 324, 851). All of this suggests that the Korean government was small and vulnerable to peasant uprisings (Jun et al. 2008, p. 250). In terms of international trade, Chosŏn entered a long period of relative isolation, which was strengthened by Confucian ideology (Lee and Temin 2010, p. 565). Besides the tribute missions to Beijing, there was some trade along the northern border with Manchuria. The Japan–Korea trade was confined to the southern port of Pusan and a monopoly on this trade was granted to the *daimyo* of Tsushima – an island situated between Japan and Korea. All private trade was conducted by Japanese ships and there was no direct trade with Europeans.

Thus, in contrast to most other parts of the globe, relatively strong states meant that they were able to keep the world market at a comfortable distance; the states themselves were heavily involved in regulating trade flows. Only in the nineteenth century would these countries have to yield to the might of American and European gunboats forcing them to open up to the world economy on terms that were favourable to Westerners.

Large Economies

The states we find in this part of the world were rooted in developed market economies. Sixteenth-century Ming China witnessed a 'commercial revolution' during its 'silver century'; the state (which had been very influential during the early Ming) withdrew from direct involvement and increasingly relied on the market to take care of production and distribution. This had strong positive effects on the economy: agriculture flourished, small market towns boomed, and cities expanded again. After a difficult transition, the Qing continued these policies. A similar transition towards a commercial economy occurred in seventeenth-century Japan, although in this case without the stimulating effect of international trade. The Osaka region became the economic powerhouse of the Tokugawa state, as the Yangtze delta was the economic core of the Chinese economy, while the Seoul region was the most dynamic part of the Korean economy.

Demography

What these three societies had in common was that these were, by the standards of the period, large states and economies, boasting significant populations. Demographic estimates for early modern East Asia are obviously subject to some margin of error (see Brandt et al. 2014, Gruber 2014, Jun et al. 2008). Based on many decades of research into government census data and family genealogies, the following trends can be sketched, even if we should take them with a grain of salt.

In 1500, the population of China was about 100 million, or almost one-quarter of the entire population of the world; it increased dramatically to 380 million in 1820, close to 40 per cent of the global total (Maddison 2003). China's rapid population growth was made possible only by the rapid adoption of New World crops, like maize and

potatoes (Flynn and Giraldez 2004; Nunn and Qian 2011). Perhaps
Maddison's (2003) estimates, that we use here, are somewhat too high
for China in 1820, but even taking into account some margin of error,
it is clear that, in terms of population, it was many times larger than
any other country in the world. Japan was much smaller, of course, but
still counted some 10.5 million inhabitants in 1450. The population
consequently rose rapidly in the sixteenth and seventeenth centuries to
28 million in 1700 and grew much more slowly to just over 30 million
around 1800 (Bassino et al. 2015),[3] making it of a similar size to the
largest European country: France. Korea's population stood at roughly
10 million around 1500 and increased to 18.6 million in the early
nineteenth century (Jun et al. 2008), making its population base substantially larger than Spain and England. Demographic expansion was
particularly rapid from the fourth decade of the seventeenth century, as
the population recovered from a series of wars with the Japanese and
Chinese, but was relatively stable over most of the eighteenth century. It
is in any case obvious that over the entire early modern period, the East
Asian population constituted between 30 to 40 per cent of the entire
world population. So, in terms of simple population numbers, East Asia
was the centre of the world – and only India with its 200 million people
at the end of the eighteenth century was a serious competitor.

These societies have often been characterized as Malthusian societies suffering from high population pressures (e.g. Chao 1986; Gruber
2014). Another interpretation is, of course, that population growth is
a sign of prosperity and human well-being: resulting from lower death
rates and higher longevity (e.g. Lee and Fang 2001; Hanley 1997).
Bassino et al. (2015) suggest an increase in arable land in Japan due to
Tokugawa land reclamation programmes. Nonetheless, average population densities increased from 690 to 800 people per square km of
arable land in the period 1600–1800. In China, population growth
was also greater than increases in arable land and population densities increased from about 83 per square km around 1700 to 194 per
square km in 1812. In Korea, population density in 1800 was possibly
around 500 people per square km.[4] This number had increased from
the sixteenth century because the population had increased but the
amount of arable land remained roughly the same (Lee 1997). To compare these numbers, this figure stood at 134 people per square km of
total land area in early seventeenth-century England.[5] This means that
pressure on the land in Japan and Korea was very large indeed. Were

the high and increasing population/land ratios pushing down living standards? How did incomes develop during this period of population growth? And how does this relate to the international economy.

Economic Development and Standards of Living

China and Japan had all the ingredients for successful economic performance: stable institutions, highly developed market economies, high levels of human capital, a very productive agriculture based on rice cultivation, and a large, dynamic urban sector. China was the economic engine of the region long before 1500, and continued to form its core region after that date, but its economy showed signs of long-term stagnation. There are no reliable, detailed estimates of the development of GDP per capita, but there are many recent attempts to chart its development path, which we will discuss below. Perhaps the only thing that seems to be certain is that China was more wealthy than the global average in 1500, and poorer than this in 1820 – a 'reversal of fortune' that still is in need of a convincing explanation. Japan, relatively backward in 1500 and 1600, did much better, and showed remarkable GDP growth during the seventeenth and eighteenth centuries. Korea's level of economic development was lagging behind both Japan and China, and there was probably almost no growth over the eighteenth century.

One of the most contentious issues raised in the Great Divergence debate was the relative level of GDP per capita in China in the eighteenth and early nineteenth centuries. Pomeranz (2000) argued that there was no substantial gap in welfare between China and Europe as a whole, a hypothesis which has led to much detailed research in recent years. One approach to this issue was to reconstruct the development of the real wage of urban, unskilled labourers. Allen et al. (2011) have shown that in the eighteenth century, real wages in China (Suzhou, Canton, Beijing) were indeed much lower than in London or Amsterdam, but that the gap with the rest of Europe was relatively small or absent. Real wages in Japan (Kyoto and Tokyo) were even lower in the middle of the eighteenth century, and often below the 'subsistence minimum' defined in these studies (the bare-bones basket of consumption goods necessary for a family to survive). Around 1800, Chinese and Japanese real wages were on a par. For Korea, we currently do not have estimates of welfare ratios, but there are series on wages and rice prices from the late sixteenth century. Myung Soo Cha (2009) combined evidence on market and public-sector wages and rice prices and suggests that wages declined over the entire seventeenth and eighteenth centuries. Wages were probably at their highest in the early seventeenth century, due to labour shortages resulting from the population losses of the wars with Japan (1592–1598) and China (1627–1637).[6] After that, wages fell from over 6 kg of rice in the 1690s to around 4 kg in the early nineteenth century. Another recent study by Jun and Lewis (2004) shows both silver wages and rice prices and puts these in a comparative perspective. These figures suggest that at the end of the eighteenth century, Korean unskilled wages could pay for some 2.2 kg of rice (a slightly lower estimate than that by Cha), which was comparable to the rice wage in China and the grain wage in the European periphery (Italy).

In their paper, Allen et al. (2011) focused on the period after 1738, and did not take into account observations before that year. If we include these as well, we see that real wages declined sharply during the eighteenth century in Beijing and in particular in Suzhou (observations for Canton only start in 1741) (Figure 8.1). If we follow the real

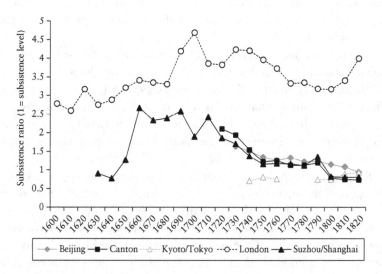

Figure 8.1 Real wages in China and Japan (compared with London), 1600–1850
Source: Allen et al. (2011)

wages of Suzhou back in time to the middle decades of the seventeenth century, we see low real wages before the final years of the dynasty (which were characterized by rampant inflation), a very sharp rise of the real wage starting in the mid-1650s – resulting in very high real wages in the 1670s and 1680s (years of sharp deflation) – and then a declining trend which results in real wages close to the subsistence minimum after the middle of the eighteenth century.

It is difficult to interpret this development of Chinese real wages in the long run. Was the level we find in the 1640s and after the 1740s – close to the bare-bones minimum – the 'normal' level, and were real wages between the 1650s and 1730s 'temporarily' out of equilibrium due to population decline and chaos resulting from the violent Ming–Qing transition, during which perhaps as much as one-third of the population died and the Chinese population level declined accordingly, and/or sharp deflation due to the falling supply of silver from abroad and Qing policies which stabilized the currency after the inflation of the 1640s? Richard Von Glahn, the expert on Chinese monetary history, has described the second half of the seventeenth century as 'a prolonged depression during which deflation spread throughout the economy' (1996a, p. 212), and silver scarcity was one of the causes of this trend. As a contemporary, T'ang Chen, observed:

More than fifty years have passed since the founding of the Qing dynasty, and the empire grows poorer each day. Farmers are destitute, artisans are destitute, merchants are destitute, and officials too are destitute. Grain is cheap, yet it is hard to eat one's fill. Cloth is cheap, yet it is hard to cover one's skin.[7]

Symbolically, this period ended with the opening of Chinese ports for international trade in 1685; one of the explicit aims of this move was to increase the inflow of silver to reduce the 'silver famine'.

This still leaves open the question of how to interpret the very high real wages in south China during the 'prolonged depression' between 1660 and 1690. If we take these estimates seriously, and interpret the high real wages between 1660 and 1740 as more than an incident, the gap in real wage levels between the North Sea area and southern China only opens up in the early decades of the eighteenth century, as can be seen by comparison with the London real wage series. Real wages are only one component of real income, and their representativeness is still the subject of debate. The Chinese labour market was probably less 'deep' and 'wide' than that of Western Europe; estimates suggest that only a small per cent of the labour force was involved in wage labour, whereas in Western Europe this share was probably much higher – up to 50 per cent in the North Sea area (Van Zanden 2009). Similarly, the extent of the Japanese labour market was relatively small, and concentrated in cities, while in rural areas the labour market functioned to satisfy the seasonal demands of agriculture as the Tokugawa economy generally relied on family labour (Saito 2009). The Korean labour market was dominated by widespread *corvée* labour for the state as well as slave labour: about a third of the population consisted of slaves (Cha 2009, p. 1140).[8] Real wages may therefore not be representative for real incomes in the economy at large.

Estimates of GDP per capita are probably more suitable for charting long-term economic development, but these require much more data – or much more assumptions to substitute for missing data. There are two recent attempts to quantify China's GDP for this period (shown in Figure 8.2), which use historical data to make inferences concerning economic growth. Figure 8.2 shows both of these estimates. The study by Broadberry, Guan and Li (2014) ('China 1' in Figure 8.2)

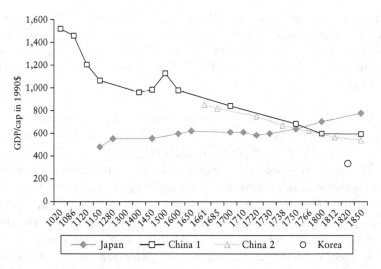

Figure 8.2 GDP per capita in East Asia, 1020–1850
Sources: Japan: Bassino et al. (2015); China 1: Broadberry et al. (2014); China 2: Yi et al.(2015); Korea: Bolt and Van Zanden (2014).

also covers the Ming and Song periods, and shows a dramatic long-run decline, from over $1,500 around 1000, to $1,127 in 1500 via $977 in 1600 and down to $597 in 1800. As usual, the quality of the underlying data does not improve when going back in time, so the precise extent and timing of Chinese decline is still unclear, but these estimates at least suggest that that real incomes were trending downward in the long run.[9] The second (and more detailed) trend in GDP ('China 2' in Figure 8.2) by Yi et al. (2015) focuses on the Qing period, and shows that estimated GDP per capita declined similarly over the seventeenth and eighteenth centuries – a total decline of 40 per cent in 150 years. Both these estimates for the level of GDP per capita at the start of the nineteenth century fit rather well with the more detailed comparison of the structure and size of GDP in two highly developed 'regions', the Yangtze delta and the Netherlands in the 1820s by Bozhong Li and Van Zanden (2012). They find that GDP per capita in the Netherlands was about 85 per cent higher than in the Yangtze delta, a gap that is completely due to the much lower productivity of industry and services as, in agriculture, Chinese productivity was on a par with that in the most developed parts of Western Europe (see also Li 2012; Allen 2009a).

A decline of GDP per capita by 40 to 50 per cent is a dramatic story, almost unheard of in economic history (by comparison, northern Italy, the most spectacular example of decline in Europe in the same period, saw its GDP per capita fall by 22 per cent between 1400 and 1800). Agricultural productivity in output per worker as well as output per land, while on a high level in the seventeenth and eighteenth centuries, did not improve over time (Allen 2009a).[10] Estimates of the urbanization rate, perhaps the best proxy of the level of economic development in the early modern period, point in the same direction, however. Between 1200 and 1600 China was among the most urbanized countries in the world, with about 4 per cent of its population living in large cities; in the Yangtze delta this share was about double the national average (Yi, Van Leeuwen and Van Zanden 2015). After that urbanization stagnated. When including smaller cities of 2,000 inhabitants (or more) in the analysis, the stagnation and decline becomes more evident. Whereas around 1600 the percentage of population living in smaller cities had been 12 per cent, this changed during the Qing, and in 1776 this figure had fallen to 7 per cent, at which level it more or less remained until about 1900. There were a number of reasons for this decline: the share of port cities in total urban population fell, in particular in the Yangtze delta, possibly as a result of the limitations on international trade (which were, however, lifted during the period of de-urbanization).

The share of the capital city in total population also declined; during the Song and the Ming the capital city was about the same size (1 million inhabitants) as during the Qing, but the total population was much larger in the latter dynasty. This may be related to the declining capability of the Chinese state to raise taxes (see also Brandt et al. 2014). The stagnation and decline in the urbanization ratio also seems to run parallel with the long-term fall in GDP per capita.

The story of Chinese stagnation, if not long-run decline, is dramatic. The contrast with Japan is extreme: the available estimates of GDP per capita suggest a clear upward trend from $554 in 1450 to $641 in 1800 (further moving up to $681 in 1850, when Japan had clearly surpassed the Chinese level) (Bolt and Van Zanden 2014; Bassino et al. 2015). An important part of this growth came from increased agricultural output; as the pressure on land increased, agricultural production intensified and increased output per worker and hectare of arable land. This growth was probably the result of increased working time on the land per worker, 'self-exploitation' – as Akira Hayami (2010) notes – advances in the quality of the land, more use of fertilizer, and greater crop diversification (Miyamoto 2004, p. 43). Fixed taxes provided an incentive for the peasants because all increases in production accrued to them (Iwahashi 2004, p. 100).

At the same time, the level of urbanization doubled from about 6 per cent in 1600 to 12 per cent in 1700, after which it stabilized. With about 700,000 inhabitants in 1700, the capital of Tokyo (then Edo) was by far the largest city, but the commercial metropolis of Osaka was second-best, with almost 400,000 people. The duality between the north-eastern capital and the commercial south-west nicely illustrates the complexity of Japan's development, characterized by a big state and a growing commercial community. This is confirmed by more qualitative evidence: under the Tokugawa, Japan developed into a 'market economy' – an 'economic society' is the term used by Hayami (2004) for the changes observed: markets had spread and developed, monetization ensued and domestic trade flourished, allowing a greater division of labour. Human capital formation also increased strongly, as is for example evident from the rapid growth of book production and consumption in the seventeenth and eighteenth centuries (Van Zanden 2009) and a decreasing skill premium (Saito 1978). By looking at indicators of physical well-being – heights and longevity – and elements of material culture – housing, furniture and clothing – Susan

Hanley (1997) suggests that the standard of living of the Japanese improved over the seventeenth and eighteenth centuries. In addition, this may have led to decreased inequality as the income of *samurai* did not improve to a similar extent (Hanley 1997).

No recent attempts have appeared to estimate long-term trends of GDP for Korea, beyond Maddison's (2007) guestimate for the 1820s of $335, suggesting it was likely the poorest of the three societies. There is some debate on the trends in Korean economic development over the seventeenth and eighteenth centuries. Whereas Jun et al. (2008, 2009), mainly on the basis of commodity prices, suggest that the seventeenth century can be seen as a period of economic growth resulting from growing agricultural productivity as observed from low and stable food prices, the eighteenth century was an era of stagnation and the nineteenth century showed decline. Cha (2009) on the other hand suggests that Korean productivity declined from the later seventeenth century onwards, as suggested by trends in rents and wages, while Hochol Lee (1997) suggests growing agricultural productivity until the late eighteenth century and decline thereafter. We tend to side with Jun et al. (2008), as they reasonably argue that the trends in factor prices shown by Cha (2009) are not indicative of trends in the markets, while trends in the commodity prices probably are. Lee (1997) is unable to show whether rising agricultural productivity kept pace with population growth. Seoul was the only large city in Korea and grew from some 125,000 inhabitants in 1500 to 200,000 around 1650, but after that the size of the city stagnated and even slightly declined to about 188,000 inhabitants in 1800 (Buringh 2016). This corroborates the eighteenth-century stagnation thesis. When we include the information on other cities, we can sketch trends in urbanization between 1500 and 1800 and, consistent with what we know about levels of development from wages and the GDP estimate for the early 1800s, urbanization rates were somewhat lower in Korea than in the other East Asian countries (Table 8.1).

As noted above, all these figures should be taken with a grain of salt, as the estimates are dependent on imperfect data, refer to unrepresentative groups, or were based on a multitude of assumptions. Nonetheless, as the estimates of three different studies suggest more or less similar levels and trends (in the case of GDP for China) and the trends in different indicators point in the same direction (for Japan and Korea), we may have some confidence in the overall picture sketched.

Table 8.1. *Urbanization in East Asia: percentage of total population in cities with 10,000 or more inhabitants, 1500–1800*

	1500	1600	1700	1800
China	3.8	4.0		3.8
Japan	3.5	6.1	12.0	13.3
Korea	2.1	2.9	4.8	3.6
W. Europe	5.8	7.9	9.5	10.2

Sources: Western Europe, China: Maddison (2007); Korea: Buringh (2016); Japan: Bassino et al. (2015).

China was in long-term decline – stagnant urbanization, declining real wages and GDP/cap – during the Ming and Qing, while Japan experienced slow but persistent economic growth as evidenced by various indicators. Korea probably had the lowest levels of economic development in this period – possibly showed growth over the seventeenth century and stagnated in the eighteenth.

Our focus in this book is on the effects of the world market on these developments. First, we will review the case of China and ask the question whether its relative decline was related to its complex interaction with the world market. Next, we will look at Japan and discuss the reverse question; was its success due to its successful isolation from world trade?

Interaction with the Global Market

American Silver and the Chinese Money Supply

In *China Upside Down*, Man-houng Lin (2007) described the deep crisis China went through in the first half of the nineteenth century, resulting in the Taiping rebellion of 1850–1861. This was at the time probably the greatest human catastrophe in history and may have cost 20 to 30 million lives. This large-scale destabilization of social and political life in China had economic roots. The story starts with the collapse of silver mining in Spanish America after about 1810; due to the independence struggle and political disintegration the mining industry in both Peru/Bolivia and Mexico all but stopped working, and global silver output declined dramatically. The Mexican minting industry also came to a halt, as did exports of Spanish *peso*'s to Asia (and Europe). From the 1570s a large part of the silver surpluses of the region flowed into China – via the Philippines – but this flow suddenly dried up. Before 1800 the silver inflow into China was used to pay for its exports – tea, silk, porcelain – but at the same time imports of opium tended to grow to such a magnitude that silver was no longer necessary to pay for those commodities. Instead, from the mid-1820s onwards, silver increasingly flowed out of the country, which destabilized the monetary system. This was to a large extent based on a more or less fixed exchange rate between copper coins (for small transactions) and silver (for large ones). Since the start of the Qing dynasty this exchange rate was set at 1,000, but in practice it was usually 10–20 per cent below this level. Towards the end of the eighteenth century – during the White Lotus rebellion (1794–1804) – the exchange rate began to trend upwards (resulting in a temporary ban on silver exports), but only after 1820 did it start to move up dramatically – to around 1,350 in the late 1820s, 1,600 at about 1840 and more than 2,000 after 1844 (Lin 2007).

The point that the various parts of the world economy were closely interconnected can probably not be better illustrated than by this link between declining American silver production and monetary problems in China. Silver became increasingly scarce, but because taxes had to be paid in silver, taxation levels increased accordingly – in particular for the 'common man' who earned an income in copper. One of the responses by the government was to limit the coinage of copper in order to make it scarcer and balance the copper–silver ratio, but this was clearly counter-productive, and reduced the supply of money even more.

The outflow of silver (or in fact already the coming to a standstill of the inflow of American silver) created a number of problems. The money supply was sharply reduced, and the level of taxation increased dramatically – at least, in terms of the copper coins which were the usual medium of exchange for peasants and craftsmen. This led to large-scale social unrest, worsened by the fact that the state was becoming increasingly corrupt and unable to keep law and order. Lin (2007, p. 13) cites an observer in 1850 – just before the outbreak of the Taiping rebellion – stating: 'Commoners are so ignorant about what is happening, they cannot help but despair when they observe the exchange rate of silver relative to copper coins increasing every year. The disturbances in Fenghua in Zhejiang and in other places can largely be attributed to this problem.' In short, the monetary contraction that resulted from the fall in American silver production (and the output of its minting industry), strongly destabilized the Chinese economy and led to the civil war of the 1850s. In its turn, this sparked the Second Opium War (1856–1860), further undermining the state, which only barely survived the events of the 1850s.

The big question is: why was China so vulnerable? Why did its economy suffer so much from the cessation of the inflow of silver? It was, moreover, not the first time that such a scenario was enacted. There are striking similarities with the socio-political crisis of the 1630s and 1640s that resulted in the downfall of the Ming and the takeover by the Qing in 1644. Already during the 'silver century' between 1550 and 1630 the Chinese economy had become hooked on the inflow of silver from, initially, mainly Japan, and after 1570 increasingly also from Latin America. Scholars like William Atwell (1982, 1986, 2005) and Frederic Wakeman (1986) have suggested that, as a result of the Japanese turn towards autarky and the decline in Spanish American production in the 1630s, imports of silver into China fell, setting in motion the same kind of mechanisms that were in operation after 1810. Von Glahn (1996a, 2016) has, however, demonstrated that while there was a decrease in supply, there is no evidence for a *large enough* decline in the silver inflow into China to have impacted total stocks in this period. But what did happen is that the growing financial difficulties of the Ming state resulted in a debasement of the copper coinage in order to maximize state income from *seigniorage*. This had a similar effect: the copper coin/silver ratio shot up, from less than 1,000 before 1640 to more than 2,000 in the early 1640s (Von Glahn 1996a, pp. 106–109). The copper inflation resulted in rising (copper) prices of basic foodstuffs and an increase in taxation (which followed the market rate of the copper/silver ratio) – two destabilizing factors which contributed to the disintegration of the Ming state in these years. This greatly aggravated the difficulties resulting from harvest failures between 1638 and1642 that led to popular revolts and played a part in the demise of the Ming.[11]

Why did the Chinese economy need such large imports of silver to function properly? In older literature, it was suggested that the Chinese had a preference for hoarding silver as an alternative store of wealth; as a result, silver disappeared quickly from circulation (the same literature suggests that India suffered from a similar appetite for silver). The story is more complex than that, however. If one combines an estimate of the amount of silver in circulation by a Chinese official, Jiang Chen, in 1643 of 9,375 tons[12] with estimates of the imports of silver between 1550 and 1800 and the output of domestic mines, one can guestimate the 'silver supply' (per capita) in this period.[13] This shows a moderate increase from 4 to 6 grams of silver between 1550 and 1650. As domestic silver output by this time was small,[14] this was largely the result of growing imports. This growth was followed by a slow decline to slightly more than 5 grams in 1800 as imports faltered (data from Von Glahn 1996b). Note that the population of China in the same period grew from about 120 million to 340 million; the main reason for importing such large quantities of silver was to supply the growing population with the necessary means of exchange. If a large part of imported silver had been hoarded – that is, disappeared from circulation – the silver supply per head would have declined even further. Five grams of silver was, by international standards, not much. In 1500, before the inflow of American silver, the comparable European figure is about 7 grams of silver and 0.6 grams of gold; because gold had 11 times the price of silver, the total value of this was about 13 grams of silver (estimates from Palma 2015). If we assume that about half of American imports remained in Europe, this 'silver supply' would rise to 22 grams in 1550 and 46 grams in 1600 (but European prices were by that time higher than in China).

China, first of all, needed silver imports to keep the per capita money supply at a moderate – perhaps even rather low – level, while the population grew rather rapidly. Furthermore, during the Song, Yuan and early Ming, paper money had been used on a large scale, to the admiration of Marco Polo, for example. The Yuan had linked the issuing of paper money initially to the underlying cash reserves of the state, but this link disappeared from the 1270s onwards – and the temptation to print money to finance state expenditure in times of need became simply too big. During the Ming, the value of paper money collapsed, and silver was accepted by the merchant community and the state as the obvious alternative (Von Glahn 1996a). From the early Ming onwards a transition process started in which payments in silver became increasingly important, stimulated by the state which increasingly demanded the payment of taxes in silver (as noted above). The famous Single Whip tax reform of 1581 which demanded payment of the land tax in silver consolidated this change. Silver imports, which boomed from the 1570s onwards (thanks to the establishment of the link between Spanish America, Manila and China), played a key role in this internal transition to a silver-based economy (Flynn and Giraldez 1995, 2002a).

The switch from paper money to silver for large transactions is only part of the story. Initially, during the Song period (and before), the money supply had consisted of small copper coins, which could be combined in strings (of 1,000 pieces) to take care of large transactions. During the Song, huge quantities of copper coins were manufactured by the state. These coins also became extremely popular outside China, and flowed in large numbers to Japan, Korea and Southeast Asia where they dominated exchange until well into the eighteenth and nineteenth centuries. During the commercial revival of the East and Southeast Asian economies between 900 and 1200, these small copper coins were used on a very large scale. But the popularity of these coins abroad also meant that a constant supply of new coins was necessary to keep the money stock intact. The dynasties after the Song failed to produce sufficient numbers (Von Glahn 1996a). In the fifteenth century the scarcity of small coins led to a rise in the private manufacture of debased bronze coins; during the final decades of the Ming dynasty the state also produced sharply debased coins, leading to inflation in these years. But efforts, also by the Qing, to produce more copper coins, continued to remain far below the levels required by the economy.

An important difference with Western Europe was that gold was not monetized, and it was only used for decorative purposes. The almost continuous money supply issues in China translated themselves into a shift in the relative price of silver versus gold; this price ratio, which was 10 or more in Western Europe and in China during the Song, fell to 5–6 after 1350, when confidence in paper money had evaporated and the crisis in the copper coin supply worsened (Von Glahn 1996a, p. 61). When, after 1500, China acquired access to foreign supplies of silver from Japan and Spanish America, a large part of the exchange consisted of the swapping of Chinese gold for imported silver. The gold/silver prices ratio began to move up to 7–8 after 1550, but remained at a level (much) lower than in Europe.

It is impossible to deal with all the complexities of Chinese monetary history in detail, but a few conclusions can be drawn. China was relatively vulnerable to swings in silver production and exports/ imports because of certain institutional weaknesses. The state failed to regulate the most important part of the money supply – silver. It, paradoxically, demanded silver for the payment of taxes, but did not mint silver coin nor intervene actively in the supply and standardization of silver to the domestic market. After the Song, it also failed to supply the private economy with sufficient copper coinage – a form of money for which it did take responsibility, but in a rather unsuccessful way. These problems emerged against the background of the failure of Song/Yuan/Ming experiments with paper money, which in a way set in motion the transition towards the silver-based economy of the eighteenth century. Finally, China did not make use of the monetary possibilities of gold, which would have added flexibility to the system (for example: Great Britain responded to the monetary problems of the 1810s by switching to the gold standard, which solved part of the silver scarcity problem). In sum, China was vulnerable because the Chinese state was incapable of solving the many interrelated issues of the money supply. This offers a perfect example of the more general problem of the declining capacity of the state to monitor and steer the economy; as G. William Skinner observed: 'Chinese history saw a secular decline in government effectiveness from mid-Tang on to the end of the imperial era' (cited in Brandt, Ma and Rawski 2014, p. 66).

Commodity Trade from Canton

Silver imports thus had significant effects on the Chinese state and economy, but what about the export trade? By 1683, the Qing dynasty had consolidated its control over China and after the defeat of Taiwan by the Qing armies, the ban on maritime trade was lifted by the Kangxi emperor (r. 1667–1722). Over the course of the eighteenth century, international trade grew once more. Von Glahn (1996b, p. 442) shows how trade with Japan soared immediately following the lift of the ban. Furthermore, trade with Southeast Asia flourished (again – see Chapter 7) and has been estimated at a value of 22–52 metric tons of silver per annum in the first half of the eighteenth century (Von Glahn 2016, p. 319). Via Southeast Asia, trade was also conducted with Europeans, e.g. the VOC bought tea from Chinese *junks* (see Figure 8.3) in Batavia, but direct trade with Europeans from Canton also grew from the late

Figure 8.3 A variety of Chinese ships. Engraving by Jan Luyken. Chinese *junks* were employed in the Asian trade.
Source: Cornelis van Yk, *De Nederlandsche scheepsbouw-konst open gestelt.* (Amsterdam: 1697). Courtesy of Rijksmuseum, Amsterdam.

seventeenth century onwards. Ramon H. Myers and Yeh-chien Wang (2002, p. 587) note that between 1719 and 1806, this trade grew at 4 per cent per year.

Paul van Dyke (2005) sketches a lively picture of the eighteenth- and early ninteenth-century Cantonese trading system and the actors involved. Foreign trade was always conducted via intermediaries, the *Cohong* merchants, a clear indication that even while opening its doors to the world, the Chinese government tried to keep control. Despite such restrictions, direct trade with Europe expanded impressively. The consumption of tea expanded enormously in Europe (see

Chapter 9), while China remained the only major supplier on the global market until the middle of the nineteenth century (Liu 2007, p. 69). Tea exports to Britain increased from 400 tons annually in the 1720s, to 1,700 tons in the 1750s to a staggering 8,200 tons in the 1790s.[15] Dutch exports meanwhile increased from some 70 tons per annum in the first decade of the eighteenth century to over 1,500 tons in the 1770s. Among the other goods exported globally were Chinese silk and cotton cloths, and porcelains (in return for which imports of silver, but also raw cotton and opium from India, expanded over the eighteenth century). The export of silk from Canton increased from 5 tons to 163 tons per annum between the early 1720s and early 1790s, while prices consistently increased over the same period (Myers and Wang 2002, p. 622). In addition, sugar was cultivated mainly for the Asian market, but was also transported to Europe. While sugar production was mostly in the hands of small peasants who had shifted from rice cultivation, there may have been some wealthy peasants and merchants who ran large 'plantations' employing waged labour (Marks 1998, p. 173). Trade growth thus spurred the commercialization of the region in the immediate vicinity of Canton. Already in the early eighteenth century, about half of the arable land in the Guangdong province was devoted to commercial agriculture and this percentage likely increased over the remainder of the century (Marks 1998, p. 184).

Yet, besides in the immediate hinterland of Canton, the Pearl River delta and the Fujian hills (where the tea was grown), the impact of the trade on China's overall economy was limited. It has been estimated that by 1788, the total value of long-distance traded goods was 173 million *taels* (or 65 million kg of silver), or 0.5 *tael* (0.19 kg silver) per capita (Myers and Wang 2002, p. 583). Brandt et al. (2014 p. 56) neatly summarize what is known about interactions between the Chinese economy and the world market before 1800:

Apart from the effect of silver inflows, which exerted major influence on China's monetary system from the sixteenth century onward, the impact of international trade on Chinese prices, incomes, organization, and production remained small prior to 1800. Sketchy data suggest 1 per cent of GDP as a generous upper bound to China's trade ratio (imports plus exports divided by GDP).

Silver for Silk

From 1638 to 1858, the Tokugawa adopted a policy of *sakoku*, officially closing off the country from the world market. Much recent
research, however, suggests that the isolation was not as absolute as
the use of the term might suggest. In fact, Japan played a role of significance in the early modern global economy, in particular for Asian
monetary flows (as we have seen above – transporting large sums of
money) as well as for the business of the Dutch East India Company.
As such, Japan had an important effect on intercontinental trade flows.

The Dutch started trading with Japan in 1609 – initially from
Hirado – and obtained their privileged position as the only Europeans
allowed to conduct trade with the Japanese from the artificial island of
Deshima – originally built for trade with the Portuguese by Nagasaki
in 1639. After the Shimabara uprising of 1637–38, in which a Catholic
Japanese *daimyo* rose against the shogun, the Portuguese were banned
from Japan. Christianity had spread quite impressively in the sixteenth
century, as a result of Jesuit activity: by the early 1580s there were
some 150,000 Christians in Japan (Elisonas 1991, p. 333). Nagasaki
was the centre of Jesuit activity and in the early seventeenth century
almost all of its 25,000 inhabitants were Christian (ibid., p. 368). The
Tokugawa were fervently anti-Christian, banning the practice and
preaching of Christianity and ordering the persecution of Jesuits and
Christians. Eager to please the shogun, as well as to quell Catholicism
and hinder the Portuguese, the protestant Dutch aided Tokugawa
forces in quelling the uprising. Some 37,000 Christians were killed in
the Shimabara uprising (Gordon 2003, p. 17) and by the second half
of the seventeenth century, virtually no Christians were left in Japan
(Elisonas 1991, p. 370).

Figure 8.4 shows the island of Deshima. The number of VOC
employees manning Deshima rarely exceeded 20 (Goodman 2013,
p. 20). These Europeans – many of the VOC employees were not
Dutch – lived in great isolation. As one of Deshima's European inhabitants wrote:

A European condemned to spend the rest of his life in this solitude would
truly be buried alive. News of great upheavals of empires never reaches this
place. The journals of Japan and still less those of foreign countries do not
arrive. One can vegetate here in the most absolute moral nullity, foreign to
all that is taking place on the world scene.[16]

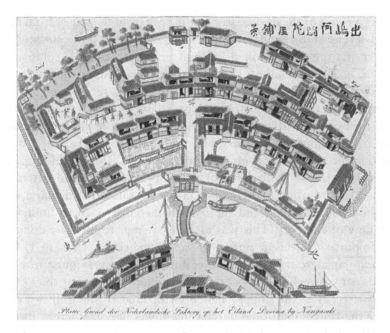

茶碗屋陀崎阿嶋出

Platte Grond der Nederlandsche Faktory op het Eiland Desima by Nangasaki

Figure 8.4 Deshima Island off the coast of Nagasaki: an artificial island that was Japan's only gateway to the rest of the world
Source: I. Titsingh, *Bijzonderheden over Japan*, The Hague, 1824–1825.

The trade in Nagasaki was closely monitored by the Japanese, who feared smuggling as well as the spread of Christianity. In the late sixteenth century, a large proportion of exports consisted of silver (to China, as discussed above) as a result of a sudden increase in silver mining in the same decades. In a careful study of the Japanese mining industry Schreurs (2015) has documented the growth of output and exports over the years between 1596 and the early seventeenth century, and the steady decline thereafter. The industry was heavily monitored by the state, which acquired most of the silver in the form of taxation and exported large quantities to China in return for luxury imports such as silk. Only a small part of the output found its way into the domestic economy but, still, this expansion of silver production had a strong effect on the relative price of silver, which declined dramatically (or alternatively, the price of rice increased strongly). We know that the price of rice in silver values increased continuously over the seventeenth century (Schreurs 2015).

As a result of the decline in silver output from the mines from the mid-seventeenth century, the Tokugawa tried to limit the outflow of silver and therefore banned VOC silver exports in 1668 (Shimada 2006, p. 14). After that, copper became the leading export commodity from Deshima, the exports of which increased rapidly from an average of 500 tons in the 1650s to over 4,000 tons at the turn of the century, yet declined to half that figure in the middle of the eighteenth century, and amounted to only about 1,000 tons at the end of that century (Schreurs 2015). This decline, again, was the result of deliberate Tokugawa policies to curtail external trade. Urbanization and commercialization raised the demand for bullion within Japan, and the *bakufu* therefore tried to limit the outflow of currency. This was also an attempt to increase domestic import-substitution agriculture and handicrafts. Thus, in 1715, Dutch–Japanese trade was further curtailed to a maximum of two ships per year, while in 1790 this was reduced to one. For the VOC, Japanese silver and copper had been of crucial importance as it gave the Dutch additional purchasing power in Asia, thereby limiting the shipments from Europe. Much of the copper was spent by the VOC in India, where Japanese copper was in strong demand and prices for copper increased continuously over much of the eighteenth century; as a consequence, the VOC derived a fine profit from the copper trade (Shimada 2006).

While Nagasaki was under direct control of the Shogunate and the *bakufu* was able to effectively curtail the trade by the Dutch (and Chinese) there, trade with Ryukyu and Korea (and via Korea with China), from the domains of Satsuma and Tsushima, respectively, was harder to regulate. The export of precious metals was crucial for obtaining Chinese raw silk (Hayami 2004, p. 16), which was in high demand for the Japanese silk textile industry: 'Silk products were the most highly valued commodities in the Japanese domestic market' (Tashiro 2004, p. 116). While the amount of silk imported from Nagasaki declined as a result of *bakufu* restrictions, initially the trade via the Korea–Tsushima and Ryukyu–Satsuma routes rose: almost 1,000 tons of raw silk entered Japan via Tsushima between 1684 and 1700.[17] Yet even these trades declined substantially shortly after that. This provided room for the growth of domestic silk production, which increased throughout Japan in the eighteenth century. A similar story can be told for sugar, of which the import was gradually reduced in the second half of the eighteenth century. Throughout the seventeenth and eighteenth centuries, Japan curtailed the inflow of foreign goods in order to spur its domestic industries.

Even Korea, despite its policy of isolation, imported substantial quantities of copper and silver via Tsushima, yet much of this silver consequently flowed to China. At its height in the late seventeenth and early eighteenh centuries some 90–110 tons of silver per annum were transferred through Korea (Lee and Temin 2010, p. 559). Yet, in their attempt to spur domestic industries, the Tokugawa Shogunate tried to curtail this trade as well, by setting quota and high exchange rates on silver. From the 1730s onwards, silver exports from Japan to Korea slowly died out.

Conclusion

Summing up, China, Japan, and Korea were – given the constraints of the period – well-functioning economies which, however, were highly inward-looking. Overall living standards were lower than in Western Europe and were more influenced by domestic agricultural conditions, and possibly increasing pressures on the land, rather than by external factors. Their isolation was also due to the efforts of both states to remain independent economically and politically. Japan found out in the sixteenth and early seventeenth centuries that external economic and political forces – including the spread of Western ideas embodied in Christianity – could destabilize society and state. Its inward turn, in combination with the stabilization of the polity under Tokugawa rule, resulted in two centuries of rapid economic change, in processes of commercialization, market integration, and the growth of human capital. In many respects, it was 'catching up' with China as it started off at much lower levels of real income, urbanization and human capital, but in the process it gradually managed to overtake its 'big brother' in terms of levels of urbanization, literacy, effectiveness of the state and, eventually, GDP per capita. Paradoxically, the two and a half centuries of inward-looking policies appear to have been the 'best' preparation for a radical transformation of economy and society that would begin with the Meiji Revolt of 1867. Trade restrictions had the clear purpose of stimulating domestic industries – as in the case of silk and sugar. And, after Perry opened the country for international trade in 1854, the Japanese elite were willing and the state was able to learn from Western experience. In this, it could to some extent build on the contacts it had had with the Dutch trading post in Deshima, which had been a source of Western knowledge and ideas. Already in the eighteenth century Japanese scholars tried to compare Chinese (Confucian) and Western ideas and technologies, and this empirical approach may have helped them to prepare for the shock of 1854.

China consistently walked in the opposite direction, abandoned its inward-looking policies during the Ming and the Qing dynasties and became, particularly during the eighgteenth century, more dependent on international exchange – especially on the inflow of silver. Increased commercialization and growing imports of silver in the eighteenth century meant heightened vulnerability to world market fluctuations. Especially as Qing taxes had become almost entirely monetized, the fortunes of the state were connected to the world market. This gradual turn to more openness was, apparently, not the right 'preparation' for the challenges of the ninteenth century, when international competi- tion (military, economic) accelerated dramatically. During the Qing dynasty the Chinese elite arguably lacked the curiosity that was char- acteristic of Japanese scholars. The Opium Wars (1839–42, 1856–60) did not trigger the same kind of response as Perry's intervention in Japan. After 1850, China became the sick man of the world econ- omy and Japan the young upstart. The comparison suggests that in the early modern period, for strong, centralized states and well-developed economies, openness did not really pay off and keeping the world mar- ket at arm's length may have been the better strategy.

Suggested Reading

Allen, Robert C., Jean-Pascal Bassino, Debin Ma, Christine Moll-Murata and Jan Luiten van Zanden (2011).'Wages, Prices, and Living Standards in China, 1738–1925: In Comparison with Europe, Japan, and India', *Economic History Review* 64, pp. 8–38.
Brandt, Loren, Debin Ma and Thomas G. Rawski (2014). 'From Divergence to Convergence: Re-evaluating the History Behind China's Economic Boom', *Journal of Economic Literature* 52, pp. 45–123.
Gruber, Carmen (2014). 'Escaping Malthus: A Comparative Look at Japan and the "Great Divergence"', *Journal of Global History* 9, pp. 403–424.
Hayami, A., O. Saito and R.P. Toby (eds.) (2004), *The Economic History of Japan: 1600–1990. Vol. 1: Emergence of Economic Society in Japan, 1600–1859*. Oxford: Oxford University Press.

Jun, Seong Ho, J.B. Lewis and Kang Han-Rog (2008). 'Korean Expansion and Decline from the Seventeenth to the Nineteenth Century: A View Suggested by Adam Smith', *Journal of Economic History* 68, pp. 244–282.

Pomeranz, K. (2000). *The Great Divergence. China, Europe and the Making of the Modern World Economy*. Princeton: Princeton University Press.

Von Glahn, Richard (2016). *The Economic History of China. From Antiquity to the Nineteenth Century*. Cambridge: Cambridge University Press.

9 | Europe and the Spoils of Globalization

Introduction

Around the year 1000, Western Europe was a relatively poor and backward region at the fringes of the world economy. It traded cloth and wine for furs, grains and timber from Eastern Europe through the Baltic Sea and via cities of the Hanseatic League (Findlay and O'Rourke 2007). The most valuable trade was that of slaves with the Islamic world – then the centre of the global economy. In return, Europe imported Southeast Asian spices, textiles and silk from across the Mediterranean. This trade became increasingly dominated by the Italian city states, in particular Venice and its main rival Genoa, which occupied the most lucrative routes. Yet the horizon of European merchants was limited, because once the commodities landed on the shores of the Middle East, Arabic merchants took over. Trade over the Atlantic was non-existent, and African overland trade was dominated by Islamic merchants (and along the coast of Africa trade was very limited). Yet, soon after the *Reconquista* – the recapture of the Iberian peninsula from the Muslims – was completed, the newly established Iberian kingdoms, Portugal in particular, sought ways to circumvent the joint trading monopoly in spices controlled by Venice and the Mamluk Sultanate (which occupied Egypt and the Levant). Over the course of the fifteenth century, the Iberians would lead the way in seafaring explorative missions that would change this structure dramatically.

After the 1490s, global trading networks came into existence dominated by, at first, Portuguese and Spanish merchants who traded in all the oceans of the world – from Brazil to the Moluccas. The final stage of this process of the formation of a global trading network was the linking of the Americas with Asia in the 1570s – with the Philippines and, more specifically, Manila as the main linchpin (Flynn and Giraldez (1995, 2002a). Of course, Chinese and Japanese merchants

238

remained important in the Chinese sea; they continued to form a dense network in the triangle between southern China, Indonesia and Japan. Similarly, Indian and Arabic merchants dominated trade in large parts of the Indian Ocean, with cities like Malacca and Surat as hubs. After the initial Portuguese expansion, their networks often rebounded and at the end of the sixteenth century, the Portuguese had become marginal players in that region. The arrival of the Dutch and English in around 1600 changed this to some extent, but Asian trade remained in many ways as competitive and dynamic as that of the European intruders. Yet, Europeans were almost everywhere, and their horizon expanded to include all continents in the late eighteenth century, when Australia was also incorporated.

Whereas in other regions globalization was dominated by one or two key developments, such as the slave trade, colonization and export expansion, exploitation of mineral resources, or the growth of money supply, all these elements of the process can be found in the European experience. Europe profited enormously from the exploitation of the American silver mines and the increased money supply which resulted from it, but it also harvested most of the 'fruits' of the expansion of world trade – with Africa, North America and Asia. It profited as an intermediary – carrying almost all the intercontinental trade on its ships – as a source of supply of European export products and as a major source of demand of new luxury commodities that revolutionized tastes and industries. The growth of silk and, in particular, cotton textiles, are classic cases of import substitution that played a large role in the industrialization of Western Europe. It has also been argued that the introduction of new commodities such as sugar, coffee and tea (and tobacco) changed consumer patterns and induced households to increase their efforts to earn a market income (De Vries 2008). All dimensions of globalization seem to have supported the development of a highly productive, market-oriented and dynamic economy concentrated in the north-western corner of the continent.

The key question, therefore, is: why did this happen? Why did everything come together in the rise of Europe, and more specifically the North Sea region, eventually resulting in the Industrial Revolution that took off in the second half of the eighteenth century? Some scholars have argued that this difference was already visible in the late medieval period, when the various parts of Europe responded differently to

the shock of the Black Death. Recent research into the development
of GDP in these years, has indeed shown that the regions of Europe
responded differently to the sudden fall in the population, which was
usually in the magnitude of one-third to, sometimes, one half (Bolt and
Van Zanden 2014). In a Malthusian economy – after Thomas Malthus
(1798), who famously proposed that economic growth is always
checked by population growth and limited resources – one would
expect GDP per capita to rise dramatically: a sudden drop in population numbers means that labour becomes suddenly much scarcer,
whereas the supply of capital and land does not change in the short
run. This translates into changes in relative prices (wages go up, while
land prices and interest rates go down), that are well documented
in the economic historical literature (e.g. Clark 2005, 2007). These
changes in relative prices then drive the adaptation of production processes (which become less labour- and more capital-intensive) leading
to a rise in GDP per capita. Such a process appears to have happened
particularly in England and Holland – where estimates of GDP per
capita show a consistent rise after 1348, the year of the Black Death –
whereas in Spain, France, Italy and Sweden nothing similar seems to
have happened (De Pleijt and Van Zanden 2016). The explanation for
the absence of a surge in GDP per capita in Spain is that this was a
'marginal', underpopulated country – similar to a frontier economy, as
suggested by Carlos Alvarez Nogal and Leandro Prados de la Escosura
(2013). The decline in population numbers meant that the commercial
infrastructure had to be paid for by a much smaller population, resulting in high transaction costs and a decline in commercialization. Italy,
the region with the highest GDP per capita at the time, is a different
case; GDP per capita did go up, but only to a limited extent according
to Paolo Malanima (2011).

Reactions to the Black Death in a way foreshadowed developments
between 1500 and 1800. It is ironic that the two regions that reacted
in the classical Malthusian way, by strongly increasing their GDP
per capita, appear to have been the 'real' market economies which
produced higher levels of income and output after this exogenous
shock, and thereby more or less freed themselves from Malthusian
constraints. Holland and England would – after the break in 1348 –
show more-or-less consistent economic growth between 1348 and
1800 (and beyond) (Broadberry et al. 2015; Van Leeuwen and Van
Zanden 2012). But why were other regions in Europe less successful?

Why did Poland fall behind, and why did Italy, after a splendid perfor-mance during the Middle Ages, decline over the early modern period?

Thus, we are going to argue that globalization was key to the long-term success of Europe in general, and north-western Europe in par-ticular, during the early modern period. We will suggest, however, that the degree to which regions profited from this, was not determined by the globalization process as such, but by institutional structures and changes that facilitated economic development – as happened in north-western Europe.

American Silver and the Price Revolution

For Adam Smith the discovery of the Americas was the most important turning point in the economic history of Europe – as a result of, amongst others, the large imports of silver (and gold) that followed. We have seen in Chapter 3 that the massive growth of silver production was one of the dominant features of the glo-balization process in Latin America. Whereas in the sixteenth cen-tury, on average, just over 100 tons of silver were transported to Europe from America per annum, this figure had risen to 270 in the seventeenth century and increased to over 315 tons per annum in the eighteenth century (see Chapter 2). In many ways, this bonus contributed to Europe's wealth. It may therefore be surprising that Spain – the direct beneficiary of the silver inflows – was probably negatively affected by it, whereas other parts of Europe actually profited (see Map 9.1 for a map of early modern Europe).

The inflow of silver and gold from Spanish America potentially had a number of important economic consequences. It meant, first of all, a sudden increase in purchasing power, as both metals formed the basis of the money supply. Purchasing power, moreover, that became available at the discretion of the Spanish crown, greatly enhanced its ability to finance its activities – which first and foremost meant that it allowed the crown to pay for its many wars. American silver therefore had consequences for the political economy of the Spanish state (it strongly reinforced the position of the king), but the long-term effects of this change were mixed (to say the least), and the terms 'resource curse' and 'Dutch disease' have been used to describe them.[1] At the European level, the inflow of American silver could have three economic effects. First, prices might go up,

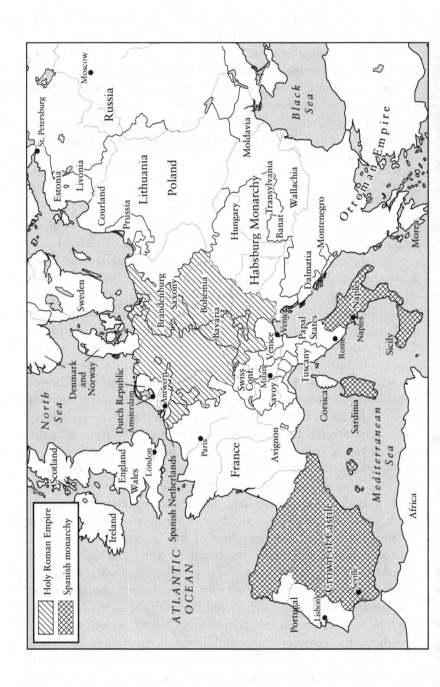

particularly if the supply of commodities did not increase much in response (if the supply was *inelastic*); then the growth in the money supply might simply translate itself into inflation. Second, and more positively, the money could be absorbed into the commercial circuits of the economy, raising the level of commercialization and stimulating specialization. Third, the money could be used to subsequently buy imports from other regions, in particular from regions that were not interested in European commodities (such as large parts of Asia). In this third way, Spanish silver facilitated global market exchange and strengthened the role that European merchants – who had access to this 'new' resource – played in world trade.

We will now discuss how important each of these effects were, and then return to the pivotal role Spain played in all this. The question that is easiest to answer is the effect the increased silver supply had on the price level. As a result of research by Robert Allen (2001), we can now chart the silver value of a basket of the same, or very similar, consumer goods over time. At about 1500, the south of Europe was already more expensive than the north, but this gap grew sharply until the middle of the seventeenth century (demonstrated by the data series of Valencia compared to that of London and Amsterdam). Between 1500 and 1600 prices in Valencia increased by a factor of 4, whereas in London, Vienna and Cracow they merely doubled (Figure 9.1).

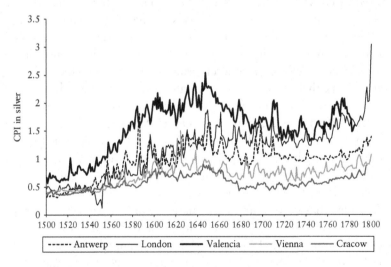

Figure 9.1 Consumer price indices in Europe 1500–1800
Source: Allen (2001).

The immediate effect of this was that Spain became a relatively expensive part of the European economy (the 'Dutch disease' effect), a logical result of the fact that American silver entered the region via Spain and was used to finance Spanish warfare. Yet it may also reflect the supply constraints of the Spanish economy, which increasingly needed imports from other parts of Europe. Not accidentally, perhaps, the source of these supplies was often the North Sea area. Thus, ironically, during the height of the Dutch–Spanish War (1568–1648), the Spanish were dependent on grain imports from the Baltic, organized by the Dutch who financed a large part of their war effort in this way (Van Tielhof 2002).

A doubling of the price level – as happened in large parts of Europe – was a modest response to the great increase in the money supply. Nuno Palma (2015) has estimated that the per capita money supply of Europe increased by almost a factor of 10 between 1492 and the first half of the seventeenth century, which, corrected for inflation, would still mean a substantial growth of 'real' money. It is not easy to determine whether the increased money supply drove the commercialization and specialization of the economy that must have occurred given the sharp increase in the real money supply. Developments during the 1500–1800 period contrasted sharply with those during the fifteenth century, when silver flowed out of Europe to the East (possibly caused by conversion from paper money to silver that was happening in China at the same time), price levels stagnated or even declined in real terms over extended periods of time, and silver shortage was a common complaint of merchants and state officials alike, constraining not only the development of international trade but also the ability of states to tax their citizens. As Smith also remarked, the years around 1500 were indeed a turning point, as this monetary constraint was suddenly lifted in a dramatic way. Or, as Palma (2016b) concluded: 'American precious metals permitted a dramatic increase in English monetization, which in turn generated *Smithian growth*,[2] supported state-building, eased the transition to a paper money system and facilitated the transition into modern economic growth.'

The idea that silver inflows stimulated economic growth in Europe is not new, of course. The arguably most famous version of this argument was launched in 1934 by Earl J. Hamilton, who pointed at the link between sixteenth-century inflation and the decline of real wages in the same period, and argued that the latter development must have improved the profitability of enterprise, thus creating more favourable incentives for capital accumulation and growth. In the 1950s and 1960s, this monetary interpretation of the price revolution (as suggested by Hamilton (1934)) was replaced by a Malthusian approach stressing the growth of population as the main driving force of both the increase in the general price level and the decline of real wages. In the background to this debate, there is a much more fundamental discussion about the 'neutrality' of money, dominated by (monetary) economists who usually argued that in the long run the money supply only affected the price level and did not have an impact on the real economy (a summary can be found in Palma 2015). Since the 1990s, this debate has switched back to Keynesian ideas that increased money supply may affect the real economy beneficially (as John Maynard Keynes, arguably the most influential economist of the twentieth century, also stressed). In economic history, this recent interpretation is taken up most forcefully by Palma (2015, 2016a, 2016b) who argues in favour of the growth-enhancing effects of American silver in a number of recent papers.

To return to Hamilton (1934), we can now try to determine if the European experience fits his predictions. If the decline of real wages is driving economic expansion, we would expect that in the North Sea area, real wages declined most, but this is clearly not the case (as we know from the work of Allen 2001; shown below in Figure 9.2). By contrast, there is a positive link between real wages and economic growth: in the North Sea area, real wages hardly declined at all in the long run – despite increases in population in these centuries – and even went up in times of fast economic growth (Antwerp in sixteenth century, Amsterdam in the seventeenth century and London after 1650). Real wages, on the other hand, went down quite sharply in Spain (Valencia) and Central Europe (Vienna). The gap is clearly visible by the end of eighteenth century. The decline of real wages, that was possibly caused by the inflow of silver – pushing up prices – from the Americas, cannot therefore help to explain the divergent development of Western Europe.

Finally, American silver also solved a crucial constraint on the development of world trade by providing Europeans with the purchasing power necessary to buy desired Asian commodities. Fifteenth-century intercontinental trade had been handicapped by the fact that Europeans wanted goods – spices from the Moluccas, silk from China – but did

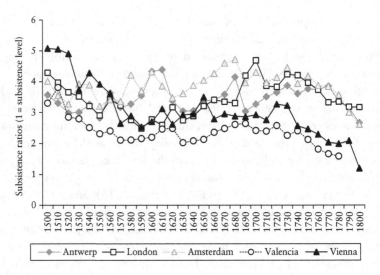

Figure 9.2 Real wages expressed as subsistence ratios in Europe, 1500–1800
Source: Allen (2001).

not have much to offer in return. Instead, silver leaked out of the continent, as we saw already, creating shortages of silver money. Portuguese ventures towards the coast of West Africa in the fifteenth century were already motivated by the desire to access the sources of the trans-Saharan gold trade that supplied Europe with at least some precious metals. This constraint was radically lifted after 1492, when the silver inflows from Spanish America exploded. Palma and Silva (2016) estimated the effects of this windfall, and concluded that 'European imports of Asian goods were up to thirteen times higher than they would have been without new routes and without precious metals. The effect of American precious metals is six times larger than that of the discoveries of new trading routes.'

In short, American silver and gold had many positive effects on the European economy: it made possible the rapid expansion of trade with Asia, it stimulated growth and commercialization, and lifted constraints caused by the limited availability of money for economic growth. Yet not all countries profited equally, and it was probably Spain that payed the highest price. 'Dutch disease' may have played a role: due to the dominant position of the silver export, prices in Spain increased more than elsewhere, which resulted in a deterioration of

Spanish competitiveness (Drelichman 2005). It might also have had consequences for the political economy of the Spanish state, a link that has become known as the 'resource curse'. States that have access to such large external funds do not have to turn to their citizens any longer to negotiate about taxes or increase their legitimacy. Such states become more autocratic and tend to neglect the education of their population (Drelichman and Voth 2008). Summing up, the Spanish state 'suffered from becoming too rich too fast. American treasure overwhelmed the country's institutional setup, resulting in a fully-fledged "resource curse" that affected the economy, domestic and foreign policy, and the structure of client networks' (Drelichman and Voth 2008). The most telling examples of this are the many bankruptcies the Spanish state underwent during the period of 'silver addiction', resulting in a loss of confidence in the currency and a crippling of its capital markets. Holland and England, by contrast, gradually became hallmarks of monetary stability, with booming capital markets.

Luxury Consumption and the 'Industrious Revolution'

One of the key consequences of the growth of global commodity trade for Europe was the rise of luxury consumption and a consumer culture. Besides the silver discussed in the previous section, Europe imported a host of luxury goods. In the sixteenth century, the main luxury imports into Europe were pepper and fine spices from Asia: in the period 1500 to 1550, between 80 and 90 per cent of the total trade volume carried by the Portuguese into Lisbon was made up of pepper, while the remainder comprised of spices like ginger, cloves and nutmegs (Findlay and O'Rourke 2003, p. 18). The dominance of pepper declined slightly, as imports of indigo and textiles rose. After the entry of the northern companies in the Asian trade after 1600, further changes took place in the composition of Europe's overseas import trade. Pepper and Indonesian spices continued to be a substantial part of return cargoes of the VOC in terms of volume, but, in terms of total values, textiles actually became the single most important commodity imported by the Dutch, British and French companies (Gottmann 2016, p. 22). In the eighteenth century, in particular, we see a spectacular rise in the import of cocoa, coffee, sugar, tea and tobacco. These goods were also imported from the Americas (except tea), and that

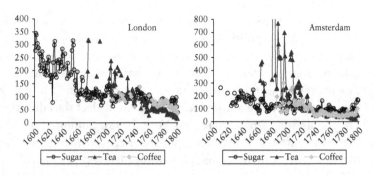

Figure 9.3 Real sugar, tea and coffee prices, London and Amsterdam (index: 1735 = 100), 1600–1800
Sources: Clark (2006) and De Zwart (2016b).

trade was much bigger than the trade with Asia. In the later eighteenth century, annual average imports into Europe stood roughly at these numbers: 7,500 tons of tea, 14,000 tons of coffee and a whopping 170,000 tons of sugar (see Chapter 2, and De Vries 2015, p. 28).

As a result of this dramatic increase in supply, prices of these luxuries in Europe came down relative to domestically produced goods like grains, peas and meat. In Chapter 2, we saw this in terms of a long-run decline for pepper prices, especially in the sixteenth century, but in Figure 9.3 this is also demonstrated for coffee, sugar and tea. Sugar prices declined by factor of 4 in England over the seventeenth and eighteenth centuries, while the price of tea decreased by a factor of 10, relative to the price of a basket of goods (Allen 2001). Even more dramatic was the decline in the price of tea on the Amsterdam market.

These price declines meant that the consumption of such luxuries, once the privilege of only the wealthiest inhabitants of Europe, now came within the reach of the middling and even the lower classes. As could be seen in the previous section, low-skilled workers in many cities of Europe had some money to spare; in the eighteenth century, wage labourers in Antwerp, Amsterdam and London earned between three and four times the subsistence level. Of course, this did not mean that they would simply buy more of the goods that reflected a subsistence lifestyle (cheap grains, peas and beans), but instead consumers started to purchase a wider variety of goods. In particular, consumers in the North Sea area became highly addicted to these products. Hanna Hodacs

(2016, p. 2) noted that most of the tea imported by the Scandinavian Company actually ended up with consumers in Britain and the Low Countries.

A Frenchmen visiting England in the 1780s noted that:

[t]hroughout the whole of England the drinking of tea is general. You have it twice a day and, though the expense is considerable, the humblest peasant has his tea twice a day just like the rich man; the total consumption is immense.

He figured that the average English person consumed about four pounds of tea (Macfarlane and Macfarlane 2011, p. 147). In the same period, Sir Frederick Eden wrote that in southern England 'in poor families, tea is not only the usual beverage in the morning and evening, but is generally drunk in large quantities at dinner' (ibid., p. 148) (see Figure 9.4: a Dutch girl drinking tea at breakfast). The consumption of sugar in England was even greater than that of tea. A working-class family in the period 1788–1792 spent some 7 per cent of its budget on sugar, and 3 per cent on tea (Feinstein 1998); English per capita consumption in that period was actually about 2 lbs of tea and over 20 lbs of sugar annually (Hersh and Voth 2011). Similarly, regarding luxury consumption in the Dutch Republic, the minister François Valentijn (1666–1727) noted that coffee had 'broken through so generally in our land that maids and seamstresses now had to have their coffee in the morning or they could not put their thread through the eye of their needle' (cited in McCants 2008, p. 177). Developments were, however, not restricted to the North Sea area, as a Frenchman observed in the eighteenth century:

Consumption [of coffee] has tripled in France; there is no bourgeois household where you are not offered coffee, no shopkeeper, no cook, no chambermaid who does not breakfast on coffee with milk in the morning. In public markets and in certain streets and alleys in the capital, women have set themselves up selling what they call *café au lait* to the populace (cited in Hersh and Voth 2011, p. 13).

Such remarks by contemporaries have recently been confirmed by quantitative research. In a thorough study of after-death inventories in eighteenth-century Amsterdam, Anne McCants (2008) has shown that

Figure 9.4 A Dutch Girl at Breakfast. Tea was often consumed domestically. Painting by Jean-Etienne Liotard *c*.1756. Courtesy of Rijksmuseum, Amsterdam.

the consumption of coffee was widespread even among families with relatively humble backgrounds. These inventories show that 60 per cent of these Amsterdam households had coffee wares (and were thus, presumably, drinking coffee on a regular basis), while some 50 per cent had owned tea pots. Other studies of material culture in the Dutch Republic have come to similar conclusions, also for smaller towns, stating that by '1750 coffee and tea wares were altogether commonplace' (Dibbits 2001). A study on eighteenth-century Antwerp showed that even among the lowest income groups (living in one-room houses) more than half owned tea wares in 1730 (Blondé and Van Damme 2010). It is now well established that the rise in consumption of these goods was not limited to the wealthy elites, nor that these developments were entirely limited to the North Sea region (although they were most pronounced there) (Ogilvie 2010).

The rise of consumption has been described as a 'consumer revolution' that changed consumption patterns and created new social practices. The most well-known aspect of this was the rise of coffeehouses, where people gathered not only to indulge in their new habit of drinking coffee, but also to socialize, conduct business and/or engage in intellectual debate. By the eighteenth century, there were between 600 and 700 *cafés* in Paris (Hersch and Voth 2011, p. 11). Drinking tea, on the other hand, was a domestic activity that became a regular ritual promoting household interaction over the eighteenth century (Berg 2005, p. 230). Both coffee and tea consumption were associated with polite and desired behaviour. New consumer patterns replaced older ones as, for example, beer consumption in the Dutch Republic between 1675 and 1800 declined from 200 to 40 litres per capita (De Vries 2008, p. 165). The latest arrivals of printed Indian calicoes, and Chinese blue and white porcelains were advertised in newspapers in order to further fuel consumers' desires (Berg 1999). It became important to be fashionable. The craze for Ottoman tulips ('tulip mania', or *tulpenmanie*) famously led to the first speculative bubble on Dutch financial markets in 1637. Changing consumer demands also had important effects on European production. Not only did imported sugar, coffee and tea compete on European markets with domestically produced food and beverages, but the import of Asian cloth and ceramics stimulated the production of imitations in Europe (which we will discuss at greater length on pp. 257–261). The consumer revolution was facilitated by a rise in retailers and various studies have shown that the numbers of shops increased over the seventeenth and eighteenth centuries (e.g. Blondé and Van Damme 2010), thereby reducing transaction costs and generating new jobs and economic growth.

All of this points to an ongoing process of commercialization leading to changes in the consumer behaviour of households. The availability of luxury commodities led to a greater degree of consumer aspiration and may therefore have increased incentives to work harder and longer, as Jan de Vries (2008) has argued. This resulted in an 'industrious revolution' that led to higher (market) incomes and specialization.

Sir Dudley North wrote in 1691 that the desire for the new luxuries 'disposes [people] to work, when nothing else will incline them to it; for did men content themselves with bare necessities, we should have a poor world' (cited in De Vries 2008, p. 66). This helps to explain why labourers in England, for example, worked more days than ever before. Whereas in the fifteenth century, English farm labourers possibly worked only 165 days per year, this increased to between 210 and 260 days by the late sixteenth century, further rising to 280 days by the end of the eighteenth century (Allen and Weisdorf 2011, p. 721). Urban workers in London may even have extended their working year to over 300 days around 1800. Not only did men work more days, but women and children may also have diverted time from domestic labour to market work. We know that in late eighteenth- and early nineteenth-century England the contribution of women and children to household incomes was substantial (Horrell and Humphries 1995). There are indications that the participation of women in the wage labour market in the Dutch Republic rose in the seventeenth and eighteenth centuries (Van Nederveen Meerkerk 2008). More pessimistically inclined authors, however, suggested that the decline of real wages in the second half of the eighteenth century may also have played a role in the rise of eighteenth-century work efforts (Motavasseli and Smulders 2017 present the best overview of this debate).

Finally, Jonathan Hersh and Hans-Joachim Voth (2011) argue in a recent paper that real wage indices, based on an unchanging basket of goods, as shown above, do not reflect the actual increase in living standards caused by people's increased ability to consume a wider variety of goods. They use a variety of quantitative techniques to show that the import of sugar, coffee and tea had a significant positive impact on the standard of living of early modern Europeans.

Thus, while scholars like O'Rourke and Williamson, as well as Wallerstein, have doubted that the import of luxuries could have substantial economic effects (like the trade in staples), most recent research points in the direction that it did: it led to a consumer revolution, impacted European production patterns, pushed work efforts and specialization, and increased living standards.

Institutional Change and Growth

Recent research has re-emphasized the direct and indirect effects that the expansion of international trade had on, in particular, the

Table 9.1. *Urbanization in Europe: percentage of total population in cities with 10,000 or more inhabitants, 1400–1800*

	1400	1500	1600	1700	1800
England	2.7	2.1	5.9	11.3	23.1
Netherlands	1.3	16.2	26.3	31.0	29.4
Belgium	31.7	22.0	16.1	23.0	13.8
France	6.3	6.2	7.0	8.7	9.0
Spain	10.0	10.4	13.2	19.3	15.2
Italy	12.9	12.8	17.5	15.7	17.3
Germany	5.5	4.7	5.2	4.8	7.6
Poland	2.2	3.3	4.6	3.1	3.1
Sweden	0.0	0.0	0.0	2.7	4.0
Ottoman Empire	5.8	7.4	10.1	12.2	9.2

Source: Bosker et al. (2013)

two most successful economies of the early modern period: the Dutch Republic and England. Detailed studies of the determinants of the process of urbanization have shown that the increase in urbanization in Western Europe in the seventeenth and eighteenth centuries was closely linked to the growth of international trade (Bosker et al. 2013). Urbanization levels increased in Europe as a whole, but this trend was strongest in the Netherlands and England, which had relatively low levels of urbanization in 1400, but the highest in 1800 (see Table 9.1). The area that is now Belgium was in 1400 the most urbanized part of Europe, but it lost its position during the sixteenth century to the Netherlands (the Dutch Republic). The decline of Belgium was closely connected to the rise of the northern Netherlands, however. The centre of gravity of the North Sea economy was in Flanders in the late Middle Ages; it first moved to Brabant (Antwerp) in the first half of the sixteenth century and, after 1585, shifted to Holland (when, as part of the fighting following the Dutch Revolt of 1572 the Spanish forces conquered Antwerp, and many merchants from the southern Netherlands fled to Holland and Zeeland) (Gelderblom 2000). The growing gap between north-western Europe and the rest of Europe was arguably even more significant than these changes within the North Sea area. In almost all regions, urbanization increased slowly between 1400 and

1800 (northern Italy, for which we do not have separate estimates, was probably the exception to this rule), but the increase in the urban ratio was slower and more erratic than in the north-west. Table 9.1 shows the estimates of urbanization – the percentage of the population living in cities with more than 10,000 inhabitants – in this period.

The causes of the spectacular increase in urbanization levels in the North Sea area, compared with relative stability elsewhere, have been identified in a number of papers studying the structure of the urban system of Europe. Allen (2003) emphasizes the role of intercontinental trade in this development, suggesting that over half of England's urban expansion in the seventeenth and eighteenth centuries was due to trade with the empire. As England and Holland captured most of the profits in global trade, they forged ahead of the rest. The finding that the growth of overseas colonial trade spurred urban growth has been confirmed by recent studies (Acemoglu et al. 2005; De Pleijt and Van Zanden 2016).The growth of overseas trade in these cities meant more job opportunities; it increased demand for dockworkers and sailors, ship-owners, merchants and brokers, customs duties officials, craftsmen that built and maintained ships, as well as all those supplying the networks of international commerce. As a result of their global connections, cities like Amsterdam and London grew rapidly. Amsterdam's population grew particularly rapidly during the Dutch 'Golden Age' in the seventeenth century, from 54,000 to 200,000 inhabitants, while London's population multiplied by a factor of 20(!) between 1500 and 1800 – increasing from some 50,000 in 1500 to almost 1 million in 1800 (Buringh 2016).

A comparison of the urban systems in the Arabic world and Western Europe between 800 and 1800 also points to the role of international trade and its institutions for the rise of urbanization (Bosker et al. 2013). The Arabic world switched to a new technology in long-distance transport – the camel – in combination with an infrastructure of caravans, which was innovative but in the long run not very dynamic; productivity did not increase any more once the switch to camels and caravans had been made. Western Europe became increasingly dependent on transport via the seas, and managed to develop new technologies – new ship designs amongst others – that sharply reduced transport costs. Access to the sea became increasingly important in this context, and, in particular, access to the Atlantic became, after 1500, a main driver of urban growth. The political economy of the two urban systems was also quite different. The flowering of the Arabic urban system was closely linked to the growth and expansion of the Abbasid Empire; when this started to disintegrate, the urban system of the Arabic world showed signs of fragmentation. At the same time in Western Europe, an urban system emerged that was rooted in independent cities (communes), which were able to deal with the problems of the political fragmentation of Europe quite successfully.

Similarly, Acemoglu et al. (2005) found that access to the Atlantic Ocean and to trade with the Americas, Asia and Africa was a main determinant of urban growth in the early modern period. Moreover, the urban growth that resulted from this trade also stimulated institutional changes that were conducive to economic growth. As a seventeenth-century Englishman observed about Dutch economic success during its Golden Age: 'It is no wonder that these Dutchmen should thrive before us. Their statesmen are all merchants. They have travelled in foreign countries, they understand the course of trade, and they do everything to further its interests' (cited in Hart 1993, p. 25). Between 1500 and 1800, the rise of global trade 'enriched and strengthened the commercial interests outside the royal court, such as overseas merchants, slave traders, and colonial planters' which allowed them to demand and obtain institutional changes that were in their interests, constraining the power of the monarchy and protecting private property rights (Acemoglu et al. 2005, pp. 562–563). A very influential literature suggests the importance of political institutions that place constraints on political power, preventing the government from using its power arbitrarily and thereby creating insecure private property, which has a negative effect on investment and economic growth (North and Weingast 1989; Acemoglu and Robinson 2012). Additionally, overseas trade spurred innovations in commercial and financial institutions: by giving out shares to fund its operations starting in 1602, the VOC played an important role in the rise of the Dutch capital market (Gelderblom and Jonker 2004).

But why did international trade push institutional change and economic growth in England and the Dutch Republic more than in the countries of other Atlantic traders, like France, Portugal and Spain? The reason is that the former countries already had more checks on royal power when they started trading across the Atlantic. In France, Portugal and Spain, on the other hand, most trade was in the hands of the state and it was the kings and their cronies who benefitted the most from it. This is also confirmed by the development of parliamentary activity in Europe (Van Zanden et al. 2012): northern Europe had more active parliaments already from the fourteenth century on, and the gap increased significantly until 1800 as absolutism actually grew stronger in France, Spain and Portugal. Between 1614 and the Revolution in 1789, the French parliament (Estates General) did not meet once.

Of course, there are a multitude of other differences between these economies that are unrelated to international trade. This can also be illustrated by the estimates of GDP per capita that have in recent years been constructed by economic historians working on the various countries of Europe (Table 9.2). In the late Middle Ages, northwestern Europe had relatively low levels of GDP per capita (but we do not have estimates for Flanders, which was the wealthiest part of the region). By about 1800 the situation had reversed, and England and Holland had (much) higher levels of GDP per capita. After the Black Death, incomes rose in the North Sea area. The emergence of the European Marriage Pattern (EMP) – entailing the higher average age of marriage and smaller families – in the North Sea area is one possible factor affecting this (De Moor and Van Zanden 2010).

Table 9.2. *GDP per capita in nine European countries, 1350–1800* ($ of 1990)

	1350	1400	1500	1600	1700	1800
England/Great Britain	786	1099	1086	1082	1513	2097
Netherlands	876	1195	1454	2662	2105	2609
Belgium			1467	1589	1375	
Spain	907	819	846	892	814	916
Italy	1515	1751	1533	1363	1476	1363
Germany			1146	807	939	986
Poland			702	810	569	634
Sweden	787		1107	865	1182	929
Ottoman Empire	580		660		700	740*

Sources: Bolt and Van Zanden (2014); Malinowski and Van Zanden (2016); Krantz (2017) and Schön and Krantz (2015).
*Data for 1820

The EMP may have allowed increased investment in education of (the lesser number of) children.[3] We know that in terms of human capital formation, as estimated by literacy (Allen 2009b, p. 53) and book consumption (Baten and Van Zanden 2008), the North Sea region had the highest levels of Europe in the eighteenth century. The region was also leading in terms of agricultural productivity per worker (Allen 2000). As a result, the rest of Europe gradually fell behind. Northern Italy, the richest region in the fourteenth and fifteenth centuries, slowly declined. The European periphery – Sweden, Poland, the Ottoman Empire and even Germany – witnessed a gradual erosion of its real income. Only France seems to have stabilized and continued to occupy a position close to the Western European average.

In combination with these factors, international trade allowed Western Europe to attain remarkable economic success over the early modern era. Trade expansion created strong incentives for the further development of capital markets; low interest rates and the stability of the capital market were key factors in industrialization. Joel Mokyr (2009) has suggested an entirely different link: the global expansion of European networks produced much new knowledge about the peoples of the globe, which tended to undermine established views. It demonstrated that the classics may have been wrong, and that new ideas were required for a better understanding of the new facts. This new knowledge therefore played a role in the Scientific Revolution of the seventeenth century, and in the growth of new attitudes – aimed at developing and empirically testing new ideas – that furthered the kind of practical knowledge that lay behind many techniques of the Industrial Revolution. The Enlightenment and the Enlightenment economy that was inspired by the new ideas were to some extent rooted in the 'Great Discoveries' of the fifteenth and sixteenth centuries.

Import Substitution and the Industrial Revolution

As we have seen in the introduction, the idea that the early modern expansion of European trade and influence resulted in a new international division of labour, has been most forcefully articulated by Wallerstein in the 1970s and 1980s. In his view, Western Europe became the 'core region' specializing in high value-added manufacturing and services activities (a process that set the region on the road to modern industrialization), whereas the other parts of the world – from

Poland to Latin America – developed into peripheries, focused on the exports of raw materials and used forms of labour coercion to acquire these commodities. In sum, the growth of world trade in the 'long sixteenth century' laid the basis for the global inequality that we still see today. As noted, many scholars, like O'Brien (1982) as well as O'Rourke and Williamson (2002a, 2004), have criticized such a view, mainly based on the argument that, quantitatively, the overseas trade amounted to too little to have such far-reaching effects. Nonetheless, it is clear that by the end of the eighteenth century, this pattern was emerging as a result of the Industrial Revolution. But what role did international trade play in the industrialization process?

One of the effects of importing luxury commodities from the East (particularly those from India and China) was that it created opportunities for import substitution as it spurred the development of European imitations of Eastern goods (see Berg (2005) for various British examples). Silk had been a highly valued import from China, but in the late Middle Ages European producers learned to copy the technologies involved, and in Italy and France silk industries emerged that successfully catered for the needs of European consumers. Porcelain is a similar story: when the supply was interrupted in the middle decades of the seventeenth century due to political instability in China, European producers (particularly in Delft) started to imitate the Chinese product, with mixed success. The original Chinese product remained clearly superior until the setting up of a factory in Meissen (Germany) in 1710, which produced the first European porcelain.

There are many examples of Europeans trying to copy – in due course often successfully – the technologies that had been developed in Asia for the mass production of luxury products. The invention of the printing press by Johannes Gutenberg can be seen as another example – the Chinese and Koreans had developed moveable type printing before – but in this case the 'imitator' in one stroke of genius developed a set of technologies that were at least on a par with those of the East. Similarly, Europeans were quick to see the advantages of gunpowder, and soon appear to have superseded the East in the development of canon and guns that made effective use of the innovation.

The most spectacular example of import substitution was cotton. Before 1800 India was the cotton capital of the world, producing large quantities of high-quality textiles for large parts of Asia. For example, as we saw in Chapter 7, the trade with the Moluccas – the famous Spice Islands – was based on the exchange of spices for Indian textiles. European merchants arriving in the Indonesian archipelago needed textiles from India to do their business, and therefore established trading factories in India as well. Moreover, the European companies in the seventeenth century began to import large amounts of textiles for the European market, where cotton became increasingly fashionable; the European companies combined imported some 100,000–200,000 pieces of textile to Europe in the 1660s and 1670s, and this number had increased to 1.4 million pieces a century later (Berg 2015, p. 124). In various parts of Europe, a cotton industry was already emerging – sometimes making use of imports of cotton yarn from India and Indonesia – often making mixed cloth by combining cotton with linen. In 1721, the English Parliament started an experiment with import tariffs on cotton textiles, ostensibly for increasing tax revenues, but with the side effect of making it more lucrative to produce cotton textiles on English soil (Griffiths, Hunt and O'Brien 1991). It allowed the rise of the industry that would, more than any other, become the symbol of the Industrial Revolution of the late eighteenth century. New technologies were developed to solve constraints in the production process – spinning was 'mechanized' thanks to James Hargreaves' spinning jenny and Richard Arkwright's water frame, both invented in the 1760s. In the 1770s, Samuel Crompton combined these inventions into a machine that became known as the 'mule' that allowed British textile producers to face up against Indian competition (Allen 2009b, p. 185).

Why were these inventions British? An important role in this story is played by the relative prices of the factors of production – land, labour and capital. The sudden decline of the population due to the Black Death created an economy characterized by the availability of cheap capital (interest rates all over Europe declined to about 5 per cent, a historic low), an abundant supply of skilled labour (the skill premium in industry also fell strongly after 1350) and high real wages. High wages also meant that British textile producers were uncompetitive compared with low-cost Indian producers (see Chapter 6). The import of large amounts of Indian textiles threatened the British textile industry and the above-mentioned protective measures did nothing to improve the position of British textiles in third markets (Broadberry and Gupta 2009). It did, however, allow a domestic industry to survive and eventually rise. In combination with low energy prices – the result of favourably located coal and the expansion of the British coal industry – high wages and cheap capital constituted the right mix of relative prices to stimulate labour-saving technology such as, eventually, the steam engine (Allen 2009b). The rapid growth of international trade played a large role in this, as it created the demand for labour which kept real wages at a relatively high level. Furthermore, Allen (2009b) argued that international trade created large trade hubs where the division of labour was more refined, pushing labour productivity and wages in these cities. He also demonstrated that real wages in England and the Low Countries remained at a high level during the early modern period, thereby creating the incentives for mechanization.

Thus, as Maxine Berg (2005, p. 327) concluded:

Europe responded to a commodity trade with the wider world; inventing, producing and consuming new European, and especially British goods provoked changes in technologies, the uses of new materials and forms of energy, and the reorganization of labour that became the industrial revolution. World markets stimulated this process in the first place; success then led to global ascendency.

The long-term consequences of its success are well documented: after about 1820 the industry conquered world markets as distant as China, Indonesia and even India. Indigenous cotton production could hardly cope with the intense competition from Lancashire, where output growth was spectacular – cotton was by far the most dynamic industry of the first phase of the British Industrial Revolution until, after the development of railways and steamships, coal and steel took over. Also, in Continental Europe the cotton industry was often the first to pioneer the industrialization process, and very soon comparable factories were set up in Flanders, Twente, the Ruhr area and other industrializing regions. In the Global South, however, the 'cotton invasion' of the 1820s marked the beginning of the process of deindustrialization that would characterize these economies during much of the nineteenth century (see also Chapter 6 on South Asia).

To what extent did the profits earned in international trade in general, and the Atlantic slave trade and the plantation system in particular, fuel the Industrial Revolution? This is the subject of the still classic book by Eric Williams (1944), who argued that profits earned in the slave trade and the plantation economies helped to explain the Industrial Revolution of the eighteenth century, suggesting a link between exploitation in the periphery and economic success in the core areas. Most research that has investigated the profits from the slave trade and the plantation system disputes whether the profits in these sectors were in fact substantially higher than those from other (domestic) sectors of the economy and whether these profits were actually invested in those sectors crucial to the Industrial Revolution, i.e. the iron, coal and textile industries (Eltis and Engerman 2000). At the same time, however, it does seem to be the case that Western African slave-exporting regions, as well as the plantation colonies in the Americas, played an important role as export markets for British manufactures. Of the total cotton textile production, we know that exports vis-à-vis domestic consumption rose from about 30 per cent of total production in 1760 to 60 per cent around 1800. America and West Africa were already the most important export markets for British cotton textiles in the early eighteenth century: 80–90 per cent of total exports went there (Inikori 2002). These areas were similarly the dominant markets for British woollens, linens and metals in the eighteenth century. Furthermore, the export industries were also growing faster than most other industries of the British economy; cotton textile manufacturing grew by 9 per cent per year between 1770 and 1800 (Solow 1985, p. 112; Riello 2003, p. 212). Another aspect of Williams' hypothesis, namely that the slave trade was abolished because of the decline of the plantation economies from the 1780s onwards, has been refuted by Seymour Drescher (1977, 2009).

Stagnation in Eastern Europe and the Ottoman Empire

So far, we have focused on Western Europe and particularly on the success story of the North Sea area. Its economic performance was not representative of Europe as a whole, however; it was in fact only a tiny minority of Europeans – a few million inhabitants of the Low Countries and the British Isles – that really improved its standard of living thanks to, amongst others, the forces of globalization. Most Europeans were probably not better off in 1800 compared with 1500: their real wages went down in the very long run (but in 1500 they were probably still inflated by the long-term consequences of the Black Death) and their GDP per capita also did not show growth (and perhaps on average some decline). On the other hand, they had access to new consumer goods such as coffee, tea and sugar, but probably consumed much less meat (and fish) than in 1500 (Van Zanden 1999). More important for the standard of living of the poor was probably the spread of maize (in the south) and the potato (in the north), as these goods supplied cheap calories for the labouring poor. In that sense, the poor may really have profited from the Atlantic exchange, but as the disastrous consequences of the potato blight in nineteenth-century Ireland demonstrate, the strategy to concentrate on potatoes alone would have disastrous consequences in the long run. Inequality of wealth and income had probably increased in the long run (Alfani and Ryckbosch 2016) – land, for example, rose much more in value than labour, and the gender wage gap tended to increase as well (De Pleijt and Van Zanden 2016). In the late eighteenth century, the 'golden age of the craftsmen' and the 'golden age of the female labourers' of the fifteenth century, when all profited from labour scarcity, were a very distant memory. At the same time, growing cities had created new opportunities for migrants from the countryside, and international migration – to the Americas, or the Cape Colony – made it possible to really improve one's (material) lot.

Inequality also had a spatial dimension. Poland is perhaps the classic example of a country that did not profit from the growth of the world market, in spite of the important role the Polish economy played in its initial rise. In the fifteenth century, Poland became the main supplier of cereals (rye in particular) for Western Europe, a trade that was channelled via the port of Gdansk, at the mouth of the Vistula. The city had developed close ties with Amsterdam, which controlled a large part of the international trade of the Baltic. In the sixteenth century, population growth and stagnating agricultural production in Western and Southern Europe led to the rapid growth of demand for foodstuffs, and to a spectacular expansion of the grain trade between the Baltic (Gdansk in particular) and Amsterdam (the western hub of the grain trade) (Van Tielhof 2002). The Polish economy – and especially the Vistula catchment area (including cities like Warsaw and Cracow) – profited as well from the export boom. The Polish state simultaneously experienced a 'Golden Age'; it was the largest state of Europe at the time, also thanks to the commonwealth with Lithuania, and for example incorporated large parts of present-day Ukraine. Poland's golden age did not last long, however. It probably led to a modest increase in GDP per capita, but after the peak in the 1560s and 1570s, things started to go downhill (Malinowski and Van Zanden 2016). Political instability was part of the problem, but in the long run the loss of export markets, perhaps in combination with supply constraints in Poland itself, resulted in much-reduced export earnings. GDP per capita declined during the first half of the seventeenth century and stagnated until the early ninteenth century. By then, Poland had become one of the poorest regions in Europe. The Polish state was unable to redress the decline, and during the eighteenth century it became part of the problem. It was unable to compete with the increased powers of its neighbours – Austria/Hungary in the south, Prussia in the west and Russia in the east. Concerted actions by these countries led to a number of partitions of the Polish Kingdom, resulting in the dissolution of the state in 1795. No part of Europe, probably, would change fate so dramatically as Poland.

The debate about the political and economic decline of Poland is complex and still ongoing. An important interpretation of the causes of this decline focuses on the link with the world market. For Wallerstein (1974), Poland was the best example of the fate of a region that became part of the periphery in his world system: it exported raw materials in the form of grains to the core (the Dutch Republic/the Netherlands) in return for products of manufacturing (textiles for example) and international services. But this specialization in agricultural exports proved to be a dead end. This exchange stimulated structural change and specialization in the Netherlands – with the dynamic effects that we analysed in the previous sections. It did not have the same dynamic effects on the Polish economy, which concentrated even more on agricultural products. Political factors, however, played a role as well. Poland, and Central and Eastern Europe in general, saw the 'return of serfdom', including the reintroduction and extension of labour duties peasants were forced to perform for their lords. This began in the fifteenth century – perhaps related to the labour scarcity after the Black Death (although it is still unclear what the impact of the Black Death on the Polish population had been). But labour services clearly intensified in the sixteenth century, when the demand for them increased due to the high and very profitable export of grains. Serfdom is generally considered to be ineffective and inefficient – compared with free market transactions – but as Mikolaj Malinowski (2016) has argued, in a society with high transaction costs and low levels of commercialization, it may be an 'optimal' way to extract a surplus from the agricultural sector. He suggests that in this way an urban sector could survive a period of poor market conditions. The long-term effects of a transition towards coerced labour under serfdom may however have been quite negative. In the interpretation suggested by Malinowski (2016), these institutional changes interacted with the growing (sixteenth century) and declining (seventeenth century) possibilities of the world market to produce economic outcomes that were, in the long run, quite disappointing.

Poland played, in particular in the sixteenth century, a key role in the expansion of international trade – feeding the growing population of Western Europe – but was not really rewarded for it. Its eastern neighbour, Russia, remained much more marginal in trade networks. During the early Middle Ages the trade between the highly developed Middle East and the north of Europe had been carried out via the Russian river system, organized by Viking/Swedish merchants who set up communes in various strategic places (Novgorod for example). In the late Medieval period, these trade routes had declined, perhaps in absolute terms, but clearly relative to the growth of trade via the Italian city states. The expansion of the Polish-Lithuanian state in the sixteenth century, the rise of Sweden as the new power in the Baltic, and the decline of the independent republic of Novgorod in a way sealed off access to the West. The Grand Duchy of Moscow (as Russia was called at the time) tried to reopen trading connections with the West by making use of the northern port of Archangel. In the 1550s, English merchants established trade contacts via this northern route (Veluwenkamp 1995). They set up the Muscovy Company – the first chartered company which acquired a royal monopoly on the trade with Russia – to organize it. In the 1570s they were followed by the Dutch, who managed to take over most of the trade in the next decades. Products of agriculture and forestry were exchanged against textiles and metal from the West and the large deficit of Russian trade was made up for by silver coins (Veluwenkamp 1995). During the seventeenth century, Russian trade with the West was mainly channelled via this route; in 1721 this changed, when, after the Great Northern War, Russia opened the new port of St Petersburg, which became the new gateway to the Russian hinterland.

The exports from Russia to the world markets (or rather, the European markets) were however much smaller than those of Poland,

and hardly affected the internal organization of agriculture. This was characterized by a similar movement towards the enserfment of the rural population, who were more or less free during the fifteenth century, but became increasingly oppressed by the state and the nobility who demanded heavy labour services. Moreover, in contrast to Western Europe, a not insignificant part of the population (5–15 per cent) were slaves without any rights, until Peter the Great in 1724 transformed all slaves into serfs (but by then the difference had become quite small) (Hellie 2006b). As in Poland the late fifteenth and first two-thirds of the sixteenth centuries were periods of relative stability and peace – almost a Russian 'Golden Age' of recovery after the consolidation of the state of Moscow between 1453 and 1480. After 1565, periods of violent internal warfare often led to a further deterioration of the position of the peasantry – in 1592 they lost almost all rights, thanks to a decree by Boris Gudunov (one of the more capable tsars during the long period of troubles between 1565 and 1614). In a way, the enserfment of the Polish and the Russian peasantry followed more or less the same trajectory in time (i.e. a gradual worsening of their position between the late fifteenth and the late seventeenth centuries), albeit that serfdom in Russia was on average much more oppressive, and closer to actual slavery, than in Poland (Hellie 2006a). This parallel development, however, does cast some doubt on the idea that Polish enserfment was driven by, or connected with, the development of export production and developing links with world markets in general.

The Ottoman Empire – the third state to be discussed here, which covered a large part of south-eastern Europe – saw its position in the world economy change dramatically. Until about 1500, the core of the world economy consisted of the 'golden band' of urbanization and relatively highly developed states that ran from the Mediterranean to southern China – including the Middle East, Persia and northern India. This is where the Neolithic Revolution had emerged 10,000 years ago, and where the first great civilizations came into existence. The silk route was (and still is) the symbol of the vibrant zone of high economic activity. The Ottoman Empire in 1500 played a key role in this system of exchange. Particularly after the conquest of Istanbul in 1453, European influence was on the defensive again, and merchants from Egypt or Syria could dominate the flows of goods between the East and the West.

As we described in Chapter 1, this all changed in the sixteenth century; the initial push of the Portuguese in the early decades of that century already dealt a big blow to the trade via the Caravan routes of the Middle East. The taking over of Asian trade routes by the Dutch and the British after 1600 did the rest and marginalized the region in terms of global trade. Economically and politically, the Ottoman Empire went through a cycle that was to some extent comparable with that of the Polish state: it had its golden age in the late fifteenth and first two-thirds of sixteenth centuries, when it was expanding strongly in Eastern Europe and many a battle was fought to end the expansion of the Turks (the Battle of Lepanto of 1571 which stopped the advance of the Ottomans in the Mediterranean is probably the most famous). As had been the case in Poland and Russia, Ottoman fortunes eventually declined. The death of Suleiman the Magnificent (r. 1520–66) is often seen as a turning point. While recent scholarship questions this, in terms of real wages and GDP per capita there is still some truth in the hypothesis that things went downhill after the 16th century, as both stagnated until the 1800s (Ozmucur and Pamuk 2002; Pamuk and Shatzmiller 2014).

The loss of centrality within international trading networks may be part of the explanation for this relative decline of the region. Reflecting this, in the eighteenth century the gap in terms of technology and capabilities of the state between the Ottoman Empire and Western Europe became increasingly obvious.

As in Poland, changes in the social and political structures of the country, may have contributed to the decline. Political power be came more fragmented after the sixteenth century, partly due to the rise of a decentralized system of taxation, the *timar* system, which delegated much power (in this respect) to local authorities. The Ottoman Empire never tried to impose high indirect taxes on international trade (as Britain and, to an extent, the Dutch Republic did), as its policy towards trade was mainly governed by the wish to stabilize the flow of imports into the country, preferably at low costs. To further that end, it granted merchants from foreign countries extensive rights – the 'Capitulations' – which, however, did not really strengthen the position of the Ottoman trading class (Bulut 2002). By the eighteenth century, all Ottoman trade with Europe was carried on Western ships (Kuran 2003, p. 414). This mercantilism-upside-down (or 'reversed' mercantilism) in which the interests of consumers (including the household of the sultan) predominated over those of producers, did not really help to strengthen the Ottoman economy. Other policies – such as the ban on printing books – did not help either (for institutional explanations of Ottoman decline see also Kuran 2003 and Pamuk 2004).

An entirely different policy to deal with the changes in global inequalities was developed by Peter the Great (r. 1682–1725), tsar of the Russians, who was one of the first monarchs in history to develop a set of polices to modernize the country and to try to bridge the gap with the rapidly developing North Sea region. After having spent considerable time abroad (in Holland and England) he became convinced that customs and institutions in the West were superior to those at home. It became his mission to use the power of the state to modernize Russia, and he imported many skilled craftsmen and experts to facilitate the transfer of technology he had in mind. Reorganizing the army to be more successful in his many wars was an important objective, but he also, for example, tried to abolish forced weddings (of which he considered himself a victim) and to ban the large beards that Russian men preferred to wear. As mentioned already, his perhaps most strategic move was the building of St Petersburg as a window to the West. In order to be effective, he used the oppressive power of the Russian state to carry out his ideas, and he strengthened his own position as the undisputed ruler of this state, eliminating all opposition (he for example terminated the meetings of the duma in which local nobility could criticize and perhaps even oppose him). This dilemma – that modernizing monarchs needed absolute power to carry out their programmes, and in that way tended to undermine them – would be a critical problem for all attempts to 'modernize from above' in the nineteenth and twentieth centuries.

Conclusion

Without doubt, Europe was the part of the world economy that profited most from the globalization process between 1500 and 1800. Most regions experienced the expansion and integration of the world market as an exogenous force. For Africans who were caught up in the slave trade, *mita* workers in Potosí who dug out the silver ore, or the inhabitants of Banda Islands who fell prey to the VOC, it was, by and large, forces outside their control that pulled them into the world market under conditions that often had long-term negative effects. For

Europe, the development of world trade was, mostly, an endogenous development – the result of the growth of markets and the adaptation of institutions that had begun already during the high Middle Ages. That, of course, did not mean that all Europeans participated voluntarily in the process, or that, for example, Africans did not have agency in shaping these processes. Moreover, within Europe there were contrasts as well in the degree to which regions profited from the new opportunities. Central and Eastern Europe and the Mediterranean fared much less well than north-west Europe, which became the economic powerhouse of the continent. This 'Little Divergence' between the North Sea area and the rest was a remarkable development, which in itself cannot be solely explained by the rise of globalization in the same period. In a way, Italy, Portugal and Spain were better placed to profit from the growth of international trade; Italy because it already had the commercial infrastructure and traditionally was the commercial centre of Western Europe; Portugal and Spain because they initiated the 'Discoveries' and dominated the new trade routes (and the linked territorial empires) in the sixteenth century. Yet, in the seventeenth and eighteenth centuries the economic core of Europe moved to the north-west and economic growth was increasingly concentrated there.

It is this combination of factors that drove Western Europe forward: since the later Middle Ages the region had become more commercialized and more urbanized; there were higher levels of human capital, and there were stronger constraints on executive power. After 1500, a virtuous circle of increased trade, growth of purchasing power, consumption, work ethics, institutional change and innovation took place in Western Europe, pushing the region towards global economic dominance. Long-distance trade on its own cannot explain the first Industrial Revolution; neither can it be explained without it.

Suggested Reading

Allen, Robert C. (2009b). *The British Industrial Revolution in Global Perspective*. Cambridge: Cambridge University Press.

Berg, Maxine (2005). *Luxury & Pleasure in Eighteenth-Century Britain*. Oxford: Oxford University Press.

De Pleijt, A.M. and J.L. van Zanden (2016). 'Accounting for the Little Divergence: What Drove Economic Growth in Pre-Industrial Europe, 1300–1800?' *European Review of Economic History* 20, pp. 387–409.

De Vries, Jan (2008). *The Industrious Revolution. Consumer Behavior and the Household Economy, 1650 to the Present.* Cambridge: Cambridge University Press.

McCants, Anne M. (2008). 'Poor Consumers as Global Consumers: The Diffusion of Tea and Coffee Drinking in the Eighteenth Century', *Economic History Review* 61, pp. 172–200.

Palma, Nuno (2016a). 'Sailing away from Malthus: Intercontinental Trade and European Economic Growth, 1500–1800', *Cliometrica* 10, pp. 129–149.

Pamuk, Sevket (2004). 'Institutional Change and the Longevity of the Ottoman Empire, 1500–1800,' *Journal of Interdisciplinary History* 35, pp. 225–247.

Van Zanden, Jan Luiten, Maarten Bosker and Eltjo Buringh (2012). 'The Rise and Decline of European Parliaments, 1188–1789', *Economic History Review* 65, pp. 835–861.

10 | Conclusion

We have seen that all regions of the world were affected by the development and the changing geography of international exchange. Some were more fundamentally changed than others, obviously, and nothing compares with the overwhelming impact on the Americas. Even by the standards of O'Rourke and Williamson (discussed in Chapter 1, pp. 2–3) who define globalization in terms of market integration only, there was in fact a whole lot of 'hard globalization' going on, in the first place over the Atlantic (where transaction costs had been infinite before 1492), but also on major Eurasian trade routes (as De Zwart (2016a) has demonstrated). Moreover, O'Rourke and Williamson's argument that international trade before 1800 was mainly concerned with luxury products, that did not affect economic outcomes and the standard of living of the population, seems to be contradicted by the 'consumer revolution' of the eighteenth century, the 'industrious revolution' that followed it, as well as the import-substitution industrialization in Britain that was stimulated by the spread of new consumer goods over these centuries. Of course, there had been substantial interaction between Europe, Africa and Asia before the 1500s, across the famous Silk Road, for example, but in the sixteenth century this exchange became truly global; with the inclusion of the Americas, trade came to be conducted overseas rather than overland, it flowed in every direction and total volumes increased consistently (and faster than the growth of population and other indicators of economic activity).

This is, of course, not to deny that things changed dramatically after 1800 as globalization and market integration accelerated in the early 1800s. As we saw in Chapter 2, between 1500 and 1800 the average rate of growth of long-distance trade was about 1 per cent in the long term. This changed after 1820, when the growth of international trade accelerated to over 3 per cent per year in the nineteenth century (Federico 2016). Initially this sudden acceleration may have been caused by a rebounding effect after the slump in international exchange during the Napoleonic wars, when France tried to block all trade with Britain. But soon the new rate of growth was supported by new technologies – railways, steamships – and advanced trading practices, including much lower tariffs. Measures of market integration also show a break at about 1820, pointing to rapidly improving conditions for international trade (Federico and Chilosi 2015). Price convergence was much faster and more consistent in the nineteenth century. Transport costs declined to such levels that it became economical to start shipping bulk goods like grains across the Atlantic (Sharp and Weisdorf 2013), thereby reducing food prices as well as solving the land constraint of the European, especially the British, economy (O'Rourke and Williamson 2002a). The huge amounts of land in the New World were used for the production of land-intensive agricultural production, while Europe could focus on capital and labour-intensive industrial production. The ratio of world trade to world GDP increased from somewhere between 2 and 8 per cent around 1800 to roughly 20 per cent by the end of the nineteenth century (Estevadeordal et al. 2003, p. 360). Anyway, there is no disagreement that the 1820s saw radical changes in the growth path of many Europe countries, also resulting from the start of 'catching up' growth on the Continent, trying to emulate the Industrial Revolution that had occurred in Britain.

Between Columbus and Napoleon there was a 300-year period during which, we argue, the growth of international exchange – of flows of money (silver/gold), of commodities and people – strongly affected economic development and well-being in large parts of the world. A worldwide web of trade came into existence that was largely dominated by Europeans. This trade involved the shipping of bullion from the Americas, first to Europe and then on to India or China. There the silver was used to purchase cotton or silk textiles, which were either transported back to Europe, or were shipped to Southeast Asia to barter for spices, which were then brought back to Europe. Indian cotton textiles could also be used in Africa to buy slaves, who were in turn transported to the Caribbean or Brazil where they were sold in exchange for sugar, or coffee, or some other plantation produce. Connections were so strong, that it makes sense to think in terms of a world system. Moreover, following Wallerstein (and many others), we have shown that this creation of a world market had important consequences for the long-term economic prospects of the regions involved.

In the overview presented in Chapters 3 to 9, we chose to focus on different regions in the world, to study the impact of globalization on the societies there. The disadvantage of such an approach is that the interconnections between, and the common patterns among, the various regions received less attention. We bring it all together in this concluding chapter.

Global Currency

The argument that due to long-distance trade the world economy was developing into one 'global system' is perhaps most convincing when we look at the flows of money – of silver and gold – in the world economy. Because there was limited desire for European goods, American silver provided the Europeans with the purchasing power in Asia that kept the wheels of commerce spinning. As we have seen, the rhythm of the world economy was to a large extent determined by the ups and downs of silver production in Bolivia/Peru and Mexico. Silver flowed in large streams to Europe and to Manila, and continued its journey in the hands of, often, European merchants to Russia, or to India, Indonesia and China, where it helped to sustain commercialization and the switch to a silver-based economy. As huge amounts of silver were pumped through the world economy, relative values of silver converged across the globe (see Flynn and Giraldez 2004). While in some areas, Spain most notably, the increased supply of silver may have pushed inflation and caused 'Dutch disease', in many parts of the world it had the positive effect of spurring monetization and commercialization, increasing purchasing power and increasing production. Silver and gold were transported as bullion but also as coin and Spanish *reals* and *pesos* were used widely throughout Asia and Europe. It is difficult to find a more convincing case for the unity of the global networks of the world in this period.

Global Production

Of course, silver flows were only one side of the coin; silver was used to pay for commodities that could not be bought otherwise (if the silver flow was not the result of blatant unequal exchange as it, of course, was quite often between Spain and Spanish America).

Silk, porcelain and tea, for example, flowed in the other direction, from China to Europe and the Americas. European products were imported on a large scale in Spanish America. Geographical changes and the development of chains of supply and demand of these commodities can also be used to illustrate the interconnectedness of the world system. Across the globe, centres of production of commodities shifted from one place to another. Coffee, for example, was initially 'discovered' by the Ethiopians, and spread to Arabia in the fifteenth century, where Mocha became the main exporter of the product (which was grown mainly in Yemen). In the early seventeenth century, the first Europeans became consumers of the product – its consumption started in Malta and Venice, from where it spread gradually to the north. In the seventeenth century, Mocha continued to dominate the trade in this product; its growing popularity meant that the commodity became increasingly scarce. This brought the VOC to the introduction of the crop in Java around 1700, soon followed by similar initiatives to grow it in Surinam, the American colony of the Dutch. Both initiatives were highly successful and led to a growing supply of coffee from Java and the Americas – at the expense of Mocha, which became marginal in international trade. The history of coffee beans and trees nicely illustrates how scarcities in the world economy at one place (in Mocha) might lead to dramatic changes in crops grown and work performed in very distant places (Surinam and Java).

Other crops and products had similar global networks of production, distribution and consumption – from whale oil and furs from the Far North to sugar and cotton from the Deep South. Perhaps cotton is the best example of a commodity that became truly global in reach and impact, in which the production of the raw fibre spread to all continents and the output was dramatically relocated from India – the centre of the global industry in the seventeenth and eighteenth centuries – to England, where it became the symbol of the Industrial Revolution (see also Beckert 2015). It was, in short, the 'first global consumer commodity' (Lemire 2011), with dense international networks for the production of raw materials and the spinning and weaving of the cloth. Its spatial organization in 1600 differed dramatically from that in 1800, when the southern colonies of the United States had just emerged as the most important producers of the fibre. Economic,

technological and geographical forces were behind such drastic reloca-
tions of production processes, demonstrating the dynamics of a system
of which the different parts were connected by links of trade, networks
of merchants and information flows.

Cotton textile production in Europe had existed since the Middle Ages,
albeit on a relatively modest scale as woollen and linen textile production was more important. In the seventeenth and eighteenth centuries,
the massive inflow of cotton and silk textiles from India and China put
pressure on Europe's textile industries. This led to the adoption of pro-
tectionism measures, as we have seen for England. This experience was
not confined to Europe, however. As early as 1582 it was remarked by a
Spanish official in New Spain (Mexico) that because of large imports of
silk and clothing from China via the Philippines, Mexico's silk culture
and clothing industries were having difficulties (Atwell 1998, p. 401),
while in the eighteenth century, Spanish America's woollen textile
industry also fell victim to the forces of globalization (see Chapter 3).
For most of the sixteenth to eighteenth centuries India's cotton textiles
circulated throughout Africa and Southeast Asia, yet with the rise of
industrialization in Britain it was the Indian textile manufacturers that
came to feel the heat from global competition.

Furthermore, while Wallerstein sketched a global economy with
labour at the core, that is Western Europe, characterized as 'free' labour
for wages and self-employment, and slavery and servitude as common
forms of labour in the periphery, we have seen that this picture was
much more nuanced. Of course, a substantial part of the labour in
American silver mines was coerced, as was Javanese coffee production.
Slavery dominated sugar production in the Caribbean as well as the
production of mace and nutmeg on the Banda Islands. However, forms
of coerced labour also continued to exist in Europe, while Chinese and
Indian textiles were produced by either self-employed men and women
or wage labourers. In regions like Latin America, we have observed
an increase in free wage labour over the early modern era. Increased
amounts of small coins in circulation seem to point at the growth
of wage labour in China and India (Lucassen 2017). Perhaps a safe
overall conclusion is that the rise of world trade led to more free and
unfree labour for the market, at the expense of subsistence work and
unemployment or leisure.

Global Consumption

As global production of commodities developed, so did consumption. In the previous chapter, we discussed how global trade spurred the rise of luxury consumption in Europe. The European coffeehouse has been described as 'the world economy in miniature, an international emporium joining coffee from Java, Yemen or the Americas, tea from China, sugar and rum from Africa's Atlantic islands or the Caribbean, and tobacco from North America or Brazil' (Topik and Pomeranz 2013, p. 83). Other parts of the world did not miss out on this development entirely, however. Luxury consumption spread to settler societies in North America and South Africa. There is convincing quantitative and qualitative evidence to suggest substantial consumption of Chinese tea and porcelains as well as Indian cotton manufactures in eighteenth-century North American colonies (Breen 1988; Berg 2005). Per capita consumption of tobacco, sugar and coffee, at the same time, was even higher than in the metropole. Native Americans joined in the consumer revolution and bought increasing amounts of alcohol, as well as European cloth from the colonists over the eighteenth century (Carlos and Lewis 2010). At the same time, the Native American habit of smoking tobacco spread throughout Europe and Asia from the early seventeenth century on. Probate inventories show substantial amounts of luxury items in the Cape Colony; these included European paintings and timepieces, but also sugar from Java and even furniture from China (Fourie 2013).

Regarding Asia, there is evidence of rising and then declining sugar and spice consumption in eighteenth-century Surat in India (Nadri 2008b). Yet the rise of a luxury consumption culture seems to have been limited to India's commercial elites (Gommans 2015). In China, there was substantial consumption of sugar, tobacco and tea, as well as a rise in the quantity of 'home furnishings, elaborate clothes' and 'eating utensils' among the richer groups in society (Pomeranz 2000, p. 127). In contrast to Europe, however, these were almost always domestically produced, and thus had little to do with trends in international commerce. We find an expansion in the amount of furniture in Japanese houses over the Tokugawa period, again unrelated to patterns of trade (Hanley 1997). Indian cotton textiles were in high demand in Southeast Asia throughout the early modern period.

In Europe, we have seen that the desire to consume such exotic luxuries led to an increased work effort to obtain the income necessary to buy such goods. Pomeranz (2000) argues that China in the same period shared in this rise in industriousness as spurred by consumer desire. Native Americans intensified their efforts at hunting beavers for the global fur trade, in order to satisfy their increased desire for luxury goods, to such an extent that they depleted the beaver stocks (Carlos and Lewis 2010). While Hayami (2015) finds an increase in work efforts in Tokugawa Japan, this development was unrelated to global markets and its 'industrious revolution' was the result of low incomes. Similarly, there is substantial evidence of work efforts by women and children in eighteenth-century India, yet more likely in response to declining real wages rather than as a means of increasing luxury consumption (De Zwart and Lucassen 2015).

Global Populations

The 'Columbian exchange' had a huge demographic impact on the Americas due to the spread of infectious diseases from Eurasia. In some areas almost the entire indigenous population was wiped out. Over the course of the early modern era, population numbers in America were restored, but a large part of the American population now consisted of people who themselves, or their forefathers, were born in Europe or Africa. Because most of the initial migrants to the Americas were men, there was a rise in the amount of *mestizos* – people of mixed European and Amerindian descent. Thus, as a result of globalization, the entire population of the Americas was transformed; its American population became a global population. On a different scale, throughout Asia, there were small numbers of Europeans, while different groups of Chinese, Indian, Japanese and Arab merchants could be found scattered across Southeast Asia. In Europe, journeymen trekked from city to city to learn their trade, and large numbers of people boarded ships from England and Holland as sailors and soldiers, and visited distant continents. The exchange of flora and fauna that was also part of the Columbian exchange had a further effect on demographic developments as New World crops like the potato, maize and tomato, were integrated with Old World agriculture and supplemented existing diets. In particular, the potato was high-yielding and nutritious and was adopted on a large scale in China, thereby playing an important role in the population growth that took place there.

Global Cities

Similarly, the urban system of the world was revolutionized in this period. In 1500 the urban belt of the world stretched from the Mediterranean to the Yangtze delta; it was in essence the first urban civilizations that had emerged after the Neolithic Revolution – from the Levant to southern China – that still dominated the global distribution of cities and, probably, of income and wealth as well. After 1500, this pattern changed as a result of the rapid rise of rival urban centres along the Atlantic coast, the economic growth that occurred there, and the stagnation, if not decline, of the ancient centres of civilization. Cities sparked up in those areas fully engaged in global maritime commerce. We have seen that the rise of Antwerp, Amsterdam and London was related to increased job opportunities as a consequence of the growth of global commerce. In India, coastal cities like Bombay and Calcutta grew rapidly in size, while the population in administrative centres like Delhi and Agra declined. In general, on the basis of the figures of urbanization we have shown in previous chapters, it is safe to conclude that the world became more urbanized between 1500 and 1800, and that considering the above, world trade contributed to this development. It was also in the cities that populations were most 'global'. Early modern cities were full of immigrants – in fact, because death rates tended to exceed birth rates in these filthy cities, urban growth was only possible with high immigration rates. Most of this immigration was from nearby rural areas, but many people also came from further away. In Amsterdam, at least a third of the population was foreign-born; most were Germans or Scandinavians, but among them were Africans, Turks, Frenchmen and many others (Shorto 2013, p, 145). If you could walk the streets of eighteenth-century Batavia, you would see, amongst others, Javanese, Malays, Ambonese, Balinese, Indians, Chinese, as well as various Europeans roaming about (Ota 2014).

Global Divergence

The realignment of production and distribution that occurred during these three centuries of globalization had large consequences for the well-being of the peoples involved. As always, there were winners and losers. In general, it can be said that the winners were mainly located in Western Europe, where economic growth accelerated when regions became part of the core of the international trading system. Urbanization was highest there, real incomes – particularly of the merchant groups – increased, but, at the same time, income and wealth inequality went up as well. Even in the North Sea region, where the standard of living of the population diverged positively from that of the rest of Europe, and the European 'consumer revolution' demonstrates that purchasing power was on the rise, the gains were modest, especially compared with the spectacular economic growth of the nineteenth and twentieth centuries. Outside Western Europe economic growth was limited to Japan (the one country that managed to largely steer away from world markets), Spanish America (but at the prize of a huge decline in the native population) and North America, where new settler societies realized relatively high levels of well-being, largely as a result of producing for the global market.

Compared with these modest gains in well-being achieved by the 'winners' of globalization, there were also real losers in the process who suffered immeasurably. Slaves who were captured in Africa to feed the slave trade, and their sons and daughters who were born in slavery in European colonies, witnessed a dramatic decline in their well-being, arguably much bigger than the gains achieved elsewhere in the system. Perhaps we should add the serfs of Poland to this as well, and the decline in well-being of the inhabitants of the Middle East who bore some of the burden of the relocation of world trade. The inhabitants of the Moluccas who lost their 'independence' should also be included – the genocide of the Banda Islands by the VOC constitutes another tragic episode in the story of globalization. The Aztec and Incas, and in fact almost all 'Indian' people inhabiting the pre-Columbian Americas, were badly affected by the Conquest and occupation. Entire societies collapsed under the violence of the invaders and the biological weapons they accidentally brought with them. There is not much doubt that the net effect of globalization on global well-being – particularly when we include the effects of warfare and conquest – was strongly negative.

Probing slightly deeper into the distribution of the benefits and detriments of early globalization, the story of the winners and losers becomes more complex. The consequences could differ substantially between various regions within the continents, as well as between social groups. In Africa, regions like Angola and Congo were more heavily affected by the slave trades than the Gold Coast. We saw how the North Sea area in Europe picked up on the growth that in the medieval era had accrued to the Mediterranean. While in Southeast Asia, the rise of Batavia as an important hub of the Dutch East India Company trade occurred at the expense of neighbouring Banten (situated just 13 miles east of Batavia), which had been an important commercial centre in the fifteenth and sixteenth centuries. Even in Africa there were groups – slave traders and raiders, and coastal elites – who benefitted from a trade that brought so much harm to the rest of the population, as well as to the region's long-term growth prospects. Dutch merchants benefitted more from rising global trade than the sailors they employed. Even between different merchant groups, the results of early globalization could vary. For India, for example, we noted that there were some merchants who benefitted from the growth of international exchange after 1500 (and especially after 1600), due to increased demand for local and regional trade. At the same time, the bigger Indian merchants (the Gujarati's) who had been more active in long-distance trade in the fifteenth and sixteenth centuries were in full decline by the eighteenth century.

The data that we have shown in this book, on real wages, GDP and urbanization, suggest that between 1500 and 1800, a gap in economic performance emerged between Western Europe and the North American colonies on the one hand, and the rest of the world on the other, a development that is known as the 'Great Divergence'. In this book, we have focused on the role that global trade may have played in this development. As we have also seen, for many parts of the globe, long-distance maritime trade formed only a small part of the economy. In some cases, this meant that the effect of trade on the 'Divergence' was small (like in China, India, and Japan). Over the past decades, a stimulating literature has emerged that has attempted to explain the Great Divergence by emphasizing a variety of factors, such as geographical conditions, demographic patterns, institutions and human capital formation (see the literature cited in this book). Such endogenous developments are necessary to explain, for example, the persistent rise of north-western Europe as the central hub of world trade in this period and why this part of the world profited so much from the new opportunities of globalization (see Van Zanden 2009).

Global Empires

The early modern era was also an age of empires; large land-based empires in most of Asia and Eastern Europe, smaller land empires in Africa, and, of course, European maritime empires that stretched across the globe from the metropoles in Western Europe, over much of the Americas, and along the coasts of Africa and Asia. Overall, the period was one of increasing political centralization. Early modern Europe saw the emergence of state building and fiscal states related to the growth of commerce. We have seen the growth of states like Oyo, Dahomey and Asante that was related to the rise of Atlantic commerce; exporting slaves and gold, often in return for firearms. For the Southeast Asian mainland, we observed how rising global trade may have aided the process of centralization there. In East Asia, relatively large states were mostly closed off from the global economy for much of the early modern era. The income of these states was to a greater degree dependent on land-based income. But even for a state like China, an increasing dependence on global silver influenced politics and economics in the long run and can be seen as one reason for its nineteenth-century instability. In some parts of the world, the colonization that was related to long-distance trade may be seen as a force driving political centralization.

Long-distance trade was conducted under widely different conditions across the globe. In northern India (until the second half of the eighteenth century) and China, due to the existence of large and strong states, European companies had no influence on trading conditions. In areas with smaller and weaker states – for example, south-western India and Sumatra – Europeans allied themselves with local potentates, providing them with military assistance against their rivals in exchange for favourable trade deals. In yet other areas, like the Americas and some parts of the Indonesian archipelago, the Europeans established themselves as colonial overlords. But even among these areas, there were large differences.

There was no such thing as one early modern model of colonization because the characteristics of European colonialism differed widely across the globe. These differences were driven by a variety of factors, such as disease conditions and the size of indigenous populations. This is the interpretation of Acemoglu et al. (2001, 2002) who suggest that variations in economic development trajectories among Europe's former colonies are related to the different patterns of colonization that occurred: in densely populated areas (like Indonesia, India, Peru and Mexico), the European colonizers imposed extractive institutions to exploit the population as much as possible, thereby creating the 'wrong' set of institutions for long-term economic growth. In scarcely populated regions (such as North America and Australia) the same colonizers became settlers who brought 'inclusive' European institutions with them, creating a much more favourable environment for growth.

Others have emphasized differences in the legal systems of the colonizers; with the British transplanting the apparently more benign common law system that protected investors, over the Roman law system transplanted by the Spanish (La Porta et al. 1998, 2008). J.H. Elliot (2006, p. 137) stressed that the colonies in North America had more institutions of political representation 'partly because voting was an established feature of joint-stock companies, and was therefore likely to be transferred with relative ease to colonial settlements operating under company charters'. Recent research has emphasized the agency of local elites in the development of colonial institutions, even in Spanish America, where a supposedly more 'absolutist' variant of colonialism took root (see e.g. Grafe and Irigoin 2012). In Asia, colonization was in the hands of joint-stock trading companies, but it did not lead to the rise of representative institutions of government or to policies that were conducive to long-run economic growth. On Java, the VOC implemented a system of forced deliveries of coffee in return for low prices that would foreshadow the infamous Cultivation System of the nineteenth century. Disease environment, as well as suitability of the soil for the cultivation of particular cash crops may have further influenced institutional developments there (De Zwart 2016b).

This focus on the 'colonial origins' of global inequality also stresses – like Wallerstein's 'world system' approach – the continuity between the economic fate of countries during the early modern period and during the period of 'modern economic growth' in the nineteenth and twentieth centuries.

Global Consequences

Thus far, we have been pre-occupied by the 'short-term' consequences, on well-being in the period itself. As Wallerstein has already argued, the 'long-term' consequences may have even been more important. Globalization created a division of labour that to a large extent perpetuated itself in the period after 1800: Western Europe became the centre of the world economy and achieved high rates of economic growth in the age of industrialization, whereas many other regions were fixed into a subordinate position. In parts of the world it installed a set of institutions that was really unfavourable for long-term growth; the plantation economies of the Caribbean are the most telling examples of this. The long-term effects of slavery on Africa were also negative, while India suffered in the long run due to the loss of its cotton textile industry (which might not have been the case if the region had remained independent). Spanish colonial rule imposed institutions to recruit labour on societies in Latin America that were not conducive to economic growth, but in many ways these institutions were copies of similar structures of labour coercion that existed under the Incas and the Aztecs, and at some point labour coercion was followed by more market-oriented institutions – like wage labour – that were more efficient and less oppressive. The institutional heritage of the early modern period is not entirely negative, and the tendency to stress path dependency over free agency of social groups and societies should not be exaggerated. There is no linear development from sixteenth-century institutions to twenty-first-century income distribution and there have been many moments in which history could have taken another turn (see Austin (2008a) on the 'compression of history'). There is, for example, great variation in the way in which plantation economies of the Caribbean have dealt with their history, ranging from the 'success stories' of Cuba and the Dominican Republic to the bitter fate of Haiti (Frankema and Masé 2014).

Finally, globalization contributed, as we discussed in the previous chapter, to the emergence of the Industrial Revolution in Britain, and in that way to the start of modern economic growth in the 1820s. This was the great watershed in world history, resulting in the modern world economy with, on average, much higher standards of living than before 1820 (in Maddison's estimates, average GDP per capita has risen by a factor of 12 since that year). Not only has GDP per capita increased tremendously, but human well-being as measured by a range of indicators – life expectancy, real wages, heights, literacy – has improved tremendously over the past two centuries (Van Zanden et al. 2014). This improvement occurred across the globe, even if not everyone shared in this development equally. If there is absolution for the sins that early modern globalization committed – and it committed many sins – then it is perhaps for this long-term effect; it was a stage in the development of the world economy which helped pave the way for the industrial society that came into existence after 1820.

Notes

Chapter 1

1 See, for example, the Google Books Ngram viewer that allows to chart the usage of words in books since the 1800s: https://books.google.com/ngrams/, visited on 27 May 2018.

2 Term coined by De Vries (2010).

3 Except for North America: where cities were so small we showed urbanization with at least 5,000 inhabitants.

4 See: *The Economist*, 'The world's shifting centre of gravity', 28 June 28 2012.

5 New institutional economics emphasizes the role of institutions in economic development. Institutions are defined as 'the rules of the game in a society or, more formally, the humanly devised constraints that shape human interaction' (North 1990, p. 3).

6 See Giraldez (2015) on Asian sailors on European ships.

7 Words of Roger Williams, a colonial governor in New England in the seventeenth century, cited in Parker (1988, p. 118).

Chapter 2

1 Why the Dutch East Indiamen were so slow is discussed in a recent paper by Solar and De Zwart (2017).

2 Based on Dutch-Asiatic Shipping Database (Bruijn, Gaastra and Schöffer 1987).

3 For example, the exports from America to Europe shown here around the turn of the eighteenth century actually exceed the estimates of American production shown in Chapter 3.

4 Barrett (1990) puts forward 50 tons on average for the entire period 1600–1800.

5 Using the total import figures for the years 1695–1705 from Chaudhuri (1978) which should reflect the export of bullion flows.

6 Using the invoice values of the VOC from different parts of Asia from De Zwart (2016a) for the period 1650–1790.

7 For a discussion of different measurements of price convergence, see De Zwart (2016a).

8 The Moluccas are in the eastern part of the Indonesian archipelago.

9 Thanks to Leo Lucassen for making an early version of his work available to us.

10 European settlement in Australia started only in earnest at the end of the eighteenth century and is left out of the discussion here.

11 In the early seventeenth century, some of these migrations had coercive elements (McKeown 2011, p. 313). See also Chapter 8 on Chinese expansion.

12 Relative to the total population, the ratio of Russian migration, on the other hand, was higher (McKeown 2014). A share of this flow was coerced (Richardson 2011).

13 Transatlantic Slave Trade Database: www.slavevoyages.org/, visited on 31 August 2017.

Chapter 3

1 The term Latin America is used here for the entire Middle and Southern American mainland, as well as the Caribbean. The term 'Spanish America' excludes Brazil.

2 In his later work, *ReOrient* (1998), referred to in the chapters on Asia, Frank, however, doubts the existence of a European-led world system before 1800.

3 Words of Columbus, cited in Thomas (2003, p. 11)

4 On the causes of the decline see: Livi-Bacci (2006, 2008).

5 See Dell (2010) for a map of the region from which the labour was drafted.

6 We draw on previous work put forward in Arroyo Abad et al. (2012).

7 See the discussion by Bauer (1979a) and (1979b) and Loveman (1979).

8 Prices of goods differ across the globe, also when currencies are converted via exchange rates. To take into account the differences in the purchasing power of various currencies over time and across countries, the Geary-Khamis dollar (GK$) was created. This is a fictional currency unit used to compare wealth and incomes between countries at the same purchasing power parity of the US dollar at a given point in time. In this book, we express values in GK$ of 1990, reflecting the purchasing power of a dollar in the United States in 1990.

9 The evidence on slave health before 1807 is limited. Stanley Engerman (2000, p. 501) notes: 'rates of natural population decrease were highest

in the earliest stage of settlement [...] after a period of adjustment, the rate of natural decrease slowed, and, in the case of Barbados, a small natural increase became possible even before slave emancipation'. Experts like David Eltis, Frank Lewis and David Richardson (2005, p. 684) suggest that life expectancy was probably higher around 1800 than in the seventeenth century.

Chapter 4

1 Although some scholars have found support for the high profits and consequently a large role in investment (Solow 1985).
2 This database is the result of a large international project that has resulted in a number of important works on the slave trade since the 1960s, see Curtin (1969), Lovejoy (2011), Klein (2010). For our brief summary in this chapter, we are indebted to the work on this project. While their numbers are still subject to change as more research is being done, they have captured such a large part of the total that they deem it 'unlikely that future scholars will dramatically increase the size or scale of the trans-Atlantic slave trade'.
3 All figures mentioned in this paragraph and the next are based on data from Eltis et al. (2013), accessed 26 June 2016.
4 This is the subject of some debate, see e.g. Rodney (1972); Thornton (1992).
5 Van den Boogaart (1992) suggested that already in the seventeenth century the value of slaves exceeded that of the other exports. Such conclusions have been refuted by Eltis (1994). The valuation of the West African trade is complex as many of the transactions were bartered, meaning that monetary values are depending on European or American values and can include or exclude freight and insurance charges. Transport costs of slaves were obviously higher than those of gold and ivory.
6 Richards (1980) notes that Inikori underestimates the total number of guns imported.
7 Recent research, however, has shown that much of the provisions of slave ships were already bought in Europe, limiting the demand in Western Africa (Dalrymple-Smith and Frankema, 2017). E.g. the Dutch in the last decades of the eighteenth century bought all their needed provisions in Europe.
8 Or further away, in neighbouring areas, if the state was strong enough to protect its own citizens, e.g. in Asante and Dahomey (these states were located in the regions of current Ghana and Benin, respectively).

9 Polygyny is the practice of having more than one wife, which is a form of polygamy, the practice of having more than one spouse. Polyandry is the practice of having more than one husband.
10 See e.g. Austin (2008a), Acemoglu and Robinson (2010); Frankema and Van Waijenburg (2012).
11 Paragraph based on De Zwart (2013).

Chapter 5

1 Quebec, Nova Scotia and Newfoundland.
2 Quebec, Nova Scotia and Newfoundland.
3 Total population numbers linearly extrapolated from 1780.
4 We thank Bob Allen and Eric Schneider for generously sharing their data with us.

Chapter 6

1 Correa, *Three Voyages*, cited in: Giraldez (2015, p. 42).
2 This includes shipping to and from other areas in Asia, besides India.
3 Roy (2013)'s high estimate is based on the assumption of a 1 per cent GDP growth per annum between 1750 and 1860, yet new estimates suggest stagnation or declining GDP in this period.
4 Datta (1999) provides different figures for those later years, which are disputed by Bowen (2010).
5 Prakash (1998, p. 98) gives incomplete figures.
6 Total treasure from Bruijn et al. (1979, pp. 226–244); bullion into India for the years 1701–1702, 1711–1712, 1722–23, 1731–1732, 1741–1742, 1751–1752, 1761–1762, 1770–1771, 1784–1785 from Prakash (1998, p. 98). This includes bullion flowing in via Batavia and other Asian VOC establishments. It is not clear from these figures what percentage of this silver was re-exported to China (see Flynn and Giraldez (2004, 2008) who note that China was the principal end market of American silver).
7 In 1765, the EIC obtained so-called *diwani* rights in Bengal, Bihar and Orissa (north and north-eastern India), which legally acknowledged their rule and granted the Company the right to collect revenues.
8 Fisher equation: $MV = PT$, where M = money supply, V = velocity of circulation, P = price level and T = trade.
9 Van Santen (1982) came to similar conclusions about the lack of inflation in seventeenth-century Gujarat.

10 Growth rates were computed by estimating the linear trend of the logs of the series shown in Figure 6.2.
11 Value reported was 2.85 million *xerafins*, according to Souza (1986): 1 *xerafin* = 0.75 *tael* = 0.028 kg.
12 For this section, we draw on the work by Ashin Das Gupta (1982), the main expert on Indian early modern shipping.
13 Bairoch (1982, p. 296) gives a figure of 25 per cent of total manufacturing output in 1750, declining to 2 per cent in 1900, but the accuracy of these figures may be disputed.
14 Discussed by Frank (1998, pp. 267–268).
15 Broadberry, Custodis and Gupta (2015) focus on the decline in industrial output rather than employment. If we would assume some increases in labour productivity, this would mean that the declines in employment would be greater than those in output. Parthasarathi (2011, pp. 203–213) discusses various technological innovations in India that may have led to increased labour productivity.
16 Different positions in this long-standing debate often had political connotations. Whereas both Marxist and 'nationalist' scholars emphasized the role of British colonial policies, more liberal, or mainstream, writers stress the effects of changing global market conditions that affected the terms of trade (see Ray 2016).
17 C.A. Bayly (1983) also notes the ecological stress in the mid-eighteenth century and this point is taken up more recently by Geoffrey Parker (2013), who, however, emphasizes poor climate conditions in the seventeenth century.
18 For a deeper analysis of the wages and the occupations they pertain to, we refer to the sources mentioned in the table.
19 Based on the 'bare-bones' basket as put forward by Allen et al. (2011); see our Introduction.
20 Heitzman (2008) believes the urban population was between 10 and 20 per cent, while Habib (1982) suggests an urbanization rate that declined from 15 to 13 per cent between 1600 and 1800. Our numbers are more in line with Blake's (1987) suggestion of an urban population of about 5 per cent in the seventeenth century.

Chapter 7

1 This includes exports to other parts of Asia, but not exports and imports between the different Southeast Asian countries.
2 Mace is the dried aril and nutmeg the seed core of the fruit of the nutmeg tree. In its prime, after about 13 years, a nutmeg tree yields 10 *pond* of peeled nutmegs and 1.5 *pond* of dried mace (Jacobs 2006, p. 20).

3 Based on figures from the Bookkeeper-General database; this is in contrast to the suggestion by Bulbeck et al. (1998, p. 21) that only half of the nutmeg and mace were sold in Europe (based on Hanna 1978). Similarly, Reid (1993a, pp. 19–20) cites Knaap (1987) to suggest that Europe took one-third to half the world supply of Moluccan spices.

4 Bulbeck et al. (1998, p. 6) note that 0.95 million represents 11 per cent of the total trade, but 33 per cent of total exports; total exports can thus be estimated at 2.9 million Spanish *reals.*

5 This is an imperfect measure of population density as the total land area differs from the total amount of arable land (excluding for example desert, inland water bodies, tundra and rugged mountain slopes). For East Asia and England, we do have such estimates of arable land (see next chapter).

6 His range varies between 2.7 (for a slave) and 650 (caulker) times the daily rice requirement. The average of 25 is taken from Boomgaard (1990, p. 44).

Chapter 8

1 Sng and Moriguchi (2014, p. 441) give per capita tax revenue in koku of rice: around 1700 this was approximately 0.3 and 0.16 koku. One koku is 150 kg of rice (Schreurs 2015).

2 When the American Commodore Perry forced the opening of Japan with his Black Ships. Unarmed peasant uprisings did occur frequently, especially in the second half of the Tokugawa era (Hayami and Kitô 2004, p. 235).

3 Also in the case of Japan, estimates of population differ widely (see Gruber 2014).

4 4,259,000 ha. around 1775 (Lee 1997) against a population of 18.6 million in 1807 (Jun et al. 2008).

5 In 1700, England's population was 5.2 million with 9.56 million square km of arable land (Broadberry et al. 2015).

6 The wage series for the seventeenth century cited by Cha (2009) stems from government (palace) records that are considered unreliable by Jun et al. (2008).

7 Cited in Myers and Wang (2002, pp. 564–565).

8 The increasing land–labour ratios in Korea, and the concentration of land in the hands of fewer people, also meant increases in the size of the labour market and in the northern parts of the country hired labour may have become cheaper than slave maintenance (Deuchler 1997, p. 306).

9 In a recent paper, Deng and O'Brien (2016) are highly critical about the possibility of estimating GDP per capita for China in the long run, given the absence of reliable primary data. GDP estimates for periods further

back in the past are always contentious, yet the fact that these estimates are rather close and show roughly similar trends gives some confidence in these estimates.

10 Li (1998, 2005) suggested agricultural productivity in the Yangtze delta actually rose in this period. This claim, however, is based on gross ouput, while Allen (2009a)'s study shows stability in net output due to increased fertilizer costs.

11 Adverse climate conditions played a part in these harvest failures. See the book by Parker (2013) on the global seventeenth-century crisis.

12 250 million *taels* (Wang 1992, p. 60); Von Glahn (1996b, p. 432) notes that this figure is probably too low.

13 Obviously, such figures are subject to a large margin of error, they should only be seen as indicative of a trend and provide a very rough indication of the overall level.

14 Domestic output was 4–6 tons per annum in the sixteenth and seventeenth centuries (Von Glahn 1996a, p. 114).

15 Cheung (2013, pp. 259-260): 8.9 million pounds in 1720s, 37.3 million pounds in 1750s. Bowen (2010): total 1790–1799 = 182 million pounds. Figures in this paragraph were transformed to annual estimates by dividing by 10.

16 Words of Karl Pieter Thunberg (1743–1828), physician and botanist of Deshima in 1776, cited in Goodman (2013, p. 22).

17 1.62 million *kin*, 1 *kin* = 0.59 kg (Tashiro 2004, pp. 109, 112).

Chapter 9

1 The term 'Dutch disease' stems from the 1970s, when it was used to describe the decline of the Netherlands manufacturing industry as a result of the boom in exports of natural gas after the discovery of a giant gas field in Groningen (in the north of the Netherlands) which pushed the value of the guilder up and thereby reduced the competitiveness of manufacturing.

2 After Adam Smith, who emphasized the effects of increased trade volumes and geographical expansion of markets on specialization, and of specialization on growth; as more countries focus on producing what they are good at, and importing what they are not good at making, overall productivity increases.

3 Following Becker's (1981) quality–quantity trade-off hypothesis which predicts a negative relationship between the number of children and the investment in their education.

Bibliography

Abu-Lughod, J.L. (1989). *Before European Hegemony. The World System AD 1250–1350*. Oxford: Oxford University Press.

Acemoglu, Daron, Simon Johnson and James A. Robinson (2001). 'The Colonial Origins of Comparative Development: An Empirical Investigation', *American Economic Review* 102, pp. 3077–3110.

(2002). 'Reversal of Fortune: Geography and Institutions in the Making of the Modern World Income Distribution', *Quarterly Journal of Economics* 117, pp. 1231–1294.

(2005). 'The Rise of Europe: Atlantic Trade, Institutional Change, and Economic Growth', *American Economic Review* 95, pp. 546–579.

Acemoglu, Daron and James A. Robinson (2010). 'Why Is Africa Poor?', *Economic History of Developing Regions* 25, pp. 21–50.

(2012). *Why Nations Fail: The Origins of power, Prosperity and Poverty*. New York: Crown Business.

Alfani, Guido and Wouter Ryckbosch (2016). 'Growing Apart in Early modern Europe? A Comparison of Inequality Trends in Italy and the Low Countries, 1500–1800', *Explorations in Economic History* 62, pp. 143–153.

Allen, Richard B. (2008). 'The Constant Demand of the French: The Mascarene Slave Trade and the Worlds of the Indian Ocean and the Atlantic during the Eighteenth and Nineteenth Centuries', *Journal of African History* 49, pp. 43–72.

Allen, Robert C. (2000). 'Economic Structure and Agricultural Production in Europe, 1300–1800', *European Review of Economic History* 3, pp. 1–25.

(2001). 'The Great Divergence in European Wages and Prices from the Middle Ages to the First World War', *Explorations in Economic History* 38, pp. 411–447.

(2003). 'Progress and Poverty in Early Modern Europe', *Economic History Review* 56, pp. 403–443.

(2007), 'India in the Great Divergence', in Timothy J. Hatton, Kevin H. O'Rourke and Alan M. Taylor (eds), *The New Comparative Economic History: Essays in Honor of Jeffrey G. Williamson*. Cambridge, MA: MIT Press, pp. 9–32.

(2009a). 'Agricultural Productivity and Rural Incomes in England and the Yangtze Delta, *c*.1620–*c*. 1820', *Economic History Review* 62, pp. 525–550.

(2009b). *The British Industrial Revolution in Global Perspective.* Cambridge: Cambridge University Press.

Allen, Robert C., Jean-Pascal Bassino, Debin Ma, Christine Moll-Murata and Jan Luiten van Zanden (2011). 'Wages, Prices, and Living Standards in China, 1738–1925', in Comparison with Europe, Japan, and India', *Economic History Review* 64, pp. 8–38.

Allen, Robert C., Tommy E. Murphy and Eric B. Schneider (2012). 'The Colonial Origins of the Divergence in the Americas: A Labor Market Approach', *Journal of Economic History* 72, pp. 863–894.

Allen, Robert C., and Roman Studer, 'Prices and Wages in India 1595–1930'. Datafile from Global Prices and Income History Database, http://gpih .ucdavis.edu/, visited on 25 May 2018.

Allen, Robert C. and J.L. Weisdorf (2011). 'Was There an "Industrious Revolution" before the Industrial Revolution? An Empirical Exercise for England, *c*.1300–1830', *Economic History Review* 64(3) pp. 715–729.

Alpers, Edward A. (1975). *Ivory and Slaves in East Central Africa. Changing Patterns of International Trade to the Later Nineteenth Century.* London: Heinemann.

(1976). 'Gujarat and the Trade of East Africa, *c*.1500–1800', *International Journal of African Historical Studies* 9, pp. 22–44.

(1977). 'Eastern Africa', in Richard Gray (ed.) *Cambridge History of Africa*. Cambridge: Cambridge University Press.

Álvarez-Nogal, C. and L. Prados de la Escosura (2013). 'The Rise and Fall of Spain (1270–1850)', *The Economic History Review*, 66(1), pp. 1–37.

Andaya, Leonard (1993). 'Interactions with the Outside World and Adaptation in Southeast Asian Society, 1500–1800', in Nicholas Tarling (ed.) *The Cambridge History of Southeast Asia Vol. 1: From Early Times to c.1800*. Cambridge: Cambridge University Press, pp. 341–401.

Arasaratnam, S. (1988). 'The Rice Trade in Eastern India 1650–1740', *Modern Asian Studies* 22, pp. 531–549.

Arroyo Abad, Leticia, Elwyn Davies and Jan Luiten van Zanden (2012). 'Between Conquest and Independence: Real wages and demographic change in Spanish America, 1530–1820', *Explorations in Economic History* 29(2), pp. 149–166.

Arroyo Abad, Leticia, and Jan Luiten van Zanden (2016). 'Growth under Extractive Institutions? Latin American Per Capita GDP in Colonial Times', *Journal of Economic History* 76, pp. 1182–1215.

294 *Bibliography*

Attman, A. (1986). *American Bullion in European World Trade*. Uppsala: Almqvist and Wiksell.

Atwell, William S. (1982). 'International Bullion Flows and the Chinese Economy circa 1530–1650', *Past and Present* 95, pp. 68–90.

 (1986). 'Some Observations on the "Seventeenth-Century Crisis" in China and Japan', *Journal of Asian Studies* 45, pp. 223–244.

 (1998). 'Ming China and the emerging world economy, c.1470–1650', in Denis C. Twitchett (ed.), *Cambridge History of China, Vol. 8: The Ming Dynasty, Part 2: 1368–1644*. Cambridge: Cambridge University Press, pp 376–416.

 (2005). 'Another Look at Silver Imports into China, ca.1635–1644', *Journal of Global History* 16, pp. 467–489.

Austin, Gareth (2008a). 'The "Reversal of Fortune" Thesis and the Compression of History: Perspectives from African and Comparative Economic History', *Journal of International Development* 20, pp. 996–1027.

 (2008b). 'Resources, Techniques and Strategies South of the Sahara: Revising the Factor Endowments Perspective on African Economic Development, 1500–2000', *Economic History Review* 61, pp. 587–624.

 (2009). 'Factor Markets in Nieboer Conditions: Pre-Colonial West Africa, c.1500–c.1900', *Continuity and Change* 24, pp. 23–53.

 (2013). 'Commercial Agriculture and the Ending of Slave-Trading and Slavery in West Africa, 1780s–1920s', in: Robin Law et al. (eds) *Commercial Agriculture, the Slave Trade and Slavery in Atlantic Africa*. Woodbridge: James Currey.

Bagchi, A.K. (1976). 'De-Industrialization in India in the Nineteenth Century: Some Theoretical Implications', *Journal of Development Studies* 12, pp. 135–163.

Bairoch, P. (1982). 'International Industrialization Levels from 1750 to 1980', *Journal of European Economic History* 11, pp. 268–333.

Bakewell, P. (1984). *Miners of the Red Mountain, Indian Labor in Potosí, 1545–1650*. Albuquerque: University of Mexico Press.

Barendse, R.J. (2000). 'Trade and State in the Arabian Seas: A Survey from the Fifteenth to the Eighteenth Century', *Journal of World History* 11, pp. 173–225.

Barrett, Ward (1990). 'World bullion flows, 1450–1800', in J.C. Tracy (ed.), *The Rise of Merchant Empires: Long-Distance Trade in the Early Modern World, 1350–1750*. Cambridge: Cambridge University Press, pp. 224–254.

Bassino, Jean-Pascal (2007). 'Market Integration and Famines in Early Modern Japan 1717–1857'. Mimeo: http://federation.ens.fr/ydepot/semin/texte0708/BAS2007MAR.pdf

Bassino, Jean-Pascal, S. Broadberry, K. Fukao, B. Gupta and M. Takashima (2015). 'Japan and the Great Divergence, 725–1874', *Mimeo*. CEPR Discussion Paper No. DP10569. Available at SSRN: https://ssrn.com/abstract=2602806

Baten, J. and M. Blum (2014). 'Human Height since 1820', in J.L. van Zanden et al. (eds.), *How Was Life? Global Well-Being since 1820*. Paris: OECD Publishing.

Baten, J. and J.L. Van Zanden (2008). 'Book Production and the Onset of Modern Economic Growth', *Journal of Economic Growth* 13(3), pp. 217–235.

Baten, J., D. Ma, S. Morgan, Q. Wang (2010). 'Evolution of Living Standards and Human Capital in China in the 18–20th Centuries: Evidences from Real Wages, Age-Heaping and Anthropometrics', *Explorations in Economic History* 47, pp. 347–359.

Baten, J., M. Stegl, and P. van der Eng (2013). 'The Biological Standard of Living and Body Height in Colonial and Post-Colonial Indonesia, 1770–2000', *Journal of Bioeconomics* 15, pp. 103–122.

Bauer, A.J. (1979a). 'Rural Workers in Spanish America: Problems of Peonage and Oppression', *Hispanice American Historical Review* 59, pp. 34–63.

(1979b) *Expansion económica y sociedad rural: El caso chileno en el siglo XIX*. Santiago: Ediciones Nuestra America.

Bayly, C.A. (1983). *Rulers, Townsmen, and Bazaars. North Indian Society in the Age of British expansion, 1770–1870*. Cambridge: Cambridge University Press.

Becker, Gary, (1981). *A Treatise on the Family*. Cambridge, MA: Harvard University Press.

Beckert, Sven (2015). *Empire of Cotton. A Global History*. New York: Vintage.

Bentley, Jerry H., Sanjay Subrahmanyam and Merry E. Wiesner-Hanks (eds) (2015). *The Cambridge World History, Volume 6: The Construction of a Global World, 1400–1800 CE, Part 1: Foundations*. Cambridge: Cambridge University Press.

Berg, Maxine (1999). 'New commodities, luxuries and their consumers in eighteenth-century England', in Maxine Berg and Helen Clifford (eds), *Consumers and luxury. Consumer culture in Europe 1650–1850*. Manchester: Manchester University Press.

(2005). *Luxury and Pleasure in Eighteenth-Century Britain*. Oxford: Oxford University Press.

(2009). 'Quality, cotton and the global luxury trade', in Giorgio Riello and Tirthankar Roy (eds.) *How India Clothed the World. The World of South Asian Textiles, 1500–1850*. Leiden: Brill.

(2015). '"The merest shadows of a commodity". Indian Muslins for European markets', in Maxine Berg, Felicia Gottmann, Hanna Hodacs, and Chris Nierstrasz (eds.), *Goods from the East 1600–1800. Trading Eurasia*. London: Palgrave Macmillan, pp. 119–137.

Bezemer, D., J. Bolt and R. Lensink (2014). 'Slavery, Statehood and Economic Development in Sub-Saharan Africa', *World Development* 57, pp. 148–163.

Black, Jeremy (2011). *Fighting for America: The Struggle for Mastery in North America, 1519–1871*. Bloomington: Indiana University Press.

Blake, S.P. (1987). 'The Urban Economy In Pre-Modern Muslim India: Shahjahanabad, 1639–1739', *Modern Asian Studies* 21(3), pp. 447–471.

Blondé Bruno and Llja Van Damme (2010). 'Retail Growth and Consumer Changes in a Declining Urban Economy: Antwerp', *Economic History Review* 63(3), pp. 638–663.

Blussé, Leonard (1981). 'Batavia, 1619–1740: The Rise and Fall of a Chinese Colonial Town', *Journal of Southeast Asian Studies* 12, pp. 159–178.

(2008). *Visible Cities. Canton, Nagasaki, and Batavia and the Coming of the Americans*. Cambridge, MA: Harvard University Press.

Bolt, J. and J.L. van Zanden (2014). 'The Maddison Project: Collaborative Research on Historical National Accounts', *Economic History Review* 67, pp. 627–651.

Bookkeeper-General Database from Huygens ING: http://bgb.huygens .knaw.nl/, visited on 25 May 2018.

Boomgaard, Peter (1990). 'Why Work for Wages? Free Labour in Java 1600–1900, *Economic and Social History in the Netherlands* 2, pp. 37–57.

(2009). 'Labour, Land and Capital Markets in Early Modern Southeast Asia from the Fifteenth to the Nineteenth Century', *Continuity and Change* 24, pp. 55–78.

Boshoff, W. and J. Fourie (2010). 'The Significance of the Cape Trade Route to Economic Activity in the Cape Colony: A Medium-Term Business Cycle Analysis', *European Review of Economic History* 14, pp. 469–503.

Bosker, Maarten, Eltjo Buringh and Jan Luiten van Zanden (2013). 'From Baghdad to London, Unraveling Urban Development in Europe, North Africa and the Middle East, 800–1800', *Review of Economics and Statistics* 95, pp. 1418–1437.

Bosma, Ulbe (2013). *The Sugar Plantation in India and Indonesia. Industrial Production, 1770–2010*. Cambridge: Cambridge University Press.

Bowen, H.V. (2008). *The Business of Empire: The East India Company and Imperial Britain, 1756-1833*. Cambridge: Cambridge University Press.

(2010). 'Bullion for Trade, War, and Debt-Relief: British Movements of Silver to, around, and from Asia, 1760–1833', *Modern Asian Studies* 44, pp. 445–475.

Boyajian, J.C. (1993). *Portuguese Trade in Asia under the Habsburgs, 1580–1640*. Baltimore: Johns Hopkins University Press.

Brading, D.A. (1971). *Miners and Merchants in Bourbon Mexico, 1763–1810*. Cambridge: Cambridge University Press.

Brandt, Loren, Debin Ma and Thomas G. Rawski (2014). 'From Divergence to Convergence: Re-evaluating the History Behind China's Economic Boom', *Journal of Economic Literature* 52, pp. 45–123.

Braudel, Fernand (1982). *Civilization and Capitalism 15th–18th century. Vol. II: The Wheels of Commerce*. Berkeley and Los Angeles: University of California Press.

Breen, T.H. (1988). '"Baubles of Britain": The American and Consumer Revolutions of the Eighteenth Century', *Past and Present* 119, pp. 73–104.

Broadberry, S. and B. Gupta (2006). 'The Early Modern Great Divergence: Wages, Prices and Economic Development in Europe and Asia, 1500–1800', *Economic History Review* 59, pp. 2–31.

(2009). 'Lancashire, India, and Shifting Competitive Advantage in Cotton Textiles, 1700–1850: The Neglected Role of Factor Prices', *Economic History Review* 62, 279–305.

Broadberry, S., B. Campbell, Alexander Klein, Mark Overton, and Bas van Leeuwen (2015). *British Economic Growth, 1270–1870*. Cambridge: Cambridge University Press.

Broadberry, S., J. Custodis and B. Gupta (2015). 'India and the Great Divergence: An Anglo-Indian Comparison of GDP Per Capita, 1600–1871', *Explorations in Economic History* 55, pp. 58–75.

Broadberry, S., Hanhui Guan and David Daokui Li (2014). 'China, Europe and the Great Divergence: A Study in Historical National Accounting, 980–1850', *EH.net Working Paper*: http://eh.net/eha/wp-content/uploads/2014/05/Broadberry.pdf

Bruijn, J.R. (1980). 'Between Batavia and the Cape: Shipping Patterns of the Dutch East India Company', *Journal of Southeast Asian Studies* 11, pp. 251–263.

(1990). 'Productivity, profitability, and costs of private and corporate Dutch ship owning in the seventeenth and eighteenth centuries', in *The Rise of Merchant Empires. Long-Distance Trade in the Early Modern World, 1350–1750*, J. D. Tracy (ed.). Cambridge: Cambridge University Press, pp. 174–194.

Bruijn, J.R., F.S. Gaastra and I. Schöffer (1979–1987). *Dutch-Asiatic Shipping in the 17th and 18th Centuries*. Vols. 1–3. The Hague: Nijhoff.

Bruijn, Jaap R. and Femme S. Gaastra (1993). 'The Dutch East India Company's shipping, 1602–1795, in a comparative perspective', in ibid. (eds.) *Ships, Sailors and Spices. East India Companies and Their Shipping in the 16th, 17th and 18th Century*. NEHA: Amsterdam.

Bulbeck, David, Anthony Reid, Lay Cheng Tan and Yiqi Wu (1998). *Southeast Asian Exports since the 14th Century. Cloves, Pepper, Coffee and Sugar.* Leiden: KITLV.

Bulut, Mehmet (2002). 'The Role of the Ottoman and Dutch in the Commercial Integration between the Levant and Atlantic in the Seventeenth Century', *Journal of the Economic and Social History of the Orient* 45(2), 197–230.

Buringh, Eltjo (2016). Clio Infra Urbanization Hub, www.cgeh.nl/urbanisation-hub-clio-infra-database-urban-settlement-sizes-1500-2000.

Burnard, Trevor, and John Garrigus (2016). *The Plantation Machine: Atlantic Capitalism in French Saint-Domingue and British Jamaica. Early Modern Americas.* Philadelphia, PA: University of Pennsylvania Press.

Carlos, Ann M. and Frank D. Lewis (1993). 'Indians, the Beaver, and the Bay: The Economics of Depletion in the Lands of the Hudson's Bay Company, 1700–1773', *Journal of Economic History* 53, pp. 465–494.

(2001). 'Trade, Consumption, and the Native Economy: Lessons from York Factory, Hudson Bay', *Journal of Economic History* 61, pp. 1037–1064.

(2010). *Commerce by a Frozen Sea. Native Americans and the European Fur Trade.* Philadelphia, PA: University of Pennsylvania Press.

Carmagnani, M. (1963). *El salariado minero en Chile colonial: su desarrollo en una sociedad provincial: el Norte Chico 1690-1800.* Santiago: Editorial Universitaria.

Cha, Myung Soo (2009). 'Productivity Trends in Korea from the Seventeenth to Nineteenth Century: A Comment on Jun, Lewis, and Kang', *Journal of Economic History* 69, pp. 1138–1143.

Challú, Amílcar E. (2010). 'The Great Decline: biological well-being and living standards in Mexico, 1730–1840', in R.D. Salvatore, J.H. Coatsworth and A.E. Challú (eds.), *Living Standards in Latin American History, Height, Welfare and Development 1750–2000.* Cambridge, MA: Harvard University Press.

Chandler, Tertius, and Gerald Fox (1974). *3000 Thousand Years of Urban Growth.* New York and London: Academic Press.

Chandra, B. (1992). 'The colonial legacy', in B. Jalan (ed.), *The Indian Economy: Problems and Prospects.* New York: Viking, pp. 1–32.

Chao, Kang (1986). *Man and Land in Chinese History: An Economic Analysis.* Stanford, CA: Stanford University Press.

Chaudhuri, K.N. (1978). *The Trading World of Asia and the English East India Company, 1660–1760.* Cambridge: Cambridge University Press.

(1993). 'The English East India Company's shipping (c.1660–1760)', in J.R Bruijn, and F.S. Gaastra (eds), *Ships, Sailors and Spices. East India Companies and Their Shipping in the 16th, 17th and 18th centuries.* Amsterdam: NEHA, pp. 49–80.

Chaudhury, S. (1995). *From Prosperity to Decline: Eighteenth-century Bengal*. Delhi: Manohar.

(1999). 'The Asian merchants and companies in Bengal's export trade, circa mid-eighteenth century', in S. Chaudhury and M. Morineau, (eds) *Merchants, Companies and Trade : Europe and Asia in the Early Modern Era*. Cambridge: Cambridge University Press, pp. 300–320.

Cheung, Sui-wai (2013). 'Copper, Silver and Tea. The Question of Eighteenth-Century Inflation in the Lower Yangzi Delta', in Billy, K.L. So (ed.), *The Economy of Lower Yangzi Delta in Late Imperial China. Connecting money, markets, and institutions*. London and New York: Routledge.

Clingingsmith, D. and J.G. Williamson. (2008) 'Deindustrialization in 18th and 19th Century India: Mughal Decline, Climate Shocks and British Industrial Ascent', *Explorations in Economic History* 45, pp. 209–234.

Clark, Gregory (2005). 'The Condition of the Working Class in England, 1209–2004', *Journal of Political Economy* 113(6), pp. 1307–1340.

(2006). 'England prices and wages since 13th century', *Global Price and Income History group*, http://gpih.ucdavis.edu/

(2007). *A Farewell to Alms. A Brief Economic History of the World*. Princeton: Princeton University Press.

Clio-Infra (2015). 'Total Population', www.clio-infra.eu/Indicators/Total Population.html

Coatsworth, John H. (1998). 'Economic and institutional trajectories in nineteenth-century Latin America', in John Coatsworth and Alan M. Taylor (eds), *Latin America and the World Economy since 1800*. Cambridge, MA: Harvard University Press, pp. 23–54.

(2004). 'Globalization, growth and welfare in history', in M. Marcelo Suárez-Orozco and Desirée Qin-Hilliard (eds), *Globalization: Culture and Education in the New Millennium*. Oakland, CA: University of California Press.

(2005). 'Political economy and economic organization', in V. Bulmer-Thomas, J. Coatsworth and Robert Cortes-Conde (eds), *Cambridge Economic History of Latin America*. Cambridge: Cambridge University Press, pp. 237–273.

(2008). 'Inequality, Institutions and Economic Growth in Latin America', *Journal of Latin American Studies* 40, pp. 545–569.

Coclanis, Peter A. (1989). *Shadow of a Dream: Economic Life and Death in the South Carolina Low Country, 1670–1920*. Oxford: Oxford University Press.

Crosby, Alfred W. (1972). *The Columbian Exchange: Biological and Cultural Consequences of 1492*. Westport, CO: Greenwood Press.

Curtin, Philip D. (1969). *The Atlantic slave trade: A census*. Madison, WI: University of Wisconsin Press.

Dalrymple-Smith, Angus and Ewout Frankema (2017). 'Slave Ship Provisioning in the Long 18th Century: A Boost to West African Commercial Agriculture?', *European Review of Economic History* 21, pp. 185–235.

Dalrymple-Smith, Angus and Pieter Woltjer (2016). 'Commodities, Prices and Risk: The Changing Market for Non-Slave Products in Pre-Abolition West Africa', *African Economic History Network Working Paper* 31.

Dalton, John T. and Tin Cheuk Leung (2014). 'Why Is Polygyny More Prevalent in Western Africa? An African Slave Trade Perspective', *Economic Development and Cultural Change* 62, pp. 599–632.

Das Gupta, A. (1982). 'Indian Merchants and the trade in the Indian Ocean, *c.*1500–1750', in T. Raychaudhuri and I. Habib (eds) *Cambridge Economic History of India*, vol. 1, pp. 407–433.

Datta, R. (1999). 'Markets, bullion and Bengal's commercial economy: an eighteenth century perspective', in O. Prakash and D. Lombard (eds.), *Commerce and Culture in the Bay of Bengal, 1500–1800*. Delhi: Manohar, pp. 329–359.

Davis, Lance E., Richard A. Easterlin and William N. Parker, et al. (1972). *American Economic Growth: An Economist's History of the United States*. New York: Harper and Row.

Davis, R. (1962). *The Rise of the English Shipping Industry in the Seventeenth and Eighteenth Centuries*. London: Macmillan & Co.

De Moor, T. and J.L. Van Zanden (2010). 'Girlpower: The European Marriage Pattern and Labour Markets in the North Sea Region in the Late Medieval and Early Modern Period', *Economic History Review* 63(1), pp. 1–33.

De Pleijt, A.M. and J.L. van Zanden (2016). 'Accounting for the Little Divergence: What Drove Economic Growth in Pre-Industrial Europe, 1300–1800?', *European Review of Economic History* 20, pp. 387–409.

De Vries, Jan (2003). 'Connecting Europe and Asia: a quantitative analysis of the Cape-route trade, 1497–1795', in D. O. Flynn, A. Giraldez, and R. von Glahn (eds), *Global cConnections and Monetary History, 1470–1800*. Aldershot: Routledge, pp. 35–106.

(2008). *The Industrious Revolution: Consumer Behavior and the Household Economy, 1650 to the Present*. Cambridge: Cambridge University Press.

(2010). 'The Limits of Globalization in the Early Modern World', *Economic History Review* 63, pp. 710–733.

(2015). 'Understanding Eurasian trade in the era of the trading companies', in Maxine Berg, Felicia Gottmann, Hanna Hodacs, and Chris Nierstrasz (eds), *Goods from the East 1600–1800. Trading Eurasia*. London: Palgrave Macmillan, pp. 7–39.

De Zwart, Pim (2011). 'South African Living Standards in Global Perspective, 1835–1910', *Economic History of Developing Regions* 26, pp. 49–74.

(2012). 'Population, Labour and Living Standards in Early Modern Ceylon: A Contribution to the Divergence Debate', *Indian Economic and Social History Review* 49, pp. 365–398.

(2013). 'Real Wages at the Cape of Good Hope: A Long-term Perspective, 1652–1912', *Low Countries Journal of Social and Economic History* 10, pp. 28–58.

(2016a). 'Globalization in the Early Modern Era: New Evidence from the Dutch-Asiatic Trade, *c.* 1600–1800', *Journal of Economic History* 76, pp. 520–558.

(2016b). *Globalization and the Colonial Origins of the Great Divergence.* Leiden and Boston: Brill.

De Zwart, Pim and J. Lucassen (2015). 'Poverty or Prosperity in Bengal? New Evidence, Methods and Perspectives *c.*1700–*c.*1870', *Paper Presented at the WEHC 2015 in Kyoto.*

De Zwart, Pim and J.L. van Zanden (2015) 'Labor, Wages and Living Standards in Java, 1680–1914', *European Review of Economic History* 19, pp. 215–234.

Dell, Melissa (2010). 'The Persistent Effects of Peru's Mining Mita', *Econometrica* 78, pp. 1863–1903.

Deng, Kent, and Patrick O'Brien (2016). 'Establishing Statistical Foundations of a Chronology for the Great Divergence: A Survey and Critique of the Primary Sources for the Construction of Relative Wage Levels for Ming-Qing China', *Economic History Review*, 69, pp. 1057–1082.

Den Heijer, Hendrik (1997). *Goud, ivoor en slaven. Scheepvaart en handel van de Tweede Westindische Compagnie op Afrika, 1674-1740.* Zutphen: Walburg Pers.

Deuchler, Martina (1992). *The Confucian Transformation of Korea: A Study of Society and Ideology.* Cambridge, MA: Harvard University Press.

(1997). 'Social and economic developments in eighteenth-century Korea', in Anthony Reid (ed.) *The Last Stand of Asian Economies. Responses to Modernity in the Diverse States of Southeast Asia and Korea, 1750–1900.* London: Macmillan, pp. 299–320.

Dibbits, H.C. (2001). *Vertrouwd Bezit. Materiele Cultuur in Doesburg en Maassluis 1650-1800.* Nijmegen: Sun.

Dijk, Wil. O (2002). 'The VOC's Trade in Indian Textiles with Burma, 1634–80', *Journal of Southeast Asian Studies* 33, pp. 495–515.

Dincecco, Mark and Mauricio Prado (2012). 'Warfare, Fiscal Capacity, and Performance', *Journal of Economic Growth* 17, pp. 171–203.

Dobado-Gonzáles, Rafael and Gustavo A. Marrero (2011). 'The Role of the Spanish Imperial State in the Mining-Led Growth of Bourbon Mexico's Economy', *Economic History Review* 64, pp. 855–884.

Dobado Gonzáles, Rafael, Alfredo Garcia-Hiernaux and David E. Guerrero (2012). 'The Integration of Grain Markets in the Eighteenth Century: Early Rise of Globalization in the West', *Journal of Economic History* 72, pp. 671–707.

Dobado Gonzáles, Rafael, A. Gómez Galvarriato and J.G. Williamson (2008). 'Mexican Exceptionalism: Globalization and De-Industrialization, 1750–1877', *Journal of Economic History* 68, pp. 758–811.

Drelichman, Mauricio; (2005). 'The Curse of Moctezuma: American Silver and the Dutch Disease', *Explorations in Economic History* 42, pp. 349–380.

Drelichman, Mauricio and Hans Joachim Voth (2008). 'Institutions and the resource curse in early modern Spain', in Helpman, Elhanan (ed.), *Institutions and Economic Performance*. Cambridge: Harvard University Press, pp. 120–147.

Drescher, Seymour (1977). *Econocide: British Slavery in the Era of Abolition*. Pittsburgh, PA: University of Pittsburgh Press.

   (2009). *Abolition: A History of Slavery and Antislavery*. New York: Cambridge University Press.

Duin, P. van, and R. Ross (1987). 'The Economy of the Cape Colony in the Eighteenth Century', *Intercontinenta* 7. Leiden.

Egnal, Marc (1998). *New World Economies: The Growth of the Thirteen Colonies and Early Canada*. Cary, NC: Oxford University Press.

Elisonas, Jurgis (1991). 'Christianity and the Daimyo', in J.W. Hall (ed.) *Cambridge History of Japan. Vol. 4: Early Modern Japan*. Cambridge: Cambridge University Press, pp. 301–372.

Elliott, J.H. (1984). 'The Spanish conquest and settlement of America', in Leslie Bethell (ed.), *Cambridge History of Latin America*. Cambridge: Cambridge University Press, pp. 147–206.

   (2006). *Empires of the Atlantic World. Britain and Spain in America 1492–1830*. New Haven and London: Yale University Press.

Eltis, David (1989). 'Trade Between Western Africa and the Atlantic World before 1870: Estimates of Trends in value, Composition and Direction', *Research in Economic History* 12, pp. 197–239.

   (1994). 'The Relative Importance of Slaves and Commodities in the Atlantic Trade of Seventeenth-Century Africa', *Journal of African History*, 35, pp. 237–249.

   (1995). 'The Total Product of Barbados 1664–1701', *Journal of Economic History* 55, pp. 321–338.

Eltis, David, and S.L. Engerman (2000). 'The Importance of Slavery and the Slave Trade to Industrializing Britain', *Journal of Economic History* 60, pp. 123–144.

Eltis, David, and Lawrence C. Jennings (1988). 'Trade Between Western Africa and the Atlantic World in the Pre-Colonial Era', *American Historical Review* 93, pp. 936–959.

Eltis, David, Frank Lewis and David Richardson (2005). 'Slave Prices, the African Slave Trade, and Productivity in the Caribbean, 1674–1807', *Economic History Review* 58, pp. 673–700.

Eltis, David, David Richardson, Stephen Behrend, Manolo Florentino and Martin Halbert (2013). *The Trans-Atlantic Slave Trade Database*, www.slavevoyages.org, visited 31 August 2017.

Eltis, David, Frank Lewis and Kimberly McIntyre (2010). 'Accounting for Traffic in Africans: Transport Costs on Slaving Voyages', *Journal of Economic History* 70, pp. 940–963.

Engerman, Stanley L. (2000). 'A Population History of the Caribbean', in Richard Steckel (ed.) *Population History of North America.* Cambridge: Cambridge University Press.

Engerman, Stanley L. and Robert E. Gallman (eds.) (1996). *Cambridge Economic History of the United States. Vol. 1: The Colonial Era.* Cambridge: Cambridge University Press.

Engerman, Stanley L. and K.L. Sokoloff (2000). 'History Lessons. Institutions, Factor Endowments, and Paths of Development in the New World', *Journal of Economic Perspectives* 14, pp. 217–232.

Estevadeordal, A., B. Frantz and A. M. Taylor (2003). 'The Rise and Fall of World Trade, 1870–1939', *Quarterly Journal of Economics* 118, pp. 359–407.

Fage, John D. (1997). *A History of Africa.* London: Hutchinson. [First edition: 1978].

Federico, Giovanni and David Chilosi (2015). 'Early Globalizations: The Integration of Asia in the World Economy', *Explorations in Economic History* 57, pp. 1–18.

Federico, Giovanni and Antonio Tena-Junguito (2016). 'World Trade, 1800–1938: A New Dataset', *EHES Working Papers* 93: http://www.ehes.org/EHES_93.pdf

Feenstra, Alberto (2014). 'Dutch Coins for Asian growth. VOC-duiten to Assess Java's Deep Monetisation and Economic Growth, 1724–1800', *TSEG/ Low Countries Journal of Social and Economic History* 11, pp. 153–184.

Feinstein, Charles (1998). 'Pessimism Perpetuated. Real Wages and the Standard of Living in Britain during and after de Industrial Revolution', *Journal of Economic History* 58, pp. 625–658.

Fenske, James, and Namrata Kala (2014). '1807: Economic Shocks, Conflict and the Slave Trade', *Mimeo*, www.csae.ox.ac.uk/workingpapers/pdfs/csae-wps-2014-02.pdf?

Ferguson, Niall (2011). *Civilization. The West and the Rest.* London: Allen Lane.

Findlay, Ronald (1990). 'The "Triangular Trade" and the Atlantic Economy of the Eighteenth Century: A Simple-Equilibrium Model', *Princeton Studies in International Economics* 177.

Findlay, Ronald and Keven O'Rourke (2003). 'Commodity market integration', in Michael D. Bordo, Alan M. Taylor and Jeffrey G. Williamson (eds), *Globalization in Historical Perspective*. Chicago, IL: University of Chicago Press.

(2007). *Power and Plenty. Trade, War, and the World Economy in the Second Millennium.* Princeton: Princeton University Press.

Flynn, Dennis O. and A. Giraldez (1995). 'Born with a "Silver Spoon": The Origin of World Trade in 1571', *Journal of World History* 6, pp. 201–221.

(2002a). 'Cycles of Silver: Global Economic Unity through the Mid-Eighteenth Century', *Journal of World History* 13, pp. 391–427.

(2002b). 'Silver and Ottoman Monetary History in Global Perspective', *Journal of European Economic History* 31, pp. 9–43.

(2004). 'Path Dependence, Time Lags and the Birth of Globalization: A Critique of O'Rourke and Williamson', *European Review of Economic History* 8(1), pp. 81–108.

(2008). 'Born Again: Globalization's Sixteenth Century Origins (Asian/Global versus European Dynamics)', *Pacific Economic Review* 13, pp. 359–387.

Fourie, J. and J.L. van Zanden (2013). 'GDP in the Dutch Cape Colony: The National Accounts of a Slave-Based Society", *South African Journal of Economics* 81, pp. 467–490.

Fourie, J. (2013). 'The Remarkable Wealth of the Dutch Cape Colony: Measurements from Eighteenth-Century Probate Inventories', *Economic History Review* 66, pp. 419–448.

Francks, Penelope (2016). *Japan and the Great Divergence. A Short Guide.* London: Palgrave Macmillan.

Frank, Andre Gunder (1969). *Capitalism and Underdevelopment in Latin America: Historical Studies of Chile and Brazil.* New York: Monthly Review Press.

(1970). *Latin America: Underdevelopment or Essays on the Development of Underdevelopment and the Immediate Enemy.* New York: Monthly Review Press.

(1978). *World Accumulation, 1492–1789.* London: Macmillan.

(1979). *Dependent Accumulation and Underdevelopment.* London: Macmillan.

(1998). *ReOrient: Global Economy in the Asian Age*. Berkeley, CA: University of California Press.

Frank, Andre Gunder and Barry, Gills (1993). 'The 5000-year world system: an interdisciplinary introduction', in: ibid. (eds), *The World System: Five Hundred Years or Five Thousand?* Routledge: New York and London, pp. 3–57.

Frankema, Ewout, and Aline Masé (2014) 'An Island Drifting Apart. Why Haiti is Mired in Poverty while the Dominican Republic Forges Ahead', *Journal of International Development* 26, 1, 128–148

Frankema, Ewout and Marlous van Waijenburg (2012). 'Structural Impediments to African Growth? New Evidence from Real Wages in British Africa 1880–1965', *Journal of Economic History* 72, pp. 895–926.

French, Cristopher, (1987). 'Productivity in the Atlantic Shipping Industry: A Quantitative Study', *Journal of Interdisciplinary History* 17, pp. 613–618.

Gaastra, F.S. and J.R. Bruijn (1993). 'The Dutch East India Company's shipping, 1602–1795, in a comparative perspective', in J.R Bruijn, and F.S. Gaastra (eds), *Ships, Sailors and Spices. East India Companies and Their Shipping in the 16th, 17th and 18th centuries*. Amsterdam: NEHA, pp. 177–208.

Galenson, David W. (1996). 'The Settlement and growth of the colonies: population, labor and economic development', in Stanley Engerman and Robert E. Gallman (eds), *Cambridge Economic History of the United States. Vol. 1: The Colonial Era*. Cambridge: Cambridge University Press, pp. 135–207.

Garner, Richard L. (1988). "Long-Term Silver Mining Trends in Spanish America: A Comparative Analysis of Peru and Mexico", *American Historical Review* 93, pp. 898–935.

Gelderblom, Oscar (2000). *Zuid-Nederlandse kooplieden en de opkomst van de Amsterdamse stapelmarkt (1578-1630)*. Hilversum: Verloren.

Gelderblom, Oscar and Joost Jonker (2004). 'Completing a Financial Revolution: The Finance of the Dutch East India Trade and the Rise of the Amsterdam Capital Market, 1595–1612', *Journal of Economic History* 64(3), pp. 641–672.

Geloso, Vincent (2016). 'The Seeds of Divergence: The Economy of French North America, 1688 to 1760', PhD Thesis London School of Economics.

Ghosh, Shami (2015). 'How Should We Approach the Economy of "Early Modern India"?', *Modern Asian Studies* 49, pp. 1606–1656.

Giddens, Anthony (1990). *The Consequences of Modernity*. Stanford, CT: Stanford University Press.

Giraldez, Arturo (2013). 'A two-year merchant strike (1636–1637) and the Chinese in Manila: the seventeenth-century crisis in the Philippines', in N. Kim and K. Nagase-Reimer (eds), *Mining, Monies and Culture in Early Modern Societies: East Asian and Global Perspectives.* Leiden: Brill, pp. 261–288.

— (2015). *The Age of Trade. The Manila Galleons and the Dawn of the Global Economy.* Lanham, MD: Rowman & Littlefield.

Global Slavery Index (2016). www.globalslaveryindex.org/data/. Visited 8 August 2016.

Gøbel, Erik, (1993). 'Danish companies' shipping to Asia, 1616–1807', in J.R Bruijn and F.S. Gaastra (eds), *Ships, Sailors and Spices. East India Companies and Their Shipping in the 16th, 17th and 18th centuries.* Amsterdam: NEHA, pp. 99–120.

Gómez-Galvarriato, Aurora (2005). 'Premodern manufacturing', in V. Bulmer-Thomas, J. Coatsworth and Robert Cortes-Conde (eds), *Cambridge Economic History of Latin America.* Cambridge: Cambridge University Press, pp. 357–395.

Gommans, Jos, (2015). 'For the home and the body: Dutch and Indian ways of early modern consumption', in Berg et al. (eds) *Goods from the East.* London: Palgrave Macmillan, pp. 331–349.

Goodman, G.K. (2013). *Japan: The Dutch Experience.* London: Bloomsbury.

Gordon, A. (2003). *A Modern History of Japan. From Tokugawa Times to the Present.* New York and Oxford: Oxford University Press.

Gottmann, Felicia (2016). *Global Trade, Smuggling, and the Making of Economic Liberalism. Asian Textiles in France 1680–1760.* London: Palgrave Macmillan.

Grafe, Regina, and Alejandra Irigoin (2006). 'The Spanish Empire and its legacy: Fiscal Redistribution and Political Conflict in Colonial and Post-Colonial Spanish America', *Journal of Global History* 1, pp. 241–267.

— (2012). 'A Stakeholder Empire: The Political Economy of Spanish Imperial Rule in America', *Economic History Review* 65, pp. 609–651.

Grant, Susan M. (2012). *A Concise History of the United States of America.* Cambridge: Cambridge University Press.

Greenfield, G.M. (1994). *Latin American Urbanization Historical Profiles of Major Cities.* Westport, CT: Greenwood Press.

Griffiths, T., D. Hunt and P.K. O'Brien (1991). 'Political Components of the Industrial Revolution: Parliament and the English Cotton Textile Industry, 1660–1774', *Economic History Review* 44, 394–432.

Gruber, Carmen (2014). 'Escaping Malthus: A Comparative Look at Japan and the "Great Divergence"', *Journal of Global History* 9, pp. 403–424.

Habib, Irfan (1975). 'Colonialization of the Indian Economy 1757–1900', *Social Scientist* 3, pp. 23–53.

(1982). 'The monetary system and prices', in T. Raychaudhuri and I. Habib (eds), *Cambridge Economic History of India*, vol. 1, pp. 360–381.

(1985). 'Studying a Colonial Economy without Perceiving Colonialism', *Modern Asian Studies* 119, pp. 355–381.

Haines, Michael and Richard Steckel (eds) (2000), *A Population History of North America*. Cambridge: Cambridge University Press.

Haider, Najaf (1996). 'Precious Metal Flows and Currency Circulation in the Mughal Empire', *Journal of Economic and Social History of the Orient* 39, pp. 298–364.

Hall, Kenneth R. (1985). *Maritime Trade and State Development in Early Southeast Asia*. Honolulu: University of Hawaii Press.

Hamilton, Earl J. (1934). *American Treasure and the Price Revolution in Spain, 1501–1650*. Harvard Economic Studies, 43. Cambridge, MA: Harvard University Press.

Hanley, Susan B. (1997). *Everyday Things in Premodern Japan. The Hidden Legacy of Material Culture*. Berkeley, CA: University of California Press.

Hanna, Willard A. (1978). *Indonesian Banda. Colonialism and its Aftermath in the Nutmeg Islands*. Philadelphia: Institute for the Study of Human Issues.

Harley, C. Knick (1988). 'Ocean Freight Rates and Productivity 1740–1913: The Primacy of Mechanical Invention Reaffirmed', *Journal of Economic History* 48, pp. 851–876.

Hart, Marjolein 't (1993). *The Making of a Bourgeois State. War, Politics and Finance during the Dutch Revolt*. Manchester: Manchester University Press.

Hayami, A., O. Saito and R.P. Toby (eds) (2004). *The Economic History of Japan: 1600–1990. Vol. 1: Emergence of Economic Society in Japan, 1600–1859*. Oxford: Oxford University Press.

Hayami, Akira (2004). 'Introduction: the emergence of "economic society"', in A. Hayami, O. Saito and R.P. Toby (eds), *The Economic History of Japan: 1600–1990. Vol. 1: Emergence of Economic Society in Japan, 1600–1859*. Oxford: Oxford University Press, pp. 1–35.

(2010). *Population and Family in Early-Modern Central Japan*. Kyoto: International Research Centre for Japanese Studies.

(2015). *Japan's Industrious Revolution: Economic and Social Transformations in the Early Modern Period*. Japan: Springer Japan.

Hayami, Akira, and Hiroshi Kitô (2004). 'Demography and living standards', in A. Hayami, O. Saito and R.P. Toby (eds), *The Economic History of Japan: 1600–1990. Vol. 1: Emergence of Economic Society in Japan, 1600–1859*. Oxford: Oxford University Press, pp. 213–246.

Heitzman, J. (2008). 'Middle Towns to Middle Cities in South Asia, 1800–2007', *Journal of Urban History* 35, pp. 15–38.

Held, David, Anthony G. McGrew, David Goldblatt and Jonathan Perraton (1999). *Global Transformations. Politics, Economics and Culture.* Stanford, CA: Stanford University Press.

Hellie, R. (2006a). 'The peasantry', in M. Perrie (ed.), *The Cambridge History of Russia.* Cambridge: Cambridge University Press, pp. 286–297.

(2006b). 'The Economy, Trade and Serfdom', in M. Perrie (ed.), *The Cambridge History of Russia.* Cambridge: Cambridge University Press, pp. 539–558.

Herbst, J. (2014). *States and Power in Africa. Comparative Lessons in Authority and Control.* Princeton and Oxford: Princeton University Press.

Hersh, Jonathan and Hans-Joachim Voth (2011). 'Sweet diversity: colonial goods and the rise of European living standards after 1492', https://econ-papers.upf.edu/papers/1163.pdf, visited on 27 May 2018.

Hirth, Kenneth G. (2016). *The Aztec Economic World Merchants and Markets in Ancient Mesoamerica.* Cambridge: Cambridge University Press.

Hodacs, Hanna (2016). *Silk and Tea in the North Scandinavian Trade and the Market for Asian Goods in Eighteenth-Century Europe.* London: Palgrave Macmillan.

Hoerder, D. (2015). 'Global migrations', in J.H. Bentley, S. Subrahmanyam and M.E. Wiesner-Hanks (eds), *The Cambridge World History* 6(2), pp. 3–28.

Hoffman, Philip T. (2015). *Why Did Europe Conquer the World?* Princeton and Oxford: Princeton University Press.

Holcombe, Charles (2017). *A history of East Asia. From the Origins of Civilization to the Twenty-First Century.* Cambridge: Cambridge University Press.

Hopkins, A.G. (1973). *An Economic History of West Africa.* London: Longman.

Horrell, Sara and Jane Humphries (1995). 'Women's Labour Force Participation and the Transition to the Male-Breadwinner Family, 1790–1865', *The Economic History Review,* 48(1), pp. 89–117.

Iliffe, John (1995). *Africans: The History of a Continent.* Cambridge: Cambridge University Press.

Inikori, Joseph E. (1977). 'The Import of Firearms into West Africa, 1750 to 1807: A Quantitative Analysis', *Journal of African History* 18, pp. 339–368.

(2002). *Africans and the Industrial Revolution in England. A Study in International Trade and Economic Development.* Cambridge, Cambridge University Press.

(2007). 'Africa and the Globalization Process: Western Africa, 1450–1850', *Journal of Global History* 2, pp. 63–86.

(2011). 'Transatlantic Slavery and Economic Development in the Atlantic World: West Africa, 1450–1850', in D. Eltis and S. Engerman (eds), *Cambridge World History of Slavery vol. 3*. Cambridge: Cambridge University Press, pp. 650–674.

(2014). 'Reversal of fortune and socio-economic development in the Atlantic world. A comparative examination of West Africa and the Americas, 1400–1850', in Emmanuel Akyeampong, Robert H. Bates, Nathan Nunn and James A. Robinson (eds), *Africa's Development in Historical Perspective*, Cambridge: Cambridge University Press, pp. 56–88.

Inikori, Joseph E. and Stanley L. Engerman. (1992) 'Introduction: gainers and losers in the Atlantic slave trade', in ibid. (eds), *The Atlantic Slave Trade. Effect on Economies, Societies, and Peoples in Africa, the Americas and Europe*. Durham, NC: Duke University Press, pp. 1–24.

Jacobs, Els M. (2006). *Merchant in Asia: The Trade of the Dutch East India Company During the Eighteenth Century*. Leiden: CNWS Publications (School of Asian, African, and Amerindian Studies).

Jerven, M. (2016). 'Capitalism in Pre-Colonial Africa: A Review', *AEHN Working Paper* No. 27.

Jun, Seong Ho and J.B. Lewis, (2004). "Labour costs, land prices and interest rates in the southern region of Korea (1700 to 1900)", *Mimeo* www .iisg.nl/hpw/papers/jun.pdf, visited on 27 May 2018.

Jun, Seong Ho, J.B. Lewis and Kang Han-Rog (2008). 'Korean Expansion and Decline from the Seventeenth to the Nineteenth Century: A View Suggested by Adam Smith', *Journal of Economic History* 68, pp. 244–282.

(2009). 'Stability or Decline? Demand or Supply?', *Journal of Economic History* 69, pp. 1144–1151.

Kathirithamby-Wells, J. (1977). *The British West Sumatran Presidency 1760–1785. Problems of Early Colonial Enterprise*. Kuala Lumpur: Penerbit Universiti Malaya.

Katz, F. (1978). 'A comparison of some aspects of the evolution of Cuazco and Tenochtitlán', in S.J. Hardoy, and N. Scott-Kinzer (eds), *Urbanization in the Americas from its Beginning the to the Present*. The Hague: Mouton.

Keegan, T. (1996). *Colonial South Africa and the Origins of the Racial Order*. Charlottesville: University Press of Virginia.

Klein, Herbert S. (2010). *The Atlantic Slave Trade*. (2nd ed.). Cambridge: Cambridge University Press.

Knaap, Gerrit (1987). *Kruidnagelen en Christenen de Verenigde Oost-Indische Compagnie en de bevolking van Ambon 1656–1696*. Dordrecht: Floris.

(1999). 'Shipping and Trade in Java, c.1775: A Quantitative Analysis", *Modern Asian Studies* 33, pp. 405–420.

(2006). 'All about Money: Maritime Trade in Makassar and West Java around 1775', *Journal of the Economic and Social History of the Orient* 49, pp. 482–508.

(2015). 'Semarang, a colonial provincial capital and port city in Java, *c.* 1775', in U. Bosma and A. Webster (eds), *Commodities, Ports, and Asian Maritime Trade since 1750*. Basingstoke: Palgrave Macmillan.

Knaap, Gerrit and Heather Sutherland (2004). *Monsoon Traders. Ships, Skippers and Commodities in Eighteenth-Century Makassar*, Leiden: KITLV Press.

Koninckx, C. (1993) 'The Swedish East India Company (1731–1807)', in J.R. Bruijn, and F.S. Gaastra (eds), *Ships, Sailors and Spices. East India Companies and Their Shipping in the 16th, 17th and 18th Centuries*. Amsterdam: NEHA, pp. 121–138.

Krantz, Olle (2017). 'Swedish GDP 1300–1560: A Tentative Estimate.' *Lund Papers in Economic History* 152, Lund University.

Kulikoff, Allen (1986). *Tobacco and Slaves: The Development of Southern Cultures in the Chesapeake, 1680–1800*. Chapel Hill: University of North Carolina Press.

Kulikoff, Alan (2000). From *British Peasants to Colonial American Farmers*. Chapel Hill, NC: University of North Carolina Press.

Kuran, Timur, (2003). "The Islamic Commercial Crisis: Institutional Roots of Economic Underdevelopment in the Middle East", *Journal of Economic History* 63(2), 414–446.

La Porta, Rafael, Florencio Lopez-de-Silanes, Andrei Shleifer, and Robert W. Vishny (1998). 'Law and Finance', *Journal of Political Economy* 106, pp. 1133–1155.

La Porta, Rafael, Florencio Lopez-de-Silanes, Andrei Shleifer (2008). 'The Economic Consequences of Legal Origins', *Journal of Economic Literature* 46, pp. 285–332.

Larsen, C.S., et al. (2002). 'A biohistory of health and behavior in the Georgia Bight', in R. Steckel and J.C. Rose (eds), *The Backbone of History. Health and Nutrition in the Western Hemisphere*. Cambridge: Cambridge University Press, pp. 406–438.

Law, Robin (1992). 'Posthumous Questions for Karl Polanyi: Price Inflation in Pre-Colonial Dahomey', *Journal of African History* 33, pp. 387–420.

(2013). '"There's nothing grows in the West Indies but will grow here": Dutch and English projects of plantation agriculture on the Gold Coast, 1650s–1780s', in Robin Law, Suzanne Schwarz and Silke Strickrodt (eds), *Commercial Agriculture, the Slave Trade and Slavery in Atlantic Africa*. Rochester: James Currey, pp. 116–137.

Lee, Hochol (1997). 'Agriculture as a generator of change in Late Choson Korea', in Anthony Reid (ed.), *The Last Stand of Asian Economies*.

Responses to Modernity in the Diverse States of Southeast Asia and Korea, 1750–1900. London: Macmillan, pp. 57–82.

Lee, Hun-Chang and Peter Temin (2010). 'The Political Economy of Preindustrial Korean Trade', *Journal of Institutional and Theoretical Economics* 166, pp. 548–571.

Lee, Susan and Peter Passell (1979). *A New Economic View of American History.* New York: W.W. Norton.

Lemire, Beverly (2011). *Cotton.* Bloomsbury: London.

Levin, P., L. Arroyo Abad and M. Cuesta (2007). 'Brazil, 1550–1769'. *Datafile from Global Prices and Income History Database*, http://gpih .ucdavis.edu., visited on 23 May 2018.

Li, Bozhong (1998) *Agricultural Development in Jiangnan, 1620–1850.* Houndsmills: Macmillan Press.

(2005). 'Farm labour productivity in Jiangnan, 1620–1850', in: R.C. Allen et al. (Eds.) *Living Standards in the Past: New Perspectives on Well-Being in Asia and Europe.* Oxford: Oxford University Press.

Li, Bozhong and Jan Luiten van Zanden (2012). 'Before the Great Divergence? Comparing the Yangzi Delta and the Netherlands at the Beginning of the Nineteenth Century', *Journal of Economic History* 72, pp. 956–989.

Lieberman, Victor (1990). 'Wallerstein's System and the International Context of Early Modern Southeast Asia', *Journal of Asian History* 24, pp. 70–90.

(1993). 'Local Integration and Eurasian Analogies: Structuring Southeast Asian history, c.1350–c. 1830', *Modern Asia Studies* 27, pp. 475–572.

(1995). 'An Age of Commerce in Southeast Asia? Problems of Regional Coherence – A Review Article', *Journal of Asian Studies* 54, pp. 796–807.

(2003). *Strange Parallels. Southeast Asia in Global Context, c. 800–1830. Vol. 1: Integration on the Mainland.* Cambridge: Cambridge University Press.

(2009). *Strange Parallels. Southeast Asia in Global Context, c. 800–1830. Vol. 2: Mainland mirrors: Europe, Japan, China, South Asia and the Islands.* Cambridge: Cambridge University Press.

Lin, Man-houng (2007). *China Upside Down. Currency, Society and Ideologies, 1808-1856.* Cambridge, MA: Harvard University Press.

Lindert, Peter H. and Jeffrey G. Williamson (2016). *Unequal Gains. American Growth and Inequality since 1700.* Princeton: Princeton University Press.

Liu, Yong (2007). *The Dutch East India Company's Tea Trade with China, 1757-1781.* Leiden and Boston: Brill.

Livi Bacci, M. (2006). 'The Depopulation of Hispanic America after the Conquest', *Population and Development Review* 32, pp. 199–232.

(2008). *Conquest: The Destruction of the American Indios*. Cambridge: Polity Press.

Lovejoy, Paul E. (1989). 'The Impact of the Atlantic Slave Trade on Africa: A Review of the Literature', *Journal of African History* 30, pp. 365–394.

(2011). *Transformations in Slavery. A history of slavery in Africa*. (3rd ed.). Cambridge: Cambridge University Press.

Lovejoy, Paul E. and Jan S. Hogendorn (1993). *The Slow Death of Slavery: The Course of Abolition in Northern Nigeria, 1897–1936*. Cambridge: Cambridge University Press.

Loveman, B. (1979). 'Critique of Arnold J. Bauers, "Rural Workers in Spanish America: Problems of Peonage and Oppression"', *Hispanic American Historical Review* 49, pp. 478–485.

Lucassen, Jan (2007). 'Introduction: Wages and Currency, 500 BCE–2000 CE', in Jan Lucassen (Ed.) *Wages and Currency Global Comparisons from Antiquity to the Twentieth Century*. Bern: Peter Lang, pp. 9–58.

(2017). 'Labour and Deep Monetization in Eurasia, 1000 to 1900', in K. Hofmeester and P. de Zwart (eds), *Colonialism, Institutional Change, and Shifts in Global Labour Relations*. Amsterdam: Amsterdam University Press.

Lucassen, J. and R. Unger (2000). 'Labour Productivity in Ocean Shipping 1500–1850', *International Journal of Maritime History* 12, pp. 127–124.

Lucassen, Leo (2016). 'Connecting the world. Migration and globalization in the second millennium', in C.A. Antunes and K.J. Fatah-Black (eds), *Explorations in History and Globalization*. London: Routledge, pp. 19–46.

Ma, Debin (2012). 'Political institutions and long-run economic trajectory: some lessons from two millennia of Chinese civilization', in Mashiko Aoki, Timur Kuran and Gerard Roland (eds) *Institutions and Comparative Economic Development*. New York: Palgrave Macmillan, pp. 78–98.

(2013). 'State Capacity and Great Divergence, the Case of Qing China (1644–1911)', *Eurasian Geography and Economics* 54, pp. 484–499.

Ma, Debin and Jared Rubin (2016). 'The Paradox of Power: Understanding Fiscal Capacity in Imperial China', *EH.net*: http://eh.net/eha/wp-content/uploads/2016/08/MaRubin.pdf, visited on 27 May 2018.

Macfarlane, A. and I. Macfarlane (2011). *Green Gold: The Empire of Tea*. London: Ebury Press.

Machado, Pedro. (2009). 'A wash in a sea of cloth: Gujarat, Africa, and the Western Indian Ocean, 1300–1800', in Giorgio Riello and Prasannan Parthasarathi (eds), *The Spinning World. A Global History of Cotton Textiles, 1200–1850*. Oxford: Oxford University Press.

Maddison, Angus (2001). *The World Economy: Historical Statistics*. Paris: OECD.

(2007). *Contours of the World Economy, 1–2030 AD*. Oxford: Oxford University Press.

Malanima, P. (2011). 'The Long Decline of a Leading Economy: GDP in Central and Northern Italy, 1300–1913', *European Review of Economic History* 15(2), pp. 169–219.

Malinowski, M. (2016). 'Little Divergence Revisited: Polish Living Standards in a European Perspective, 1500–1800', *European Review of Economic History* 20(3), pp. 345–367.

Malinowski, M. and J.L. Van Zanden (2016). 'Income and Its Distribution in Preindustrial Poland', *Cliometrica* 11, pp. 1–30.

Mann, Charles C. (2005). *1491: New Revelations of the Americas Before Columbus*. New York: Knopf.

Mancall, Peter, Joshua Rosenbloom and Thomas Weiss (2006). 'Exports and Slow Economic Growth in the Lower South Region, 1720–1800', *NBER Working Paper* 12045. Cambridge, MA: NBER.

(2008). 'Commodity Exports, Invisible Exports and Terms of Trade for the Middle Colonies, 1720 to 1775', *NBER Working Paper* 14334. Cambridge, MA: NBER.

Manning, Patrick (1990). *Slavery and African Life. Occidental, Oriental, and African Slave Trades*. Cambridge: Cambridge University Press.

(2014). 'African population 1650–2000: comparisons and implications of new estimates', in Emmanuel Akyeampong, Robert H. Bates, Nathan Nunn and James A. Robinson (eds), *Africa's Development in Historical Perspective*. Cambridge: Cambridge University Press, pp. 131–152.

Manzel, Kerstin, Joerg Baten, and Yvonne Stolz (2012). 'Convergence and Divergence of Numeracy: The Development of Age Heaping in Latin America from the Seventeenth to the Twentieth Century', *Economic History Review* 65, pp. 932–960.

Marks, Robert (1998). *Tigers, Rice, Silk and Silt. Environment and Economy in Late Imperial South China*. Cambridge: Cambridge University Press.

Marquez, Graciela (2005). 'Commercial monopolies and external trade', in V. Bulmer-Thomas, J. Coatsworth and Robert Cortes-Conde (eds.), *Cambridge Economic History of Latin America*. Cambridge: Cambridge University Press, pp. 395–422.

McCants, Anne M. (2008). 'Poor Consumers as Global Consumers: The Diffusion of Tea and Coffee Drinking in the Eighteenth Century', *Economic History Review* 61, pp. 172–200.

McCusker, John J. and Russell Menard (1985). *The Economy of British America, 1607-1789. Needs and Opportunities for Study*. Chapel Hill, NC: University of North Carolina Press.

314 Bibliography

McKeown, A. (2011). 'Different Transitions: Comparing China and Europe, 1600–1900', *Journal of Global History* 6, pp. 309–319.

(2014). 'A different transition: human mobility in China, 1600–1900', in J. Lucassen and L. Lucassen (eds), *Globalising Migration History. The Eurasian Experience (16th–21st centuries)*. Leiden and Boston: Brill, pp. 279–305.

McNeill, J.R. (2010). *Mosquito Empires. Ecology and War in the Greater Caribbean 1620–1914*. Cambridge: Cambridge University Press.

McNeill, J.R. and Kenneth Pomeranz (2015) *Cambridge World History*. Volume 7: Production, Destruction and Connection, 1750–Present, Part 1: Structures, Spaces, and Boundary Making Cambridge: Cambridge University Press.

Meilink-Roelofsz, M.A.P. (1962). *Asian Trade and European Influence in the Indonesian Archipelago between 1500 and about 1630*. Dissertation University of Amsterdam. The Hague: Martinus Nijhoff.

Menard, Russell (1973). 'Farm Prices of Maryland Tobacco, 1659–1710', *Maryland Historical Magazine* 86, pp. 80–85.

(1976). 'A Note on Chesapeake Tobacco Prices, 1618–1660', *The Virginia Magazine of History and Biography* 84, pp. 401–410.

(1991). 'Transport costs and long-range trade, 1300–1800: was there a european transport revolution in the early modern era?', in J.D. Tracy (ed.), *The Political Economy of Merchant Empires*. Cambridge and New York: Cambridge University Press, pp. 228–276.

(1996). 'Economic and social development of the South', in Stanley Engerman and Robert E. Gallman (eds), *Cambridge Economic History of the United States. Vol. 1: The Colonial Era*. Cambridge: Cambridge University Press, pp. 249–295.

Meredith, Martin (2014). *Fortunes of Africa: A 5,000 Year of History of Wealth, Greed and Endeavour*. New York: Public Affairs.

Miyamoto, Matao (2004). 'Prices and macroeconomic dynamics', in Akira Hayami, Osamu Saito and Ronald P. Toby (eds), *The Economic History of Japan: 1600–1990. Volume 1: Emergence of Economic Society in Japan, 1600–1859*. Oxford: Oxford University Press, pp. 119–158.

Mokyr, Joel (2009). *The Enlightened Economy. An Economic History of Britain 1700–1850*. New Haven, CT: Yale University Press.

Monteiro, John M. (2005). 'Labor systems', in V. Bulmer-Thomas, J. Coatsworth and Robert Cortes-Conde (eds), *Cambridge Economic History of Latin America*. Cambridge: Cambridge University Press, pp. 185–233.

Moosvi, Shireen (1987a). *The Economy of the Mughal Empire c.1595. A Statistical Study*. Oxford: Oxford University Press.

(1987b). 'The Silver Influx, Money Supply and Revenue Extraction in Mughal India', *Journal of the Economic Social History of the Orient* 30, pp. 47–94.

Moraley, William (2005). *The Unfortunate. The Voyage and Adventures of William Moraley, an Indentured Servant.* Susan E. Klepp and Billy G. Smith (eds) Pennsylvania State University Press. 2nd Edition. Original published in 1743.

Morris, Ian (2010). *Why the West Rules – For Now. The Patterns of History, and What They Reveal About the Future.* London: Profile.

Motavasseli, Ali and Sjak Smulders (2017). 'Urban and Rural Labour Supply and Home Production, 1750–1830', Working Paper Tilburg University.

Mukherjee, Tilottama (2011). 'Markets in Eighteenth Century Bengal Economy', *Indian Economic and Social History Review* 48, pp. 143–176.

Munro, John H. (2003). 'The monetary origins of the "price revolution": south German silver mining, merchant banking, and Venetian commerce, 1470–1540', in Dennis O. Flynn, Arturo Giráldez and Richard von Glahn (eds), *Global Connections and Monetary History, 1470–1800.* Aldershot, pp. 1–34.

Myers, R.H. and Y-C. Wang (2002). 'Economic Developments 1644–1800', in W.J. Peterson (ed.) *Cambridge History of China.* Vol. 9, part 1. Cambridge: Cambridge University Press, pp. 563–645.

Nadri, Ghulam (2008a). 'The Dutch Intra-Asian Trade in Sugar in the Eighteenth Century', *International Journal of Maritime History* 20, pp. 63–96.

(2008b). *Eighteenth-Century Gujarat. The Dynamics of Its Political Economy.* Leiden: Brill.

Nagtegaal, L. (1996). *Riding the Dutch Tiger. The Dutch East Indies Company and the Northeast Coast of Java, 1680–1743.* Leiden: KITLV Press.

Newson, Linda (2005). 'The demographic impact of colonization', in Victor Bulmer-Thomas, *The Cambridge Economic History of Latin America. Volume 1: The Colonial Era and the Short Nineteenth Century.* Cambridge: Cambridge University Press, pp. 143–184.

North, Douglass (1968). 'Sources of Productivity Change in Ocean Shipping, 1600–1850', *Journal of Political Economy* 76, pp. 953–970.

(1990). *Institutions, Institutional Change and Economic Performance.* Cambridge: Cambridge University Press.

North, Douglass, and Barry Weingast (1989). 'Constitutions and Commitment: The Evolution of Institutions Governing Public Choice in Seventeenth-Century England', *Journal of Economic History* 49(4), pp. 803–842.

Northrup, David (2005). 'Globalization and the Great Convergence: Rethinking World History in the Long-Term', *Journal of World History* 16(3), pp. 249–267.

Nunn, Nathan (2008). 'The Long-Term Effects of Africa's Slave Trades', *Quarterly Journal of Economics* 123, pp. 139–176.

(2009). 'The Importance of History for Economic Development', *Annual Review of Economics* 1, pp. 65–92.

Nunn, Nathan and Nancy Qian (2011). 'The Potato's Contribution to Population and Urbanization: Evidence from a Historical Experiment', *Quarterly Journal of Economics* 127, pp. 593–560.

Öberg, Stefan and Klas Rönnbäck (2016). 'Mortality among European settlers in pre-colonial West Africa: The "White Man's Grave" revisited', *Göteborg Papers in Economic History* No. 20.

O'Brien, Patrick K. (1982). 'European Economic Development: The Contribution of the Periphery', *Economic History Review* 35, pp. 1–18.

(2005). 'The global economic history of European expansion overseas', in V. Bulmer-Thomas, J. Coatsworth and R. Cortes-Conde (eds) *Cambridge Economic History of Latin America*. Vol. 1. Cambridge: Cambridge University Press, pp. 7–42.

O'Grada, C. and M. Kelly. (2014) 'Speed under Sail, 1750–1850', *UCD (University College Dublin) Working Paper Series*.

Oguchi, Yujiro (2004). 'The finance of the Tokugawa shogunate', in Akira Hayami, Osamu Saito and Ronald P. Toby (eds), *The Economic History of Japan: 1600–1990. Volume 1: Emergence of Economic Society in Japan, 1600–1859*. Oxford: Oxford University Press, pp. 192–212.

O'Rourke, Kevin H. and Jeffrey G. Williamson (2002a). 'When did Globalisation Begin?', *European Review of Economic History* 6, pp. 23–50.

(2002b). 'After Columbus: Explaining Europe's Overseas Trade Boom, 1500–1800', *Journal of Economic History* 62, pp. 417–456.

(2004). 'Once More: When Did Globalisation Begin?', *European Review of Economic History*, 8, pp. 109–117.

(2009). 'Did Vasco da Gama Matter for European Markets?', *Economic History Review* 62, pp. 655–684.

Ogilvie, Sheilagh (2010). 'Consumption, Social Capital, and the "Industrious Revolution" in Early Modern Germany", *Journal of Economic History* 70(2), 287–325.

Ostkamp, Sebastiaan (2014). 'The Dutch 17th-century porcelain trade from an archaeological perspective', in J. van Campen and T. Eliëns (eds) *Chinese and Japanese porcelain for the Dutch Golden Age*. Nijmegen: Bart, pp. 53–85.

Osterhammel, J. and N. Petersson (2005). *Globalization. A Short History*. Princeton: Princeton University Press.

Ota, Atsushi (2014). 'Toward cities, seas, and jungles: migration in the Malay Archipelago, c.1750–1850', in J. Lucassen and L. Lucassen (eds),

Globalising Migration History. The Eurasian Experience (16th–20th Centuries). Leiden and Boston: Brill.

Ozmucur, Süleyman and Şevket Pamuk (2002). 'Real Wages and Standard of Living in the Ottoman Empire', *Journal of Economic History* 62, pp. 293–321.

Palais, James B. (1996). *Confucian Statecraft and Korean Institutions: Yu Hyongwon and the Late Choson Dynasty*. Seattle, WA: University of Washington Press.

Palma, Nuno (2015). '*Harbingers of modernity: monetary injections and European economic growth, 1492–1790*'. Dissertation, The London School of Economics and Political Science (LSE).

(2016a). 'Sailing away from Malthus: Intercontinental Trade and European Economic Growth, 1500–1800', *Cliometrica* 10, pp. 129–149.

(2016b) 'The existence and persistence of liquidity effects; evidence from a large-scale historical experiment'. *GGDC (Groningen Growth and Development Centre) Research Memorandum* 158.

Palma, Nuno, and Jaime Reis (2014). 'Portuguese Demography and Economic Growth 1500–1850', presented at *Accounting for the Great Divergence* conference, Venice.

Palma, Nuno, and Andre Silva (2016). "Spending a windfall: American precious metals and Euro-Asian trade 1531–1810". *GGDC Research Memorandum* 165.

Pamuk, Şevket (2004) 'Institutional Change and the Longevity of the Ottoman Empire, 1500–1800', *Journal of Interdisciplinary History* 35(2), pp. 225–247.

Pamuk, Şevket, and Maya Shatzmiller (2014). 'Plagues, Wages, and Economic Change in the Islamic Middle East, 700–1500', *Journal of Economic History* 74(1), 196–221.

Parthasarathi, Prasannan (1998). 'Rethinking Wages and Competitiveness in the Eighteenth Century: Britain and South India', *Past and Present* 158, pp. 79–109.

(2011). *Why Europe Grew Rich and Asia Did Not. Global Economic Divergence, 1600–1850*. Cambridge: Cambridge University Press.

Parker, Charles H. (2010). *Global Interactions in the Early Modern Age, 1400–1800*. Cambridge: Cambridge University Press.

Parker, Geoffrey (2013). *Global Crisis. War, Climate Change and Catastrophe in the Seventeenth Century*. New Haven: Yale University Press.

(1988). *The Military Revolution. Military Innovation and the Rise of the West, 1500–1800*. Cambridge: Cambridge U.niversity Press.

Pearson, Michael N. (1998). *Port Cities and Intruders: The Swahili Coast, India, and Portugal in the Early Modern Era*. Baltimore, MD: Johns Hopkins University Press.

Phelan, J.L. (1959). *The Hispanization of the Philippines: Spanish Aims and Filipino Responses, 1565–1700.* Madison WI: University of Wisconsin Press.

Polanyi, Karl. (1966). *Dahomey and the Slave Trade: An Analysis of an Archaic Economy.* Seattle, WA: University of Washington Press.

Pomeranz, Kenneth (2000). *The Great Divergence. China, Europe and the Making of the Modern World Economy.* Princeton: Princeton University Press.

Pomet, Pierre, *A Complete History of Drugs. Written in French by monsieur Pomet.* London, 1748.

Ponzio, Carlos Alejandro (2005). 'Globalisation and Economic Growth in the Third World: Some Evidence from Eighteenth-Century Mexico', *Journal of Latin America Studies* 37, pp. 437–467.

Prakash, Om (1981). 'European trade and South Asian economies: some regional contrasts, 1600–1800', in Leonard Blussé and Femme S. Gaastra (eds), *Companies and Trade. Essays on Overseas Trading Companies during the Ancien Régime.* Leiden: Leiden University Press, pp. 189–205.

(1985). *Dutch East India Company and the Economy of Bengal 1630–1720.* Princeton, NJ: Princeton Legacy Library.

(1998). *European Commercial Enterprise in Pre-Colonial India.* Cambridge: Cambridge University Press.

(2004). *Bullion for Goods: European and Indian Merchants in the Indian Ocean Trade, 1500–1800.* Delhi: Manohar Publishers.

(2007). 'Long distance trade, coinage and wages in India, 1600–1960', in J. Lucassen (ed.), *Wages and Currency. Global Comparisons from Antiquity to the Twentieth Century.* Bern: Peter Lang.

(2009). 'From Market-Determined to Coercion-Based: Textile Manufacturing in Eighteenth-Century Bengal', in Giorgio Riello and Tirthankar Roy (eds), *How India Clothed the World. The World of South Asian Textiles, 1500-1850.* Leiden and Boston, MA: Brill, pp. 217-251.

Ramaswamy, V. (1985). *Textiles and Weavers in Medieval South India.* Delhi, Oxford University Press.

Ray, Indrajit (2016). 'The myth and reality of deindustrialisation in early modern India', in Latika Chaudhary, Bishnupriya Gupta, Tirthankar Roy and Anand V. Swamy (eds) *A New Economic History of Colonial India.* London and New York: Routledge.

Raychaudhuri, Tapan (1982). 'Inland trade', in Tapan Raychaudhuri and Irfan Habib (eds), *Cambridge Economic History of India. Vol. 1.* Cambridge: Cambridge University Press.

Reid, Anthony (1988). *Southeast Asia in the Age of Commerce 1450–1680. Vol. 1: The Lands Below the Winds.* New Haven and London: Yale University Press.

(1990). "An "Age of Commerce" in Southeast Asian History", *Modern Asian Studies* 24(1), pp. 1–30.

(1993a). *Southeast Asia in the Age of Commerce 1450–1680. Vol. 2: Expansion and Crisis.* New Haven and London: Yale University Press.

(1993b). 'Economic and social change', in N. Tarling (ed.), *Cambridge History of Southeast Asia.* Cambridge: University Press, pp. 460–507.

(2009). 'Southeast Asian consumption of Indian and British cotton cloth, 1600–1850', in G. Riello and T. Roy (eds) *How India Clothed the World. The World of South Asian Textiles, 1500–1850.* Leiden and Boston: Brill.

(2015). *A History of Southeast Asia: Critical Crossroads.* Oxford: Wiley Blackwell.

Reid, Richard J. (2012). *Warfare in African History.* Cambridge: Cambridge University Press.

Reinhard, Wolfgang (ed.) (2015). *Empire and Encounters; 1350–1750.* Cambridge, MA: Belknap Press/Harvard University Press.

Richards, John F. (1997). 'Early Modern India and World History', *Journal of World History* 8, pp. 197–209.

(2003). *The Unending Frontier. An Environmental History of the Early Modern World.* Berkeley: University of California Press.

Richards, W.A. (1980). 'The Import of Firearms into West Africa in the Eighteenth Century', *Journal of African History* 21, pp. 43–49.

Richardson, David (1991). "Prices of Slaves in West and West-Central Africa: Toward an Annual Series, 1698–1807", *Bulletin of Economic Research* 43, pp. 21–56.

(2011). 'Involuntary migration in the early modern world, 1500–1800', in D. Eltis, Stanley Engerman (eds), *The Cambridge World History of Slavery.* vol. 3. Cambridge: Cambridge University Press, pp. 563–593.

Riello, Giorgio (2009). 'The globalization of cotton textiles', in G. Riello and Prasannan Parthasarathi (eds) *The Spinning World. A Global History of Cotton Textiles, 1200–1850.* Oxford: Oxford University Press, pp. 261–289.

(2013). *Cotton: The Fabric that made the Modern World.* Cambridge: Cambridge University Press.

Riello, Giorgio and T. Roy (2009). *How India Clothed the World. The World of South Asian Textiles, 1500–1850.* Leiden: Brill.

Roberts, Callum (2007). *The Unnatural History of the Sea.* Washington DC: Island Press.

Rodney, Walter (1972). *How Europe Underdeveloped Africa.* London: Bogle-L'Ouverture Publications.

Roessingh, H.K. (1976). *Inlandse Tabak. Expansie en contractie van een handelsgewas in de 17e en 18e eeuw in Nederland.* Unpublished PhD thesis, Wageningen University.

Rönnbäck, K. (2009). 'Integration of Global Commodity Markets in the Early Modern Era', *European Review of Economic History* 13, pp. 95–120.

(2012). 'The Speed of Ships and Shipping Productivity in the Age of Sail', *European Review of Economic History* 16, pp. 469–489.

(2014). 'Living Standards on The Pre-Colonial Gold Coast: A Quantitative Estimate of African Laborers' Welfare Ratios', *European Review of Economic History* 18, pp. 185–202.

Rosenbloom, J.L. and Thomas Weiss (2014). 'Economic Growth in the Mid-Atlantic Region: Conjectural Estimates for 1720 and 1800', *Explorations in Economic History* 51, pp. 41–59.

Roy, Tirthankar (2002). 'Economic History and Modern India: Redefining the Link', *Journal of Economic Perspectives* 16, pp. 109–130.

(2010). 'Economic Conditions in Early Modern Bengal: A Contribution to the Divergence Debate', *Journal of Economic History* 70, pp. 179–194.

(2012). *India in the World Economy. From Antiquity to the Present.* Cambridge: Cambridge University Press.

(2013). *An Economic History of Early Modern India.* London and New York: Routledge.

Saito, Osamu (1978). 'The Labor Market in Tokugawa Japan: Wage Differentials and the Real Wage Level', *Explorations in Economic History* 15, pp. 84–101.

(2009). 'Land, Labour and Market Forces in Tokugawa Japan', *Continuity and Change* 24, pp. 169–196.

Salisbury, Neal (1996). 'The history of Native Americans before the arrival of Europeans and Africans until the American Civil War', in Stanley Engerman and Robert E. Gallman (eds.), *Cambridge Economic History of the United States. Vol. 1: The Colonial Era*, Cambridge: Cambridge University Press, pp. 1–52.

Samper, M., and R. Fernando (2003). 'Historical statistics of coffee production and trade from 1700–1960', in S. Topik and W.G. Clarence-Smith (eds), *The Global Coffee Economy in Africa, Asia and Latin America 1500–1989*. Cambridge: Cambridge University Press.

Sánchez-Albornoz, N. (1994). 'The first transatlantic transfer: Spanish migration to the New World, 1493–1810', in N.P. Canny (ed.), *Europeans on the Move: Studies in European Migration, 1500–1800*. Oxford: Oxford University Press, pp. 26–38.

Schön, Lennart and Olle Krantz (2015). 'New Swedish Historical National Accounts since the 16th Century in Constant and Current Prices', *Lund Papers in Economic History* 152. Lund University.

Schottenhammer, A. (2012). 'The "China Seas" in world history: a general outline of the role of Chinese and East Asian maritime space from its origins to c.1800', *Journal of Maritime and Island Cultures* 1, pp. 63–86.

Schreurs, Geert (2015). 'Mountains of the State: Precious metal Production in Tokugawa Japan', *Working Paper*, Hitotsubashi University, Japan.

Schwartz, Stuart B. (1985). *Sugar Plantations in the Formation of Brazilian Society: Bahia, 1550–1835.* Cambridge: Cambridge University Press.

Sharp, Paul, and Jacob Weisdorf (2013). 'Globalization Revisited: Market Integration and the Wheat Trade between North America and Britain from the Eighteenth Century', *Explorations in Economic History* 50, pp. 88–98.

Shepherd, James F. and Gary M. Walton (1972). *Shipping, Maritime Trade, and the Economic Development of Colonial North America.* Cambridge: Cambridge University Press.

Sheriff, Abdul (1987). *Slaves, Spices and Ivory in Zanzibar. Integration of an East African Commercial Empire into the World Economy, 1770–1873.* London: James Currey.

Shimada, Ryuto (2006). *The Intra-Asian Trade in Japanese Copper by the Dutch East India Company during the Eighteenth Century.* Leide: Brill.

Shorto, Russel, (2013). *Amsterdam. A History of the World's Most Liberal City.* London: Abacus.

Sivramkrishna, S. (2009). 'Ascertaining Living Standards in Erstwhile Mysore, Southern India, from Francis Buchanan's Journey of 1800–01: An Empirical Contribution to the Great Divergence Debate', *Journal of the Economic and Social History of the Orient* 52, pp. 695–733.

Skinner, G. William (1957). *Chinese Society in Thailand: An Analytical History.* Ithaca, NY: Cornell University Press.

Sng, Tuan-Hwee, and Chiaki Moriguchi (2014). 'Asia's Little Divergence: State Capacity in China and Japan before 1850', *Journal of Economic Growth* 19, pp. 439–470.

Solar, Peter M. (2013). 'Opening to the East: Shipping between Europe and Asia, 1770–1830', *Journal of Economic History* 73, pp. 625–661.

Solar, Peter M., and Luc Hens (2015). 'Ship Speeds during the Industrial Revolution: East India Company ships, 1770–1828', *European Review of Economic History* 20, pp. 66–78.

Solar, Peter M., and Klas Rönnbäck (2015) 'Copper Sheathing and the British Slave Trade', *Economic History Review* 68(3), pp. 806–829.

Solar, Peter M., and Pim de Zwart (2017). 'Why were Dutch East Indiamen so Slow?', *International Journal of Maritime History* 29(4) 2017, pp. 738–751.

Solow, Barbara L. (1985). 'Caribbean Slavery and British Growth. The Eric Williams Hypothesis', *Journal of Development Economics* 17, pp. 99–115.

Souza, George B. (1986). *The Survival of Empire. Portuguese Trade and Society in China and the South China Sea 1630–1754.* Cambridge: Cambridge University Press.

Stearns, Peter N. (2010). *Globalization in World History*. London: Routledge.

Steensgaard, N. (1965). 'Freight Costs in the English East India Trade 1601–1657', *Scandinavian Economic History Review* 13, pp. 143–162.

(1973). *The Asian Trade Revolution of the Seventeenth Century. The East India Companies and the Decline of the Caravan Trade*. Chicago and London: University of Chicago Press.

(1995). 'Commodities, bullion and services in intercontinental transactions before 1750', in H. Pohl (ed.), *The European Discovery of the World and its Economic Effects on Pre-Industrial Society, 1500–1800*. Stuttgart: Franz Steiner.

Storey, Rebecca and R. J. Widner (2005). 'The pre-Columbian economy', in V. Bulmer-Thomas, J. Coatsworth and Robert Cortes-Conde (eds), *Cambridge Economic History of Latin America*. Cambridge: Cambridge University Press, pp. 73–106.

Tandeter, E. (1993). *Coercion and Market Silver Mining in Colonial Potosi, 1692–1826*. Albequerque: University of Mexico Press.

(2005). 'The mining industry', in V. Bulmer-Thomas, J. Coatsworth, Robert Cortes-Conde (eds), *Cambridge Economic History of Latin America*. Cambridge: Cambridge University Press, pp. 315–356.

Tashiro, Kazui (2004). 'Foreign trade in the Tokugawa period – particularly with Korea', in Akira Hayami, Osamu Saito and Ronald P. Toby (eds), *The Economic History of Japan: 1600-1990. Volume 1: Emergence of Economic Society in Japan, 1600–1859*. Oxford: Oxford University Press, pp. 105–118.

Te Paske, John. J. and Kendall W. Brown (2010). *A New World of Gold and Silver*. Leiden: Brill.

Teso, Edoardo (2014). 'Long-term effect of demographic shocks on the evolution of gender roles: evidence from the trans-Atlantic slave trade'. Mimeo Harvard.

Thomas, Hugh (2003). *Rivers of Gold: The Rise of the Spanish Empire*. London: Penguin.

Thornton, John (1980). 'The Slave Trade in Eighteenth Century Angola: Effects on Demographic Structures', *Canadian Journal of African studies* 14, pp. 417–427.

(1992). *Africa and Africans in the Making of the Atlantic World, 1400–1680*. Cambridge: Cambridge University Press.

Tilly, Charles (1990). *Coercion, Capital and European States, A.D. 990–1990*. Oxford: Wiley-Blackwell.

Titsingh, Isaac (1824). *Bijzonderheden over Japan*. Netherlands: The Hague.

Topik, Steven (2003). 'The integration of the world coffee market', in W.G. Clarence-Smith and S. Topik (eds), *The Global Coffee Economy in*

Africa, Asia and Latin America, 1500–1989. Cambridge: Cambridge University Press.

Topik, Steven and Kenneth Pomeranz (2013). *The World That Trade Created. Society, Culture, and the World Economy, 1400 to the Present.* (3rd ed.). London and New York: M.E. Sharpe.

Unger, R.W. (2001). *A history of brewing in Holland 900–1900. Economy, technology and the state.* Leiden: Brill.

Van den Boogaart, Ernst (1992). 'The Trade between Western Africa and the Atlantic World, 1600–90: Estimates of Trends in Composition and Value', *Journal of African History* 33 (1992), pp. 369–385.

Van Goor, Jurrien (1994). *De Nederlandse Koloniën: geschiedenis van Nederlandse expansie, 1600–1975.* The Hague: SDU.

Van Leur, Jacob C. (1955). *Indonesian Trade and Society.* Brussel: A. Manteau.

Van Lottum, J. and J.L. van Zanden (2014). 'Labour Productivity and Human Capital in the European Maritime Sector of the Eighteenth Century', *Explorations in Economic History* 53, pp. 83–100.

Van Nederveen Meerkerk, Elise (2008). 'Couples Cooperating? Dutch Textile Workers, Family Labour and the "Industrious Revolution", *c.*1600–1800', *Continuity and Change* 23(2), pp. 237–266.

Van Santen, H.W. (1982). *De Verenigde Oost-Indische Compagnie in Gujarat en Hindustan, 1620-1660.* PhD thesis Leiden.

Van Stipriaan, Alex (1993). *Surinaams Contrast. Roofbouw en Overleven in een Caraibische Plantagekolonie, 1750–1863.* KITLV, Leiden.

Van Tielhof, M. (2002). *The Mother of all Trades.* Leiden: Brill 2002.

Van Young, Eric (1981). *Hacienda and Market in Eighteenth-Century Mexico.* Berkeley, CA: University of California Press.

Van Zanden, Jan Luiten (1999). 'Wages and the Standard of Living in Europe, 1500–1800', *European Review of Economic History* 3(2), pp. 175–198.

(2009). *The Long Road to the Industrial Revolution. The European Economy in a Global Perspective, 1000–1800.* Leiden: Brill.

Van Zanden, Jan Luiten, Maarten Bosker and Eltjo Buringh (2012). 'The Rise and Decline of European Parliaments, 1188-1789', *Economic History Review* 65, pp. 835–861.

Van Zanden, Jan Luiten, and Bas van Leeuwen (2012). 'Persistent but not Consistent: The Growth of National Income in Holland 1347–1807', *Explorations in Economic History* 49, pp. 119–130.

Van Zanden, Jan Luiten, Marco Mira d'Ercole, Auke Rijpma, Conal Smith and Marcel Timmer (eds) (2014). *How Was Life? Global Well-Being Since 1820.* Paris: OECD.

Van Zanden, Jan Luiten, Reinoud Bosch, Michail Moatsos, Vyacheslav Tikhonov, Jerry de Vries and Gaele Strootman (2016). *Clio Infra. Reconstructing Global Inequality*, www.clio-infra.eu, visited on 8 August 2016.

Veluwenkamp, J.W. (1995). 'The Murman Coast and the Northern Dvina Delta as English and Dutch Commercial Destinations in the 16th and 17th Centuries', *Arctic* 48, pp. 257–266.

Vickers, Daniel (1996). 'The northern colonies: economy and society 1600–1775', in Stanley Engerman and Robert E. Gallman (eds), *Cambridge Economic History of the United States. Vol. 1: The Colonial Era*, Cambridge: Cambridge University Press, pp. 209–248.

Von Glahn, Richard (1996a). *Fountain of Fortune: Money and Monetary Policy in China, 1000–1700*. Berkeley, CA: University of California Press.

(1996b). 'Myth and Reality of China's Seventeenth-Century Monetary Crisis', *Journal of Economic History* 56, pp. 429–454.

(2016). *The Economic History of China. From Antiquity to the Nineteenth Century*. Cambridge: Cambridge University Press.

Vries, Peer (2013). *Escaping Poverty. The Origins of Modern Economic Growth*. Vienna: Vienna University.

(2015). *State, Economy and the Great Divergence. Great Britain and China, 1680s–1850s*. London, etc.: Bloomsbury.

(2017). 'A very brief history of economic globalization since Columbus', in R.C. Kloosterman, V. Mamadouth and P. Terhorst (eds), *Handbook Geographies of Globalization*. Cheltenham: Edward Elgar Publishing. (Forthcoming).

Wade, Geoff (2009). 'An Early Age of Commerce in Southeast Asia, 900–1300 CE', *Journal of Southeast Asian Studies* 40, pp. 221–265.

(2015). 'Chinese engagement with the Indian Ocean during the Song, Yuan, and Ming dynasties (tenth to sixteenth centuries)', in M.N. Pearson (ed.) *Trade, Circulation, and Flow in the Indian Ocean World*. London: Palgrave Macmillan.

Wakeman, Frederic Jr (1986). 'China and the Seventeenth-Century Crisis', *Late Imperial China* 7, pp. 1–26.

Wallerstein, Immanuel (1974). *The Modern World-System I. Capitalist Agriculture and the Origins of the European World-Economy in the Sixteenth Century*. New York and London: Academic Press.

(1986). 'Incorporation of Indian Subcontinent into Capitalist World-Economy', *Economic and Political Weekly* 21, pp. 28–39.

(1989). *The Modern World-System. Vol. III. The Second Era of Great Expansion of the Capitalist World Economy, 1730–1840s*. San Diego: Academic Press.

(2011). *The Modern-World System, 3 vols*. Berkeley, CA: University of California [original 1974–1989].

Walsh, L.S. (2000). 'The African American population of the colonial United States', in M.R. Haines and R.H. Steckel (eds), *The Population History of North America*, Cambridge: Cambridge University Press.

(2010). *Motives of Honor, Pleasure and Profit: Plantation Management in Colonial Chesapeake, 1607–1763*. Chapel Hill, NC: University of North Carolina Press.

Walton, G. (1967). 'Sources of Productivity Change in American Colonial Shipping, 1675–1775', *Economic History Review* 20, pp. 67–78.

(1970). 'Obstacles to Technical Diffusion in Ocean Shipping, 1675–1775', *Explorations in Economic History* 8, pp. 123–140.

Walton, Gary M. and Hugh Rockoff (1998). *History of the American Economy*. (8th Ed.). Oak Brook, IL: Dryden Press.

Wang, Yeh-chien (1992). 'Secular trends of rice prices in the Yangzi Delta, 1638–1935', in T.G. Rawski and L.M. Li (eds), *Chinese History in Economic Perspective*. Berkeley, CA: University of California Press, pp. 36–69.

Washbrook, David (2001). 'Eighteenth-Century Issues in South Asia', *Journal of Economic and Social History of the Orient* 44, pp. 372–383.

(2007). 'India in the Early Modern World Economy: Modes of Production, Reproduction and Exchange', *Journal of Global History* 2, pp. 87–111.

Watson Andaya, Barbara (1993). 'Political development between the sixteenth and eighteenth centuries', in N. Tarling (ed.), *Cambridge History of Southeast Asia. Volume 1: From Early Times to c.1800*. Cambridge: Cambridge University Press, pp. 402–459.

Wendt, Ian C. (2009). 'Four centuries of Decline? Understanding the Changing Structure of the South Indian Textile Industry', in G. Riello and T. Roy (eds) *How India Clothed the World. The World of South Asian Textiles, 1500–1850*. Leiden and Boston: Brill.

Wicks, Robert S. (1986). 'Monetary Developments in Java between the Ninth and Sixteenth Centuries: A Numismatic Perspective", *Indonesia* 42, pp. 42–77.

(1992). *Money, Markets and Trade in early Southeast Asia: The Development of Indigenous Monetary Systems to AD 1400*. Ithaca, NY: Cornell University Press.

Williams, Eric (1944). *Capitalism and Slavery Richmond, Virginia*. Chapel Hill, NC: University of North Carolina Press.

Williamson, Jeffrey (2011). *Trade and Poverty: When the Third World fell behind*. Cambridge, MA: MIT Press.

(2015). 'Trade, growth and distribution in Southeast Asia, 1500-1940', in I. Coxhead (ed.) *Routledge Handbook Southeast Asian Economics*. New York: Routledge, pp. 22–42.

Wong, R. Bin (1997). *China Transformed. Historical change and the limits of the European experience*. Ithaca, NY: Cornell University Press.

(2012). 'Taxation and good governance in China, 1500–1914', in Bartolomé Yun-Casalilla and Patrick K. O'Brien (eds) *The Rise of*

Fiscal States. A Global History, 1500–1914. Cambridge: Cambridge University Press, pp. 353–377.

Woodruff, W. (1981). *The Struggle for World Power 1500–1980*. London: Macmillan Press.

Yi, Xu, Bas van Leeuwen and Jan Luiten van Zanden (2015). 'Urbanization in China, *ca*. 1190–1900', *CGEH (Centre for Global Economic History) Working Paper* No. 63. Utrecht University.

Yi, Xu, Zhihong Shi, Bas van Leeuwen, Yuping Ni, Zipeng Zhang, and Ye Ma (2015). 'Chinese National Income, *ca*. 1661–1933', *MPRA (Munich Personal RePEc Archive)*.

Yuping, Ni (2016). *Customs Duties in the Qing Dynasty, ca. 1644–1911*. Leiden: Brill.

Zavala, S. (1935). *La encomienda Indiana*. Madrid: Imprenta Helenica.

Index

Printed in the United States
By Bookmasters